To Jessica, Elizabeth, and all my sisters

Cooking Fish and Shellfish

BY RUTH A. SPEAR

Illustrated by Mona Mark

DOUBLEDAY & COMPANY, INC.
GARDEN CITY, NEW YORK

Portions of this book originally appeared in *The East Hampton Cookbook*. Copyright © 1975 by Ruth A. Spear.

Library of Congress Cataloging in Publication Data

Spear, Ruth A.
  Cooking fish and shellfish.

  Includes index
  1. Cookery (Fish) 2. Cookery (Shellfish)
I. Title
TX747.S59   641.6′9′2
ISBN: 0-385-13098-8

Library of Congress Catalog Card Number 78-1248
Copyright © 1980 by Ruth A. Spear
All Rights Reserved
Printed in the United States of America

Grateful acknowledgment is made for permission to reprint the following recipes:

"Richard Olney's Squids and Leeks in Red Wine" from *Simple French Food* by Richard Olney. Copyright © 1974 by Richard Olney. Reprinted by permission of Atheneum Publishers.

"Oyster Pan Roast" from Grand Central Oyster Bar Restaurant, Grand Central Station, N.Y., N.Y. Used with permission.

"Baked Shad with Almond-stuffed Dates," adaptation of "Fish Baked with Stuffed Fruit" (pp. 169–170), in *Couscous and Other Good Food from Morocco* by Paula Wolfert. Copyright © 1973 by Paula Wolfert. Reprinted by permission of Harper & Row, Publishers, Inc.

"Pike and Spinach Pâté" from Windows of the World, atop the New York World Trade Center. Used with permission.

"Gage and Tollner's Soft Clam Belly Broil" from Gage and Tollner's Restaurant, Brooklyn, N.Y. Used with permission.

"Raw Scallops Le Duc" from Le Duc Restaurant, Paris, France. Used with permission.

"Clams on the Half Shell," "Pan-Fried Clams," "Clams Casino," "Clam Hash," "Steamed Spiced Crabs," "Baked Crab Mornay," "Cold Curried Lobster Salad," "Oysters Remick," "Oyster Loaf—La Mediatrice," "Coquilles Saint-Jacques à la Parisienne," "Shrimp Tempura," "Shrimp 'Scampi,'" "Fish Cakes," "Fish Croquettes" are from *The Doubleday Cookbook* by Jean Anderson and Elaine Hanna. Copyright © 1975 by Doubleday & Company, Inc. Reprinted by permission of the publisher.

Contents

Acknowledgments

There are a number of people who aided me in this endeavor, to whom I owe deep thanks: Reva Wurtzburger, my devil's advocate, along with Shirley Williams and Paola Lucentini gave invaluable help in testing and evaluating recipes; Monique Eastman and Christine Hall contributed marvelous recipes and Christine much advice on Scandinavian fish cookery. I am especially indebted to cookbook author and friend Paula Wolfert for sharing with me her stupendous scholarly knowledge of Provençal and Mediterranean cooking and to chef Jean-Louis Todeschini, who patiently answered endless questions on French cooking techniques. Thanks are also due Robert and Paul Neumann of the Rosedale Fish & Oyster Market, New York City, for their generous time and advice, Anne Kirkland for typing the manuscript and its many drafts and revisions, Jean Goddard for her patient, loyal help in the kitchen, Karen Van Westering, my editor at Doubleday, and the others who were instrumental in one way or another in helping me collect information: Sal San Cimino of Swann's Oyster Depot, Joseph Weiner and Beth Burstein of San Francisco, John Van Glahn, the Fishery Council, New York, Bob Finley, director of the National Fishery Education Center, Chicago, E. C. Fullerton, director, California Department of Fish and Game, and Michael E. Somers, chairman, Biology Department, University of Bridgeport. The biggest thanks I've saved for last: to my husband Harvey Spear, for his unflagging enthusiasm and support, his impartial taste-testing and his prodigious consumption of fish!

Author's Note

The problem with a book on fish, says Jane Grigson in her excellent book, *Fish Cookery,* is how to stop writing it. You'll have some idea of the dimensions of the difficulty if I tell you that over 195 varieties of fish and shellfish passed through New York's Fulton Market alone in 1978. In choosing recipes, I tried to keep in mind the average cook looking for an appealing way to prepare what's locally available as well as those who want a *pièce de résistance* for Saturday night.

I cooked and ate an awful lot of fish during the book's preparation, the recipes culled from fish cookery repertoires of many countries. A number were discarded on grounds of not being special enough. By the same token I tried to include enough of the tried-and-true preparations to aid in planning simple family meals. I hope I have straddled both extremes and provided enough *données* so that any fish, even if a recipe for it does not appear here, may be approached without fear.

R.A.S.

Introduction

My childhood memories of eating fish are not particularly negative but are quite limited. It was rarely cooked in our house and simply had no fixed position in our gastronomic firmament as did, say, lamb chops. Even when my father or a family friend went fishing, the point of the exercise was the sport, and the fish were given away or thrown back. They were hard to clean, hard to store properly, and not all that interesting to eat.

Going out for dinner, on the other hand, was almost synonymous with going to one of the seafood restaurants that abounded in Philadelphia, where I grew up. There were some wonderful ones, ranging from small and immaculate "oyster houses" to the notable Bookbinder's, of which there were two, the "old" and the "original." (The difference between these two terms remains a mystery to me to this day: I only knew that the merits of each passionately divided my parents and their friends.) What "seafood" meant to us was lobster, lots of melted butter, and wearing a funny bib, or fried oysters in any month with an R in it. They were heavily breaded yet crisp on the outside, steamy, succulent, and juicy on the inside, and ritualistically obliterated with both catsup and tartar sauce. I vaguely recall that various fish were listed on these menus, but certainly no one of us ever ordered it unless lacking imagination or gastrointestinal fortitude. I think the reason was that it was quite boring, with the exception of shad and shad roe in the spring. As a child I was not allowed to eat shad, however, because of the bones, so the occasional forkfuls that were proffered me constituted my major fish consumption. Very occasionally, we ventured into crab cakes, when the crab came in from nearby Maryland. We also ate cherrystone clams smothered in spicy red cocktail sauce, and when I got older I learned from my parents the exquisite joy of sucking them off the half shell at the clam bars in the Reading Terminal Market. I also learned to eat oysters raw, which I thought a very grown-up thing.

It was another kettle of fish altogether when the fish was smoked or pickled. Thanks to Russian grandparents, some of my fondest food memories have to do with a spectacular array of smoked and pickled salmon, moist, sweet morsels of belly lox, pickled herring, *schmaltz* herring, chubs, whitefish, sable, and eel, the fatty and delectable white salmon trout, known by its Russian name *byalo ribitsa* and the elusively flavored *chubak,* or smoked shad. We feasted on these delicacies with cucumbers, tomatoes, sweet onions, and three or four kinds of bagels and densely moist black bread, slathered with cream cheese with chives in it. I liked them all, and they served further to seal my notion that fish required some terrific elaboration before being fit for consumption. I cannot recall eating just plain fish at home, so if we had it, clearly it was not memorable.

Indeed the very smell of fish frying was associated with the smell of poverty. This may have been because there were some children at school who, as it happened, were poor and also Catholic, and as I vaguely knew they *had* to eat fish on Friday in a sort of penance, this served to reinforce its backseat-to-meat position. Perhaps in those homes where I encountered it, the fish was not the freshest, the treatment unkind or uninformed, and the ventilation poor. Who knows how these ideas persist? Anyway, we always had roast chicken on Friday.

My husband grew up in Rhode Island, which has large Portuguese and Italian colonies, and he recalls having fried flounder on Fridays even though he was not Catholic, because that was when it was fresh at the market. Presumably the religion of those two ethnic groups dictated this rather than their marvelous national ways with fish; otherwise why only flounder, and why *only* Friday? Clearly the fact that Narragansett Bay was teeming with an incredible variety of finned creatures did not govern, in the last analysis, how they were eaten.

Deploring the paucity of fish in her childhood, the outstanding food writer M. F. K. Fisher, in *With Bold Knife and Fork,* remembers only "an occasional finnan haddie and codfish, always boiled until almost tasteless and then swimming in a 'white sauce' and served with little pale potatoes." "Surely," she ponders, "there must have been people all about us in Whittier, California, who caught or bought and then cooked the creatures of the nearby Pacific and our deep occasional lakes?"

To be fair, people in those days were scared of fish; freezing was unknown or at least in its infancy and, fragile fish, with its unfortunate connotation as a potential poisoner of the unwary, was treated indelicately, subjected to overlong sojourns in the oven, fried to petrifaction or boiled to lifelessness, all smelly pursuits with unendearing results.

Cookbook author Julia Child, who also grew up in California, did not fare much better. They had the usual broiled fish on Friday, panfried trout when they camped in the High Sierras, and boiled salmon on the Fourth of July. Occasionally, codfish balls with egg sauce were served on Sunday mornings as a gesture to her mother's New England origin. She recalls being quite overwhelmed in France by a *sole meunière* "handsomely browned and still sputteringly hot under its coating of chopped parsley, and around it swirled a goodly amount of golden Normandy butter. It was heaven to eat, the flesh so very fresh, with its delicate yet definite texture and taste that blended marvelously with the browned butter sauce."* A few days later, her senses

*From *Julia Child's Kitchen,* Alfred A. Knopf, 1975.

were again pleasantly assaulted by a *sole normande*, "a poem of carefully poached and flavored fillets surrounded by oysters and mussels, napped with a winy creamy buttery sauce that tasted subtly of the sole, with hints of the garnishing shellfish, and of the fluted mushrooms that topped it. I had simply never seen nor eaten anything like that before, and neither did I imagine fish could be taken so seriously and sauced so voluptuously."

Like Julia Child, my first experience with fish cooked seriously was in France; it was also a *sole meunière* and I almost swooned at its goodness. My real education (and love) began then, ranging from the hushed temples of gastronomy in Paris to the *cervecerías* of Madrid, where shellfish is eaten by the dozen out of hand and where one went expressly for that purpose. The sweet morsels of *cigalas* (crayfish) and *percebes* (barnacles!), several kinds and sizes of shrimp and clams and oysters were washed down with great quaffs of beer, while the general bonhomie increased in direct proportion to the growing pile of shells under the table. It was in Spain, too, that I learned to eat tiny baby eels with their dear specks of blue eyes, sizzling in lethally hot oil and utterly sublime. And the delicacy of *coscochas*, the fatty sweet cheeks of the hake, a giggle on English menus as "hake jowls," and then all those glorious regional fish stews and *zarzuelas* with their cadenzas and obbligatos of flavors. I never dreamed that people actually ate mussels, and I still remember clambering over rocks on the Asturian coast with friends, gathering them in ancient baskets and rushing home amid great hilarity to help prepare a gigantic Spanish version of *moules marinière* swabbed up with lots of crusty country bread. It was interesting to note in Spain in those days, where a certain *mañana* aspect could be said to prevail in commerce, that the giant *centolla* crabs and crayfish and the sweet-fleshed fish and shellfish were sped from the icy Cantabrican waters with the most amazing alacrity and dispatch. Fish was taken very seriously there, and the inland mountain capital of Madrid, where I lived, profited greatly.

Taking fish seriously is what we are learning to do of late, and it is the underlying theme of this book.

How to Use This Book

The various forms in which fish are available at market and which are specified in the recipes in this book are explained in Chapter I. In that chapter, cooking techniques are also defined and described; this material should be consulted before attempting a recipe based on a procedure with which you are not familiar.

Basic information on shellfish will be found in Chapter VI.

Specific procedures that apply to one particular fish or shellfish, e.g., soaking salt cod, shucking oysters, are detailed in the short discussion that precedes each recipe grouping.

Occasionally you will see this symbol ❁ following an item in a list of ingredients, for example:

> Lemon Butter Sauce ❁
> Beurre Manié ❁

This means that the recipe for *lemon butter* sauce or a description of *beurré manié* appears in another part of the book; see the Index for the page number.

Many of the recipes in this book can be made successfully with fish other than the one specified, but having similar characteristics. Substitutions are often suggested in the general information preceding the recipe groupings and in the recipes themselves, so that you may take advantage of local availabilities and seasonal abundance.

ONE
General Information

I cannot think of any other area of cooking permeated by as much general insecurity as the preparation of fish. Yet it is among the simplest, easiest, and fastest foods to prepare, besides being one of the most nutritious. About the worst thing you can do to it is overcook it. Ultimately, all you really have to know about a fish in the absolute sense is that it is fresh, not poisonous, and what cooking methods apply. Choosing the cooking method depends on the type of fish and its market form, about which you will read more presently. One's fish-cooking repertoire and general feeling of ease in handling fish can be greatly enhanced by being familiar with both, as well as by knowing that a great many fish of similar type are interchangeable in a given recipe. Thus, there are pleasant culinary and economic dividends to be gotten by choosing some of the less popular fish, which, due to less demand, are often half the price of those better known and more interesting.

These simple objectives may be clouded by the fact that of the twenty thousand species of fish in the world, there are literally hundreds in American waters alone and any one of these may have more than one name, depending on the locality and who is doing the calling. The porgy of Long Island Sound, for example, and the scup of Narragansett Bay are identical fish. To confuse things further, one fish name may apply to other fish as well; redfish, for example, is the name for the red drum in the South but in California is another name for bass. Certain fish have names that change according to size: a lemon sole is a winter flounder or blackback when it weighs less than three and a half pounds; scrod, thought by many to be a distinct species, is merely a cod under three pounds. Tomcod is also a name for a small cod, but on the Pacific coast is another name for a croaker!

Then there is the case of *whitefish*, a freshwater fish, and *white fish*, which is any fish with white flesh . . . and the fish that have nothing to do with each other save that someone, somewhere, thought they looked alike, for example, the trout, a fresh water fish with numerous varieties and the sea trout, a saltwater fish, also called weakfish, a member of the wrasse family, related to the bass but speckled like a trout.

Bream, a name that anglers in the South sometimes use for various small freshwater game fish called sunfish, is also a name for members of the saltwater *Sparidae* family, which includes the porgy. The *daurade* or *dorade* family of France is the prized fish called "sea bream" in Great Britain, yet in that country one can also see at the fish dealer's fish labeled "bream" that are neither porgies *nor* sea bream but a kind of cod called redfish, vastly different in flavor. All entitled to be called bream, the *daurade,* the sunfish, and porgy are miles apart, literally and figuratively, from a culinary point of view.

If all this seems an impossible confusion, never mind—these distinctions are amusing but not vital. Let us start with knowing how to buy fish and prepare it for cooking.

BUYING FISH

Fish are most commonly available to the consumer in the following ways. The list includes all the forms mentioned in the recipes in this book. Collectively they are often referred to as "market forms."

Whole fish or *"round" fish:* Technically this is a fish just as it comes from the water. A recipe will often call for a fish that is "whole." This really means "whole dressed."

WHOLE OR ROUND FISH

Whole dressed: A whole fish, eviscerated, scaled, with fins removed (which is done routinely in most markets, although the fins are easily pulled out after cooking).

A whole dressed fish is split in the process of dressing; however, it may also be had whole, dressed, backbone out, if you are planning to stuff it. Otherwise, the backbone routinely remains. So do the head and tail unless you ask that they be removed. (*Dressed* is another way of saying "cleaned," a word that some people object to because it implies that the fish was "unclean" to start with.)

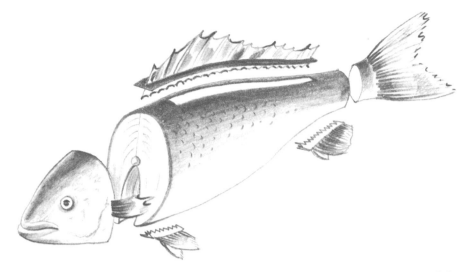

DRESSED: Scaled and eviscerated fish, usually with head, tail, and fins removed.

Drawn: A whole fish (usually a small one such as smelt, herring, mackerel, or trout, having a small ventral or belly cavity) that is gutted through a small neck slit and therefore remains unsplit.* Usually the milt, the male reproductive glands or the roe of the female, remains. The gills are removed, as are the scales if any.

DRAWN: Whole fish from which entrails are removed.

Pan dressed: Similar to whole dressed, but used for smaller fish three quarters of a pound to one and a half pounds. It means scaled, eviscerated, and usually the head, tail, and fins removed. With very small fish such as the smelt, the head and tail are usually left on unless you specifically request otherwise.

Steaks: Cross-section slices of large round-bodied fish that have been

*For instructions on drawing trout see Index, recipe for Skewered Trout.

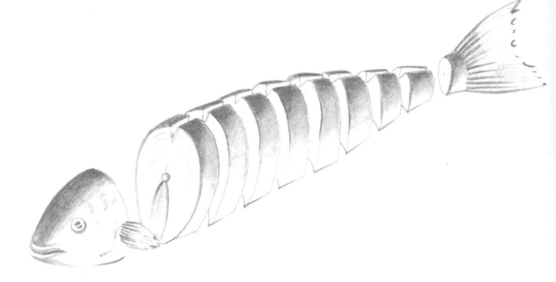

STEAKED: Large-size dressed fish may be cut into cross-section slices called steaks.

previously dressed. They contain a piece of the backbone that should be left intact. Very large flat fish such as halibut are also cut into steaks.

Fillets (also spelled filet): Sides of dressed fish cut lengthwise. Usually they are practically boneless. The skin may be left on or removed, depending on the recipe.

When a fish is filleted and the skin left on and intact along the back, it is called a "butterfly" fillet. If the fillets are joined by belly skin, it is a "kited" fillet.

FILLETED: The sides of a fish cut lengthwise away from the backbone.

BUTTERFLIED: The two sides of a filleted fish, held together by the skin.

A very large fillet may be divided into two pieces, known as "crosscut" fillets. A crosscut fillet cut in two gives "quartercut" fillets.

Fish sticks: Pieces of fish commercially cut from a frozen block of fish and usually sold frozen.

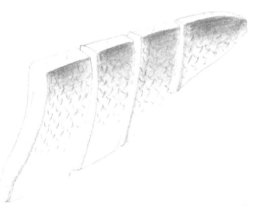

FISH STICKS.

How Much to Buy

In the absence of recipe information, here are some general rules of thumb: *Whole dressed fish:* Allow one pound per serving, except in the case of red snapper, which because of its large head will yield less than half its weight in meat. If you are going to stuff a whole fish, decrease the per-pound allowance. *Pan-dressed fish:* Allow a half pound per person. Or simply tell the fish dealer how many will be dining, and the number of those that are children. Most good markets are accustomed to advising on amounts, because what you end up with may vary, after skin, bones, etc., are removed. *Steaks:* Because there is relatively little waste, one pound serves two or three, depending on appetites. *Fillets:* Generally one pound serves two, or 3 if they are being combined with ingredients that are filling.

Remember that your phrasing is important. I once asked for *two pounds of bass fillet,* but the fishman heard *two pounds of bass filleted.* He filleted a two-pound bass, and what I had when I got home was fourteen ounces of fish to feed five people (I made a Chinese dish, which always magically stretches things). It is a good idea to stress the words "net weight" or emphasize the number of people. A fish such as red snapper has an extremely large head, so while a four-pound bass might feed six—its net yield being about three pounds—the same four pounds of snapper will yield two pounds or less. Four pounds of sole fillets, on the other hand, might feed as many as ten to twelve cooked, with a very filling sauce that incorporates other food ingredients such as mushrooms or shellfish or if served as a first course only.

Don't hesitate to ask for the head, carcasses, and other parts for making stock, when you have purchased a whole fish and had it filleted. Dealers usually have more than they know what to do with and will often throw them in for free or a nominal charge even if you're buying other fillets. Save the stock to freeze. It's economical and can be used, strained and refrozen, and kept indefinitely. In my freezer I have stock that was made from a salmon poached two years ago. For poaching and making sauces, bottled clam juice, often used in place of stock, is flat, salty, and inferior in taste, though handy in a pinch.

Storing Fish

Prior to refrigerating fresh fish, it may be washed in cold water, dried, and lightly wrapped in plastic wrap or foil. It is a good idea to use it as soon as possible, two or three days at the outside. The old saw about guests and fish going bad after three days may not be exact, at least as far as fish are concerned, but there certainly will be impairment of flavor and texture after that time. Store frozen fish in the freezer in its original wrap. To store smoked fish, handle the same way as fresh or frozen fish. (Smoking is a treatment to enhance the flavor of fish but is not sufficient to preserve it.)

Home freezing: If you are freezing fish yourself (and only freshly caught fish should be frozen), clean and gut it first. Scrape away any blood streaks and wipe inside with paper towels. Scaleless fish, such as catfish, must be skinned before freezing. Because home freezers do not achieve and maintain the low temperatures of commercial freezers, I would say that ideally three months is the longest that fish can be frozen without losing taste or texture. Six months is the maximum.

Fish with a high oil content (such as mackerel and bluefish) especially tend to develop a slightly rancid taste after three months.

The simplest way to wrap fish for the short-term freezer storage described above is to use heavy aluminum foil or freezer paper, press out all the air, seal, and label. Put the unfrozen packages in the coldest part of your freezer and try not to stack or lump them together in one place, for this could retard the internal freezing even though the outsides appear hard.

One way to lengthen freezer life and prevent liquid loss is to first dip the fish in a chilled brine solution, made by combining about five tablespoons of salt with two quarts of water. Dip the fish in it for thirty seconds, then wrap well. This method applies primarily to lean freshwater fish. Freeze oily fish, such as mackerel and bluefish, in solid blocks as described below.

If space is not a problem, another good method is to freeze the fish in lightly salted water in some container, which is then removed, so that you end up with a block of ice containing a fish. Use an empty milk carton, a fish poacher, a metal loaf pan, or a plastic container. Curl fish if necessary. If the fish has floated to the top and is not completely covered in ice, pour more water on top and refreeze. When it is frozen solid, briefly dip the container in hot water to loosen the ice block, remove the block and wrap it in plastic or aluminum wrap and seal.

A method requiring less storage space is the following: Wrap the fish (cut into its final cooking form) with plastic wrap and put it on a cookie sheet and freeze. As soon as it is completely frozen, remove it and dip it into ice water, immersing it completely. A glaze or thin coat of ice will form. Repeat three or four times, then wrap it for long-term storage. If the glaze does not form, freeze the fish a bit longer and repeat the process. This method will keep fish for about two months. After that you will have to repeat the glazing.

Do not freeze cooked fish (except shrimp, crab, or lobster) unless they are in a sauce. Cooked fish should not be kept frozen for more than three months.

Do freeze herb butters such as chive, parsley, and dill, which can then be used to dress any cooked fish. Roll the butter into long sausage shapes and freeze them. Slice off what you need, rewrap the butter, and return it to the freezer.

Freezing shellfish: ''Fresh'' shrimp have usually been frozen somewhere along the way, so buy only what you need. Of course buy and keep frozen those that are already commercially frozen. Raw clams and oysters can be frozen in their liquor in freezer containers for two to three months. People do freeze scallops, but I find that this impairs the delicate flavor and texture. Crab meat and lobster meat are available frozen commercially, lightly packed in a light brine solution, and you can duplicate this at home.

Frozen Fish

Improved freezing techniques make a variety of fish commercially available in sections of the country and at times of the year where it would not have been possible before. Commercial flash freezing, done at very low temperatures with liquid nitrogen, quick-freezes freshly caught fish that, if given reasonable care along the way, can compete favorably in quality in roughly the same way flash-frozen vegetables do with fresh ones. Among the fish you are likely to find frozen are flounder, cod, brook trout, various sole, halibut, and whiting. Local and regional markets may have skinned and dressed catfish, kingfish steaks, and grouper or mullet fillets. Pollock is often labeled simply "ocean fresh fillets," a term sometimes also applied to ocean perch, virtually the entire American catch of which is sold frozen.

Buying frozen fish: Whether whole, in fillets, or in steaks many of the same rules apply as in buying frozen meat: Make sure that the package is solidly frozen and tightly wrapped, and with little or no air space in the packing. The flesh should look firm and glossy with no discolored parts or white patches that might mean freezer burn. There should be no frost or ice crystals when the package is opened. A strong fishy taste when the fish is defrosted indicates rancidity, and if it appears lusterless, cottony, or shredded on the surface and yields liquid when pressed, it probably has been thawed and refrozen and should not be eaten. Any of these symptoms mean that you should ask for your money back.

Defrosting: Store frozen fish in the freezer in its original wrap. The best way to defrost it is to allow it a twenty-four-hour stay on the bottom (the coldest) shelf of your refrigerator. Thawing at room temperature may be quicker, but you will also lose liquid, which means leached flavor as well as nutrients, not to mention textural impairment. If you are in a hurry, partially thaw in the refrigerator, then put in a well-sealed plastic bag and let it sit in a bowl of cool water to complete defrosting. Do not thaw breaded fish items before cooking, however.

To cook frozen fish: In most cases, frozen fish, once properly thawed, can be substituted in recipes calling for the same fish in its fresh state. If you are going to fry or broil it, make sure to pat it dry first. Frying, broiling, or baking fish that is still frozen will produce a result that, while edible, is far from ideal. Plan ahead in order to allow proper defrosting time; if you can't, allow 50 per cent longer cooking time (see the Canadian Theory, noted in the Index) and if broiling, cook further away from the flame. This is to be considered an emergency measure only. If you must cook fish taken directly from the freezer, I advise poaching or baking it wrapped securely in foil, using the Canadian Theory for frozen fish and adding five extra minutes per inch for the foil.

Once defrosted, fish should never be refrozen.

PREPARING FISH FOR COOKING
Cleaning and Dressing Fish

Most fish sold in markets today are already cleaned and dressed and can be prepared for cooking—boned, filleted, steaked, butterflied—to suit the type of fish and the cook. However, if you fish or have friends who do, here are step-by-step directions for the various procedures:

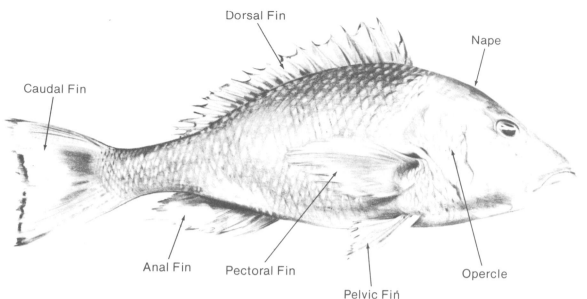

Caudal Fin

Dorsal Fin

Nape

Anal Fin   Pectoral Fin

Pelvic Fin

Opercle

ANATOMICAL DRAWING OF FISH.

REMOVE FINS: Using a sharp heavy scissors, cut off the anal, ventral, and dorsal fins. Cut around pelvic fins and pull off carefully, without tearing flesh. (Base root bones that remain in fish can be removed after cooking if fish is to be used whole.)

A FISH SCALER: The rough-toothed surface makes it easy to remove scales.

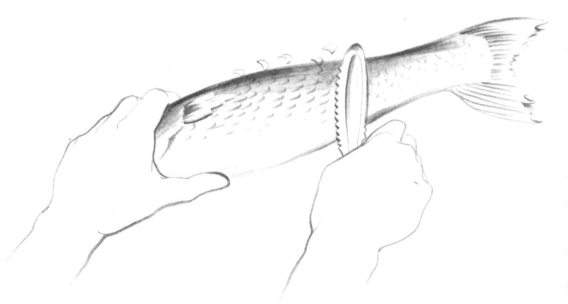

SCALING: Wash fish; scale while wet. Hold fish firmly by head on cutting board. With a scaler or knife held almost vertically, scrape off scales, starting at tail and scraping toward head. Remove all scales around fin areas and head.

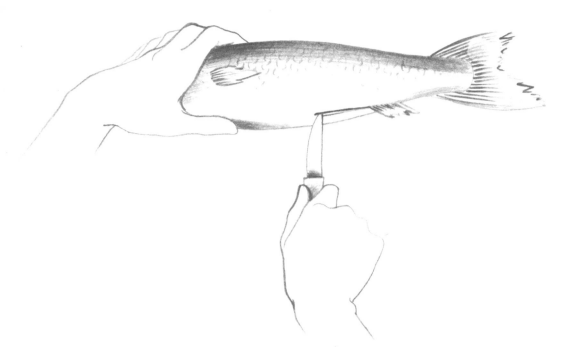

CLEANING: *With a sharp knife slit entire length of belly from vent to head, taking care not to pierce entrails. Remove intestines. If roe is to be used, remove carefully without breaking membrane casing.*

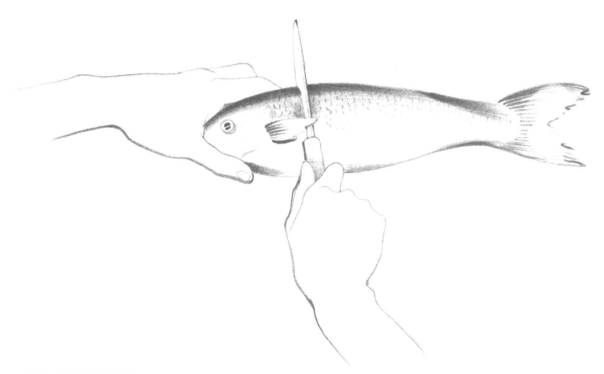

REMOVING HEAD AND TAIL: *Remove head by cutting through the backbone at the nape, then down and around the opercle to the throat. Cut off pectoral fins and tail.*

FOR LARGE FISH: Cut down through flesh to backbone on each side of fish, then place fish on edge of table with head hanging over and snap backbone by bending head down. Completely sever by cutting through any connecting flesh that remains.

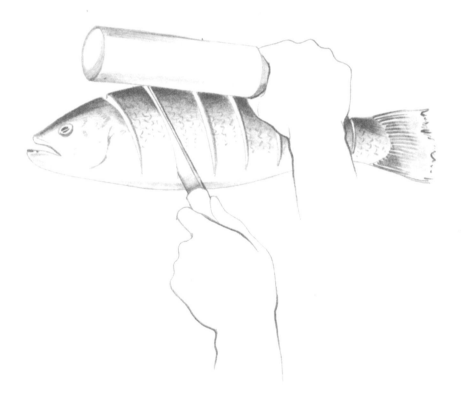

TO STEAK (a good treatment for large fish): Mark off steaks with cuts 1– 2 inches apart down to the backbone. Hold knife in cut and tap with a hammer or mallet if necessary to add force and ensure a clean cut.

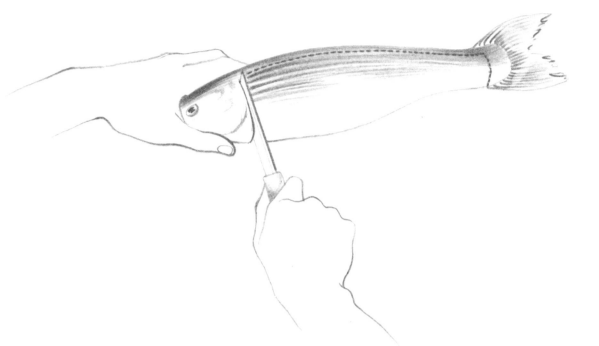

FILLETING A ROUNDFISH: Cut along back of fish from tail to head, cutting down to the backbone at the nape. Insert knife in cut, turn fish flat, and cut flesh away from backbone and rib bones with short sawing cuts.

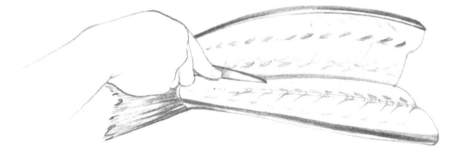

Lift away the fillet or whole side of fish in one piece. Turn and repeat on other side. Then skin or not as desired.

To bone a fish through the ventral slit, work the curved rib bones free with the fingers and use the fingers and a small knife to free the backbone from the dorsal flesh. Sever the backbone at the anal and head ends and work it free.

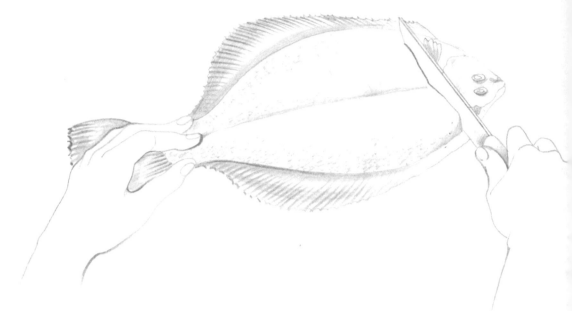

FILLETING A FLATFISH: Cut down to the backbone behind head at nape (it is not necessary to remove head).

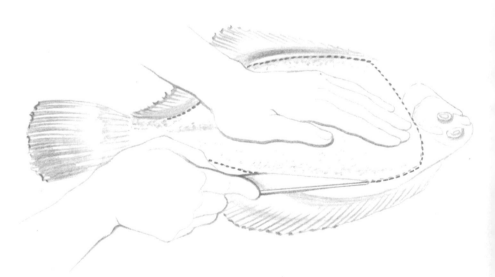

Make a cut from nape to tail along both sides (fillet portion is indicated by dotted lines). Insert knife blade and slide long backbone to loosen fillet, then lift it off.

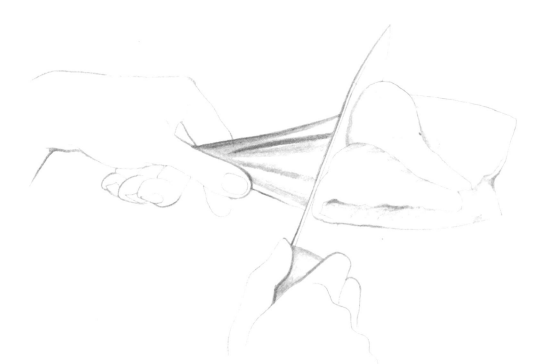

*With skin side down, hold tail of fillet, slide knife between flesh and skin,
thus removing skin. (The pressure of the* pull, *not the cut, is the key; the
skin should separate in one piece.) Cut off ribbed outside edges (skirt),
which are fatty, and discard. If half fillets are desired, divide fillet in two
along midline.*

Boning

Fish are boned because you plan to stuff them or because the bones present a problem, as in the case of shad. While you can stuff a fish that is not
boned, cutting and serving become much neater and easier if it is. Flatfish
may also be boned for stuffing, although this is a bit trickier. Small fish,
such as trout or mackerel, may be boned from the back to avoid the belly
slit, allowing you to present the fish in its swimming position rather than on
its side.

To bone a roundfish for stuffing: The backbone and ribs can be removed
either through the belly or ventral slit, the most common way, or from the

back. To bone a fish through the ventral slit, first scale fish and rinse. Remove gills by lifting them up and out through throat opening; cut out and discard. Lay fish on side with head away from you. Insert knife tip at anal end and make a ventral slit toward the head. Remove entrails, cut off fins and rinse opening. Enlarge opening to head. Holding knife almost horizontally, insert tip in opening and slide blade along upper side of backbone and rib cage, working toward tail. Carefully repeat, deepening cut until backbone is freed from top half of fish. Again working with tip and first inch of blade held horizontally, insert knife *under* backbone at head end and gently loosen bony cage from bottom half of fish, working toward tail. Carefully pull fish open as you cut, leaving as little meat as possible on bone. The backbone is now free, attached only at the head and tail. Sever with clippers or scissors at both ends; lift out and discard. Rinse fish inside and out. Fish is now ready to receive stuffing.

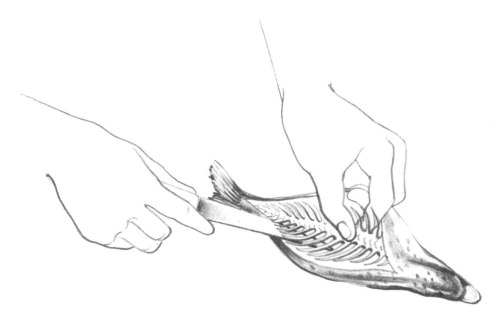

To bone a fish from the back, or dorsal method, tear gills out, insert fingers, and gently pull out viscera. Cut down each side of the backbone from the top (dorsal) side, running the blade along the backbone as you do. Take care not to pierce abdominal skin. Make a cut or break through the spine behind the head and near the tail; work bone up and out.

Boning shad: Boning the shad is, as they say, a completely different kettle of fish. Although the shad is considered a terribly bony fish because of its two sets of floating ribs, these Y-shaped "extra" bones lie neatly in two rows paralleling the backbone and can be easily excised provided you know where they are. After filleting the shad as you would any roundfish, lay the fillet skin side down and run your fingertips over the top; you can feel the extra bone sets, one lying about one half inch to one inch above the back-bone, the other the same distance below it. Remove these, following instructions in the drawings.

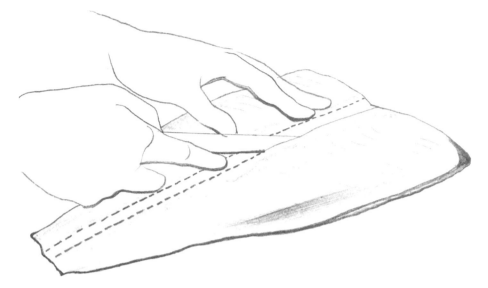

BONING SHAD: Make 2 long parallel cuts lengthwise, about ½ inch on either side of the center line of the fillet. Do not penetrate the skin.

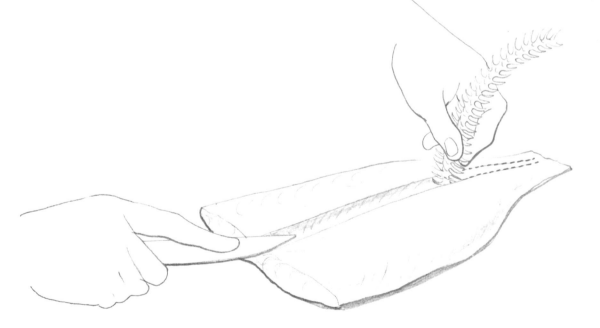

Turn fillet with tail end away from you. Insert knife tip in one cut and work underneath bone with an upward prying motion until you can grasp bone with fingers. Pull strip up and back, working loose until entire bone strip comes out in one piece. Repeat in second incision and work out second strip of bones the same way. Then repeat entire procedure on bottom fillet.

Boning a cooked whole fish: Fish always tastes better cooked whole, but Americans have what amounts to a national phobia about bones, and most people in this country do not know how to handle a whole cooked fish. The first time I was presented with a whole trout at an English luncheon, I felt a mild surge of panic, then, as everyone else tucked in with equanimity, I slyly copied my neighbor and found it really quite easy. Roundfish, such as trout and pompano, and small sea bass can be split in half with the table knife and the top half lifted aside, thus exposing the backbone, which is then lifted out. If you do not wish to eat the skin, simply fork the meat away from it, or lift the skin off first.

THE ROUNDFISH.

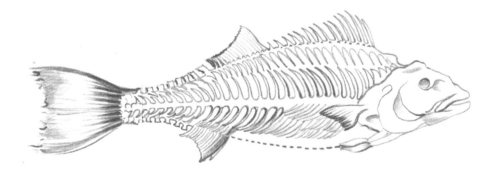

THE SKELETAL ROUNDFISH.

Flatfish, such as flounder and sole, are best handled with a draw of the knife along a mid-lateral line corresponding to the backbone. The meat can then be raised off the bone on each side of the backbone. After that is consumed, lift out the spine and bones in one piece, set them aside, and eat the rest. The bothersome tiny bones that edge a sole should be cut off and discarded before serving, but if they are not, remove them before starting to eat the fish.

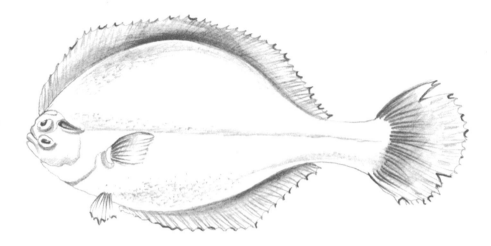

THE FLATFISH.

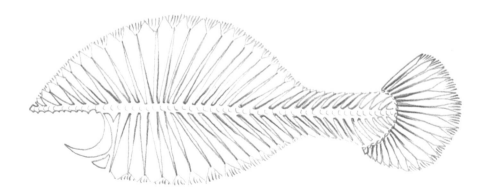

THE SKELETAL FLATFISH.

Stuffing

A whole fish, boned and stuffed with the head and tail on, makes an impressive main course that is easy to serve. The procedure is a "natural" because of the opportunities afforded by the stomach cavity, and there is no end of delicious stuffings you can use. In addition to enhancing the flavor of the fish, a stuffing, which can range from a simple bread-crumb-and-herb stuffing to an elaborate forcemeat or mousse, makes the fish go further. A roundfish is the most obvious candidate, but flatfish may also be stuffed, although removing the skeleton to do so is tricky. The completed stuffed flatfish resembles a flattened purse.

TO STUFF A BONED TROUT FROM THE BACK.

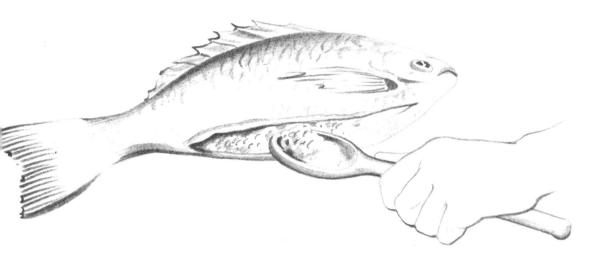

STUFFING A ROUNDFISH: Stuff loosely to allow for expansion of stuffing.

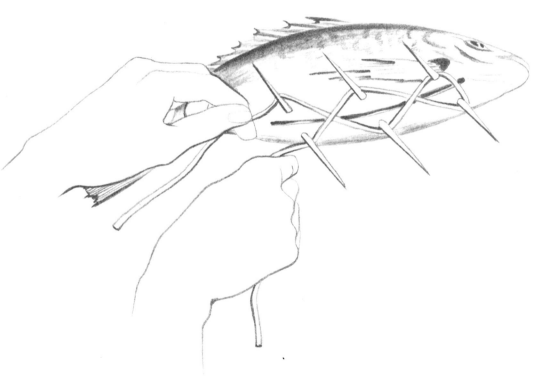

Close opening, using skewers or toothpicks and a lacing truss with either thin twine or dental floss.

STUFFING A FLATFISH: With the tip of a sharp knife, cut down center of dressed fish along backbone, from within 1 inch of head end, to tail.

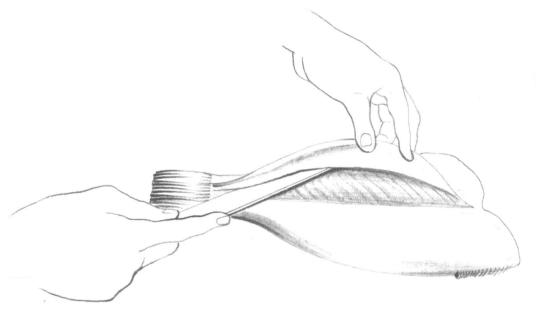

Turn knife flat and insert tip in slit; loosen flesh along one side of rib bones. Turn knife opposite way and repeat. Spine may remain or be broken in several places and lifted out.

The completed stuffed fish.

COOKING METHODS

The Canadian Cooking Theory

The single greatest culinary crime committed against fish is overcooking it. In the last few years, the Consumer Division of the Canadian Fisheries and Marine Service has come up with an exhaustively tested theory for accurately cooking fish, and this has gained wide acceptance by serious cooks. Known as the Canadian Cooking Theory and referred to in this book as ''the Canadian Theory,'' it can be applied to the four basic methods of cooking fish: dry heat (baking, broiling and grilling, and barbecuing); moist heat (poaching, steaming, and braising); panfrying or sautéing; and deep-frying. It is helpful whenever you cook without a recipe or work with one that does not give a specific cooking time.

The principle is simplicity itself: lay fish to be cooked (any form) on the counter or table (lay a whole fish on its side) and measure it at its thickest point by standing a ruler perpendicular to the table top. *Cooking time is calculated at 10 minutes per inch,* plus or minus any fraction thereof.

Add 5 minutes per inch if a sauce is involved.

Double the cooking time if the fish is frozen.

Fish should be cooked only until the translucent flesh becomes opaque. Actually, if you remove the fish from the heat when there is still a hairline of translucency in the middle (you can check this by inserting the tip of a sharp knife), it will continue to cook to perfection in its own heat. The

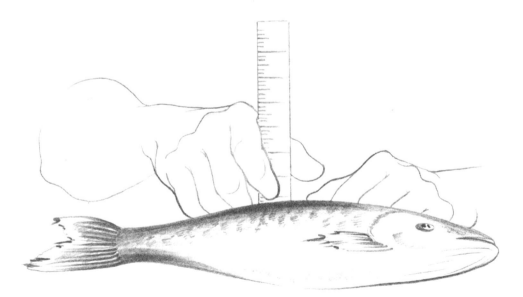

MEASURING FOR THE CANADIAN COOKING THEORY.

problem with testing for doneness by flaking with a fork, the guide given in fish recipes since time immemorial, is that your fish will flake for sure if it is overcooked, but then it is too late. The Canadian Theory, while it must be combined with common sense and a vigilant eye, gives you a good rule of thumb to start with. Once you get to know what properly cooked (but not overcooked) fish looks like, you will not need to make the fork test and can rely on timing and your eye alone.

Since fish cooked quickly at a high temperature retains maximum flavor and moistness, the Canadian Theory recommends *baking* at 450° and *broiling* at a distance of two to four inches from the flame. Bake or broil on a greased preheated broiler pan or ungreased foil, and in either case baste with melted fat or a basting sauce. It is not necessary to turn fish being broiled.

The only caveats I would add to this theory concerns its blanket application to broiling and baking in foil. Thin fillets (one half inch or less) tend to become overcooked and dry when timed by the formula, so for broiling use fillets at least three quarters of an inch thick at their thickest point. In broiling thinner fillets, watch very carefully for the moment when the flesh becomes opaque but not paper-dry. If possible try to catch the moment of the translucent hairline described above. Fillets of panfish and small flatfish will be done in 3 minutes or less; check after 2 minutes. And don't expect thin cuts to broil crispy and golden on top, unless you have been profligate with butter. Nor can you get around these aesthetics with a dusting of paprika before cooking. It will burn under the intense flame and give a bitter off-taste to the fish.

Baking

General Procedure: Any size fish or market form may be baked, and of course it is the ideal method for a stuffed whole fish. Thick steaks or fillets are also best baked. Preheat the oven to 400–450°. Place the whole fish or fillets on a buttered or oiled baking pan and dot with butter. Season with salt and pepper and bake, calculating the cooking time according to the Canadian Theory, which applies only when baking at this temperature and in an uncovered dish.

Baking in foil: The Canadian Theory prescribes adding 5 minutes per inch to fish cooked in foil. Where baking is concerned, I have found that at the high temperature enough intense heat is generated by steam forming inside the foil package to make the extra time unneccesary. The only exception would be an unusually thick center cut or a large fish over five pounds. In either case place the wrapped fish on a cookie sheet before putting in the oven.

If you have any reason to suspect that your oven temperature does not coincide with the setting, check it with an oven thermometer. For high-heat baking, such as the Canadian and Spencer methods (see below) preheat your oven for 20 minutes. Be precise about the cooking time; overbaking dries out natural juices.

The Spencer Method: Another high-heat method, also called "oven-frying," which is especially suited to cooking fillets, was developed in 1934 by government food expert Evalene Spencer and was named after her. It is a procedure that essentially reduces the size of your oven, giving you fast high heat, almost as in broiling, without the drying effects of the flame, plus the crispness of frying, without the trouble. It works as follows:
 1. Heat the oven to 550°. Put the rack in the highest position. Starting at your left, place in sequence the following:
  1. A shallow dish of salted milk (¼ cup for each pound of fish)
  2. A pan of finely sifted bread crumbs (about ¾ cup for each pound of fish).
  3. An oiled baking pan.
  4. A cup of melted butter or bacon fat (3 tablespoons for 4 fillets).
 Cut the fish into serving-size pieces. Using the left hand, dip a fish piece into the milk, then lay it on the crumbs. Use the right hand to pat the crumbs in place on both sides and transfer to the baking sheet. When all are done, drizzle the fat over the crumbs and bake for 10–15 minutes. Under no circumstances add liquid of any kind. Transfer the cooked fish with a spatula to a serving dish.

NOTE: Where very thin fillets are cooked, you might use crumbs that have previously been toasted, as the very short cooking time may not be enough to brown them.

Broiling

Broiling, being the simplest and most pristine form of fish cookery, requires impeccably fresh fish and careful attention to technique. This means precise timing and proper placement in relationship to the flame, so browning can take place without overcooking or burning the fish. The appealing surface of a properly broiled piece of fish cannot be simulated with a shower of paprika and you should look with a jaundiced eye at restaurants that try to get away with it unless dietary reasons prevent the use of fat.

General Procedure: Preheat the broiler for a full 10 minutes. (Inefficient heat will only break down the fish and sap its juices.) Adjust the rack so that the top surface of the fish is 2–4 inches from the heating unit. If using fish still frozen, allow at least 6 inches to prevent overcooking the outside before the inside is done. Measure the fish and calculate cooking time. Ideally, fish for broiling should be at least ¾ of an inch thick to avoid becoming dry. Thinner fillets benefit from having their tops dusted with flour or crumbs first. Place fish on buttered or oiled rack of the broiling pan, and brush with melted butter or basting sauce, or dot with butter. Fillets do not require turning; steaks may be browned on one side, then turned. In dividing the cooking time, allow a slightly longer time for the second side to become appetizingly brown, but take care not to exceed the total cooking time. Baste, then season after cooking. Broiling particularly suits oily fish such as shad, mullet, and mackerel.

To Broil a Split Fish: Melt some butter in the baking pan first. Place the fish in the pan, skin side down, dot the surface with butter, and broil without turning.

Broiling over Charcoal: Read the general information on charcoal grilling at the beginning of Chapter Seven.

Poaching

General Procedure: Poaching, as contrasted with boiling, is cooking in a liquid at about 205°, or just under the boil. Because of its delicate nature, fish is always poached rather than boiled. The liquid can be a previously made court bouillon or stock, milk or even lightly salted water. Almost any fish may be poached, although coarse-grained fish that flake into large pieces are less suitable. Bass, snapper, salmon, and large trout, which all have a fine flake, are best. Oily fish such as mackerel and bluefish are not good for poaching. You can poach a whole dressed fish, a thick center cut, or fillets. To prevent surface disintegration in the hot liquid, a whole fish or a thick center cut is wrapped in washed cheesecloth, which should have sufficiently long ends to give "handles" for lifting the fish in and out of the liquid. (These may then be tied together on top of the pot if they are in danger of burning.) Add the fish to the liquid, which should just cover, bring to a boil, cover, and adjust the heat so the liquid neither boils nor bubbles but just "shivers" *(mijoter*—to simmer—in French). Allow 8–10 minutes per pound or time the cooking according to the Canadian Theory. Leave the fish in the liquid after cooking is completed, until it is cool enough to handle. The cooking liquid may be strained through additional cheesecloth and refrigerated or frozen for future use.

An alternative way to poach smaller pieces of fish and fillets (still no less than one inch thick) is to bring the poaching liquid to a full boil, add the fish, turn off the heat, cover, and leave in the liquid for the alloted poaching time. Another way, best for fillets, is to oven-poach them.

The recipe for Poached Striped Bass, below, serves as a model for poaching any similar whole fish.

Oven-Poaching: Fish fillets take nicely to "oven-poaching," which can be done in fish stock, white wine, a combination of the two, or (very agreeable for children) in milk. Preheat the oven to 350° and butter a flameproof dish just large enough to hold the fish in one layer. Season the fillets with salt and white pepper and arrange them in the dish, on top of 2 tablespoons of minced shallots if you like. Bring the liquid, which should barely cover the fish, to a boil on top of the stove, cover the fish with a sheet of buttered waxed paper, and bake for 10 minutes. This method is handy when a recipe calls for cooked, flaked fish of some sort and you haven't any leftovers.

Small pieces of fish may also be oven-poached in a small amount of liquid on a bed of aromatic vegetables, a technique which is often the basis for more complicated preparations that require elaborate saucing. The vegetables (onions, carrots, celery, shallots, mushrooms) take on added flavor by being lightly sautéed or softened in butter first. The fish, which should be lightly scored so that it does not curl while cooking, is placed on top of the vegetables and a small amount of liquid added. This can be fish fumet or a combination of fumet and white wine. Cover the fish with a buttered piece of brown or wax paper, laid directly on top, to help keep it moist. Place the dish in the lower third of a preheated 350° oven. Eight to ten minutes is about right for most average-sized sole and flounder fillets; thicker fish should be cooked at 400° and timed according to the Canadian Theory.

POACHED STRIPED BASS

COURT-BOUILLON
6–8 cups water
2 cups dry white wine
¼ cup white vinegar
1 cup thickly sliced onion
2 carrots, cut in 1-inch chunks
4 celery stalks with leaves, cut in
   1-inch chunks

1 leek, trimmed, split in half, and
   well rinsed (optional)
4 parsley stems
2 bay leaves
3 branches fresh thyme or ½ teaspoon dried
2 tablespoons salt
1 tablespoon peppercorns, crushed

THE FISH
A 3- to 4-pound striped bass, cleaned, gills removed, head and tail left on (or substitute red snapper, haddock, pollock, rockfish, whitefish, or lake trout)

Combine all the ingredients for the court-bouillon in a 6- to 8-quart enameled or stainless steel soup kettle. Bring to a boil over high heat, partially cover the pot, reduce heat, and simmer for 20 minutes. Straining is not necessary. Set aside to cool.

Wash the fish inside and out under cold running water. Without drying it, wrap in a long double-thick piece of damp, washed cheesecloth or, if none is available, a clean, thin tea towel, and tie with string in 2 or 3 places. Leave at least 6 inches of cloth at each end to serve as handles for lifting. (Twisting the ends of the cloth with string will make the handling easier.)

When the court-bouillon is lukewarm, pour it into a deep roasting pan with a cover or in a fish poacher, add the fish. The court-bouillon should cover the fish by 1½–2 inches. Add water if necessary.

Cover and bring to a boil over moderate heat; immediately adjust the heat so that fish cooks barely at a simmer for 8–10 minutes, depending on the size. Remove the pan from the heat and let the fish stand in the cooking liquid for another 15 minutes or until the fish and liquid are lukewarm.

Using the ends of the cheesecloth as handles, lift the fish from the pan, let it drain for a moment, then lay it on a large cutting board or platter. Cut off the strings. Open the cheesecloth but let the fish remain on it. Carefully scrape away the skin with a sharp small knife, making a cut in the skin at the base of the tail and gently pulling off the skin in strips toward the head. Also remove the line of bones along the top side of the fish, and any along the belly. Lift up the cheesecloth and flip the fish, skinned side down, onto a serving dish. Complete the skin removal on the second side.

If the fish is to be served cold, cover it with plastic wrap and refrigerate until thoroughly chilled. Garnish as desired and serve with green mayonnaise ✳ .

If the fish is to be served hot, serve with Beurre Blanc Sauce ✳ or Hollandaise Sauce ✳ .

Steaming

Steaming is somewhat like poaching except that the food is cooked *over* the liquid and not *in* it. Steaming permits fish to cook in its own juices and keeps the skin and flesh moist. A steaming setup can be improvised by using a colander, roasting trivet, or a metal pie pan with holes punched in it, set on an upright coffee cup, or anything else that will hold the fish above the boiling liquid. Almost any fish or shellfish may be steamed. If a large fish is involved, use a roaster rack and two coffee cups for steady support. This should be done in a large, heavy pot with a tight-fitting cover, such as a Dutch oven.

General Procedure: Place the food to be steamed in a heatproof dish or on foil, and then on the rack device in the pot as described above. Add boiling water to the pot within one inch of the bottom of the rack. Place the pot over high heat, cover tightly, and commence timing from the moment the pot is covered. Time according to the Canadian Theory. If you are steaming lobsters, be sure to drain them thoroughly after steaming.

Steaming, as a fish cooking technique, figures heavily in Chinese cooking, generally with smaller fish. Various seasonings such as shredded ginger root, garlic, scallions, and soy sauce may be placed on the fish after rubbing it lightly with salt inside and out. Steam as above.

Braising

Braising is a relatively little-used technique in this country, but one that is excellent especially for lean fish, because the texture and flavor are not lost in cooking. In general, it involves cooking a fish with a small amount of liquid, usually the rendered essences of sautéed aromatic vegetables combined with fish stock or wine, so that the fish will steam as it bakes. The key to braising is to use a covered vessel of a size that will snugly hold the fish and the other ingredients. Braising can be done for a short time at high heat (425°) or a longer time at more moderate (350°) heat. Either way, it carries the bonus of divine cooking juices that can be used *au naturel* or turned into a sauce. Cooking *en papillote* could be considered a related procedure in that the fish steams in aromatic essences while baking.

General Procedure: The following recipe, Wine-Braised Striped Bass, can serve as a model for oven-braising any suitable whole large fish such as salmon, weakfish, or trout. Large fillets can be treated in a similar manner. Braising may also be done on top of the stove. For this method consult Braised Salmon (see Index).

BRAISED STRIPED BASS

A 4- to 6-pound striped bass (or weakfish, salmon, or trout) cleaned, skin on, head and tail off
Salad oil
Salt and pepper
3 tablespoons butter
3 carrots, cut julienne
2 stalks celery, cut julienne

2 onions, sliced thin (about 1 cup)
2 cloves garlic, sliced thin
1 *bouquet garni* made with parsley, 2 bay leaves, and ½ teaspoon tarragon
2 cups white wine, concentrated fish stock, or a mixture of wine and stock, or a mixture of wine and bottled clam juice

Preheat oven to 425°.

Wash and dry the fish, brush the outside with salad oil, and season inside and out with salt and several grinds of pepper. Select a flameproof baking pan the same size as the fish; set the fish and pan aside.

Melt the butter in a heavy skillet and stir in the sliced vegetables. Add the *bouquet garni,* cover the pan, and cook slowly, uncovering to stir occasionally, until the vegetables are tender but not brown—about 10 minutes. Season with additional salt and pepper.

Put the vegetable mixture and the *bouquet garni* in the bottom of the pan and lay the fish on this bed. Add enough of the braising liquid so that the bottom of the pan is covered to a depth of about ½ inch. (The dish may be prepared ahead to this point and refrigerated.)

Bring the liquid to a simmer on top of the stove over moderately high heat. Cover the fish with a buttered piece of foil or cooking parchment and bake in the preheated oven timing according to the Canadian Theory. Regulate the heat so the liquid barely simmers; baste with liquid several times.

To serve: lightly butter a hot serving platter. Slide the fish onto the platter with the aid of two spatulas, peel the skin off the top side. Pull out any fins or small bones. The fish may be served as is, with the pan juices and braising vegetables (remove the *bouquet garni*) or with a sauce made as follows: strain the pan juices and the vegetables through a *chinois* or sieve, pushing down to extract the juices. Reduce the pan juices over high heat to ⅓ their original volume and thicken with *beurre manié* made by creaming together 2 tablespoons of butter with 1 tablespoon flour. Pour the sauce over the fish. Serves 6–8.

Alternatively, you may sauce the fish with a reduction of the pan juices and puréed vegetables. Put the vegetables through a food mill set over a heavy saucepan. Add the pan juices, 3 or 4 peeled, seeded, and chopped tomatoes, and ⅛ teaspoon saffron threads. Cook the mixture over brisk heat until the sauce is reduced and thickened. Stir in ½ cup of *Crème Fraîche* or heavy cream. Season to taste with salt and pepper. Serves 6–8.

Cooking "en papillote": This technique is one that suits a whole fish (especially large ones), a center cut, or even thick fillets, is wonderfully easy and tidy, and allows a great range of inventiveness. I am always slightly astonished at how truly delicious fish is cooked this way, especially measured against the simplicity of the procedure. And cleanup is virtually nonexistent. The idea, with which you may experiment endlessly, is to enclose in parchment or aluminum foil the fish with an aromatic vegetable or vegetables that will render liquid, with condiments, and with a small amount of additional liquid, usually wine, and a bit of butter for enrichment. Aluminum foil is marvelous for this method, because it is easy to handle and can hold liquid as well. Traditionally only parchment was used. The seasoned fish is measured and baked in a 425° oven, timing according to the Canadian Theory, with 5 minutes added per inch for the foil.

The enclosures can range from sliced onions or chopped shallots, a *mirepoix* or—a combination I am particularly fond of with a whole bass—paperthin slices of zucchini and onions and a *duxelles* stuffing for the fish. Sliced scallions and grated ginger are another possibility. Parsley or any favorite herb combination might also be placed inside the fish.

The foil, which I like to butter first, should be at least 3 inches longer than the fish. Dot the top with 2–3 tablespoons of butter in thin slices. Bring the edges up on all sides and add about 3 tablespoons of white wine, then make a butcher's triple fold and roll down smoothly, following the contours of the fish. Twist the ends securely. Place the foil package on a baking sheet and bake in a preheated oven. When the fish is done, transfer it to a heated serving platter and open at the table. The juices are the sauce.

Frying

Frying—cooking quickly in fat—can be done in three different ways: sautéing, shallow fat frying, and deep fat frying. The term "panfrying" is sometimes used interchangeably with sautéing and shallow frying or merely indicates an alternative to oven methods. Each technique has its place in the fish cookery repertoire, and none, properly done, produce the leathery, greasy product often connoted by the term "fried fish."

Sautéing requires a relatively small amount of fat—sometimes just a glaze, and is done quickly (the French word means literally "to jump"). It requires, above all, a good, heavy, unwarped pan with even heat distribution. (Often the catchall term "fried" is used to describe something that really is sautéed.) Many recipes specify clarified butter (butter from which the milk solids have been removed) for this technique, because, though butter enhances the delicate flavor of fish as no other medium can, its milky sediment scorches easily. Clarified butter is easily made and, refrigerated, keeps indefinitely. Alternatively, oil, which has a higher smoking point, can be used with butter in a half-and-half proportion.

Shallow frying requires a fair amount of oil—at least one quarter inch— that may be rendered pork fat, vegetable oil, or butter and oil (not olive oil, for its flavor is too assertive for fish). The fat should be hot but not smoking before the fish is added. (Temperature is right if a small cube of bread browns in sixty seconds. If the bread blackens, the fat is too hot.) Shallow frying is a suitable method for any of the small fish (generally one pound or under) classified as panfish.

Deep frying, as a cooking technique for fish, has a very bad name. Yet, properly done, it can produce very delicious, very ungreasy fish requiring only tartar sauce, tomato sauce, or a squeeze of lemon as a complement. The two salient points are: start with oil heated to a properly high temperature (usually 375°) and maintain it by frying only a few pieces at a time so that the fat temperature is not drastically lowered. (Also note that oil over 400° tends to break down, giving an off-flavor to food.) Use a deep-fry thermometer if you do not have a thermostatically controlled deep fryer. When the oil temperature lowers, the crisp exterior crust cannot form quickly enough to prevent fat from soaking into the food. Instead of having its juices sealed in, your food becomes a sponge. It is the excessive oil content of foods fried at too low a temperature that gives rise to the notion that fried foods are greasy and hard to digest. In fact, food fried correctly is less greasy than sautéed food.

In the absence of a crumb or butter coating, do not salt fish or shellfish to be fried until after it is cooked.

Sautéing: Heat enough clarified butter or an oil-butter combination to just cover the bottom of the pan, until it is quite hot. Add the fish, time the cooking carefully (the Canadian Theory again), and keep constant watch. The heat may require several adjustments while the fish is browning, and if the burners do not respond with alacrity, simply lift the pan up off the burner now and again to compensate. When the fish is lightly golden on one side, turn with a spatula and complete the other side. The fish, which may be in fillets or slices, can be dredged in seasoned flour or cornmeal if crispness is desired, but avoid batter. The amount of heat used in sautéing will not cook the batter properly.

CLARIFIED BUTTER: Melt two sticks (½ pound) of butter cut into 1-inch pieces over low heat. Remove the pan from the heat. Let stand for 3 minutes, then skim the top. Very slowly pour the liquid butter into a jar, leaving the milky solids behind in the bottom of the pan. Or let the butter melt by placing it in a heatproof bowl in a 200° oven, then complete as above, or refrigerate and use the clear yellow fat that hardens on top. Discard the milky portion when you get to it. Clarified butter loses about one fourth of its original volume. Makes ¾ cup.

SAUTÉING À LA MEUNIÈRE: Remove cooked fish from the pan and keep warm. Melt additional, unclarified butter in the pan, and when it is golden brown add a squeeze of lemon, pour over the fish, and sprinkle with chopped parsley.

Panfrying or shallow frying: Make sure that the fish is dry. Season, dust with flour, fine cracker meal, or cornmeal if desired. Heat at least ¼ inch of rendered pork fat, vegetable oil, or oil and butter until hot but not smoking. Just after adding the fish raise the heat for about 10 seconds, then lower slightly. The fat must be very hot, but continue adjusting heat so nothing burns. Don't keep turning the fish. When one side is golden (look underneath to check), turn once and complete the other side. Do not put too many pieces into the pan at once and do not add more oil. As soon as 2 or 3 pieces are done, remove them and add more, rather than doing two distinct batches. These measures help to keep the temperature constant.

Coated fish fillets and small panfish are usually done in about 4 minutes per side. Avoid batter here too, as the heat is usually not high enough to cook it properly.

Deep frying: Heat the oil (peanut, corn, or vegetable oil is best) in the deep fryer to 375°. Dip serving-size pieces of fish in beaten egg, then coat with the flour or cornmeal or cracker crumbs. Place the pieces on a large flat platter or piece of foil so they do not touch each other, and let them dry for 5–10 minutes. Then lower several pieces into the fat. Time the immersion according to the Canadian Theory and do not overcook. Drain on paper towels and season to taste.

The oil may be strained after frying and stored in the refrigerator when cool. The bottom inch or so, which tends to collect some dark particles, should be discarded the next time and additional oil added.

Last, since most people object to the after-smell of frying, make sure that you do it with proper ventilation. Should objectionable odors linger, try burning some sugar in a clean pan. If panfrying is the culprit, pour ½ cup of vinegar into the pan and let it burn off. Cuts the grease, too!

BATTER FRYING: There are several recipes for batter and the choice depends largely on what they are to coat. In general, the purpose of coating fish or shellfish in batter before frying is to prevent the penetration of oil, while cooking, and to conserve moisture and flavor inside at the same time that a nicely contrasting crisp texture is achieved outside. The lighter the batter, the less soggy the result, and to this end some recipes for batter call for flat beer or even carbonated water. The beer batter recipe that follows is a nice all-around batter, but remember that, as you must allow time for the beer to go flat, plus time for the batter to stand, begin about 4 hours before you plan to eat.

Important note: If your fryer is equipped with a basket, do not use it with batter-coated foods.

Lightly dredge food to be fried in flour first, dip it into the batter, and then let each piece drip over the batter bowl for a few seconds. This will prevent excess batter "spin-offs." Fry only a few pieces at a time, and use a slotted spoon to turn them when they rise to the surface, so that they cook evenly. Drain on paper towels and keep the cooked pieces warm until all are completed. Serve at once to avoid sogginess.

Fish particularly suitable for batter-frying include hake, cod, whiting, shark, or any firm-fleshed white fish. The fish itself may be in chunks, 3 by 5 inch crosscuts of fillets, or smaller "fingers." Shrimp and small, whole smelt are nice in the beer batter, which of course may be used for the other fish mentioned as well.

BEER BATTER

This batter may be used as a coating to deep-fry fish or shellfish. Make it at least 1–2 hours before you want to use it, and let it stand at room temperature. Leftovers can be refrigerated for up to 3 or 4 days. Let the beer go flat first by pouring it into a bowl 2 hours before mixing the batter, and leaving it uncovered at room temperature.

A 12-ounce can of flat beer   Several dashes cayenne pepper
1¼ cups sifted flour   2 teaspoons baking powder
1 tablespoon salt

Pour the beer into a bowl. Add the flour (the mixture will foam slightly). Whisk in the salt, cayenne, and baking powder. Let the mixture stand, covered, for 1–2 hours. It will thicken as it stands. Whisk briefly before using. Makes about 2½ cups of batter.

BEER BATTER WITH EGG

2 large eggs, separated
½ cup beer
½ cup flour

½ teaspoon salt
½ teaspoon baking powder
Additional flour for dredging

In a large bowl combine the egg yolks, beer, flour, salt, and baking powder. In a second bowl beat the egg whites until stiff. Fold them into the batter gently but thoroughly. Dredge the food to be fried in additional flour and follow the dipping and frying procedure in the preceding recipe. Food fried in this batter will puff more than with other batters, so do not crowd the frying basket. You may use chopsticks to lower the food into the oil and turn it as needed. Makes about 1½ cups of batter.

TEMPURA BATTER

This batter makes only a thin film of coating on the food to be fried. The chilling is an essential part of the procedure, as the contrast between batter and oil temperatures is what produces the characteristic crisp, thin coating that seems almost a part of the food itself.

1 egg yolk
1 cup ice water

1½ cups flour

Beat the egg yolk in a bowl. Add the ice water and beat again to blend. Add the flour all at once and stir to mix. The batter will be lumpy. Chill for 2 hours. Using chopsticks or tongs, dip shrimp or other food to be fried in the batter, let the excess drip off, and lower the food into the hot oil. Let cook for 3–4 minutes, drain, and serve immediately.

Planking

Planking as a method of cooking fish originated not as a cook's conceit but as a practical, controlled way to expose a broad surface of food to a fire. It was taught to the early settlers in North America by the Indians. A kited or butterflied fish was attached to a hardwood plank by means of pegs or nails, the plank was tilted at a proper angle toward the campfire and was turned as necessary to cook the fish evenly. This is the method in a nutshell, and the only other requirement even today is to baste it with some oil or sauce. Shad, whitefish, trout, and salmon are the fish most frequently planked.

A fish to be butterflied and plank-cooked at a campfire will of course not be skinned, since this is what holds the double fillets together. It need not be scaled either—the meat may be simply forked away from the skin when it is cooked. To cook, put the fish, skin side down, on the wood and pin all around the edges with tacks, real or makeshift. Prop the wood upright near the fire, play around with the distance, which is difficult to prescribe, and check the fish for doneness after 10–15 minutes. Its thickness will determine the cooking time.

Whole fish may be plank-cooked in the oven, as well, as often steaks are, and then served with a wreath of duchess potatoes. Preheat the plank by putting it in a cold oven and turning on the heat to 425°, leave for 15 minutes. Then oil the plank, which should be large, preferably grooved,* and made of a nonresinous hardwood that has been initially oil-seasoned. Put a whole, cleaned fish on the hot plank, brush with melted butter, margarine, or oil, and season. Bake uncovered, timing according to the Canadian Theory.

Remove the plank from the oven, pipe mashed or duchess potatoes around the fish (a recipe can be found in any good general cookbook), raise the heat to "broil," and broil for 2–3 minutes, 4 inches from the flame, until the potatoes are flecked with brown. Empty spaces may be filled in with various vegetable garnishes such as bouquets of cherry tomatoes, green peas, string beans, broiled mushrooms, or parsley and lemon clusters. Serve directly from the plank.

Sushi and Sashimi

In the making of *sashimi* and *sushi,* the Japanese have developed the preparing of raw fish to a high art, one for which only the freshest, cleanest fish will do. This is part of a venerable tradition of food designed to please the eye as well as the palate, in which a highly developed art of cutting and slicing is part of the aesthetic. In Japan, *sashimi*—morsels of fresh fish, shellfish, and the like, ritually cut according to density and flake, and *sushi,* which is fish in combination with vinegared rice and sometimes seaweed— is made with fish no more than a day out of the water—and pollution-free water at that. With rare exceptions, you cannot control the absolute freshness of market fish here, and if you fish yourself, you probably would not have the needed variety. Frozen fish simply will not do because the texture is impaired.

So, although I adore *sushi* with a passion (as do many others, witness the fact that there are 150 Japanese restaurants serving it in New York at this writing), and even assuming that I could pass on to you the various cutting techniques that are an inseparable part of its preparation, I have decided this is not for the home cook. But I urge you if you like fish—as well you must or why would you be reading this book?—to find a good Japanese

---

*Planks for this purpose can usually be purchased in housewares departments, grooved with a well-and-tree pattern, and accompanied by directions for seasoning the wood.

restaurant of impeccable reputation and treat yourself to this unique experience.

Smoking

Fish flesh is extremely perishable, and one way to prolong its life is to smoke it. Fish to be smoked is generally brined first, then as the moisture content of the fish is lowered through the gentle, continuous application of smoke, it is replaced by the salt, which acts as a preservative. The degree of preservation depends on the amount of salt used, plus the length of smoking time. The chemical action of the formaldehyde in the smoke also firms the muscle fiber of the fish and helps to preserve it by inhibiting the growth of bacteria. The way the fish is brined, the temperature at which it is smoked, and the fuels used to fire the smoke are all factors in flavoring the finished product.

Types of smokers: Smokers can be anything from old refrigerators and barrels to specially constructed smokehouses and commercially made smoke boxes. Basically they all act on the same principle of distributing smoke evenly over the fish. The U.S. Bureau of Marine Fisheries* provides a pamphlet containing excellent information on the construction of several types of varying complexity.

Any nonresinous wood may be used to fuel your smoker—oak, ash, hickory, maple, and alder. Sawdust is a favored fuel for cold smoking because it burns slowly, wood chips may be used in either process, and small logs may be used for hot smoking.

Smoking falls into two categories: *hot smoking,* in which fish is exposed to temperatures of 120–180° over a six- to eight-hour period with gradual increases in temperature, and *cold smoking,* in which fish is exposed to a temperature range of 70–90°, for up to thirty-six hours. Hot smoked fish actually cooks and will keep for only a few days. Cold smoked fish is not so much cooked as cured by drying out in the warm (not hot) smoke. Cold smoking can be done over a period of several days.

Kippered is an adjective used in America to describe certain hot-smoked fish such as sablefish (also called black cod), sturgeon, and salmon. A kipper, on the other hand, is a brined, air-dried, cold-smoked herring, with a distinctive mahogany color that comes from the slow six-day cure.

Preparation for smoking: However fish is to be smoked, it should be gutted and cleaned well, washed with cold water, and put first into a cleaning brine, consisting of two cups of salt to four gallons of water. (Table salt is no good for this process because of the chemical additives it contains. Use coarse or kosher salt.) Soak the fish in this solution for thirty minutes

*Write to the National Marine Fisheries Service, 100 East Ohio Street, Chicago, Illinois 60611.

to remove or leach impurities from the flesh. Wash again in cold water; it is now ready for the brine.

A proper salting brine is one that will float a potato—a 70 per cent solution made with one pound or two cups of coarse salt to one gallon water. Add one cup of brown sugar for flavor and, if you like, as they do in the South, some Tabasco and pickling spices for a piquant flavor. Put the fish in an earthenware crock or plastic tub, add the brine, cover, and leave for fifteen minutes to four hours, depending on the fish size. Then remove, rinse, drain, and hang the fish in a cool, shady place for at least three hours until a thin, shiny skin forms on the surface. This skin, or pellicle, which seals in the moisture and keeps the fish intact, is essential for fish to be smoked. Air drying with the aid of an electric fan helps the pellicle to form.

What fish to smoke: Almost any fish can be smoked, including game fish such as sailfish and marlin. In addition, one can smoke peeled raw shrimp, oysters, and clams. I have heard of smoking frozen fish, but it is risky in terms of flavor and texture loss. Small fish may be gutted and left whole, others cut into fillets or chunks. Oily skins should be removed. Sides of very large fish may be dry salted rather than brined, a procedure that is frequently done commercially.

Dry salt method: A crust of salt into which brown sugar and spices may be mixed, as in brining, is patted on both sides of the fish and left for eight to 10 hours. Then the fish is rinsed, air-dried on a rack or old screen until the pellicle forms, and hot smoked.

For more detailed information about smoking procedures for fish, consult your local library.

TWO

Broths and Sauces

BROTHS FOR POACHING

A *court-bouillon* is a flavored liquid in which fish or shellfish is completely immersed and cooked. Court-bouillons can be a simple water-vinegar-lemon combination for plain white fish, or be flavored with various herbs, condiments, or aromatic vegetables appropriate to the fish or shellfish to be cooked in it. They may also contain red or white wine.

The word "bouillon" comes from the French *bouillir*—to boil. (A bouillon itself is any liquid in which meat, fish, or vegetables have been cooked. All bouillons are broths.)

Fish stock is a concentrated broth made from fish trimmings, bones, and cleaned skins and heads, which after cooking give the required gelatinous quality to the liquid. The liquid may be white or red wine combined with water, usually in equal quantities, or sometimes wine alone. Aromatics such as onion, parsley, and bay leaf are added, and good French housewives save mushroom peelings to throw in as well. Fish stock is used as the base of fish sauces or as a moistener for fish in braising. Very little salt is used in its preparation, since it is usually intended to be reduced.* Fish stock is also called broth.

Fumet de poisson and *fumet* are terms that can be used interchangeably with "stock," especially in recipes of French origin, but technically a fumet is a fish stock concentrated through reduction and is primarily used as a base for sauces to accompany fish, the simplest of which is the great basic, *velouté de poisson*. The *velouté,* in turn, is the foundation for a number of classic sauces such as Mornay, Bercy, and the traditional chaud-froid, a cream-colored aspic used to coat cold poached fish.

Once a fish has been poached in a court-bouillon, that liquid, too, may be reduced to one third of its volume and becomes a fumet in the sense that it is now an enriched and concentrated stock. Fumet can be further reduced and used with various fish as a sauce on its own; some sauces requiring an intense fish flavor will also call for this highly reduced fumet.

*Sometimes known as "boiling down." In the context of cooking, to reduce means to lessen the volume of a liquid by evaporation. Sauces are reduced to heighten their flavor and also make them thicker in consistency.

COURT-BOUILLON 1

This is a good simple broth in which to cook shellfish or poach fish such as bass and snapper, which will then be sauced.

2 quarts water
1 cup dry white wine
1 tablespoon salt
3–4 sprigs parsley
1 small bay leaf

½ teaspoon dried thyme
2 stalks celery, ribs with leaves, sliced in 2 or 3 pieces
1 small carrot, coarsely chopped
Several peppercorns

Combine all ingredients in a 6-quart enameled or stainless steel pot and bring to a boil over high heat. Partially cover the pot, reduce heat, and simmer for 30 minutes. Strain through a large, fine sieve and cool.

COURT-BOUILLON 2

This is a more highly flavored poaching broth ideal for poaching fish to be served cold.

2 quarts water
2 cups dry white wine
¼ cup wine vinegar
3 onions, sliced
2 carrots, cut in 1-inch chunks
3 stalks celery with leaves, chopped

6 parsley stems, chopped
2 bay leaves, broken up
½ teaspoon dried thyme
2 tablespoons salt
8–10 peppercorns

In a 6- to 8-quart enameled or stainless steel soup pot, bring all the ingredients for the court-bouillon to a boil over high heat. Partially cover the pot and simmer for 40 minutes to 1 hour. Let cool and strain before using. Makes about 2 quarts, enough to poach a 3-pound fish.

FISH STOCK (Fumet de poisson)

2 pounds fishbones and trimmings
2 tablespoons butter
1 medium carrot, sliced
1 medium onion, sliced
½ teaspoon dried thyme
½ bay leaf

Several parsley sprigs
1 celery stalk, coarsely chopped
1 cup dry white wine
4 cups water
Salt and freshly ground black pepper

Rinse and roughly chop the fish trimmings. Melt the butter in a heavy pot and sauté the sliced carrot and onion for 5 minutes. Add the fish trimmings, the thyme, bay leaf, parsley, celery, wine, and the 4 cups of water, boil for

25 minutes. Strain the fish broth, return it to the saucepan, and let it reduce over high heat for about 10 minutes or until reduced to 2½ cups (or less if you wish a stronger flavor). Taste and season with salt and pepper. Makes about 2½ cups.

The bones of sole and flounder are particularly good for making fumet (Paul Bocuse* maintains that only sole backbones can produce a "real fish stock"), don't hesitate to beg them from your fish dealer. Fish stock can be kept for a few days in the refrigerator or frozen indefinitely.

NOTE: Bottled clam juice may be used as an emergency substitute for fish stock. To make it more interesting, bring the clam juice to a boil with a *bouquet garni* of parsley, thyme, celery, and bay leaf. Some white wine can be added if appropriate to the recipe.

PREPARING A FISH IN ASPIC

Whole poached fish that are intended for use on a buffet are often coated with aspic, which gives the fish an appealing shine and enhances as well as fixes the decorations. Aesthetics apart, an aspic-coated fish is an especially good choice for a buffet or for serving large numbers of people because the aspic also keeps the fish from drying out. The entire fish may be prepared the day before the party and refrigerated. Essentially the procedure consists of poaching the fish in a court-bouillon, making the aspic from the poaching liquid, decorating the fish (this is the fun part), and then giving it several thin coats of aspic, each of which is allowed to set before the next is applied. Whole salmon, large trout, salmon trout, and bass, as well as small trout for individual first-course servings, may be treated this way.

Making the court bouillon and *poaching the fish:* Prepare court-bouillon 2 (see Index), doubling the quantities if required. Poach the fish in it as directed in Poaching (see Index), remove it from the liquid, let cool, then refrigerate. While the fish cools, reduce the poaching liquid until it has a good flavor, strain, and reserve 2 cups. Make the aspic according to the following recipe and then proceed with coating and decorating the fish.

BASIC ASPIC

2 cups reserved stock from
   poaching fish (see Note 1 p.
   46)
2 egg whites and the eggshells

1 tablespoon gelatin or more (see
   Note 2 p. 46)
½ cup white wine

Put the fish stock into a saucepan. Beat the egg whites lightly and add them to the pan; crush the eggshells and add. Add gelatin and wine. Over low

Paul Bocuse's French Cooking, Random House, 1977.

heat, beat the mixture with a wooden spoon to circulate the egg whites; continue beating until the stock begins to boil.

Let it simmer gently, uncovered, for 5 minutes, then remove from heat and let stand for 15 minutes undisturbed. The whites will rise to the surface and form a crust and at the same time draw impurities from the liquid that would otherwise cloud the aspic; this procedure is called clarifying.

Rinse a thin tea towel or double thickness of cheesecloth in cold water, wring it out, and use it to line a colander set over a large bowl. Skim off the crust and discard. Carefully pour the aspic into it and let drip through slowly, undisturbed, until only some crusty residue remains in the cloth. Pour the aspic into a small bowl and set this into another bowl, filled with ice. Stir occasionally over a 10-minute period until heavy and syrupy. It is now ready to be used to coat the fish.

NOTE 1: An exception would be the stock from poaching salmon, which does not work well in aspic. In this case make a separate stock from white fishbones (sole and flounder bones are the best).

NOTE 2: Although fish broth, when cold, may jell on its own, gelatin must be added to ensure a firm set. In using it, careful measurements are required; *one package of unflavored gelatin (about 1 tablespoon) will jell 2 cups of liquid.* Too much gelatin will produce a rubbery aspic; too little will prevent it from setting properly so that it will puddle around the base of the fish. To check, make this jell test: chill a saucer in the refrigerator, put a tablespoon of stock on it, and refrigerate for 10 minutes. If the liquid jells completely in that time, do not add any gelatin. If it half jells, that is, if it develops a set film but is liquid underneath, add a half envelope of gelatin. If it does not jell at all, add the whole package.

Coating and decorating the fish: Put the chilled, skinned fish on a platter. Spoon the syrupy aspic over it. If the aspic becomes too thick to spoon, warm it slightly and stir until syrupy again. Let the excess aspic that runs off the fish remain on the platter; it is delicious when set. Chill the glazed fish for about 10 minutes in the refrigerator. Decorate the fish in any of the ways mentioned in Decorating and Garnishing Fish, immediately following. Serve the fish with Green Mayonnaise *(Sauce Verte).*

Leftover aspic jelly may be chopped for garnish or used to make aspic diamonds. See instructions in Decorating and Garnishing Fish.

DECORATING AND GARNISHING FISH

Other foodstuffs provide the materials for attractive ways to decorate and garnish fish, both cold and hot. The simplest, of course, is to use bunches of parsley or watercress and lemon wedges or halves. If you are presenting a whole fish at the table, the eye should be replaced with a black olive or a small cherry tomato. A ruff of parsley may be placed around the neck. If

A LEMON HALF DECORATIVELY CUT FOR GARNISH.

you have the patience, lemon halves cut in a sawtooth pattern are pretty around both cold and hot fish.

Garnishes for cold fish are endless; you can use deviled hard-cooked egg halves, plain hard-cooked egg halves or quarters, or the whites only, stuffing them with salmon caviar and reserving the yolks for another use. Tomato halves filled with *salade russe* or cooked green peas that have been mixed with sour cream and snippets of dill or chives are especially pretty. For a poached whole salmon, crescents of lemon rind cut out with a truffle

A COLD FISH DECORATED WITH STUFFED TOMATO HALVES, WATERCRESS, AND TARRAGON LEAVES.

A DECORATED COLD POACHED TROUT IN ASPIC.

cutter can be used to represent scales. Thin slices of cucumber without the skin can also be used to simulate scales: soak the slices in salted water first so they are a bit limp. If you have time and patience and a steady hand, outline each scale with a thin line of mayonnaise mixed with a little aspic and forced through a pastry bag fitted with a small tube.

Decorating a cold fish in aspic: Using a small scissors, cut appropriately sized flower "petals" from pieces of pimiento or tomato skin that has a bit of flesh attached. Cut pointed "leaves" from watercress leaves and narrow stems from the green part of a scallion or leek or from a sliver of cucumber peel. A branch of fresh tarragon, if available, makes an attractive stem and leaves. "Daisy" petals may be cut from hard-cooked egg white to surround a center made from a round of truffle or black olive. Or create your own fantasy.

Have all your decorative materials cut and ready, as well as a bowl of cool but still liquid aspic. After the fish has been given the first coat of aspic and allowed to chill for about 10 minutes, use tweezers to dip each element of decoration in the syrupy aspic so it will stick when applied to the fish. Refrigerate to set the decoration (about 10 minutes). When set, spoon on another layer of syrupy aspic, chill again for 5–10 minutes, and repeat with another aspic coating, giving the fish three coats of aspic in all. Surround the fish with aspic diamonds (see below) or overlapping slices of lemon. Keep it chilled until serving time, and just before serving add sprigs or bunches of watercress to the platter.

Aspic diamonds: These are often used as a garnish around the base of a poached whole fish or on a platter of poached cold trout or of smoked trout fillets. To prepare: Pour liquid aspic into a metal jellyroll pan to a depth of about one quarter inch, chill until firm. In the pan cut aspic with a series of diagonal crisscross cuts at quarter-inch intervals, or turn onto a cutting board moistened with white wine or onto large brown paper bag (this increases the shine) and chop, then mound decoratively on the platter.

SAUCES

In this country the word "rich" is almost always thought of in connection with sauces; consequently they are shied away from automatically by the diet-conscious. Yet not all sauces need be rich or eaten in great quantity. In the case of fish, which can tend to blandness, a touch of sauce can make the difference between a pale meal with Calvinist overtones and one that profoundly satisfies.

Generally speaking, fish sauces fall into three categories: first, the natural "sauce" or the essences that are rendered when a fish is braised; second, one that is made from a base of reduced fish stock or poaching liquid and perhaps given a specific flavoring and enriched with egg yolk, butter, and cream (the classic French sauces fall in here), and third, sauces that make a good accompaniment to fish but are not themselves based on fish essences. Tartar sauce, cucumber sauce, and green mayonnaise are examples of these.

The French approach to sauces may appear complicated, but there is a beautiful, simple progression of logic in the system. A good example is the *velouté* (which can be made with chicken or veal stock as well, but in this book is confined to fish stock), which starts with a court-bouillon or with the liquid remaining from a fish that has been poached in white wine and aromatic vegetables. Butter and flour are cooked together to make a blond *roux* and then simmered with the cooking liquid. This sauce may be enriched with heavy cream and egg yolk or flavored in various ways.

FISH VELOUTÉ (Velouté de Poisson)

2 tablespoons butter	1 cup hot fish stock
2 tablespoons flour	Salt and freshly ground pepper

In a heavy-bottomed saucepan, melt the butter, then stir in the flour with a wooden spoon. Cook over low heat for one minute, stirring constantly. The mixture should have no more than a yellowish tan color. Remove the pan from the fire, and after the mixture stops bubbling, pour in the hot (but not boiling) fish stock all at once, whisking as you do. Return to moderate heat, bring to a slow boil, whisking constantly, then let simmer for 10 minutes. Taste and correct seasoning if necessary. Makes 1 cup.

NOTE: If you are not going to use the sauce immediately, film the surface with a tablespoon of stock so a skin does not form. Use the back of a spoon to spread it evenly. You can also press a piece of plastic wrap on the surface of the sauce.

If the *velouté* is to be served plain, that is, not used as the base of a more complicated sauce, it is usually enriched with a liaison of cream and egg yolks. Bring 2 cups of *velouté* sauce to a boil, reduce until it reaches the consistency of light cream and is reduced by about half. In a small bowl beat together 3 egg yolks and one cup of heavy cream and season with a pinch of crushed pepper and one of grated nutmeg. Add a little bit of the warm sauce to the egg mixture, then pour the mixture into the remainder of the sauce, whisking constantly. Return the sauce to the stove and heat gently, whisking continuously, but do not let the sauce boil; remove from the heat and stir until cooled. Makes about 2 cups.

The *velouté* thus enriched is sometimes called *Sauce parisienne*.

SAUCE POULETTE

1 onion, finely chopped	2 tablespoons butter
½ cup white wine	A pinch of nutmeg
1 cup Fish Velouté ❀	Juice of a half lemon
2 egg yolks	1 tablespoon chopped parsley

In a small, heavy saucepan, stew the onion in the wine until the liquid is almost evaporated. Stir in the *velouté*. Beat the egg yolks with a tablespoon of the hot sauce in a small bowl, then stir this mixture into the balance of the sauce. Stir in the butter, nutmeg, and lemon juice, add the parsley. Heat carefully but do not let the sauce boil. Makes about 1½ cups. This sauce is excellent with all white fish, especially freshwater fish.

SAUCE BERCY

1 tablespoon finely chopped shallot	2 tablespoons butter
3 tablespoons white wine	1 teaspoon finely chopped parsley
1 cup Fish Velouté ❀ made with a highly reduced fumet (see Index)	

Stew the shallot in the wine until the liquid is reduced by half, then stir into the *velouté*. Swirl in the butter and blend in the parsley. Makes about 1¼ cups. Serve with braised and broiled fish; it is especially good with fillets of salmon.

WHITE WINE SAUCE

3 tablespoons white wine
1 cup Fish Velouté ✻ made with a
 reduced *fumet* (see Index)

1 egg yolk
2 tablespoons heavy cream
2 tablespoons butter

Add the white wine to the *velouté* and cook over moderate heat, stirring occasionally, for 10 minutes. Let it cool. In a small bowl beat the egg yolk and the cream together and combine with the sauce. Cook on a very low heat until the sauce thickens a little. Swirl in the butter. Makes about 1½ cups. Use to nap poached fish.

SAUCE NORMANDE

The above white wine sauce can be turned into *sauce normande*, good with any white fish, by the addition of the reduced cooking juices of some shellfish such as shrimp, mussels, clams, or scallops. Add the reduced fumet and the reduced shellfish juice to the basic white wine sauce, stir together, and cook slowly as directed above; sprinkle with minced parsley. It is a nice idea to garnish the dish with some of the cooked shellfish that produced juices used in the sauce.

BASIC BÉCHAMEL SAUCE

4 tablespoons butter
4 tablespoons flour
1½ cups milk at room temperature

Salt and freshly ground black
 pepper
Nutmeg

Melt the butter in a heavy-bottomed saucepan. Stir in the flour and whisk until smooth (the mixture will froth). Cook, stirring constantly, over low heat for 2 minutes but do not let the mixture take on more color than pale tan. Remove from the fire and pour in all the milk, beating until smooth. Return the pan to moderate heat and stir until the sauce reaches a simmer, cook for 10–15 minutes. Season with salt, pepper, and nutmeg to taste. Makes about 2 cups of sauce.

 This sauce can be enriched with the simple egg-cream liaison described in Fish Velouté (see Index) or any of the ways listed below.

SAUCE NANTUA

2 cups Basic Béchamel Sauce ✻
 (preceding recipe)
½ cup heavy cream

4–6 tablespoons Shrimp Butter
Salt and pepper if necessary
9–10 cooked small shrimp

Put the *béchamel* in a saucepan over low heat, add the cream, and off heat swirl in the shrimp butter, stirring until melted. Season if necessary. Use the shrimp to garnish the dish with which the sauce is served. Good with any white fish. Makes about 2½ cups.

MORNAY SAUCE

Prepare the Basic Béchamel Sauce, using 1 cup milk and 1 cup fish stock for the liquid requirement. Add an additional ½ cup of stock to the sauce and heat, uncovered, over moderate heat, until reduced to about 2 cups. Over a very low flame gradually add ½ cup grated Swiss or Gruyère cheese (or a combination of grated Gruyère and Parmesan), stirring until cheese is melted. Do not let sauce boil after cheese is added. Remove from heat and swirl in 2 tablespoons of butter, one at a time. Makes about 2 cups.

Mornay Gratin for Poached Fillets: Reduce the liquid in which fillets were poached until it is almost a glaze, and add it to the basic Béchamel, prepared as above. Add ¼ cup cheese and 1 tablespoon butter as directed above. Nap the fillets with this sauce, sprinkle with 2 or 3 tablespoons of grated Parmesan, and run under the broiler until the top is flecked with brown.

EGG SAUCE

To 1 cup of Basic Béchamel Sauce ✿ add 2–3 hard-cooked eggs, chopped or sliced. Add some chopped parsley if desired. Makes about 1½ cups sauce.

HOLLANDAISE SAUCE

The only tricky thing about making a good *Hollandaise* is that the cooking must be done at a temperature hot enough to allow the eggs to emulsify but not cook. Otherwise you will have scrambled eggs and a curdled sauce. For safety's sake use a double boiler, make sure that the pan does not touch the water in the bottom part, and make sure that the water does not boil.

3 egg yolks	Several grains cayenne pepper
2 teaspoons water	Salt
¼ pound (1 stick) butter cut into small pieces	Lemon juice

Put hot water in the bottom of a double boiler and combine the egg yolks and the 2 teaspoons of water in the upper part. Whisk the eggs until they are slightly thickened. Put the double boiler over moderate heat and gradually stir in the butter with a wooden spoon or wire whisk. Make sure that the water does not boil. The sauce should be smooth, with a texture of thick custard. (If it seems too thick, it may be diluted with a little water.) If it starts to curdle, it can be restored by a tablespoon of hot water from the bottom pot, briskly whisked in over the hot water. Season to taste with the cayenne, salt, and a squeeze or two of lemon juice. Serve the sauce immediately. It can be kept warm for a time in the double boiler on very low heat but will have to be whisked again before serving.

SAUCE BÉARNAISE

A *béarnaise* is really nothing more than a tarragon-flavored *hollandaise* and is prepared in the following way: Simmer a tablespoon of finely chopped shallots, a teaspoon of dried tarragon or 2 teaspoons of chopped fresh tarragon, and a small pinch of salt in ¼ cup of vinegar. Cook it down until it is almost a glaze, that is, until the shallots are a purée and about 2 tablespoons of vinegar remain in the pan. Strain and let cool. Add this mixture to the egg yolks and then proceed as for *hollandaise*.

The sauce may be flavored with additional finely chopped tarragon, minced parsley, or minced capers. Correct the seasoning with lemon juice, additional salt, and black pepper if desired.

SAUCE MOUSSELINE

In the top of a double boiler, heat together equal amounts of Hollandaise Sauce ❋ and stiffly whipped heavy cream. Stir constantly and with great care, just until the *mousseline* is thoroughly heated. Season to taste with salt and white pepper and serve hot. For any white fish.

BEURRE BLANC SAUCE (Nantais Butter Sauce)

Beurre blanc is one of the nicest, silkiest, most delectable fish sauces there is, and it is really nothing but warm whipped butter perfumed with shallots with a light bite of vinegar. It is thought to have originated in the Loire Valley to enhance the shad and pike of that region, and is part of that body of French cooking known as *cuisine de femme*—what we might call good, straightforward, home cooking. Escoffier said that *only* a woman can make a really good *beurre blanc* sauce; we shall let the men sort that one out for themselves.

Though it is not difficult to make, it does require undivided total attention, both to it and to the intensity of the heat. The butter must be the best—and sweet. White wine vinegar might be hard to find; substitute plain white or a light cider vinegar if you have to, but remember that the latter will give you a pinkish sauce. The shallots are a must. The final straining is optional—some do, some don't. One final note: be sure that whatever fish you serve it with is very well drained.

4 tablespoons finely minced
  shallots
¼ cup white wine vinegar
¼ cup white wine
A pinch of salt

4–5 white peppercorns
½ pound (2 sticks) sweet butter at
  room temperature, cut into
  small cubes
Lemon juice (optional)

Combine the shallots with the vinegar, wine, salt, and peppercorns in a small, heavy saucepan. Simmer slowly over a *very* low flame. The liquid must evaporate very slowly until there is none free when the pan is tipped and the shallots have wilted and cooked to a moist, slightly mushy purée.

Take the pan off the heat for 30 seconds or so to cool it. (Use an asbestos mat at this point, as complete control of the heat is critical in making this sauce.) Set the heat at its lowest point. Set the pan on the mat and, using a small whisk, holding it like a pencil, slowly and gradually beat in the butter, about an ounce at a time, in 7 or 8 batches. Remove the pan from the heat frequently so the butter never melts but rather becomes the consistency of heavy cream or a custard. Add each new piece when the previous one begins to disappear and there is just a trace of solid butter left. If the butter does actually melt because the heat is too high, the sauce will break, and you will have to take corrective measures (see below). The final sauce should be satiny smooth, a creamy thick emulsion with no greasy yellow streaks. Taste for seasoning and add a little lemon juice.

Strain the sauce into a warm (not hot) bowl or sauceboat. (Leftover *buerre blanc* can be refrigerated and used as you would a flavored butter on grilled steaks and hamburgers.)

To correct a separated beurre blanc: If at any moment the sauce threatens to separate, it can sometimes be rescued by immediately setting the pan into a bowl of cold water for an instant. If this does not work and it separates, combine 2 tablespoons of cold water and 1 tablespoon of firm butter in a clean pan, whisk over low heat for 30 seconds, then slowly add the turned sauce, whisking constantly. Over low heat, beat in 3 additional tablespoons of fresh butter. If *this* doesn't work, you will just have to start over again!

LEMON BUTTER SAUCE

Melt ¼ pound (1 stick) of butter in a small saucepan over low heat. Stir in 2½ teaspoons of fresh lemon juice, ½ teaspoon salt, several grinds of white pepper, and 2 tablespoons of minced parsley. Heat for a few seconds longer. Excellent for basting broiled fish.

VARIATION: Lemon-Dill Sauce: substitute 2 tablespoons of minced fresh dill for the parsley.

Cold Sauces for Fish

MAYONNAISE

This recipe can be made in the blender or food processor.

1 egg plus 1 egg yolk
1 tablespoon lemon juice
1 teaspoon salt

¼ teaspoon freshly ground pepper
1 cup oil (can be half olive, half
    salad oil)

Put the egg, egg yolk, lemon juice, salt, and pepper in a blender or food processor. Run until blended, 2–3 seconds. With the motor running, pour the oil very slowly through the top of the blender or the feed tube of the processor. Once the mixture has the consistency of heavy cream, you can add the oil faster. Taste for seasoning. Makes about 1 cup. This mayonnaise will keep for about a week in a covered container in the refrigerator.

MUSTARD MAYONNAISE

Add 3 tablespoons of Dijon mustard to the ingredients in the blender jar before adding the oil in the recipe above. This mayonnaise is particularly good with crab claws served as an appetizer.

GREEN MAYONNAISE (Sauce Verte)

1 large handful spinach or water-
    cress leaves, washed, stems
    removed
½ cup finely chopped fresh herbs,
    made of a combination of the

following: parsley, tarragon,
    chervil, chives, and dill
2 cups homemade mayonnaise
Salt and freshly ground pepper

Blanch the spinach or watercress in boiling water for 1 minute; run cold water over, drain, and chop very finely. Combine with the herbs and chop everything together. Twist the mixture in a cheesecloth or the corner of a dish towel to remove excess liquid, mix well into the mayonnaise, and season to taste.

RÉMOULADE SAUCE

1½ cups mayonnaise, preferably
    homemade
2 tablespoons drained, minced
    capers
¼ cup grated onion
1 clove garlic, finely minced

2 teaspoons each of chopped
    parsley, tarragon, and chives, or
    1 teaspoon each of these herbs
    dried
A dab of anchovy paste
Lemon juice to taste

Mix all the ingredients and refrigerate the sauce for an hour or so. Use to dress cold poached shrimp or mussels. If desired, a tablespoon or two of chopped fresh tomato may be added.) Makes about 1¾ cups sauce.

THOUSAND ISLAND DRESSING

¼ small onion
½ stalk celery
¼ medium green pepper, seeded
2 hard-cooked eggs, cut in eighths
1 cup mayonnaise

¼ cup chili sauce
1 teaspoon paprika
½ teaspoon salt
2 tablespoons snipped chives
   (optional)

Chop finely the onion, celery, and green pepper, set aside. Chop the hard-cooked eggs, set aside. Add the remaining ingredients and mix well.

TO PREPARE IN THE FOOD PROCESSOR: With the steel blade in place and using the on-off motion, chop the onion, celery, and green pepper very finely. Remove the steel blade, insert the plastic blade, add the remaining ingredients and process briefly. Makes 2 cups.

TARTAR SAUCE

The recipe variations for this classic accompaniment to fish of all kinds are endless, so this is not *the* recipe for tartar sauce—only *a* recipe that I like very much.

2 cups mayonnaise
3 tablespoons finely chopped
   onion
2 teaspoons lemon juice
3 tablespoons finely chopped dill
   pickle or gherkin

2 tablespoons finely chopped
   parsley
2 tablespoons minced, drained
   capers
1 teaspoon Dijon-type mustard
Salt and pepper to taste

Whip the mayonnaise lightly and add the remaining ingredients. Refrigerate for 1–2 hours before serving. Serve with fried, broiled, or poached fish, or fried shellfish. This recipe may be halved.

VARIATIONS: Replace the onion with 3 shallots, finely minced, or reduce the amount of parsley and add minced tarragon and minced chervil. If you like it on the sweet side, add 1 teaspoon of sugar.
Gribiche Sauce: to the tartar sauce recipe, add one hard-cooked egg, finely chopped.
The Tadich Grill, a famous San Francisco fish restaurant, serves a superb tartar sauce, the secret of which is the addition of mashed potatoes. It makes the sauce smooth and less rich and oily. Try adding a quarter cup of plain mashed potatoes to the above recipe.

CUCUMBER SAUCE

2 large cucumbers
1 teaspoon salt
1 cup sour cream
1 cup mayonnaise
1 tablespoon cream-style
  horseradish

1 teaspoon grated onion
1 tablespoon tarragon vinegar
Salt to taste
Several grindings of fresh white
  pepper

Peel the cucumbers and slice very thinly. Put them in a 2-quart mixing bowl and cover with water. Add the salt and stir well. Let the cucumbers sit for 30 minutes, drain them, then dry them on paper towels. Combine the sour cream, mayonnaise, horseradish, grated onion and vinegar in a bowl, add the cucumbers, and stir gently. Season with salt and white pepper. Cover the bowl and place in the refrigerator for several hours or overnight. The sauce will keep for 3 to 4 days. Makes about 2½ cups.

NOTE: This sauce is delicious with hot baked or barbecued salmon and cold poached salmon or trout.

HORSERADISH CREAM SAUCE (Sauce Raifort)

½ cup heavy cream
2 tablespoons prepared horseradish
1–2 tablespoons lemon juice
1 tablespoon finely grated lemon
  rind

A pinch of cayenne pepper
Salt

Whip the cream until it holds soft peaks. Fold in the horseradish, lemon juice and rind, and pepper. Season to taste with salt. Makes about 1 cup. Superb with smoked trout.

RAVIGOTE SAUCE

In a bowl, combine ½ teaspoon salt, a grind or two of freshly ground pepper, 1 teaspoon each of prepared mustard, chopped parsley, and tarragon (or ½ teaspoon dried tarragon), 2 tablespoons of capers, slightly crushed, ¼ cup of finely minced onion, 2 tablespoons of vinegar, and 1 chopped, hard-cooked egg. Beat vigorously with a whisk while adding 5 tablespoons of olive oil. Serve with poached fish or leftover white fish of any kind.

AIOLI SAUCE

Aioli was originally made by pounding the garlic in a mortar. It is much easier in a blender; here are both methods. In either case, however, the oil and the eggs must be at room temperature to form the proper emulsion. The number of garlic cloves may be increased or decreased according to one's individual sense of adventure. For a description of *"Le Grand Aioli"* see the Index.

3 cups olive oil	Salt
10 garlic cloves, peeled	Lemon juice
4 egg yolks at room temperature	

IN THE BLENDER: Place 3 tablespoons of the oil in a small bowl. Prepare a very thick Mayonnaise ✽ (following the instructions given in the mayonnaise recipe—see Index), using 3 of the yolks and the balance of the 3 cups of oil. Season to taste with salt and a squeeze of lemon juice. Remove the mayonnaise to a bowl. In the container of the blender put the garlic cloves, the remaining egg yolk, and the reserved 3 tablespoons of oil. Blend to a paste, add the mayonnaise, and blend again briefly.

IN A MORTAR: Reduce the olive oil to 2¼ cups. Pound the garlic in a mortar until fine. Lightly beat the egg yolks, stir them into the garlic with a pinch of salt, then, without breaking the stirring rhythm, add the olive oil virtually drop by drop, always turning the pestle in the same direction. If the mixture seems to be getting too thick, add 2 teaspoons of lukewarm water. Season with a squeeze of lemon juice.

If your *aioli* should separate, that is, the oil rise to the surface, it can be corrected in this way: Pour the sauce into a bowl, clean the mortar and pestle, crush an additional garlic clove in it with a bit of salt, add a few drops of tepid water and another egg yolk at room temperature. Into this mixture blend the first sauce, a spoonful at a time, and all will be well. Serve *aioli* sauce with cold or hot poached fish, Provençal fish soups or as part of a *"Grand Aioli."*

SKORDALIA (Greek Garlic Sauce)

Skordalia is another of those interesting Mediterranean sauces like the Turkish *tarator* and the French *aioli*. It does not rely on dairy products for creaminess. The Greeks serve it over sliced fried fish, batter-fried salt cod, with fried eggplant or zucchini or even cold hard-cooked eggs. Either cooked potatoes and bread or nuts and bread can serve as the thickening agent.

4–8 cloves garlic (depending on taste), mashed	2 egg yolks at room temperature
4 1-inch slices stale French or Italian bread, crusts removed, soaked in water for a few minutes, and squeezed dry	1 hot boiled Idaho potato, peeled
	¾–1 cup olive oil
	¼ cup lemon juice
	½ teaspoon salt

Put the garlic and 2 slices of the bread in the blender and whirl to a smooth paste. Add the egg yolks and the remaining bread and blend thoroughly. Cut up the potato, add, and blend to a smooth paste. Gradually add the olive oil and lemon juice alternately to the blender with the motor running, until the sauce is as thick as mayonnaise. Add the last quarter cup of oil slowly, and if the sauce seems unable to absorb more, stop adding oil. Add salt if necessary. If the sauce seems too runny, soak another slice of bread in water, squeeze it dry, and blend in. Makes about 1½ cups, serving 4–6.

Flavored Butters

DILL BUTTER

Cream ¼ pound (one stick) butter until light and fluffy. Blend in 4 tablespoons chopped dill. Season with ½ teaspoon salt, 1½ teaspoons lemon juice. Makes about ½ cup.

TARRAGON BUTTER

Substitute 3 tablespoons chopped tarragon or 3 teaspoons dried in the recipe above.

PARSLEY BUTTER

Substitue 3–4 tablespoons chopped parsley in the first recipe above.

HERB BUTTER

Using the first recipe, omit the dill and blend in 1 tablespoon each of finely chopped fresh parsley, chives, tarragon, and chervil.

MAÎTRE D'HÔTEL BUTTER

Cream ¼ pound butter until light; blend in 2 tablespoons chopped parsley, 2 tablespoons chopped shallots, scallions, or chives, and 1 tablespoon lemon juice. Season to taste.

CHIVE BUTTER

Cream 1 stick sweet butter with 2 tablespoons chopped chives and 1 tablespoon lemon juice. Season to taste.

ANCHOVY BUTTER

Into the creamed stick of butter blend 2–3 tablespoons anchovy paste, 1 tablespoon chopped parsley and a few drops of lemon juice. Omit salt.

GARLIC BUTTER

Blend 2 garlic cloves put through a press into a stick of creamed butter. Season to taste with salt and a few dashes of lemon juice.

SHELLFISH BUTTER (Shrimp or Lobster)

Pound or purée ¼ cup cooked shrimp or lobster in a blender or food processor. Cream with a stick of softened butter, by hand or in one of the machines. Season to taste with salt and pepper.

NOTE: You can keep a flavored butter handy for use by forming it into 6–8 balls, flattened slightly, freezing briefly on a cookie sheet, and then storing them in the freezer in a labeled bag or box.

CAVIAR BUTTER

Crush 2 tablespoons red caviar and cream it with a stick of butter. Season with 1 teaspoon lemon juice and a grind of black pepper.

GREEN PEPPERCORN BUTTER

Crush or pound 1 teaspoon green peppercorns and cream them with a stick of butter. For broiled, fried, or poached fish.

THREE

Chowders, Soups, and Stews

CHOWDER

The name "chowder" is a corruption of the French *chaudière,* a large cal-dron in which communal fish stews were made in Breton fishing villages. Each fisherman contributed something of his catch to the pot. These early French efforts contained neither milk nor tomatoes. Though chowders may also be based on other shellfish, or on cod, haddock, whitefish, or eel, clam chowder is the most venerable tradition in this country. The difference between a chowder and a fish stew is not always clear, but generally the classic chowder base is pork of some kind, onions, potatoes, and milk.

The southward drift of the chowder was marked by the replacement of milk with tomatoes, a version that became known as "Manhattan," which was considered absolute heresy by New Englanders (in 1939 a bill was actually introduced into the Maine legislature to make tomatoes in chow-ders illegal). The great chowder controversy—New England vs. Manhat-tan—still exists to inflame otherwise placid individuals. Today public opin-ion seems weighted in favor of the tomato.

NEW ENGLAND CLAM CHOWDER

4 large potatoes
½ pound very lean bacon, in ¼-inch pieces
1 medium onion, minced
2 quarts heated stock, potato water, or chicken broth

1 quart shucked chowder clams plus juice
Salt and pepper
1 cup heavy cream or milk, heated
A walnut-size lump of butter
Chopped parsley

Peel the potatoes, cut into 1-inch cubes, cover with water, bring to boil, and cook for 5 minutes. Drain them and reserve the water if it is to be used in place of stock.

Cook the bacon in a big heavy pot until crisp. Remove, drain, and keep warm. Cook the onions gently in the hot bacon fat. When limp, add the drained potatoes and mix well. Add the hot stock or potato water and simmer for 15 minutes or until the potatoes begin to break apart. Add the clams and juice and season to taste. Add the cream or milk and heat just enough to blend—do not allow to boil or cook too long, as the clams will toughen. Pour into a hot tureen and top with the butter. Scatter crumbled bacon and chopped parsley as garnish. Serves 4 as a hearty main dish with crusty bread followed by salad, cheese, and a fruit dessert.

MANHATTAN CLAM CHOWDER

1 quart shucked chowder clams
   plus their liquid
½ pound bacon, cut into ¼-inch
   pieces
3 medium onions, finely chopped
1 small green pepper, finely
   chopped
2 cups peeled, seeded, and
   chopped tomatoes, or a 1 pound
   12 ounce can chopped tomatoes, juice reserved

3 medium potatoes, diced
4 carrots, diced
2 stalks celery, diced
1½ quarts water
Salt and freshly ground black
   pepper
1 teaspoon dried thyme
1 bay leaf

Drain off the clam liquid and reserve. Chop the clams finely and set aside. Cook the bacon in a heavy soup kettle until almost crisp, remove with a slotted spoon and reserve. Add the onions and green pepper to the hot bacon fat and sauté until the onions are pale gold. Add the tomatoes and their juice, potatoes, carrots, celery, and 1½ quarts of water. Season with salt (cautiously, since clams can be salty) and pepper to taste, add the thyme and bay leaf, and bring to a boil. Lower the heat and simmer gently, uncovered, for about 40 minutes or until the potatoes are tender.

Add the clams and their juice, cover, and simmer for 20 minutes longer. Correct the seasonings, add the reserved bacon, and serve. Serves 6.

CLAM CHOWDER WITH CORN

4 large potatoes, peeled, cut into
   1-inch cubes
½ pound very lean bacon, cut into
   ¼-inch pieces
1 medium onion, minced
2 cups canned cream-style corn
A 15-ounce can whole corn
2 quarts hot fish stock, potato
   water, or chicken broth

1 quart shucked chowder clams
   plus juice
Salt and pepper
½ cup sliced red pimiento
1 cup heavy cream or milk, heated
A walnut-size lump of butter
Paprika

Put the potatoes in a saucepan with water to cover. Bring to a boil, cook for 5 minutes, drain, and reserve liquid. Set the potatoes aside. Cook the bacon in a heavy soup pot; when crisp, remove with a slotted spoon, drain, and keep warm. Cook the onions gently in the hot bacon fat. When limp, stir in the potatoes. Add creamed and whole corn, mix thoroughly, then add the hot stock, potato water, or broth. Simmer for 15 minutes or until potatoes start to break apart. Add the clams and juice and season. Add the pimiento and cream or milk, heat through but do not boil. Pour into a hot tureen and top with the butter, heavily sprinkled with paprika. Scatter the bacon crumbs as a last garnish, and perhaps some chopped parsley. Serves 4 as a hearty main dish with crusty bread followed by salad, cheese, and dessert.

NOTE: Fresh clams may be replaced by 2 cups of canned clams.

NEW ENGLAND FISH CHOWDER

About 4 pounds fresh cod or halibut, pollock or sea bass, or a combination, cleaned, skinned, and filleted, heads, tails, bones, and trimmings reserved
4 ounces diced salt pork
4 tablespoons butter

1 medium onion, sliced
2 tablespoons flour
4–5 medium potatoes, sliced
1 bay leaf
2–3 cups milk
Salt and several grindings of pepper
8 unsalted crackers, split in half

Cut the fish into 2-inch pieces, set aside. Put the heads, tails, bones, and trimmings into a pot with water to cover (about 2 quarts). Bring to a boil, skim off any scum, reduce heat, and cook slowly for about 20 minutes. Strain the broth, measure off 4 cups, and reserve, keeping hot. Discard bones and trimmings.

Blanch the salt pork for 5 minutes in 2 quarts of water, drain, and discard water. Melt 2 tablespoons of the butter in the soup pot in which you will make the chowder, fry the salt pork until golden. Stir in the onion and sauté until wilted, about 8 minutes. Turn the pork-onion mixture into a sieve set over a bowl to drain off fat, then return to the pot.

Over moderate heat, blend in the flour (add a bit of the pork if the mixture seems dry), cook for 2 minutes, stirring. Off heat, blend in 1 cup of the hot fish liquid. Beat in the balance of the fish stock.

Add the potatoes, bay leaf, salt, and pepper, cook slowly, uncovered, until the potatoes are tender, about 15 minutes. (The recipe may be made ahead to this point and refrigerated when cool.) Just before serving, bring the soup base to a simmer, add the fish, and simmer for about 5 minutes (a few minutes longer if the fish is frozen).

Scald the milk, add the seasoning, and swirl in the remaining 2 tablespoons of butter. Heat until piping hot but do not boil. Crumble in the crackers if desired. Serves 4–6.

VARIATION: Fish chowder with salt cod: Soak 2 pounds of salt cod fillets and poach in milk as directed (see Index). Proceed as above, using the poaching liquid in place of the stock, and adding milk as needed.

BOB THOMAS' FISH CHOWDER

This chowder is especially adaptable to frozen fish.

2 pounds (approximately) firm white fish such as cod, halibut, pollock, blackfish, filleted and skinned

4–5 medium all-purpose potatoes (about 1¾ pounds), peeled and cut into ½-inch cubes

1 teaspoon salt

4 tablespoons butter

⅔ cup carrots cut into ¼-inch dice (2 medium carrots)

1 cup coarsely chopped yellow onions (1 large or 2 medium)

3 tablespoons chopped parsley

½ cup milk

½ cup heavy cream (see the note below)

Salt and pepper to taste

Wash the fish and cut into 2-inch pieces. Put the fish into a heavy 5-quart pot or soup kettle, add about 5 cups of water or enough to cover the fish by 1 inch. Bring to a boil and simmer, covered, for 4–5 minutes. Remove the fish with a slotted spoon, set aside.

Add the potatoes to the same liquid, bring to a boil, add 1 teaspoon of salt, cover, and cook for 12–15 minutes until the potatoes are at the point of breaking up (you may have to help them along with several mashes of a potato masher—they should appear to have almost disintegrated).

While the potatoes are cooking, melt the butter in a 10-inch skillet, add the carrots and cook, covered, over moderate heat until they are slightly softened, about 4 minutes. Uncover, add the onions and parsley, and sauté the vegetables until the onions are soft and have taken on just the slightest color, about 5 minutes.

Add the vegetable mixture to the fish-potato water, stir in the milk and cream, add the fish, and season to taste. Heat gently but do not boil and cook, uncovered, for 5 minutes. Correct the seasoning. Serves 6.

NOTE: For a richer chowder increase the heavy cream to 1 cup and omit the milk.

If frozen fish is used, a white scum may rise to the surface of the cooking liquid; this seems to be a characteristic of frozen fish and may be safely ignored, as it will eventually blend into the broth.

BOUILLABAISSE

Bouillabaisse is one of those dishes that invariably give rise to a discussion of where one has eaten the best versions and why. There are those who insist that no decent *bouillabaisse* can be made anywhere but on the southern coast of France. My friend Paula Wolfert, with whom I agree about practically everything else having to do with food, is one. Paula knows more about *bouillabaisse* than anyone else because she not only is an expert on Mediterranean cooking, but she ate fourteen different versions in this country in order to write a magazine article stating that they don't exist here.

Paula's argument is that to make a true *bouillabaisse* you must begin with a stock or base broth made from at least a hundred tiny Mediterranean rockfish; further, that you need *rascasse* to give the proper gelatinous quality, plus *grondin vives* and *galinettes* and water from the fishing grounds off Hyères. Anything else she says is *soupe de poissons*.

Obviously the fish in this country differ from those in Marseilles, where the dish originated, but since there are many variations of *bouillabaisse*, even in the short distance between Marseilles and Toulon and, still more, throughout France there is room for adaptation. The Parisian version, for example, includes clams, mussels, and oysters, which the Marseilles version does not; some people add cognac; others Pernod. By paying strict attention to those aspects of the dish which *are* unique and inflexible, namely, the basic cooking method, the classic proportions, and the use of at least five different kinds of fish, not including shellfish, a creditable version can be made on these shores as well. Thackeray, who wrote an "Ode to Bouillabaisse," mentions that in New Orleans he ate a *bouillabaisse* better than any ever encountered in Marseilles.

Three important things to remember in the preparation of *bouillabaisse* are: one, that the bulk of the fish must be firm-fleshed, as the hard boil required of the dish will cause delicate fish to disintegrate; two, that the hard boil itself is an absolute necessity for the "union" of this dish; and, three, that as it is the variety of fish and shellfish as much as anything else that gives the dish its distinctive quality, don't bother to make it for less than ten or twelve people—the ingredients add up to a lot of eating!

Fish that may be included in the first category are:

Anglerfish	Pollock
Blackfish (tautog)	Redfish or red drum
Black drum	Rockfish or Sculpin
Grouper	Scrod
Grunt	Sea Robin
Hake	Weakfish (sea trout)
Halibut	

In the second category:

Flounder	Sole
Perch	Striped bass
Rock bass	Whiting

Cleaned soft-shell crabs may replace the lobster.

BOUILLABAISSE

This particular version is an adaptation of the outstanding one served at New York's Le Cirque restaurant. The stock is prepared first, which adds immeasurably to the depth of flavor of the finished product. In a further sophisticated touch, the fish at Le Cirque is marinated for twenty-four hours before being used, which is given here as an optional step.

Approximately 3 pounds filleted and skinned fish: red snapper, halibut, eel, tail end of cod, white perch (or other firm white saltwater fish from the first category given above)
Approximately 1 pound filleted striped bass or sole or flounder
Approximately 2 pounds heads, tails, bones, and trimmings from above
2 quarts water
2 cups dry white wine
4 tablespoons butter
3 leeks (both white and pale green parts), washed and coarsely chopped
3 stalks celery, coarsely chopped
4 cloves garlic, unpeeled and cut in half
2 medium onions, coarsely chopped
¼ cup chopped parsley
4 tablespoons tomato paste
1 pound ripe tomatoes, peeled, seeded, and coarsely chopped, or a 2 pound 3 ounce can, chopped, with juice

2 bay leaves, crumbled
1 teaspoon dried thyme or 2 branches fresh
1 teaspoon fennel seed
2 pinches saffron threads
Dried or fresh rind of a half orange
2 tablespoons salt or more
White pepper to taste
½ cup olive oil plus 2½ tablespoons
3 dozen mussels or clams, or a combination of both
2 pounds lobster tails in the shells
2½ tablespoons flour
Several splashes of Pernod, Ricard, or other unsweet anise-flavored liquor (optional)
¼-inch-thick slices French bread dried in the oven (3–4 per person)
1 recipe of *Rouille* ❋ (recipe following this one)

Cut all the fish into slices or chunks roughly 2 by 3 inches. Keep the firm and delicate fish separate. (If you are planning to marinate the fish, do this step the day before and see directions for marinade in the note below.) Set aside.

Make the stock or base: wash the heads and bones well or, better still (and easier), cut up the heads and bones in pieces and let them soak overnight in cold water to cover. Discard the soaking water and rinse well. Put the heads and bones in a large, deep soup kettle and cover with the water and wine.

Melt the butter in a heavy skillet and add the leeks, celery, garlic, onions, and parsley. Cook, stirring, over moderate heat just until the vegetables are softened, about 5 minutes. Add to the stock kettle. (This step may be omitted and the vegetables mentioned added directly to the kettle without the brief sautéing, but it adds to the depth of flavor and the color to do so.)

Add the tomato paste, tomatoes, bay leaves, thyme, fennel seed, saffron, orange rind, salt, and pepper. Pour the ½ cup olive oil over. (Disregard the unappetizing appearance of the oil and water at this point; an emulsion will form during the cooking.) Bring the liquid to a boil and cook hard for 8 minutes. Then cover, lower heat, and simmer for 40 minutes.

While the stock is cooking, scrub the mussels and clams. With a heavy knife or kitchen shears cut the lobster tails into manageable pieces, cutting through shell and flesh. Set aside.

Prepare a *lié* to thicken the broth (stock): scoop out a half cup or so of the broth and put in a small, heavy saucepan. Stir in the flour and the remaining 2 tablespoons of olive oil. Set over fairly high heat, bring to a boil, and cook for 3–5 minutes. Add to the kettle at the end of cooking time and stir in well.

Strain the broth through a strainer or large sieve placed over a bowl, pressing down on the vegetables and bones to extract all the juices. Return the broth to the kettle.

Bring the broth again to a simmer and add the firm fish. Cook for 8 minutes over moderate heat, stirring frequently but gently with a wooden spoon. Add the tender fish, shellfish, and lobster pieces and cook for 8 minutes more, using the spoon judiciously to bathe any exposed pieces with liquid but not hard enough to break up the fish.

To serve: remove the fish, lobster, and shellfish to one or two serving dishes and keep warm. Add the Pernod to the broth and correct seasoning. Put bread slices in individual deep soup plates and moisten with a cupful or so of broth. Arrange a selection of fish and shellfish on top of each. Serve at once—*bouillabaise* should not be kept waiting. Pass the *rouille* separately.

NOTE: To marinate the fish: prepare the fish a day ahead. Moisten well with olive oil. In a small bowl make a mixture of 1½ cups chopped tomatoes, 2 cloves garlic, pressed, 2 tablespoons coarse salt, freshly ground black pepper, a pinch of saffron, and 1 teaspoon fennel powder, sprinkle over fish. Cover and refrigerate overnight. Then proceed with the recipe, but season more cautiously than you would had you not used a marinade.

ROUILLE

Not for alliophobes, this fiery sauce is *de rigueur* in Provence with *bouillabaisse, bourride,* and other fish dishes and soups. It is passed at the table and added to the dish according to individual preferences. A teaspoon will do to start—the bold may wish to add more. Originally made laboriously in a mortar, it is now made in a blender or food processor in a trice.

In France the most authentic version is made with liver of sea bream added. There is also a less potent version made with an egg yolk, sort of a garlic mayonnaise, which I find a bit too timid.

½ cup fresh white bread crumbs
1 cup water
4 cloves garlic, peeled
2–3 small hot red peppers, fresh or dried

¼ cup olive oil
4–5 drops Tabasco
1 tablespoon paprika
2–3 spoonfuls of broth from *bouillabaisse* or fish soup

Soak the bread crumbs in the 1 cup of water, press out excess.

IN A BLENDER: Put the soaked, squeezed-out bread in the blender with the garlic, red peppers, and olive oil, blend until pasty. Add the Tabasco, paprika, and broth, blend until creamy. Makes about 1 cup.

IN A FOOD PROCESSOR: Using the metal blade, place all the ingredients in the container and run until a smooth paste is obtained. Thin with some more fish broth if too thick. Makes about 1 cup.

NOTE: If you do not have a blender or food processor, combine all the ingredients and crush with a mortar and pestle or in a small sturdy bowl, using the handle end of a wooden spoon, until a creamy consistency is reached.

SOUPE DE POISSON

Very fresh fish is required for this soup, which is little known outside of Provence and which I, for one, prefer to *bouillabaisse,* finding it less filling and more subtly soul-satisfying—the quintessential "bouillon of the sun." Classically, its basis is an assortment of rockfish, the more the better. In this country, use any of the fish suggested for *bouillabaisse,* or a combination of those mentioned below. Crabs, if they are available, add a delicious note, and anglerfish, if you can get it, adds an authentic taste. You end up with an astonishingly small amount of broth, considering what you start with, but it is that very reduction which gives you the sublime, concentrated flavor of Provence.

2½ pounds fish fillets, skinned; any combination of rockfish, scrod, whiting, eel, anglerfish, perch
2 soft-shell crabs per person (see Note 1 p. 71)
¾ cup olive oil

1 leek (white part only), chopped
1 onion, chopped
2 cloves garlic, crushed
2 ripe tomatoes, peeled and chopped
2 quarts water

1 bay leaf

2 sprigs fennel if available or 1
    teaspoon fennel seeds, crushed

2 tablespoons or more of salt

Freshly ground black pepper

A large pinch of saffron

1 cup uncooked small pasta (see
    Note 2 below)

Grated Parmesan cheese

Wash the fish and the crabs and pat dry. Cut the fish into serving pieces about 2 inches square. Cut the crabs in half. Set aside.

Heat the oil in a 5- or 6-quart soup kettle and add the leek, onion, garlic, and tomatoes. (In Provence, this soup is often made in a marmite or earthenware pot.) Brown vegetables slightly over high heat and add the fish and crabs. When the fish starts to become opaque but is not yet brown, add the water, bay leaf and fennel, bring to a boil, and cook over medium-high heat, uncovered, for about 15 minutes.

Remove the crabs with a slotted spoon, set aside and keep warm. Pour the liquid through a strainer into a large bowl. Combine the fish and vegetable bits and the contents of the strainer; press well to extract the essence. Put through a food mill to complete the extraction.

Discard the bones, pressed-out meat, and vegetables. (If you do not know this soup and the treat that is in store for you, it will appear that you are being wasteful and throwing away valuable food; forget this concern.) Return the sauce to the kettle and season highly to taste. To what is now a smooth, silky broth, add the saffron, bring to a boil, and toss in the pasta. When it is cooked, serve the soup at once in heated soup bowls. Pass the cheese and crabs separately. If desired, serve with toasted French bread and *Rouille* ❁ (the recipe preceding this one). Serves 4–6.

NOTES: 1. Though it is not authentic, I have substituted 2 jumbo shrimp, raw and in the shell, per person for the crab, with pleasant results.

2. *Orzo,* a small rice-shaped pasta, is ideal for this. Others are *acini di pepe* and egg *pastina.*

BOURRIDE

Bourride, a thick soup of white fish, has its origins in antiquity; the Phoenicians already knew it when they landed on the southern shores of France two thousand years ago. There are many versions, but always the *aioli* is blended with the broth.

3 pounds cleaned skinned, filleted
    white fish; at least 3 from the
    following: mullet, bass, halibut,
    pollock, haddock, cod, whiting,
    redfish, rockfish

1½ cups boiling water

1½ cups dry white wine

2 leeks (white part only), sliced

1 medium onion, chopped

1 carrot, sliced

2 slices fresh fennel (optional)

2 bay leaves

Fresh or dried peel of half an
    orange

A sprig of thyme or ½ teaspoon
   dried thyme
Salt and pepper to taste
1 recipe of Aioli Sauce

1 raw egg yolk per person
8–10 slices French bread, fried in
   butter or oil until golden brown

Cut the fish into large chunks or slices, set aside. Make a court-bouillon by combining, in a 5-quart enameled or stainless steel pot, the boiling water, wine, leeks, onion, carrot, fennel, bay leaves, orange peel, thyme, salt, and pepper. Bring to a boil over high heat, partially cover the pot, reduce heat, and simmer for 15 minutes. Add the fish, bring to a second boil, and cook at a brisk simmer for 4–5 minutes. Remove the fish with a slotted spoon and keep warm. Strain and reserve the broth.

Put 2 tablespoons of *aioli* sauce for each person in a small bowl. Put the remainder of the sauce into a heavy 2-quart saucepan along with the egg yolks. Measure ½ cup of the reserved fish broth and pour it a little at a time into the saucepan while stirring constantly with a wooden spoon. Add the remaining reserved broth, stirring or whisking briskly, until all is well blended. Put the saucepan over gentle heat and continue stirring until the soup is smooth and as thick as custard. Do not let it boil or it will curdle.

Put the slices of fried bread in a heated tureen and pour the creamy soup over. Pass the fish separately along with the remainder of the *aioli*. Serves 4–5.

NOTE: Two parboiled potatoes, sliced, may be added with the fish, removed from the broth, and served with them. Also, *Rouille* ❋ may be blended in instead of *aioli,* to similar effect.

FISHERMAN'S WHARF "BOUILLABAISSE"

3 tablespoons olive oil
3 medium onions, sliced
3 cloves garlic, mashed
1 leek (including green top), sliced
5 cups Fish Stock ❋ or half stock
   and half water
1 teaspoon salt
Several grindings fresh black
   pepper
¼ teaspoon cayenne pepper
½ teaspoon powdered saffron
1 bay leaf, crumbled
¾ teaspoon dried basil

¾ teaspoon dried marjoram
1 pound raw shrimp
2 pounds haddock fillet, skinned
4 medium baking potatoes, peeled
   and cut into 1-inch pieces
8–12 small lobster tails in their
   shells
12–18 clams, scrubbed
⅓ cup dry white wine
¼ cup chopped fresh parsley
2 fresh, ripe tomatoes, peeled and
   chopped, or a 1-pound can,
   drained

In an 8-quart Dutch oven heat the olive oil over moderate heat and add the onions, garlic, and leek. Sauté, stirring frequently for 10 minutes or until limp but not browned. Add the fish stock, salt, pepper, cayenne, saffron, bay leaf, basil, and marjoram, blend well. Cover the pot and simmer over moderate heat for 15–20 minutes.

Meanwhile, shell and devein the shrimp. Remove any bones from the haddock and slice into 2-inch pieces. Add the potatoes to the stew pot and simmer for 10 minutes. Add the lobster tails and simmer for 5 minutes longer. Then add the haddock, shrimp, and clams, simmer for 10 minutes. Test to see if the potatoes are cooked; if not, simmer the soup for 5–10 minutes more. Add the wine, parsley, and tomatoes, heat for a few more minutes. Correct the seasoning. Ladle the *bouillabaisse* into large soup bowls and serve with hot French bread. Serves 6–8.

CIOPPINO

The origin of California's most popular fish stew is of great interest to its fans. Some feel that it was originally Portuguese; my feeling is that transplanted Italian fishermen probably introduced a fish stew known on the Ligurian coast of Italy as *ciuppino,* made with a variety of white fish and shellfish. The basic recipe is similar, and it is interesting to see the influence of the New World—crab makes its appearance, fish stock intensifies the flavor, and green pepper and mushrooms add their flavorsome notes. The wine, traditionally red, becomes an option. Whatever the origin, fierce battles will no doubt continue to rage among dedicated cooks as to the best combination of fish for a *cioppino,* as well as between San Francisco and San Pedro, both of which claim to have originated the dish.

CIOPPINO WITH RED WINE

A 2½–3 pound sea or striped bass, filleted and skinned
1 pound raw medium shrimp
1 cooked Dungeness crab, fresh or frozen, or a 1½-pound lobster, cooked
18 littleneck clams in the shells, scrubbed
1 quart mussels, scrubbed and debearded
3 cups red wine
½ cup olive oil
1 large onion, chopped

2 cloves garlic, chopped
3 tablespoons chopped parsley
¼ pound mushrooms, sliced (see p. 74)
1 green pepper, seeded
2–3 ripe tomatoes, peeled, seeded, and coarsely chopped
3 ounces tomato paste
Salt and pepper to taste
A dash of cayenne pepper
1 teaspoon dried basil or 2 tablespoons finely chopped fresh basil

Cut the fish into serving pieces about 2 by 3 inches. Shell and devein the shrimp. Break or cut the crab into serving pieces or, if using lobster, split and clean it, crack the claws and cut the body and tail in small serving pieces. Set these ingredients aside.

Steam the clams and mussels in a deep pot with 1 cup of the wine until they open. Discard any that have not opened. Remove from broth with a slotted spoon and reserve. Measure off 1 cup of the broth, strain it through cheesecloth, and reserve. (The broth at this point may be an odd, murky purple; it will correct itself later.)

In a heavy 7-quart soup pot, heat the olive oil and cook the onion, garlic, parsley, mushrooms, and green pepper until the onions are translucent. Add the tomatoes and cook for 4 minutes. Add the strained broth, the tomato paste, and the remaining 2 cups of wine. Season with salt, pepper, and cayenne, bring to a simmer, cover, lower the flame, and simmer very gently for about 20 minutes. Correct seasonings.

Add the basil and the reserved fish, simmer for 8–10 minutes. Add the reserved shrimp, clams, mussels, and crab or lobster. Continue cooking at a gentle simmer, covered, until the shrimp are pink, about 5 minutes. Serves 6–8.

NOTE: In the absence of fresh mushrooms, use dried ones soaked in water and drained. The canned variety is not suitable for this dish.

SAN PEDRO CIOPPINO (with White Wine)

2 tablespoons olive oil
2 tablespoons butter
3 cups chopped onions
2–4 cloves garlic, finely minced
2 green peppers, cored, seeded, and chopped
4 cups peeled, seeded, and chopped ripe tomatoes
1 cup fresh or canned tomato sauce
1 teaspoon dried basil
1 teaspoon dried oregano
Several dashes of cayenne pepper
Salt and freshly ground pepper to taste
2 cups fresh Fish Stock ✳
2 cups dry white wine

1 pound firm-fleshed fish such as striped bass, red snapper, rock cod, or sea bass, filleted, skinned and cut into bite-size pieces
1 pound raw shrimp, shelled and deveined
1 dozen small clams, washed
1 pound lobster tail cooked in the shell (and cut into serving pieces) (optional)
1 Dungeness crab fresh or frozen, cooked in the shell and broken into pieces (optional), or 3 6½-ounce cans King crab meat, or 2 10-ounce packages frozen crab meat

Heat the oil and butter in a large, heavy kettle and add the onions and garlic. Cook, stirring often, until the onions are lightly colored. Add the green peppers and continue cooking and stirring until the peppers wilt. Add the tomatoes, tomato sauce, basil, oregano, and cayenne, salt, and pepper to taste. Add the fish stock and cook slowly for about 2 hours, stirring often to prevent burning. More fish stock may be added if needed. Add the wine and continue cooking for about 10 minutes (the soup may be made ahead to this point). About 20 minutes before serving, return the soup to a boil, add the fish and cook for about 5 minutes. Add the shrimp, simmer for about 8 minutes, then add the clams, lobster tail, and crab. Cook, stirring gently, for about 5 minutes or until the clams open. Serve in very hot soup bowls with garlic bread. Serves 10.

ZUPPA DI PESCE (Italian Fish Soup)

This recipe is adapted from the excellent version served at Il Monello, in New York City. Just the opposite of *bouillabaisse,* it must be made quickly, preferably in a shallow vessel, and not allowed to boil. Making it is a quick procedure—assemble all the ingredients first.

³⁄₄ cup olive oil	8 medium shrimp, cleaned and
2 cloves garlic, minced	deveined, tails on
¹⁄₃ cup minced shallots	1 squid, cleaned and cut in rings
1 teaspoon oregano	10–12 sea scallops
1 teaspoon salt	1 cup dry white wine
Freshly ground pepper to taste	8 littleneck clams, scrubbed
¹⁄₂–³⁄₄ pound striped bass fillet,	8 mussels, scrubbed and debearded
skinned	1¹⁄₂ cups Italian plum tomatoes
¹⁄₂–³⁄₄ pound red snapper fillet,	and their juice
skinned	2 tablespoons chopped parsley

Heat the olive oil in a large, heavy skillet with a cover. Add the garlic and shallots, cook until golden. Season with salt, pepper, and oregano, cook for 2 minutes longer.

Cut the bass and red snapper fillets into 6–8 pieces each and add to the olive oil mixture. Sauté the fish pieces until they just turn milky white, keeping them moving in the skillet, using a wooden spoon. Add the shrimp, sauté until pink, stirring frequently. Add the squid, scallops, and wine, bring to a boil, lower the heat, and simmer for 2–3 minutes. Add the clams and mussels, cover the skillet with a tight-fitting lid, and cook for 10–15 minutes or until the clams open. Do not stir the contents at this time or the fish will come apart.

Break up the tomatoes lightly with a fork, add them to the skillet, and stir them in carefully so as not to break up the fish. Simmer, uncovered, until the sauce thickens, about 10 minutes. Correct the seasoning. Sprinkle with chopped parsley and serve at once. Serves 4.

ZARZUELA DE PESCADO

This Catalan seafood stew is one of the great classics of Spanish cuisine and might be considered that country's *bouillabaisse,* although it differs in the combination of fish and in the fact that they are fried first. The name *zarzuela* dates back to seventeenth-century performances at La Zarzuela, the palace of Philip IV, and is today the Spanish word for operetta. The dish can be converted into heavier going by the addition of lobster (in Spain the spiny, or rock, lobster, is used), and then it is called appropriately *"ópera de pescado."*

This version substitutes cognac for the traditional anisette.

2 pounds filleted fish: halibut, sea bass, or haddock, cut in 2-inch chunks
½ pound eel, cut into 4 pieces
2 small squid, cut into rings
Salt and pepper to taste
3 tablespoons flour
16 cherrystone clams, scrubbed
16 mussels, scrubbed and debearded
1 cup olive oil
1 pound raw medium shrimp, shelled and deveined

1 large onion, finely chopped
2 large tomatoes, peeled and chopped, or 1 cup drained and chopped canned tomatoes
2 cloves garlic, minced
2 ounces blanched almonds
A large pinch of powdered saffron
1 zwieback or other, nonsweet cracker, crushed
½ cup dry white wine
1 tablespoon minced parsley
3 tablespoons brandy or cognac

Season the fish and squid with salt and pepper, lightly flour them, and shake off the excess.

Steam open the clams and mussels, discard one half shell of each, and set aside. Strain and reserve the broth.

Put ¾ cup of the oil in a large porcelain-lined or stainless steel kettle and heat until quite hot but not smoking. Add the squid and fry for 5 minutes, then add the rest of the fish and fry everything for 5 minutes more. Remove and drain on paper towels. Next add the shrimp, cook until they turn pink; reserve. Discard the oil.

In a skillet heat 2 tablespoons of the remaining oil and sauté the onion until it is wilted. Add the tomatoes and cook for about 3 minutes longer. Add ½ cup of the clam-mussel broth and season to taste. Make a paste of the garlic and almonds in a blender and add to the tomato mixture. Add the saffron, the zwieback or cracker, wine, and parsley, simmer for 3–4 minutes. Transfer this mixture to the kettle.

Return the fish, squid, and shrimp to the kettle. Add the clams and mussels, heat the brandy, add to the casserole, and flame it. Cover and cook over medium heat for 5 minutes. Correct the seasoning and heat through. If the sauce appears too thick, a little of the reserved mussel broth or water may be added. Serve immediately, preferably from the casserole. Serves 6–8.

SOLIANKA

The sturgeon, prince of Russian fishes, is a large and meaty creature, so after the choicest, thickest parts are used, the leftovers often end up in a stew called *solianka,* which has several versions. The dish was introduced to this country by Russian émigrés who entered the United States through the Northwest and adapted it to our plentiful salmon. The *solianka* they make is more of a soup than a stew. The combination of flavors is unusual and extremely tasty. *Solianka* served over rice is not very Russian, but it makes a satisfying one-dish meal.

3 tablespoons butter
2 medium onions, finely chopped
1½ pounds salmon fillet, boned, skinned, and cut in strips
Salt and freshly ground pepper
1–1½ cups Fish Stock ❋
1 pound sauerkraut, drained
½ cup finely chopped dill pickles

1 cup fresh bread crumbs
4 tablespoons melted butter
Several black olives
2 teaspoons capers
2 tablespoons freshly chopped dill (optional)
Lemon slices

Preheat the oven to 350°.

Melt the butter in a saucepan. Sauté the onions until they just wilt, lay the fish strips on them, season, and add enough fish broth to cover. Then cover the saucepan, simmer for 10 minutes.

Butter a fairly shallow ovenproof casserole large enough to hold the fish. Put half of the drained sauerkraut on the bottom. Lift out the fish and onions from the saucepan and arrange over the sauerkraut. Strew with chopped pickles. Cover with the balance of sauerkraut and top with the bread crumbs mixed with the 4 tablespoons of melted butter. Bake for 20 minutes or until the crumbs brown. Garnish with the black olives, capers, dill, and lemon slices. Serves 4.

MATELOTE MARINIÈRE

In the Bourbonnais region of France, it was the custom for a farm to have its own artificial fishpond in a dammed-up low-lying area to provide the family with a continuous supply of fish. Every two or three years the pond was drained to thin out the fish. The draining became a gala event that culminated in a *matelote,* a stew of freshwater fish made with red or white wine, traditionally the wine of the region. This stew is also called *meurette* or *paucheuse* according to district and preparation.

3–4 pounds fish (perch, carp, bass,
   eel, filleted, skinned and cut
   into medium-size pieces
White wine to cover
1 onion, finely chopped
2 cloves garlic, minced
1 teaspoon salt
A *bouquet garni* of parsley, 1 bay
   leaf, crumbled, and ½ teaspoon
   thyme

10 small white onions
10 small mushrooms, cut in half
3 tablespoons butter
1 tablespoon flour
Slices of French bread browned in
   butter

Put the fish in a deep soup kettle and cover with wine. Add the onion, garlic, salt, and *bouquet garni*. Bring to a boil, cover, lower heat, and simmer for 15 minutes. Remove the fish with a slotted spoon and keep warm in a serving dish.

At the same time, prepare the small white onions and mushrooms. Pierce a cross on the bottom of each onion and put them together with the mushrooms in a saucepan with a half cup of water and 1 tablespoon of the butter. Cover and simmer until the onions are tender, 12–15 minutes. Set aside and keep warm.

Cream together the remaining 2 tablespoons of butter and the flour. Add this in little balls to the fish liquid, bring to a boil, and stir constantly until the sauce is thickened. Correct the seasoning.

Drain the cooked onions and mushrooms, arrange over and around the fish. Pour the sauce over all. Garnish with slices of fried French bread.

VARIATION: *À la bourbonnaise:* use red wine instead of white, and garnish with ½ pound of peeled cooked shrimp.

LA PAUCHEUSE DE VERDUN

3½–4 pounds freshwater fish (made
   of 1 pound eel plus any or all
   of pike, carp, perch, bass) filleted, skinned and cut into 2-inch
   pieces
Salt and pepper
3 cups dry white wine or to cover
1 cup diced salt pork

7 tablespoons butter
3–4 cloves garlic
½ teaspoon thyme
Several gratings of nutmeg
3 sprigs of parsley, tied together
1 bay leaf
1 tablespoon flour
6–8 slices French bread

Season the fish with salt and pepper, put in a soup kettle with the white wine. In a small saucepan, parboil the pork in water to cover for 5 minutes, then drain and remove. Melt 2 tablespoons of the butter in the saucepan, return the pork, and sauté until golden brown. Add the pork to the fish kettle along with 2 or 3 of the garlic cloves, pressed, and the thyme and nutmeg. Tie the parsley and bay leaf together and add. Bring to a boil, lower heat, and simmer for 20–25 minutes, uncovered.

Make a *beurre manié* by creaming together 3 tablespoons of the butter and the flour, add gradually in little balls to the kettle, shaking it to blend into the liquid. (Do not stir them in; this will break up the fish pieces.) Cook for 10 minutes longer.

In a skillet melt the remaining 2 tablespoons of butter. Brown the bread slices in it, rub each with the remaining cut clove of garlic, and put in a deep serving dish, tureen, or individual bowls. Arrange a piece of fish on each slice of toast, scoop out the pork dice with a slotted spoon, and scatter over fish. Surround the toast slices with the remaining fish. Remove the parsley and bay leaf. Correct the seasoning of the sauce, strain, and pour over the fish. Serves 6.

FINNISH SALMON SOUP (Lohikeitto)

A lovely, warming, satisfying main-dish soup—just the thing to make when you have a whole salmon and have filleted it or otherwise used most of it up. Remember to save some meat for the soup. Alternatively, you can ask your fish dealer to save you the necessary bones and trimmings and you buy the fillet.

Head, tail, bones, and trimmings
   from an 8–10-pound salmon
2 pounds fillet of salmon, skinned
6 cups water
8–10 peppercorns
1 bay leaf
1 tablespoon salt
1½ pounds potatoes (preferably
   red new potatoes, although any
   boiling kind will do)

2–3 onions, coarsely chopped
⅓–½ cup heavy cream
2 tablespoons butter in 4 pats
Sliced scallions (white and part of
   the green) for garnish

Wash the salmon bones and trimmings under cold running water and wash out the head well until the water is clear. Cut the salmon fillet into pieces measuring roughly 2 by 3 inches, set aside. Put the bones and trimmings into a 5-quart soup kettle, add the 6 cups of water, peppercorns, bay leaf, and salt, bring to a boil, lower the heat, and simmer, covered, for 45 minutes. Strain the broth, discard the bones and trimmings,* return to the kettle, and set aside.

Cut the potatoes into slices about ⅜ inch thick (halving these if the potatoes are large), add to the kettle along with the onions. Bring to a boil, lower the heat slightly, and simmer for 15–20 minutes or until the potatoes are

---

*The cheeks of the salmon head are considered a delicacy in Finland and would be removed and eaten before the head is discarded.

tender. Check the potatoes frequently, and 5 minutes before you judge them to be done lay the salmon pieces on top, cover, and cook for 5 minutes.

Tilt the kettle and ladle out a cup or so of the liquid into a small bowl. Add the cream and whisk in. Return the liquid to the kettle and tilt it this way and that to distribute evenly. Correct the seasoning. Ladle the soup into heated soup plates, swirl a pat of butter into each, and top with a sprinkling of scallions. Serve at once. Serves 4.

SEAFOOD GUMBO

In the Southern United States many stew-like dishes are called gumbos because they contain tomatoes and sweet peppers. In reality this only makes them "creole." Gumbos can be made of combinations of seafood and meat or solely of crab, but as one Southern cook put it, "If it ain't got okra and it ain't got filé, it ain't gumbo."

The origin of the word "gumbo" is a matter of debate: it may come from *ngombo,* the Bantu word for okra, which was introduced into Louisiana by early African slaves. But Louisiana cooks learned to season soups and stews with powdered sassafras leaves from the Choctaw Indians, and the Choctaw word for sassafras is *kombo.* Whatever its derivation, the modern version of powdered sassafras, "gumbo filé," is still very much a part of creole cooking.

½-pound piece of ham or equal amount of bacon
1 clove garlic, minced
2 medium onions, chopped
1 medium green pepper, peeled, seeded, and chopped
2½ cups chopped, peeled tomatoes, or a 35-ounce can, drained
6 ounces (1 can) tomato paste
3 cups chicken stock
1 small hot dried red pepper
16 pieces okra, sliced in rounds
1½ pounds raw shrimp, peeled and deveined
1 pound crab meat, fresh or canned
1 tablespoon filé powder

Trim the fat from the ham, cut the lean meat into cubes, set it aside, and render the fat. Put 3–4 tablespoons of the fat in a heavy skillet and reserve the remainder. If you are using bacon, fry and crumble it, set aside; reserve the fat, use 2 tablespoons as above.

Sauté the garlic and onions in the ham fat for 10 minutes, add the green pepper and cook for 5 minutes more. Stir in the tomatoes, tomato paste, stock, and hot pepper, simmer, uncovered, for 1 hour. Add the okra and shrimp and cook, covered, for 20 minutes more.

Heat some of the reserved ham or bacon fat and sauté the crab meat for about 15 minutes; stir in the filé powder, cook for 5 minutes more and add to the shrimp and ham mixture. Serve steaming hot over hot rice. (If bacon was used, top with crumbled bacon.) Serves 6–8.

VARIATION: Reduce the shrimp to 1 pound, add 2 dozen shucked oysters, and add these when you add the crab meat.

NOTE: Filé powder may be found in specialty food stores.

PORTUGUESE SEAFOOD STEW

The base of the stew as well as the rice and peas may be prepared well ahead of serving time, and the fish and shrimp added at the last minute.

1 tablespoon olive oil
1 tablespoon butter
1 large onion, chopped (about 1½ cups)
2–3 cloves garlic, minced
1 large green pepper, seeded and chopped
1 large carrot, sliced
4 medium tomatoes, peeled and chopped
1 cup beef stock
½ cup dry white wine
½ teaspoon sugar
1 teaspoon or more chopped fresh basil, or ½ teaspoon dried

⅛ teaspoon cayenne pepper or more to taste
Salt and freshly ground black pepper to taste
1 pound raw shrimp, shelled and deveined
2 pounds firm white fish fillets, skinned and cut into 1-inch cubes
1 recipe of Rice with Peas (given below)
Chopped parsley

Heat the oil and butter together in a large, deep enameled iron pot. Add the onion and garlic, cook until the onion is softened and transparent. Add the green pepper, carrot, and tomatoes, stir. Add the beef stock, wine, sugar, basil, cayenne, salt, and pepper to taste. Bring to a boil, lower the flame, and simmer for 15 minutes. (The recipe may be prepared ahead to this point.)

Just before serving, bring the sauce to a simmer and add the shrimp. Cover and cook over moderate heat just until the shrimp turn pink, about 4 minutes. Stir very gently once or twice so they cook evenly. Sprinkle the fish with salt and add, making sure that it is immersed in the sauce. Cover and cook for 3–4 minutes longer, or until the fish is opaque. Serve in large heated soup bowls spooned over the rice and peas and garnish with the chopped parsley. Serves 6.

RICE WITH PEAS

Bring 3½ cups of chicken stock or water to a boil. Add 1½ cups of long-grain rice, bring to a second boil, cover, lower heat, and cook for 15 minutes. The rice should still be moist at this point; if not, add another half cup of liquid. Then add 2 cups of fresh peas (approximately) and 3 tablespoons butter, cook until the rice and peas are tender, about 10 minutes more. Season with salt to taste.

NOTE: Fresh peas may be replaced by a 10-ounce package of frozen, French-type tiny June peas. Defrost and add at the very end, when the rice is tender, and heat through.

GRAND CENTRAL OYSTER PAN ROAST

The Oyster Bar of New York's Grand Central Station has been a landmark for travelers since it opened with this dish (a stew despite its name) in 1912. Oyster Pan Roast is still served there today, made according to this original recipe.

16 freshly opened oysters, liquor reserved
½ cup reserved oyster liquor
¼ cup clam juice
4 tablespoons butter

2 dashes celery salt
2 teaspoons Worcestershire sauce
1 cup milk
1 cup heavy cream
Paprika

This dish is very quickly made, so heat two soup bowls before you start.
Put the oysters, oyster liquor, clam juice, 2 tablespoons of the butter, celery salt, and Worcestershire sauce in the top of a double boiler and set pot over boiling water. The bottom of the pan should not touch the water. Whisk or stir briskly for about 1 minute until the oysters plump up and their edges begin to curl. Add the milk and cream and continue stirring briskly until liquid approaches the boil. Do not let it boil; remove from heat immediately, ladle into the heated bowls, and top each serving with a remaining tablespoon of butter, dusted with paprika. Serve immediately with oyster crackers. Serves 2.

CRAB STEW

This dish is high on my list of virtuous recipes; it is delicious and is actually enhanced by making it the day before, or in the morning, and gently reheating it. It is delightful at lunch and makes a satisfying one-dish Sunday supper as well as a satisfying meal before the theater or after.

4 cups chicken broth
½ teaspoon saffron threads or ¼ teaspoon powdered saffron

¼ pound butter, more if necessary
1 cup celery in medium dice
1 cup carrots in medium dice

2 leeks, diced
4 shallots, minced
1 green pepper, seeded and diced
3 tomatoes, peeled, seeded, and
  diced
¾–1 pound fresh lump crab meat

2 tablespoons Worcestershire
  sauce
Salt and freshly ground pepper
2 cups cooked rice
Freshly chopped parsley

Heat the chicken broth with the saffron, skimming any fat if necessary. In a skillet, melt the butter and gently stew the celery, carrots, leeks, and shallots for 10 minutes. Add the green pepper and continue cooking for 5 minutes longer without letting the vegetables brown, stirring occasionally. Add tomatoes and continue cooking, using more butter if necessary.

Pick over the crab, removing bits of shell or cartilage. Add to the vegetables with the Worcestershire sauce, cook for 5 minutes, stirring. Add the saffron broth with salt and pepper, simmer for a few minutes or reheat at serving time.

Place the rice (which should be a little undercooked) in a heated dish. Pour the hot stew into a heated tureen and sprinkle with parsley. Spoon the soup over the rice in heated soup plates. Serves 6.

MARISCADA AL MARINERO

24 hard-shell clams, soaked and
  scrubbed
24 mussels, cleaned and debearded
½ cup dry white wine
1 medium onion, minced
3 tablespoons olive oil

1 tomato, peeled, seeded, and
  chopped
2 tablespoons minced parsley
2 cloves garlic, minced
Salt and freshly ground pepper

Preheat oven to 400°.

Put the clams and mussels in a large kettle with the wine, bring to a boil over high heat, cover, and cook for 5 minutes or until the shellfish open. Discard any that remain closed. Transfer them with a slotted spoon to an ovenproof casserole or heavy iron pot large enough to hold all of them. Strain the cooking liquid through a sieve lined with 4 layers of cheesecloth into another bowl and reserve.

In a skillet sauté the onion in the olive oil until softened. Add the tomato, increase heat, and cook the mixture, stirring, for 3 minutes or until the liquid has evaporated. Add the parsley, garlic, reserved cooking liquid, and salt and pepper to taste, cook for 2 minutes. Pour the mixture over the clams and mussels and bake for 7 minutes or until the liquid just starts to simmer. Serve immediately in hot soup bowls over slices of garlic toast or with hot boiled rice. Serves 4.

Garlic Toast: In a skillet sauté 4 slices of day-old French bread, crusts removed, in 3 tablespoons of olive oil with 1 minced garlic clove until the bread is golden. Drain the toast on paper towels, then cut the slices into 1-inch strips.

VARIATION: On the Balearic Island of Ibiza, a version of this is made that includes shrimp. To do this, reduce the amount of clams and mussels to 12 each, and add 12 large shrimp, raw and in the shell. Following the above procedure, add the shrimp with the parsley, garlic, and broth, cook just until the shrimp turn pink, about 5 minutes. Then proceed with the recipe. It is the custom to serve the dish with the shrimp unshelled, the peeling to be done by the diner.

CHARLESTON CRAB SOUP

2 cups milk
¼ teaspoon ground mace
1 tablespoon grated lemon rind
4 tablespoons butter
1 small onion, finely chopped
1 pound fresh white crab meat,
    picked over

1 cup heavy cream
¼ cup cracker crumbs
Salt and freshly ground pepper
2 tablespoons dry sherry

Put the milk, mace, and lemon rind in the top of a double boiler, heat over simmering water for a few minutes. Melt the butter in a small skillet and sauté the chopped onion in it for a minute or two. Add the onion and butter, the crab meat, and cream to the milk, heat for 15 minutes more. Thicken with cracker crumbs, correct the seasonings, and let stand for 15–20 minutes to develop flavor. Reheat, add sherry just before serving. Serves 6.

ZUPPA DI VONGOLE

In his *Grand dictionnaire de cuisine,* Alexandre Dumas mentions *zuppa di vongole* as "the only good thing he had eaten in Naples."

40 littleneck clams, the smallest
    possible
2 tablespoons finely chopped
    shallots or onions
½ cup olive oil

2 teaspoons finely chopped garlic
2 tablespoons finely chopped
    parsley
1 cup white wine
Slices of Italian bread

Clean the clams according to instructions given elsewhere (see Index).

In a large heavy pot sauté the shallots or onions in the olive oil until wilted. Add the garlic, sauté until lightly colored, add the parsley, stir several times, add the wine, raise heat, and boil for 2 minutes.

Add the clams to the pot, stir in, and cover tightly. Continue cooking over high heat, giving the pot a vigorous shake from time to time so the clams cook evenly. The dish is done when the shells open, about 10 minutes.

Put a slice of bread for each diner in individual deep soup plates or into a large heated tureen. Spoon out the clams and broth over the bread, taking care not to disturb any sediment at the bottom of the pot in which sand may have settled. Serves 4.

SOUPE AUX MOULES

2 cups dry white wine	5 tablespoons butter
½ cup finely minced onions	4 tablespoons flour
1 clove garlic, mashed	2 egg yolks
6 sprigs parsley	½ cup heavy cream
1 small bay leaf	Salt and pepper to taste
¼ teaspoon thyme	Lemon juice
Several grindings of pepper	3 cups boiling milk
5 quarts mussels, soaked,	Minced parsley for garnish
scrubbed and debearded	

Put the wine in a large pot and add the onions, garlic, parsley, bay leaf, thyme, and pepper. Bring to a boil, cook for 2 minutes. Add mussels, cover, and cook for 5 minutes over high heat or until the shells open. Remove the mussels with a slotted spoon, shell them, and put them in a bowl. Discard any that remain closed. Set aside. Strain the kettle liquid into a saucepan, boil, uncovered, until reduced to about 1½ cups. Set aside.

In a heavy saucepan make a *roux* by melting 3 tablespoons of the butter and stirring the flour into it until it foams for 2 minutes without taking on any color. Remove from heat.

Strain the reserved mussel broth into the *roux*, taking great care to keep back any sand that may have settled in the saucepan. Whisk briskly to blend and bring to a boil. Cook for 1 minute, stirring (the sauce will be thick). Set aside.

In a bowl combine the egg yolks and cream. Beat in a little of the hot sauce very gradually, then pour the blend back into the remainder of the sauce, bring the mixture to a boil, stirring constantly. Boil no more than a minute. Correct seasoning with salt, pepper, and a few drops of lemon juice. Add the milk and the reserved mussels, stir to blend, and bring to a simmer. Stir in the remaining 2 tablespoons butter and garnish with parsley.

Serves 6.

BILLI-BI

A rich cream of mussel soup originally served at Maxim's in Paris, this soup got its name from William B. Leeds, a wealthy American tin magnate and Maxim's habitué, whose favorite it was. Craig Claiborne calls it "perhaps the greatest soup ever created."

1 cup chopped onions
4 tablespoons chopped shallots
4 tablespoons butter
1½ cups dry white wine
4 sprigs parsley
4 pounds mussels, cleaned and
    debearded

2 egg yolks
2 cups heavy cream
½ teaspoon salt
Freshly ground pepper
1 tablespoon minced parsley

In a heavy soup kettle put the onions, shallots, butter, wine, and sprigs of parsley. Lay the mussels on this bed, cover tightly, bring to a boil, and steam for 8–10 minutes over high heat or until the mussels have opened. Discard any that do not open. Scoop out the mussels with a slotted spoon and set aside. Carefully drain off the juice and strain it through 4 layers of cheesecloth into a heavy enamel-lined saucepan. Press down on the vegetables to complete extraction, then discard them.

Shell the mussels and cut or pull away the black rims. Reserve 3 of the mussels to garnish each serving, and set aside the remainder for use in some other recipe.

Bring the broth to a boil. In a small bowl beat the yolks with the cream, stir in a few tablespoons of the broth, then blend the egg mixture into the remainder of the broth, stirring constantly. Return to the heat until the soup has thickened slightly. Season with salt and pepper. Remove from heat, ladle into soup dishes, and garnish with the reserved mussels. Sprinkle with minced parsley.

To serve cold: place the pan over cold water and cool quickly. Refrigerate, then thin if necessary with a little light cream before serving. Serves 8.

BISQUE

A bisque is a purée of crayfish or other shellfish served as a soup. In the beginning of the nineteenth century bisques of pigeon and quail were popular, and only gradually did the term come to connote shellfish purées. Bisques of anything have always been considered stylish preparations and are generally highly spiced.

LOBSTER BISQUE

There are "minute" versions of lobster bisque, but the taste of the real thing is worth the effort.

Ingredients for a *mirepoix:* ✷ ¼ cup
    each finely julienned carrots,
    onions, celery, white of leek
4 tablespoons butter
2 tablespoons olive oil

A live lobster, 1½–2 pounds
1 cup white wine
¼ cup cognac
½ cup uncooked rice
4 cups Fish Stock ✷ or broth

Salt and freshly ground pepper
1 cup heavy cream

2 tablespoons sherry
Chopped parsley

In a heavy pot, make the *mirepoix* by sautéing the vegetables for 5 minutes in a mixture of 1 tablespoon of the butter and the 2 tablespoons of olive oil. Cut the live lobster in half down the back, and cut crosswise into several pieces. Remove intestinal vein and add pieces to the pot. Move them about with two wooden spoons until the shells turn red. Add the wine and cognac, cover, and simmer for 20 minutes. Remove from heat, take the lobster meat out of the shell, and reserve.

Break up the shells and either put through a food grinder, process in a food processor with the steel blade, or pound in a mortar. Return the ground shells to the pot.

Cook the rice in 2 cups of the fish stock or broth for about 30 minutes, add to the ingredients in the pot, and purée in a food processor or put through a sieve.

Dilute the mixture with the remaining stock until the consistency of very thick soup is reached and strain through a fine sieve. Season with salt and pepper to taste, reheat, adding the cream and remaining 3 tablespoons of butter. Strain again, through a double thickness of cheesecloth.

At serving time, bring the soup to a simmer and add the sherry. Add a few cubes of lobster meat to each portion (reserve the rest of the meat for another use), and a sprinkling of chopped parsley. Serves 6.

OYSTER BISQUE

½ cup uncooked rice
4 cups chicken broth
4 tablespoons butter
18 shucked oysters and their liquor
Salt and freshly ground pepper

Tabasco sauce
1½ cups heavy cream
¼ cup cognac
Chopped parsley (optional)

Cook the rice in the broth until very soft, add the butter. Put the rice through a sieve or whirl in a blender. Finely chop 12 of the oysters or whirl in a blender with their liquid. Add to the rice mixture. Season to taste with salt and pepper and 2–3 dashes of Tabasco. Stir in the heavy cream, heat just to the boiling point. Add the 6 whole oysters and heat just until they curl at the edges. Add the cognac and cook for 2 minutes. Ladle into heated soup cups, putting a whole oyster in each cup. Garnish with chopped parsley if desired. Serves 6.

CRAWFISH BISQUE

In Louisiana the body shells of crawfish are referred to as "heads." The following recipe for bisque requires 48 crawfish, which will yield about 3 cups of ground crawfish tail meat, 1 cup to be used for the bisque and the other 2 to be used for stuffing the heads. The reserved crawfish fat is an essential part of a true Creole bisque.

The recipe is given in three parts: first you must prepare the crawfish, then the bisque, and finally the stuffed heads, which go into the bisque.

THE CRAWFISH

8 pounds live crawfish (about 48)　　　　1½ cups salt

Wash the crawfish in cold water. Make a brine in a large container by dissolving the salt in about 3 gallons of water. Soak the crawfish for 15 minutes.

Bring 6 quarts of water to a boil in a 10-quart pot. Using tongs, drop in the crawfish and boil for 5 minutes. Remove them and let them cool, then shell as follows: break off the tail, snap it in half lengthwise, lift out the meat in one piece and discard the tail shell. Snap off the large claws (if you care to, break them with a nutcracker and remove the bits of meat) and the smaller legs; discard.

Cut off the top of the heat just behind the eyes, discard. Scoop the body shell clean, carefully remove and reserve the yellow fat for "butter," and discard any intestinal matter. Wash thoroughly and reserve the 48 body shells.

Chop all the tail meat by putting it through the finest blade of a food grinder or through a food processor. Makes about 3 cups ground crawfish tail meat.

THE BISQUE

¼ cup bacon fat
¼ cup butter
½ cup flour
2 cups finely chopped onion
1 cup finely chopped celery
½ cup finely chopped green pepper
2 cloves garlic, minced
4 cups hot water
2 cans (15 ounces each) tomato
　　sauce (not purée)
¼ cup chopped parsley
2 tablespoons lemon juice
2 bay leaves
1 teaspoon dried thyme
1 teaspoon salt
¾ teaspoon cayenne pepper
8 whole allspice
1 cup ground crawfish tail meat
Reserved crawfish fat
3 cups cooked rice
48 stuffed "heads"

In a 4- to 5-quart Dutch oven melt the bacon fat and butter together and blend in the flour. Cook, stirring constantly, over gentle heat until the mixture takes on some color, 10–15 minutes. Add the onion, celery, green pepper, and garlic. Cover and cook for 5 minutes.

Gradually stir in the 4 cups of hot water, blend until smooth. Add the tomato sauce, parsley, lemon juice, bay leaves, thyme, salt, cayenne, and allspice. Stir in the crawfish meat and fat. Cover, bring to a boil, lower heat, and let simmer for 1 hour.

To serve, place a large spoonful of boiled rice in heated individual soup plates. Ladle the bisque over the rice and garnish with 5 or 6 stuffed crayfish "heads" (recipe follows). Serves 6–8 as a main course.

THE STUFFED CRAWFISH "HEADS"

½ cup butter

1 cup finely chopped onion

½ cup finely chopped celery

1 clove garlic, minced

¼ cup chopped parsley

1 teaspoon salt

¼ teaspoon cayenne pepper

2 cups ground crayfish tail meat

2 cups soft bread crumbs

48 empty crawfish body shells

½ cup flour

Fat for deep frying

Start heating fat in a deep fryer to 350°.

In a 10-inch skillet melt the butter, add the onion, celery, and garlic, cover, and cook over moderate heat for 5 minutes. Stir in the parsley, salt, cayenne, and crayfish meat. Blend in the bread crumbs. Stuff the mixture into the empty crayfish head shells. Roll them in the flour and place them, 3 or 4 at a time, in a single layer in the frying basket. Fry in the preheated fat for 3 minutes or until lightly browned. Drain on paper towels. Keep warm until ready to serve.

FOUR
Saltwater Fish

ANCHOVY

The ubiquitous and dependable anchovy has a curious major-minor role in cookery—almost never starring, but often supporting as a flavoring agent, a role with roots in antiquity. The ancient Romans made a sauce called *garum* or *liquamen,* by mixing the ungutted whole fish with sea salt and letting it ferment in the sun. Similar liquified fish sauces are found today throughout Southeast Asia, such as the *nuoc man* of Vietnam.

Although there are sixteen species of anchovy in American waters, they are not particularly appreciated as a food fish here. The French and the Italians, on the other hand, use them inventively, in hors d'oeuvres, sauces, and as pastry fillings. Pimientos and anchovies are a well-known *antipasto;* equally tasty is another, called *crostini,* in which a thin slice of mozzarella and two anchovy fillets are sandwiched between thin bread slices, the sandwich gently fried in butter, then served hot. In Italian ports, fresh anchovies are boned and baked in olive oil. In Sweden, *anchovis* (actually sprats put up in salt and bay leaves) are much esteemed in a famous dish called Jansson's Temptation. Even the phlegmatic English, whose well-known gastronomic apologia, the after-dinner savoury, often includes anchovies, have also learned to enliven otherwise unremarkable meats and vegetables with anchovy-based sauces.

TOMATOES WITH ANCHOVIES AND MOZZARELLA

12 thick slices red ripe tomatoes
¾–1 pound mozzarella, fresh
   if possible
36 flat anchovy fillets

2 tablespoons dried oregano, or
   more to taste
4–6 tablespoons olive oil
Freshly ground pepper

Arrange the tomato slices on a serving dish. Cut the mozzarella into 12 more or less equal slices and arrange on top of the tomato slices. Garnish each serving with 3 flat anchovy fillets and sprinkle with equal amounts of oregano and olive oil. Add a few twists of the pepper mill and serve at room temperature. Serves 4 as a light lunch, 12 as a buffet item.

LITTLE PROVENCAL PASTRIES

A 2-ounce can anchovy fillets,
    drained, finely chopped
1 small onion, finely chopped
1 clove garlic, finely minced
3 tablespoons chopped parsley
2 tablespoons olive oil (oil from
    the anchovy can may be used)

1 cup coarsely ground or finely
    minced cooked ham or veal
2 egg yolks
Freshly ground pepper
1 recipe of Rich Pastry Dough ❋

Preheat oven to 425°.

Pound the anchovies with the onion, garlic, parsley, and olive oil to a smooth paste, or blend in a food processor using the steel blade. Blend in the meat and bind with one of the egg yolks. Add pepper to taste.

Roll out the pastry dough rather thinly and cut out 20–22 3-inch circles with a glass or a cookie cutter. Put a teaspoon of the anchovy mixture on each, fold in half, moisten edges, and press firmly together, and crimp with a fork. Brush the tops with the remaining egg yolk, lightly beaten. Place on a buttered cookie sheet and bake for 20 minutes. Serve warm as an hors d'oeuvre. Makes 20–22.

ANCHOIADE

There are many versions of *anchoiade,* including the famous *anchoiade de Croze,* which adds red peppers, walnuts, chopped figs, and a sprinkle of orange flower water to the recipe below; it is then spread inside a cut *brioche* and heated briefly in the oven before serving.

10–12 anchovies in oil
6 tablespoons olive oil
1 tablespoon lemon juice
Freshly ground pepper

1–3 cloves garlic, crushed
6 slices stale bread, crusts
    removed, toasted

Mash the anchovies with the back of a fork. Make a sauce by beating the olive oil into the lemon juice and adding several grinds of pepper and the crushed garlic. Blend the sauce with the mashed anchovies. Spread the mixture on the toast, using a piece of untoasted bread to press into the toast. Serves 6 as a first course, or, cut in triangles, makes 24 canapés.

JANSSON'S TEMPTATION

A classic smorgasbord item, popular in Sweden also as a snack or light meal anytime, this delectable casserole of potatoes, onions, cream, and anchovies is said to have tempted the Swedish religious zealot Erik Jansson to the point where he gave up his principles of austerity to gorge himself—thereby disillusioning his followers.

7 medium boiling potatoes, peeled
4 tablespoons butter
2 tablespoons vegetable oil
4 cups thinly sliced yellow onions
   (2–3)
2 tins Swedish anchovies, drained,
   liquid reserved (see the note
   below)

White pepper
2 tablespoons fine dry bread
   crumbs
1 cup heavy cream
½ cup milk
Salt

Preheat oven to 400°. Lavishly butter a soufflé dish, 1½–2 quarts, or a shallow oval baking dish. Set aside.

Cut the potatoes into matchstick strips 2 inches long and about ¼ inch thick, and place the strips in cold water to keep them from discoloring. Heat 2 tablespoons of the butter and the oil in a 12-inch skillet; when the foam dies down, add the onions and cook, stirring frequently, until they are soft but not brown, about 10 minutes.

Drain the potatoes and pat them dry with paper towels. Arrange a layer of potatoes on the bottom of the prepared baking dish, then a layer of onions and one of anchovies. Continue layering, ending with potatoes. Sprinkle each layer with a little white pepper. Pour half the reserved liquid over. Scatter the bread crumbs over the top and dot the casserole with the remaining 2 tablespoons of butter, cut into small bits. Bake for 20 minutes.

In a saucepan, combine and heat the cream and milk, then pour over the potatoes. Bake in the center of the oven for 25 minutes more or until the potatoes are tender and the liquid nearly absorbed. Halfway through the cooking, taste the cooking liquid and add salt if needed. Serves 4–6 as a light supper, or more if used as part of a smorgasbord. This dish freezes well. Bring to room temperature, then heat in a 350° oven until bubbly.

NOTE: Swedish *anchovies* are available in food specialty shops. Regular anchovy fillets do not make a good substitute.

TAPENADE

¼ cup capers
3 2-ounce cans flat anchovy fillets
A 7-ounce can tuna
1 clove garlic or more to taste
18 black olives (preferably Greek
   or Italian), pitted

Juice of 2 lemons
½ cup olive oil
3 tablespoons cognac
Freshly ground pepper

Put the capers, anchovies, tuna (plus the oil in which they were all packed), the garlic, olives, and lemon juice in a blender. Blend on medium speed, stopping the motor from time to time to push down occasionally with a rubber spatula.

With the motor running add the olive oil very gradually (when the oil is all blended in, the sauce should have the consistency of medium-thick mayonnaise).

Blend in the cognac and black pepper to taste. Serve the sauce at room temperature with hard-cooked eggs or cold poached fish. Also good as a dip for raw vegetables. Makes about 2½ cups of sauce.

PANBANIA

Panbania means "bathed bread." It is eaten as an hors d'oeuvre, for breakfast, lunch, or snack.

1 long loaf French bread
1 clove garlic, split
1 medium cucumber, peeled and sliced
1 ripe tomato, thinly sliced
3 pimientos, cut in half

A 2-ounce can flat anchovy fillets, drained
6 black olives (preferably Greek or Italian), pitted
Olive oil
Vinegar

Cut the bread in half lengthwise and rub the cut sides with garlic. Arrange the cucumber, tomato, pimientos, anchovies, and olives over half the loaf. Sprinkle with oil and vinegar. Top with the other half of the loaf and press with a heavy weight for one half to one hour. Remove the weight, slice, and serve. Serves 6.

BAGNA CAUDA

Literally *hot bath sauce,* this heated anchovy sauce from the Italian Piedmont traditionally is served with vegetables and boiled meats. Try it as a change-of-pace warm dip for raw vegetables.

6 tablespoons butter
½ cup olive oil
4–6 cloves garlic, minced

2 2-ounce cans anchovy fillets, drained and chopped
Tabasco sauce

Heat the butter, oil, and garlic in the top of a double boiler until the butter is melted and the oil is hot. Remove from the fire but keep over hot water. Add the anchovies and a dash or two of Tabasco and cook, stirring, for about 10 minutes until the mixture is like a purée. Makes about 1½ cups.

NOTE: This sauce may be kept warm in a chafing dish on a buffet and served with vegetables such as carrot sticks, sweet red peppers, cauliflower separated into flowerets, and leaves of Belgian endive. Each person cooks his or her vegetables by dipping in the sauce slightly as with a fondue. Serve with pieces of Italian bread to catch the drippings. Leftover sauce keeps for days in the refrigerator.

ANGLERFISH

It might seem odd to include recipes for a fish that is, for practical purposes, unavailable in markets (although in New York it is making a cautious whole-sale appearance largely due to the demand by chefs of fine French restau-rants). I am hoping that as people learn about the fabulous taste and prop-erties of the anglerfish it will cease to be considered a "trash" fish (one that is thrown back when it turns up in the nets of fishermen bent on gathering more commercial ones) and begin to appear regularly as the result of popu-lar demand.

Anglerfish *(Lophius americanus)* is a member of the shark family and is known by a number of names, among them monkfish, bellyfish, goosefish, all-mouth monkfish, frogfish, and sea devil. By any name, it is truly gro-tesque, in respect for which it is sold minus its ferocious head, thus looking rather like a small fishy leg of lamb. Its habit is to settle in a depression on the sea bottom and "angle" with a rod-like appendage on its head (actually a part of the dorsal fin), thus attracting small fish to its gaping and ready mouth. This gluttony produces a firm, sweet, lobster-like meat so delectable that a respected French chef once told me that he would challenge anyone to tell the difference between it, poached and masked with a good mayon-naise or *chaud-froid,* and the same dish made with lobster. There, its most common market form is the steak, generally cut from the larger anglerfish, which is thought to have a better flavor.

In France, where it is prized and is correspondingly expensive, it is called *lotte,* if taken from Atlantic waters, or *baudroie* in the Mediterranean, and is used in a variety of inventive ways.

ANGLERFISH.

Its flesh may be substituted for pike in *Quenelles,* it is good with a green sauce (the same preparation as for eel—see Eels in Green Sauce ❋ —or to give body and texture to various fish soups and stews. Its best cooking form is in small fillets or steaks, and it may be used as a substitute in any scallop recipe or any recipe calling for firm white fish; also for recipes for fish *en brochette.* Almost any sauce enhances anglerfish.

Friends in the Languedoc once treated me to a memorable lunch—a *ratatouille* made on top of the stove, then topped with seasoned anglerfish tails into which tiny slivers of garlic had been inserted. This was baked for about a half hour in a 350° oven, the fish carefully turned once or twice on its vegetable bed. It was served with a rough country bread and an equally rough red wine. Heaven!

BARRACUDA

Barracuda is included in this book for those California fans of *Pacific barracuda (Sphyraena argentea)* who would expect to find it here. *Sphyraena barracuda,* the great barracuda of the Atlantic, however, inspires fear and loathing in a number of people because it can be poisonous, even fatal, from the ciguatera toxin often—but not always—present in the larger Atlantic fish. The critical factor is size, say Bahamians, who eat them all the time. The smaller ones (two feet and under) apparently do not feed on the benthic alga thought to be the source of the toxin. Others will say that it is because smaller ones do not eat other poisonous fish, but this is not true, or is at least beside the point. The strong, dark, tuna-like meat has its following in Florida, also, and for that reason, too, I will tell you further that the Bahamians are fond of filleting barracuda, dipping it in milk and then in a half-and-half mixture of flour and cornmeal highly seasoned with salt and pepper, and frying it in oil. In California it is often barbecued after marination in a teriyaki sauce (which for me still does not disguise its disagreeable strongness). Beyond that, I disclaim responsibility and you are on your own!

STRIPED BASS

Striped bass is my second favorite fish (the first is red snapper). Its dense, flaky white flesh makes excellent eating in just about every form and it is endlessly versatile—it can be baked, stuffed, broiled, sautéed, poached, fried, or used in stews and *seviches.* Culinary versatility apart, it is also one of the most beautiful of fishes, shading from steely blue to olive green above, with a silvery white belly and distinctive horizontal stripes along the sides.

A relatively large fish, the rapid swimming bass is a native of the Atlantic Coast of North America with the greatest concentration in the Chesapeake

Bay area. It is also found in some Gulf streams and in California, where it is stocked as a game fish and prohibited from being sold for food.

In colonial times, striped bass ranked with cod as a vital fish resource and was probably the first fish to be protected by a conservation statute (in 1939).

Unfortunately, pollution often taints this magnificent fish with the flavor of petroleum. An oil-tainted bass can be recognized by a slight yellow tinge to the flesh, and darkish skin. Rubbing the scales with the thumb may produce some oil, a handy test if any doubt lingers.

White Sea Bass and California Giant Sea Bass: These fish are not bass, but rather belong to the drum family and are related to the weakfish. Giant sea bass is also called grouper bass, and its official name until recently, when it proved too confusing, was black sea bass.

STRIPED BASS DIEPPOISE

This elegant presentation of a whole fish is really quite simple to execute, and the mingling of flavorsome ingredients yields a superb natural sauce that will delight dunkers. Weakfish may be substituted with equally good results.

A 5-pound striped bass, whole, split, head and tail on
Salt and freshly ground pepper
2–3 branches fresh tarragon or ½ teaspoon dried
Several branches of parsley
6 tablespoons butter
2 medium onions, chopped
¼ pound mushrooms, sliced

¾–1 cup dry white wine
½ pound mussels, scrubbed and debearded
½ pound uncooked shrimp, shelled and deveined
⅓ cup fresh chopped parsley
3 lemons cut in half for garnish (optional)

Preheat oven to 375°.

Line a broiler pan (or baking dish large enough to hold the fish) with heavy baking foil. Set aside. Wash and dry the fish and season with salt and pepper. Stuff with tarragon and parsley branches and set aside. Melt the butter in the baking pan, add the onions, stir to coat them, and bake for 10 minutes in the oven or until soft. Add the sliced mushrooms and the wine, stir, and lay the fish on top. Return the pan to the oven and bake for 25 minutes longer.

Put the cleaned mussels around the fish, baste both with the pan juices, and bake for 10 minutes longer. Add the shrimp, baste everything again, and bake for another 10 minutes. At the end of the 45 minutes cooking time the mussels will be opened, the shrimp pink, and the fish baked through (if you are using a larger fish, increase the initial baking time accordingly). Mask the body of the fish with chopped parsley. Serve right in the baking pan, garnished with the lemon halves. Serves 6–8.

BROILED STRIPED BASS NIÇOISE

6 striped bass steaks, about ½
   pound each
4 tablespoons olive oil
1 clove garlic
Salt and freshly ground pepper
6 large slices ripe tomato

6 thin slices lemon
12 flat anchovy fillets
1 tablespoon minced parsley
6 black olives, preferably the
   imported *niçoise* type

Preheat broiler.

Arrange the fish steaks in a baking pan. Put the olive oil in a small bowl, put the garlic through a press and add. Beat to blend. Season the fish with salt and pepper and brush with 3 tablespoons of the oil. Broil for 6–8 minutes, brush the other side with oil, and broil for 6–8 minutes more or until the flesh can be easily parted from the bone. Do not overcook.

Place a tomato slice on top of each fish steak, brush with the remaining olive oil, and season it with salt and pepper. Broil for 2–3 minutes or until the tomato begins to brown. Remove the steaks to a serving platter, place a slice of lemon on top of each tomato slice, crisscross 2 anchovy fillets over that, sprinkle with parsley, and top with an olive. Serve immediately. Serves 6.

JEAN GODDARD'S STUFFED BASS

A 4–5 pound striped bass, split
   and cleaned, head and tail on
   (Snapper or weakfish may also
   be used)
½ lemon
Salt and freshly ground pepper
1½ cups fresh bread crumbs
1½ cups chopped onions

½ teaspoon thyme
½ cup finely diced celery
¼ cup finely diced green pepper
½ teaspoon salt
4 tablespoons butter
½ cup chicken broth
½ cup white wine
Lemon slices for garnish

Preheat oven to 375°.

Wash the fish, rub it all over with the cut lemon, dry well with paper towels, season with salt and pepper.

Prepare a stuffing by mixing the bread crumbs, ½ cup of the onions, thyme, celery, and green pepper. Season to taste and stuff the cavity of the fish. Sew the opening closed or secure with skewers and twine.

Line a baking pan large enough to hold the fish with heavy duty foil. Melt the butter in the pan, add the remaining 1 cup of onions, mix well, and bake for 10 minutes or until lightly golden. Add the fish and bake for 20 minutes, lower heat to 300°, add the broth and wine to the baking pan, baste the fish, and bake for 15 minutes more, basting frequently.

Remove the fish to a serving platter with the aid of two spatulas or serve in the baking pan. Decorate with a row of lemon rounds (you may dust them with paprika if you wish). Serve with pan juices. Serves 6–8.

STUFFED STRIPED BASS MIDDLE EASTERN STYLE

A 4–5 pound striped bass, whole, head and backbone removed
½ cup olive oil
½ lemon
Salt and freshly ground pepper
4 medium onions, halved and thinly sliced
1 cup dried currants
4–5 dried apricots, coarsely chopped

¾ cup lemon juice
1 teaspoon cinnamon
1 teaspoon allspice
⅓ cup chopped parsley
3 lemons, thinly sliced
A 6-ounce can whole tomatoes, drained and mashed lightly with a fork

Preheat oven to 375°.

Select baking dish large enough to hold the fish (one that can go to the table) and oil it with 2 tablespoons of the oil. Wash and dry the fish. Rub it inside and out with the lemon, then season it inside and out with salt and pepper. Set aside.

Pour the remaining oil into a heavy skillet. Sauté the onions very slowly over low heat until translucent but not brown. While they are cooking, let the currants and apricots soak in the lemon juice in a small bowl. When the onions are ready, drain the lemon juice off the currants and apricots and reserve the juice; add the currants and apricots to the onions. Add the cinnamon, allspice, and parsley, season with salt and pepper. Cook, stirring constantly, for 2–3 minutes. Remove from heat and stir in half the reserved lemon juice.

Arrange half the lemon slices in the prepared baking dish. Stuff the fish with the onion mixture, close with skewers, and lay it on the bed of lemon slices. Mix the remaining lemon juice with the tomatoes and pour over the fish. Make an overlapping row of the remaining lemon slices on top of this. Bake in the preheated oven for 45 minutes, or according to the Canadian Theory. Serve hot with plain rice, or at room temperature accompanied by a simple rice salad garnished with chopped parsley and *pignoli*. Serves 8.

POACHED STRIPED BASS WITH BEURRE BLANC SAUCE

Poach a 3–5 pound striped bass according to directions given elsewhere (see Index). Prepare a Beurre Blanc Sauce ✸ and serve immediately while the fish and sauce are both warm.

STUFFED STRIPED BASS PARMENTIER

A 3–4 pound striped bass, split, boned, head and tail on
½ pound mushrooms
6 tablespoons butter
½ cup minced shallots or minced scallion bulbs
1 teaspoon minced garlic
1 cup minced parsley
Grated rind of 1 lemon

½ cup sour cream or *Crème Fraîche* ✻
3 cups warm mashed potatoes
3¼ teaspoons salt
Freshly ground white pepper
A scant ½ teaspoon thyme
2 bay leaves
1½ cups dry white wine

SAUCE

2 cups heavy cream
4 tablespoons flour

4 tablespoons butter (½ stick) at room temperature

Preheat oven to 450°.

Line a large roasting pan with heavy duty foil. Wash the fish, pat dry, and set aside.

Cut off the stems of the mushrooms, mince the stems finely, and set aside. Slice the caps thinly and set aside separately.

Melt 2 tablespoons of the butter in a skillet. Add ¼ cup of the minced shallots or onions, sauté for about 2 minutes. Add the minced mushroom stems and garlic, sauté for another few minutes. Off heat add ½ cup of the parsley, the lemon rind, sour cream, and mashed potatoes, combine well. Season to taste with salt and white pepper.

Sprinkle the inside of the fish with salt. Stuff the cavity loosely with the potato filling. Fasten with skewers or thread according to directions (see Index). Measure the stuffed fish at its thickest point.

Melt the remaining 4 tablespoons of butter in the prepared baking pan. Sprinkle the pan with the remainder of the shallots, 2 teaspoons of the salt, several grindings of white pepper, the remaining parsley, and the thyme. Put the fish on top and add the sliced mushroom caps and bay leaves. Pour the wine over all. Bring to a boil on top of the stove, then bake, allowing 10 minutes per inch of stuffed thickness. Baste once or twice.

Carefully transfer the fish to a heated serving platter. Peel off the skin with the aid of a small knife and remove the thread or skewers. Remove the mushrooms from the baking pan with a slotted spoon and arrange them around the fish. Keep it warm.

Prepare the sauce by pouring off the liquid from the baking pan and straining it into a saucepan. To the liquid add the cream and slowly bring to a boil. While it is heating make a *beurre manié* by working the flour into 3 tablespoons of the butter. Add it to the hot sauce, bit by bit, stirring constantly with a whisk. After it has reached a boil, lower heat and simmer for 5 minutes, then beat in the remaining tablespoon of butter. Coat the fish with some of the sauce and serve the remainder in a heated sauceboat. Serve with a green salad. Serves 6.

STRIPED BASS VERACRUZANO

A 4–5 pound striped bass, cleaned, head on, gills removed (red snapper or weakfish may also be used)
2 limes, juiced, shells reserved
Salt and freshly ground pepper
3 tablespoons olive oil
3 medium large onions, thinly sliced
6 cloves garlic, minced

3 cups peeled and diced tomatoes
18–20 black olives, coarsely chopped
3 tablespoons drained capers
3–4 *jalapeño* peppers, drained, seeded, and coarsely chopped
½ teaspoon dried oregano
1 bay leaf
Fresh coriander sprigs or fresh parsley for garnish

Put the fish in a glass, enamel, or china dish and prick the skin all over with a fork or a turkey skewer. Sprinkle it with lime juice and stuff the shells in the cavity. Let stand for 2 hours. Remove the lime shells before baking.

Preheat oven to 375°.

Season the fish with salt and pepper. Place it in a large baking dish (remove the head if necessary).

Heat the olive oil in a saucepan, add the onions and garlic, and cook until the onions are wilted but not brown. Add the tomatoes, olives, capers, *jalapeños,* oregano, and bay leaf, season to taste. Simmer for about 10 minutes, uncovered.

Pour the sauce over the fish and put in the oven. Bake, uncovered, for 50–60 minutes or until the flesh flakes easily when tested with a fork. Serve garnished with coriander or parsley sprigs. Serves 8 or more.

NOTE: 1. *Jalapeño* peppers are available in cans in many supermarkets and specialty food shops, but any hot green chilies, fresh or pickled, may be used.

2. Coriander (also called cilantro and Chinese parsley) is a pungent, feathery green widely used in Chinese, Mexican, and Indian cooking. It is the same herb whose seeds, dried, are used to flavor some yeast breads and cakes.

STRIPED BASS FERMIÈRE

About 2½ pounds striped bass fillets in 2 pieces, skinned and boned
8 tablespoons butter
1 carrot, cut into thin rounds
⅓ cup thinly sliced shallots
¾ cup thinly sliced celery

¼ pound mushrooms, thinly sliced
1½ cups dry white wine
Salt and freshly ground pepper
Juice of ½ lemon
¾ cup heavy cream
Parsley

Cut the two fish fillets slightly on the diagonal into 6 equal pieces. Refrigerate.

Preheat oven to 375°.

Select a heavy, shallow heatproof casserole (a 14 by 10-inch oval works nicely) large enough to hold the fish pieces in one layer. In it melt 4 tablespoons of the butter and when it is hot add the carrots, shallots, celery, and mushrooms. Add ⅓ cup of the wine, cook over moderate heat until the wine is well reduced, about 5 minutes. Add another ⅓ cup of wine and cook for an additional 5 minutes until it is reduced. Repeat with another ⅓ cup of wine. The total cooking time for adding and reducing the wine is about 15 minutes. Sprinkle with salt and pepper.

Season the fish pieces with salt and pepper and arrange them in a single layer over the vegetables in the casserole. Pour the remaining half cup of wine over the fish and bring to a boil on top of the stove. Bake for 15 minutes.

Select an oval serving dish large enough to hold the fish in one layer and the sauce to come. Heat it in the oven and let 1 tablespoon butter melt in it. Sprinkle the fish with lemon juice, transfer with a slotted spatula to the heated platter, and keep warm.

Add the cream to the vegetables in the casserole and bring to a boil over high heat, shaking the casserole so that the cream blends with the vegetables. Cook over high heat for about 3 minutes. Swirl in the remaining 3 tablespoons of butter, piece by piece, so they melt one at a time. Pour the sauce over the fish, sprinkle with parsley, and serve immediately. Serve with hot noodles or rice. Serves 6.

NOTE: Do not be tempted to reduce the amount of shallots in this dish. They are very mild when stewed in butter and add a lovely flavor.

BASS STEAKS AL PESTO

Using 4 striped bass steaks, 1–1½ inches thick (about 2 pounds total), follow the recipe for Red Snapper al Pesto ❋ .

SEA BASS OR STRIPED BASS WITH TURKISH ALMOND SAUCE

See Red Snapper with Turkish Almond Sauce

SEA BASS IN THE GREEK MANNER

The ways of the Greeks with their plentiful fish generally require high-heat cooking or cooking in hot oil, as opposed to the blander methods of poaching and sautéing. They frequently marinate fish in oil and lemon juice, (especially if it is of a coarser variety), and then fry it in olive oil. The following recipe may be used as well with striped bass, bluefish, Boston mackerel, or fillets of halibut, haddock, or cod.

2 sea bass, about 3 pounds total,
  cleaned, head and tail intact
Salt and freshly ground pepper
1 teaspoon dried thyme or several
  branches of fresh thyme
4 medium potatoes, peeled, cut
  into ⅛-inch slices

½ cup olive oil
Juice of 1 lemon
2 medium onions, sliced
4 ripe medium tomatoes, thinly
  sliced
1 lemon, thinly sliced

Preheat oven to 425°.

Wash the fish, pat dry, and with a sharp knife make three diagonal slashes on each side of each fish. Season to taste with salt and pepper and tuck several branches of thyme inside each fish or sprinkle half the dried thyme inside each.

Cook the potatoes in boiling salted water for 10 minutes. Drain and pat dry.

Put the olive oil and lemon juice into a shallow ovenproof baking dish large enough to hold the fish. Add the onions and potato slices and gently move them about to coat them in the oil and lemon mixture. Season with salt and pepper. Lay the fish on top of the onions and potatoes, arrange the tomato and lemon slices around the fish, and season everything again with salt and pepper. Bake for 15 minutes. Serve immediately from the baking dish. Serves 4–6.

WHOLE BASS WITH FENNEL (Loup de Mer Flambé au Fenouil)

Bass (or loup de mer, as it is called in the South of France) in combination with fennel is one of the bright fixed stars in the firmament of fish cooking. An impeccably fresh whole fish is anointed with olive oil, grilled, and then perfumed in the smoke of a bundle of fennel stalks that have been set aflame with armagnac. The fennel flavor underscores the delicate freshness of the fish without disguising it in any way. There is actually a specially designed utensil for this purpose—a basket with legs top and bottom so that the fish may be turned in the smoke of the fennel stalks flaming on an oval metal tray just underneath.

The fennel used in France is not the one we know, cultivated for its celery-like, anise-flavored bulb, but one that grows in rangy stalks that, when dried, are burned for their aromatic smoke. Lacking the real thing, one can use crushed fennel seed instead.

1 striped bass, 3–5 pounds,
  cleaned whole, unscaled, head
  and tail on
Salt and freshly ground pepper
Olive oil

2 teaspoons fennel seeds
1 bunch fennel fern (see the note
  p. 106)
⅓ cup cognac or armagnac

Season the fish inside and out with salt and pepper, rub all over with olive oil. Sprinkle 1 teaspoon of the fennel seeds in the cavity. Barbecue the fish following the directions in Chapter VII. (The fish may also be baked, in which case have it scaled.) Crush the remaining tablespoon of fennel seeds, add to the cognac or armagnac, heat until small bubbles form, ignite with a match, and pour over the fish. Spoon the liquid over the fish until the flames die.

NOTE: If the fish is large, the head and cavity may be stuffed with fennel fern so that as it cooks the flavor penetrates the fish.

SEA BASS MARECHIARE

2 sea bass, about 3 pounds total,
    boned, with heads removed
Salt and freshly ground pepper
2 cloves garlic, crushed

¼ cup olive oil
¼ cup clam juice or fish stock
1 cup Fresh Tomato Sauce ❋
Chopped parsley

Wash and dry the fish on paper towels and season inside and out with salt and pepper. Set aside. In a skillet large enough to hold the fish, sauté the garlic in the olive oil until golden brown. Discard the garlic. Add the fish and sauté briefly on both sides over fairly high heat until golden. Remove the fish from the pan to a heated platter.

Add the clam juice or fish stock to the pan, scrape up any brown bits, bring the liquid to a boil, and cook until reduced by half. Stir in the tomato sauce and season to taste. Return the fish to the pan and cook gently, covered, for 10–15 minutes. If the sauce in the pan seems too thin, uncover for the last few minutes of cooking and raise the heat. Serve the fish on a heated platter liberally sprinkled with parsley. Serves 2–4.

STEAMED SEA BASS WITH GINGER SAUCE

A 1½-pound sea bass, boned, with
    head and tail on (red snapper,
    whiting, yellow pike, gray sole,
    and butterfish are also suitable)
1 tablespoon dry sherry
2 scallions (white and green)

3 tablespoons vegetable oil
2 tablespoons finely shredded
    fresh ginger root
3 tablespoons light soy sauce
½ teaspoon sugar

Clean and wash the fish, then dry with paper towels. Score the fish with several diagonal slashes through the thick part of the flesh on both sides. Make a "baking dish" out of two thicknesses of heavy duty foil, and make a rim on all 4 sides by folding up the edges. Place the fish on the foil, sprinkle with sherry.

Put a steamer rack in a large, heavy pot with a good cover (see the Index for notes on steamed fish). Fill with the appropriate amount of water. Place the fish on its foil dish on the rack (the fish should be above the water) and bring the water to a boil. Cover tightly and steam over high heat for 10–15 minutes.

Wash the scallions, dry, split, and cut into 1½-inch pieces. Set aside.

Heat a heavy skillet or a wok until very hot. Add the oil and shredded ginger. Lower the heat to moderate and let the ginger cook for 1 minute. Add the scallions, fry, stirring constantly, for 10 seconds. Stir in the soy sauce and sugar, remove from heat.

Remove the steamed fish to a heated platter. If a lot of liquid has accumulated in the foil ''dish,'' pour it off so that only 2 or 3 tablespoons remain. Add this to the contents of the pan, pour over the fish, and serve. Serves 2.

BLACKFISH OR TAUTOG

This member of the wrasse family has made a relatively recent appearance on the Eastern market as a food fish, although it has been known to sportsfishermen as a good game fish. In flavor and texture it is not unlike the tropical dolphinfish, to which it is unrelated. It is found commercially from Cape Cod to the Chesapeake, mostly around jetties and breakwaters, and averages about 3 pounds. Blackfish is delicious prepared like Country-Fried Shad ❀ , and because its silky, firm white meat does not flake or shred, it particularly lends itself to baking and broiling. Its moist sweetness does not require saucing—dieters take note!

BLUEFISH

The bluefish is well known to anglers as a spirited, savage, and voracious fish that puts up a good fight. A member of the Pomatomidae family, related to the pompano and bass-like in shape, it is common along the Atlantic Coast from Cape Cod to Florida, and in the Gulf. Bluefish average 3 to 6 pounds in weight, although they can run to 10 pounds. Juvenile blues are called ''snappers,'' and to see them travel in a large, food-frenzied topwater school, blindly devouring a school of smaller fish such as menhaden is to observe a living chopping machine. The noise of their razor-sharp teeth explains their name. Fishermen love them because it's almost impossible *not* to catch feeding blues.

Bluefish has a pronounced flavor; also a darkish, oily flesh that makes it unsuitable for long-term freezing, although it is surpassingly good when fresh. As with shad, simple preparations are best—baking whole, stuffing, or broiling or charcoal grilling in fillets. Avoid highly spiced sauces. Baby blues may be treated as panfish, gutted, scaled and cooked whole like porgy.

The bluefish fillet has a strip of dark muscle meat down the center, which on occasion can have a strongly fishy, slightly bitter taste. I rather like it and only remove it from fillets to be frozen for more than a month, as it can hasten a certain rancidity. For whichever reason it is removed, this is how it's done: make a shallow, angled, double cut along both sides of the dark strip, taking care not to cut through the meat completely. Lift out this V-shaped strip of dark meat and discard.

TO BROIL BLUEFISH: This is the ideal simple preparation. The fillets may be skinned if you wish, although I find that skin-on broiling produces tastier, moister meat. Follow basic broiling instructions (see Index). Sprinkle with lemon juice and season with salt and pepper to taste. Dot with butter and broil about 4 inches from the heat, timing according to the Canadian Theory. Baste several times but do not turn the fish while cooking.

MAYONNAISE-BROILED BLUEFISH: Thin some mayonnaise with a little dry Vermouth and spread on bluefish fillets before broiling. Time according to the Canadian Theory. It gives a nice color and flavor.

CHARCOAL-BROILED BLUEFISH: See the Index.

BLUEFISH BAKED WITH SCALLIONS AND WINE

This is a good way to prepare not only bluefish but other whole large fish such as weakfish or striped bass, especially when there are many people to be served. If the fish weighs between 6 and 10 pounds, double the recipe.

A 4–5 pound bluefish, cleaned, head and tail on
Salt and freshly ground pepper
Several sprigs of parsley
Several sprigs of fresh dill
4 slices lemon
4 tablespoons butter

1 bunch scallions, chopped (white and part of the green)
1 cup white wine
½ cup heavy cream
2 egg yolks, lightly beaten
Chopped parsley

Preheat oven to 450°.

Select a baking dish or pan large enough to hold the fish, line it with foil (a large fish may be placed diagonally across a baking pan).

Measure the fish, wash and dry it. Season the inside with salt and pepper and put the parsley and dill sprigs and lemon slices inside. Dot the interior of the fish with 2 tablespoons of the butter. Season the outside with salt and pepper.

Sprinkle the scallions in the prepared baking dish, lay the fish on top, and dot with the remaining butter. Add the wine to the pan and bake according to the Canadian Theory, basting often.

Remove the fish to a heated serving platter, remove the parsley and dill sprigs and the lemon slices. Add these to the baking pan, bring the pan juices to a boil on top of the stove, and cook for 2 minutes. Strain the juices into a small saucepan. Stir in the heavy cream and egg yolks, cook over moderate heat, stirring constantly, until thickened, but do not boil. Correct seasoning and pour over the fish. Sprinkle with chopped parsley. Serves 6–8.

DEIRDRE'S YOGURT-BAKED BLUEFISH

2 pounds bluefish fillets in 1 or
  2 pieces, skin on
¾ cup yogurt
1 tablespoon soy sauce
⅓ cup minced scallions or 2 tablespoons minced chives

1 teaspoon grated fresh ginger
1 teaspoon Dijon mustard
1 tablespoon chopped parsley

Put the oven rack in its highest position. Preheat oven to 450°. Butter or oil a baking dish large enough to hold the fish.

    Wash the fish and pat dry. Put the fillets in the prepared baking dish. Mix the yogurt with the soy sauce, scallions or chives, ginger, and mustard, spread on top of the fish. Bake in the preheated oven, timing according to the Canadian Theory. Garnish with the chopped parsley. Serves 4–5.

BAKED BLUEFISH WITH POTATOES

This is the most delectable way I know to prepare bluefish.

1½ pounds potatoes
⅔ cup olive oil
2 teaspoons chopped garlic
¼ cup chopped parsley

Salt and freshly ground pepper
2 bluefish fillets, about 1 pound
  each, skin on, or 4–5 "snapper"
  (baby bluefish) fillets, skin on

Set the oven rack in the next to highest position. Preheat oven to 450°.

    Peel the potatoes and cut in thin round slices about ⅛ inch thick, dropping them into a bowl of cold water. Select a dish large enough to accommodate the fish fillets in a single layer without overlapping (a 10- by 16-inch oval or 12- by 15-inch rectangle works well). Pat the potatoes dry with paper towels and put in the dish along with half the olive oil, half the garlic, and half the parsley. Season highly with salt and pepper to taste. Mix well, using 2 spatulas. Spread the potato slices evenly over the bottom of the dish. Place the dish in the upper third of the oven, bake until the potatoes are about half cooked, about 15 minutes.

    Remove the dish from the oven and lay the fish, skin side down, over the potatoes. Drizzle the top of the fish with the remaining oil, sprinkle with the remaining garlic and parsley, and again season well with salt and pepper to taste. Return to the oven and bake for 10 minutes more.

    Baste the potatoes and the fish with the oil in the dish. Bake for 5 more minutes. Serve immediately, scraping loose all the potatoes stuck to the dish as you serve. Serves 6.

BLOWFISH

This odd Atlantic fish that blows itself up in the presence of danger is also known as the puffer, swellfish, rabbitfish, and silver puffer. Only the tail is eaten, which has a sweet taste something like frog's legs. The internal organs can be poisonous, especially in some Southern forms, so if you catch your own, take care in extracting the edible portion. First remove the head by grasping the tail firmly in one hand and cutting through the whole fish about an inch behind the eyes. Peel back the skin and discard. Carefully cut away the entrails. You will be left with the edible tail, which somewhat resembles the third joint of a chicken wing. Sea squab, or "chicken of the sea," as it is often called at market, is best sautéed. As there are just a few bites to each one, allow 4–6 per person, depending on appetites.

SAUTÉED BLOWFISH

18–24 blowfish	3 tablespoons olive oil
⅓ cup flour	3 tablespoons butter
Salt and freshly ground pepper	Lemon wedges

Dry the fish well. Mix the flour and salt and pepper to taste in a plastic or paper bag, shake the fish in it, a few at a time, to coat them. Melt 2 tablespoons of the olive oil and 2 tablespoons of the butter in a large heavy skillet. Sauté half the fish over fairly high heat, about 5 minutes per side or until golden. Do not crowd them in the pan; rather it is better to cook 2 batches. Remove the first batch, keep warm, add the rest of the butter and oil, and do the second batch the same way. Serve with lemon wedges. Serves 6.

BONEFISH

Bonefish never appears at market in this country and is rarely eaten here. I include it for the many sportsfishermen who asked if I was going to "say something about bonefish."

Though it is prized as a game fish in the Florida waters it inhabits, it is traditional to throw back the bonefish because it is thought to be inedible, in spite of the fact that it is delicious. The problem is: bones. Bonefish is *very* bony. There is an extra set of floating ribs, as in shad, but, as with that fish, there are ways to conquer this.

You can butterfly-fillet the fish and broil it skin side down, after which, I am told, a great many bones will arch up and can be picked away. However, more will remain, and eating those fillets must be accompanied by great caution, along with the lemon. Also the length of cooking time required until the bones "arch" is a variable and the flesh can easily dry out.

Another solution is to smoke the fish, then chill it, assuming that you have a smoker or access to one. Smoked bonefish is delicious, and the bones are more easily extracted when the meat is thus firmed.

Finally, you can bone it, which requires a fair amount of dexterity with a boning knife:

1. Lay the fish on its belly. Make a double cut down its back from just behind the head to the tail. Do not penetrate the ventral flesh or cut into the rib cage—let the knife tip slide down and around the latter by using a short, sawing motion.

2. Then make a downward cut just forward of each side of the tail to free it, but *do not cut it off*. Then grasp and twist it to loosen it from the flesh.

3. Working from the tail cut forward, run the knife blade along each side of the rib cage (again, do not penetrate the belly skin, try to keep the rib cage intact).

4. Sever the backbone at the head end and lift it and the rib cage and the entrails out.

5. The fish now lies open, and you can see the tips of the floating rib sets protruding into the cavity from the dorsal sides, near the head. They are removed by cutting above and below each set.

The fish may then be marinated in lime juice and broiled according to the Canadian Theory, or spread with a savory stuffing and topped with buttered crumbs or bacon, and baked.

BUTTERFISH

Butterfish, known as pomfret abroad, is a fat but delicately flavored small fish available most of the year in the East, in fresh and smoked form. In the West it is sometimes called Pacific pompano. Seldom exceeding 8–10 inches in length, this pleasing little fish can be simply split and broiled, panfried, or prepared *en papillote*.

PANFRIED BUTTERFISH: Follow instructions for panfried Porgy. ❃ Serve with Tartar Sauce. ❃

BUTTERFISH EN PAPILLOTE

4 butterfish about ½–¾ pound each, split and boned
4 pieces baking parchment
1 tablespoon melted butter
4 thin slices ham
1 stick butter, softened
2 tablespoons anchovy paste

1 tablespoon grated onion
1 teaspoon salt
Freshly ground pepper
4 teaspoons tomato paste
2 tablespoons finely chopped parsley

Wash the fish, pat dry, and set aside.

Cut 4 wide hearts from the baking parchment (for detailed instructions on making papillotes see drawings on page 150 and read instructions in the recipe for Pompano en Papillote). Brush each with melted butter. Place 1 ham slice on the right-hand half of each heart. Mix 4 tablespoons of the softened butter with the anchovy paste and grated onion, spread on the ham. Place the fish on the buttered ham and top with the remaining butter, 1 tablespoon per fish; season with salt and several good grindings of pepper, 1 teaspoon of tomato paste per fish, and the chopped parsley. Fold the left hand of the parchment heart over and seal (recipe may be made ahead to this point and refrigerated; bring to room temperature before baking).

Preheat oven to 425°.

Place the paper packages on a baking sheet and bake for 10 minutes or until the parchment puffs. Serve in the paper, slit open with an "X." Serves 4.

BUTTERFISH IN FENNEL SAUCE

Other fish that are excellent prepared this way are butterflied mackerel, pompano or bass fillets, and swordfish steaks.

6 butterfish, split and boned
1 cup heavy cream
Salt and freshly ground pepper
1 cup fresh bread crumbs
2 teaspoons fennel seeds,
    uncrushed

1 large onion, chopped
1 tablespoon butter
½ cup dry white wine
Lemon juice

Preheat the broiler.

Wash the fish carefully and pat dry. Arrange on a foil-lined broiler pan. Brush a thin layer of heavy cream over each fish, season to taste with salt and pepper. Season the bread crumbs with salt and pepper and sprinkle over the butterflied fish, dividing equally. Set aside.

Put ½ cup of the remaining cream in a small saucepan, add the fennel seeds, and cook over fairly high heat until reduced to ¼ cup. Set aside.

In another saucepan, sauté the onion lightly in the butter and add the wine, cook over moderate heat until reduced by half. Blend the wine reduction with the reserved cream; do not strain. Correct the seasoning and keep warm. Should the sauce seem too sweet, correct with a few drops of lemon juice.

Drizzle the remaining cream over the fish fillets and broil for 5–6 minutes. Season to taste after broiling. Spoon an equal amount of sauce over each fish and serve hot. Serves 6.

COD

> . . . Boston,
> The home of the bean and the cod,
> Where the Lowells talk to the Cabots,
> And the Cabots talk only to God.

A carved wood codfish, hung like an icon in the Massachusetts legislature in 1784, is a present-day reminder of the hallowed place occupied by the cod in the hearts and pocketbooks of sea-oriented New England. A whole level of that society, known as the "codfish aristocracy," made its fortune from this abundant and versatile fish.

A ship loaded with salt cod would set out from Boston for Spain and Portugal (the fish is still a diet staple there today). The roundabout but immensely profitable voyage home included picking up slaves in West Africa and depositing them in the West Indies, where sugar and molasses were taken on for the New England market. To complete the arrangement, the slaves were fed on the substandard salt cod not good enough to be marketed. Every home larder had its board-hard piece of salt cod to be combined with pork scraps and egg sauce and dished up with boiled potatoes and beets as the Cap Cod version of a New England boiled dinner, or thriftily made into codfish cakes and balls. When it was available fresh, it was often poached and eaten with egg sauce (as it is today in Scandinavia); served in a cream sauce on toast, it became "Cape Cod Turkey." Codfish had the dietary importance then that meat has for us today.

The fish that was the basis of this extraordinary commerce, the Atlantic cod *(Gadus morhua),* has lean, firm white meat and lends itself to just about every cooking form where its large flake will not detract. Boiled cod could be said to be the national dish of Norway, and it is not far behind in Sweden.

There are many important subspecies, among them the haddock, which is more flavorful than the cod though smaller, and distinguished by a black lateral line; the hake, with numerous family members, and the pollock.

Pacific cod is a Western relative, marketed mostly frozen and labeled "true cod" to distinguish it from black cod and lingcod. It can be used in all cod recipes. "Black cod" is a market name for sablefish in the West, but lingcod, also marketed there, is not a cod at all.

Fresh cod is marketed whole, dressed, in fillets, and in steaks. The same cuts are available frozen. Other forms are: salted, smoked, air-dried (stockfish), and canned. Cod roes are sold fresh, frozen, canned, and salted. Cod tongues and cheeks have a dedicated following and, although they do not appear regularly in the average fish market, can be obtained on order. Market cod averages 2½ to 10 pounds, cod under 3 pounds being called scrod and usually eaten as fillets.

Tomcod is a miniature cod, maximum size 12 inches, prevalent in the Atlantic from November to February. Although cod is available year round, being a cold-water fish, it tends to go deeper in the warm summer months and hug the muddy bottom where, it is said, it can develop worms. I personally have never seen any.

SCROD: Scrod is cod under 3 pounds and is regarded by many as one of the great delicacies of our waters. Its sweet meat requires little embellishment besides some form of butter, and broiling the fillets is the preferred way to prepare it. Because it is so tender and has a large flake, I like to leave the skin on while cooking; it keeps the meat from separating. The Scandinavian method of soaking scrod steaks in a brine solution firms the meat slightly and enhances the flavor in a subtle and delightful way.

BROILED SCROD: Preheat the broiler well, wash the fish and dry well. Melt a stick of butter or make a lemon or dill butter (see Index) and melt it. Make two or three diagonal slashes on top of each fillet, season with salt and pepper. Brush some butter on the broiler pan and spoon some on top of each fillet, letting it sink into the slashes. Broil, skin side down, close to the flame, using the Canadian Theory for timing. Baste with additional butter during the cooking. Serve with the balance of the butter poured over and garnish with lemon slices.

COD ROMAN STYLE

A fresh cod variation of the well-known *baccalà alla romana,* this is a hearty, cheery dish that is especially nice in winter. The leftovers are delicious cold.

2 pounds fresh cod in thick fillets,
   skinned
Salt
1 large green pepper
2 tablespoons flour
Corn oil
3–4 tablespoons olive oil

2 medium onions, thinly sliced
2 cloves garlic, minced
1 pound tomatoes, fresh or canned,
   peeled, seeded, and coarsely
   chopped
Freshly ground pepper
2 tablespoons chopped parsley

Cut the fish into 2-inch squares, remove any bones that may remain. Sprinkle with salt and let stand for 30 minutes to draw out moisture.

Meanwhile, cut the green peppers in half, core and seed them, and cut into thin strips. Drop into boiling salted water, cook for 1 minute after the second boil, drain, run cold water over, and drain again. Set aside.

Pour off any liquid that has accumulated around the fish. Pat the fish pieces dry with paper towels, put the flour in a paper bag, add the fish, and shake bag to coat them. Turn into a strainer over the sink to get rid of excess flour.

Pour corn oil into a skillet to a depth of ¼ inch. Heat it, and fry the fish quickly, over high heat, on both sides, until golden brown. Remove from the pan and keep warm.

In another large skillet heat the olive oil, sauté the onions gently until pale gold. Add the garlic and tomatoes, cook slowly for about 5 minutes. Add the reserved green pepper, cover, and cook until tender. Gently add the fried fish and cook over low heat, uncovered, in the sauce for 7–8 minutes. Add pepper to taste and salt if required. Serve in a heated dish sprinkled with the chopped parsley. Serves 4–6.

COD BAKED WITH TOMATOES

A particularly nice winter dish.

½ cup olive oil
1 cup chopped onions
4 thick cod or halibut fillets (about 2 pounds), skinned
¼ cup chopped parsley
½ teaspoon oregano

Salt and freshly ground pepper
2 cups canned plum tomatoes, drained and chopped (reserve juice)
3 large potatoes, peeled, quartered, and parboiled for 10 minutes

Preheat oven to 400°.

Pour 2 tablespoons of the olive oil in a baking dish large enough to hold all the ingredients comfortably. Spread half of the onions in the baking dish and top with fish. Cover with remaining onions, parsley, and oregano, season with salt and pepper. Add the remaining oil and enough juice from the tomatoes or water to cover the fish.

Arrange the potatoes around the fish. Cover with the tomatoes and bake, uncovered, for about 30 minutes or until the potatoes and fish are tender. Serves 4.

PELLAO (Indian Fish Pilaff)

1½ pounds cod fillets, skinned
8 tablespoons (1 stick) butter
1 teaspoon turmeric
½ teaspoon chili powder
1–2 teaspoons *garam masala* (see the note p.116)
2 teaspoons lemon juice
2 medium onions sliced paper thin (about 1¾ cups)

1¼ cups uncooked long-grain rice
2½ cups water, chicken stock, or a mixture of both
1 teaspoon salt
1 bay leaf
Tomato slices for garnish

Cut the fish into chunks measuring roughly 1 by 2 inches, dry them, and set aside.

Melt half the butter in a 12-inch skillet and stir in the turmeric, chili powder, and *garam masala*. Add the fish and sauté for about 3 minutes or until it is evenly coated with the spice mixture. Add the lemon juice and cook the fish in this mixture for about 5 minutes longer or until the fish pieces are opaque. Remove them with a slotted spoon to a warm platter. Set aside the pan containing the spiced sauce.

Melt the remaining butter in a second pan and sauté the onions gently until pale gold. Add the rice and cook, stirring, for about 3 minutes. Transfer the onion-rice mixture to the pan containing the spiced sauce, add the water or stock, the salt, and bay leaf. Bring to a boil, stir, lower heat, cover, and cook over medium heat for 18–20 minutes or until the rice is tender and the liquid absorbed.

Add the reserved fish and any liquid that has accumulated in the dish to the rice. Stirring gently, remove the bay leaf, correct seasoning, and turn into a heated serving dish. Garnish with slices of tomato. Serves 6.

NOTE: *Garam masala* is a characteristic Indian food flavoring available in jars in Indian food shops. It can be made by mixing together 1 teaspoon each of ground cloves, ground cinnamon, ground black pepper, ground cumin seeds, and ground cardamom.

DANISH BOILED COD

The Scandinavians adore cod and always keep its preparation extremely simple; the elaborations are confined to the garnishes. In addition to the ones suggested below, Danes might also serve chopped pickled beets, grated apples, capers, or Hollandaise Sauce ✻ . Scrod steaks may also be used.

3 pounds fresh cod in one piece, bone in, skin on	3 hard-cooked eggs, chopped or sliced
3 tablespoons salt	8 tablespoons (1 stick) butter, melted
2 small bay leaves	½ cup chopped parsley
1 small onion, cut in two	1 cup grated horseradish (optional)
Lemon wedges	Mustard-Dill Sauce ✻
Parsley sprigs	
6–8 hot boiled new potatoes	

Wash and wipe the fish. Sprinkle with 1 tablespoon of the salt and let stand in a cool place for 1 hour. Rinse and dry. Cover with cold water, add the remaining 2 tablespoons of salt, the bay leaves, and the onion, bring to a boil, turn down the heat, and let poach, covered, for about 20 minutes or until the fish flakes when tested and is uniformly white to the bone. Drain well and place the whole fish piece on a heated platter. (If you poach the fish in a fish poacher, the rack makes the transfer easier.) Wait 1 or 2 minutes, then drain a second time if necessary.

Garnish with lemon wedges and sprigs of parsley. Serve with the boiled potatoes, and the following in small bowls: the hard-cooked eggs mixed into the melted butter; the chopped parsley; the horseradish; and the mustard-dill sauce. Cold pickled beets make the perfect accompaniment to this dish. Serves 6.

NOTE: You may remark on the fact that while the above dish is called "boiled" it is in fact poached. Some Scandinavian cooks bring the water to boil, add the fish, and when the second boil is reached, remove the pot from the heat and let the fish gently poach itself this way for 10–15 minutes or until it flakes from the bone.

RHODE ISLAND OYSTER-STUFFED COD

A 3–4 pound cod, whole, split, head and tail on
Bacon fat or vegetable oil
½ lemon
5 tablespoons butter
½ cup chopped onions
½ cup minced celery
½ pint shucked oysters, halved, their liquor drained off and reserved

½ cup chopped parsley
½ teaspoon dried thyme
1 teaspoon salt
Freshly ground pepper
1½ cups bread crumbs

Preheat oven to 425°.

Grease a baking dish with bacon fat or oil. Rub the interior of the fish with the lemon, set aside.

Melt the butter in a skillet, sauté the onions and celery for 4 minutes. Stir in the oyster liquor, then add the oysters and cook for 2 minutes more. Add the parsley, thyme, salt, and several grinds of pepper. Blend in the bread crumbs. Stuff the fish with this mixture, truss with toothpicks and string, dot or smear with additional bacon fat or butter. Bake in the prepared dish for 30–35 minutes. Baste once with pan juices. Serve with boiled potatoes and green peas. Serves 4.

SWEDISH POACHED SCROD STEAKS

The notion of brining scrod before cooking it seemed a strange one to me, but a Swedish friend assured me that I would understand it when I tasted the scrod. She was absolutely right: the end product was not salty at all and the scrod tasted like a cousin of lobster. Cold leftovers with mayonnaise have a crab-like flake and flavor. In addition, the whole preparation is very easy.

4 scrod steaks, skin on, each about   Milk
   2 inches thick   Melted butter
6 tablespoons salt   2 hard-cooked eggs, chopped, or
1 quart water   freshly shredded horseradish

Wash the scrod. Make a brine by mixing the salt and water together, soak the fish steaks in it for 2 hours. Remove them, rinse, and pat dry.

In a stainless steel or enamel saucepan combine enough milk and water in equal quantities to cover the fish. Poach, covered, timing according to basic poaching instruction.

Remove with a slotted spoon, drain, and place on a white cloth napkin on a heated platter. Serve with a small bowl of melted butter and a second bowl of chopped egg or freshly shredded horseradish. Serves 4.

CURED COD: SALT, SMOKED, AND AIR-DRIED

Although salt cod is often bad-mouthed as a poverty food by those who have not heard of it in other contexts, or by those who have eaten it badly prepared, one has only to consider the traditional eaten-every-Friday *aioli* of food-rich Provence to give the lie to that notion. True, it is an important diet staple in many poorer parts of the world, but that does not make it any less delicious when correctly handled and prepared in one of its classic forms.

Salt cod, called *morue* in French, *bacalao* in Spanish, and *baccalà* in Italian, is usually sold in fillets or pieces cut from the fillet. The thickest part of the tail section is considered the choicest. In this country dried salt cod often comes in wooden boxes with the soaking time on the box or cover. Since the degree of saltiness is a variable, it is difficult to specify an exact soaking time. The heavier the cure, the longer soaking time required. Wood-hard cod should be considered heavily cured and treated accordingly.

To soak or "freshen": Wash the cod under cold running water, then put it in a large bowl of cold water. Refrigerate while soaking, as the cod, once freshened, will be as perishable as fresh fish. Change the water regularly— about four or five times—until the cod is soft and feels almost like fresh fish. The soaking period will be from twelve to twenty-four hours, depending on the degree of salt.

To poach salt cod: Pour off the soaking water, cover with fresh water, and bring to a near boil in an enameled or stainless steel vessel over moderate heat. At the first sign of a simmer, reduce heat and poach at just under that point. Do not let the liquid boil or the cod will toughen. Skim off the froth and poach gently, uncovered, for 15–20 minutes, depending on the thickness of the fish. Drain and proceed with your recipe, and do not take literally those which call for "flaked salt cod." The fish should be damaged as little as possible and should be broken up rather than shredded, so that it appears like good quality crab meat. The cod may be served simply with melted butter, Hollandaise Sauce ❀ , or Egg Sauce ❀ .

Stockfish is another form of cured cod, but it is dried in the wind and sun without salt. Sometimes hake, a close relative, is used instead. This is the fish that can be seen stacked like boards or hanging in stiff rows in many African markets. It must be soaked for three to four days in several changes of water, and then cut into pieces before using.

Smoked cod is very similar to finnan haddie or smoked haddock, which is a member of the cod family. Cod can be distinguished from haddock because it is usually bigger, is boneless, has a larger flake, and is often crosscut (in a large chunk)—unless it is masquerading as finnan haddie, in which case it might be a thinner filleted piece from the belly or thin part of the tail—not a choice part for smoking.

CODFISH CAKES

There are many versions of this classic American delicacy: this one includes mashed potatoes.

1 pound salt cod, soaked, poached, and flaked (1½ cups cod)	2 cups hot mashed potatoes
	1 egg
	1 teaspoon salt
3 tablespoons butter	3 tablespoons oil

Make sure the cod is thoroughly drained. Beat 3 tablespoons of the butter into the mashed potatoes and combine with the cod. When thoroughly blended, add the egg and beat in with a fork. Add salt to taste. Form the mixture into round, flat cakes. Heat the oil and remaining tablespoon of butter in a heavy skillet and brown the fish cakes on both sides, turning once. Makes about 12 3-inch cakes.

BARBADIAN CODFISH FRITTERS

1 pound salt cod, treated as below	1 cup flour
2 tablespoons minced parsley	1 teaspoon baking powder
¼ teaspoon thyme	¾ cup water
2 tablespoons minced onion or scallion, white part only	Salt and freshly ground pepper
	Corn oil for frying
1 teaspoon finely minced hot green chili pepper (optional)	

Soak the cod for 6–8 hours. Discard the water, cover with fresh water, and poach for 20 minutes. Put the fish in a towel and pound with a mallet. Transfer to a bowl.

Add the parsley, thyme, onion or scallion, and hot pepper, blend well with the fish.

In another, smaller bowl, combine the flour and baking powder, stir in ½ cup of the water, and blend to make a smooth paste. Beat in the remaining ¼ cup of water. Blend into the fish mixture and season to taste (taste carefully, for the amount of salt remaining in the cod is a variable).

Heat about ¾ inch of oil in a heavy skillet. Drop heaping teaspoons of the fish mixture into the oil, and fry for about a minute per side or until golden. Keep the fritters warm until all are fried. Drain and serve. These may be served with a spicy tomato sauce for dipping. Makes about 24 2-inch fritters, that may be served as a hot hors d'oeuvre or as a first course for 4.

BRANDADE DE MORUE

The word *brandade* comes from a Provençal word meaning "stirred." The classic recipe requires pounding the cod in a marble mortar and then stirring in the oil, drop by drop, until it is all incorporated. The final result looks like and has the consistency of mashed potatoes. The traditional recipe, however, does not call for any potatoes. The following yields quite an acceptable substitute. The mounting of the *brandade* is done in an electric mixer.

2 pounds boneless salt cod
½ cup olive oil, plus ¾–1 additional cup olive oil, warmed
3 cups (approximately) freshly baked potato pulp (about 2 large potatoes)

2–4 large cloves garlic, puréed (see the note below)
1–2 cups milk, warmed
Salt and freshly ground pepper
Lemon juice

The night before, wash the cod and soak as directed under Cured Cod: Salt, Smoked, and Air-Dried. Poach and drain.

Gently flake the cod in a heavy, medium-size saucepan. Add the ½ cup of olive oil and stir briskly over moderate heat for several minutes to warm it.

Put the cod in an electric mixer, add the potato pulp and the garlic purée. Beat at moderate speed, alternately adding oil and milk until the mixture has the consistency of mashed potatoes. Season to taste with salt and pepper and 1–2 drops of lemon juice. Serve warm, not hot, with triangles of bread fried in oil if desired. Serves 6.

NOTE: To purée garlic: push the garlic through a press into a mortar, then pound with a little salt until you have a very smooth paste.

AIOLI

Aioli can be two things: a garlicky mayonnaise, the "butter of Provence," that goes superbly with poached fish; or the name given to a classic meal with which that sauce is eaten. On Fridays and certain religious holidays in

Provence this meal is regular fare in one form or another. Its most elevated version is called *Le Grand Aioli*—a prodigious feast something on the order of a New England boiled dinner—which an entire village may gather to eat on local feast days.

LE GRAND AIOLI

Choose amounts of the following that you think you will need for 8 persons. Of course you can omit one thing or another. In Provence the list below would also include a few Jerusalem artichokes as well, some snails, cockles, and winkles.

1 pound salt cod, soaked for 4
   hours in cold water
Some blanched squid
Potatoes in their jackets
Carrots
1 hard-cooked egg per person
2 beets per person
String beans

Chick-peas
Small zucchini
1 artichoke per person
Cauliflower
A whole poached fish, such as a
   weakfish or sea bass, skinned
Aioli Sauce ✿

Rinse the cod and poach gently for 15 minutes. Boil each vegetable separately. Arrange everything in attractive bouquets around the fish on one or two large platters and serve with the *aioli* sauce and crusty French bread.

   Le Grand Aioli features, in addition to the fish and vegetables listed above, a separate plate of hot or cold boiled beef and lamb from a previously made *pot-au-feu* cold fowl, and boiled pig's feet.

SMOKED COD WITH POTATOES AND ONIONS (Morue à la Boulangère)

1½ pounds smoked cod
¾ cup vegetable oil
1½ pounds potatoes, thinly sliced
3 cups thinly sliced onions

Freshly ground pepper
½ teaspoon thyme
1–1½ cups milk

Preheat oven to 350°.

   Generously oil a baking dish. Slice the smoked cod into thin fillets and arrange half of them in the prepared baking dish. Put half the potato slices over the cod, then half of the onion slices. Season with the pepper and drizzle half the oil over the onions.

   Make another layer of cod, potatoes, onions, pepper, and oil, add a sprinkling of thyme on the top. Add enough milk to almost reach the top layer of onions. Bake for about 1 hour or until the potatoes are tender. Baste frequently and thoroughly during the cooking. Serves 6.

MARINATED SMOKED COD

1 pound smoked cod   2 onions, thinly sliced
¾–1 cup vegetable oil

Cut the cod into fillets about ¼ inch thick. Oil a glass baking dish and make
a layer of half the fillets. On top of this spread half the onion slices, then
drizzle half the oil over the onion. Repeat the layering. Cover the dish
tightly and let stand unrefrigerated, for 6–12 hours, then put in a cool place
or the refrigerator for 1 week or more. Baste occasionally with the oil in the
dish.

To serve, lift the fish fillets from the oil with a slotted spatula and arrange
on a serving platter. Surround with the onion rings and serve with thinly
sliced buttered dark bread. Serves 6 as a first course.

POLLOCK

Pollock is a member of the cod family, distinguished from that fish by its
rounder body and greenish color. It does not have the following of cod and
is generally less expensive. Sometimes called "green cod" or "Boston bluefish," pollock is found all across the Atlantic, south to the Chesapeake,
frequenting shallower waters than does cod. Important commercially, pollock makes up a large percentage of the frozen fish purveyed in this country,
often under ambiguous names like "ocean-fresh fillets."

Pollock has a dark meat that becomes lighter when cooked. It may be
prepared in the same ways as cod or haddock.

LINGCOD

The lingcod (cultus cod) is not a true cod at all. Found all along the Pacific
coast the year round, it has tender white flesh, a delicate flavor, and is very
low in fat. It is also popular smoked. The best way to handle it is to have it
split and boned for baking or broiling. You can follow almost any recipe for
other fish with similar characteristics and sauce it to your liking. Lingcod
may also be poached, as striped bass.

DOLPHIN

My Boston brother-in-law sprang from the table in alarm when, shortly after
having moved to Florida, his wife served him dolphin. He calmed down

when she explained it was the very same *mahimahi,* the fish he had adored in Hawaii, and had nothing at all to do with the mammal of the same name.

This superbly flavored fish is found in almost all tropical and semitropical waters and in our country is very popular in Florida both as a game and a food fish. Because it has a very tough skin, it is always filleted, but it may be used in virtually all forms of fish cooking—baked, broiled, poached, or sauced. Dolphin chowder is excellent. Fillets may be crumbed, sautéed, and served with lemon butter, or they may be marinated in lime juice for a half hour and broiled according to the Canadian Theory, then served with garlic butter. The roe is delicious and may be used in any recipe for shad roe.

DRUMS AND CROAKERS

The *Sciaenidae,* or drums, form a large family of fish so called because of a characteristic noise they make in large groups. The volume of the noise, which often can be heard on land, increases at spawning time. The sound was believed by the American Indians to be those of departed souls. Produced by the rapid contraction of abdominal muscles against a resonating air bladder, the noise comes across as more of a croak among the smaller members of the family—hence their name.

Drums and croakers are found along the entire East Coast and include the choicest, the red drum or redfish, the channel bass, the bony black drummer, the Northern, Southern, and Gulf kingfish (unrelated to the mackerel of the same name), the Atlantic croaker, the silver perch, the spot and the gray, silver and spotted sea trouts (weakfish). These last make exceptionally good eating and all cooking methods apply except poaching.

The Atlantic croaker has become an important food fish recently, and the black drum is popular in the South for making chowder. The totuava, a large (45–60 pounds) drum found on the West Coast, is similar to the giant sea bass. It is sold in large, thick steaks—one steak poached or baked, can feed 6 people. There is also one freshwater drum, the sheepshead, often marketed as "white perch" although it is not a member of the perch family.

The sweet, lean white meat of the croaker, the *grondin* of the French, was known until recently only to anglers, who considered it a great treat, especially the California spotfin and yellowfin varieties. Croakers have made a relatively recent appearance at markets on both coasts and may be filleted and broiled, panfried or sautéed as in the recipe that follows, Lemon Garlic Croaker. Larger whole fish may be charcoal-grilled.

LEMON GARLIC CROAKER

2 pounds croaker fillets, skinned
¼ cup lemon juice
1 teaspoon salt
1 clove garlic, minced

1½ cups white or yellow cornmeal
4 tablespoons butter
¼ cup cooking oil

Wash the fillets and pat dry. Combine the lemon juice, salt, and garlic in a shallow dish. Coat the fillets with this marinade and place them in the dish skin side up. Cover and place in the refrigerator to marinate for 30 minutes.

Remove the fish from the marinade and roll in the cornmeal. In a heavy skillet melt the butter, add the oil, and heat together until hot but not smoking. Sauté the fish over moderate heat until brown on one side, turn carefully, and brown on the other side for a total cooking time of about 7–8 minutes, depending on the thickness of the fish. Drain on paper towels and serve immediately on a hot platter. Serves 6.

EEL

People tend to squirm uncomfortably when eel is mentioned, no doubt for psychological reasons that I am not equipped to analyze. If you are one of them, I urge you to review your feelings, for eel has a number of admirable qualities: it is nutritious and is neatly and easily cooked in a variety of pleasing ways, its flesh is delicate and sweet, and there are virtually no bones other than the easily removed long backbone. Culinary matters apart, eel is the star of one of nature's greatest natural phenomena, a marathon instinct-programmed migration that makes the annual dash of the lemmings pale in comparison.

The fact that the eels do not have gonads at certain stages of their life cycle has caused many scholars to speculate on their origins, including Sigmund Freud who wrote a paper on their chemical makeup in 1877. Altogether a fascinating fish.

The American eel is our only catadromous fish, one that matures in fresh water and then moves downstream to spawn in salt water—just the opposite of anadromous fish such as salmon and shad, which develop in salt water and swim up rivers and streams to spawn in fresh. What is truly remarkable about the eel, however, is that not just any salt water will do; both the American and European eel find their way, by instinct, to a particular spot in the Sargasso Sea (in the center of what is now known as the Bermuda, or Devil's, Triangle), where spawning and fertilization occur. The larvae are distributed by ocean currents over a range of water reaching from the Gulf of Mexico to Northern Canada and eastward across the Atlantic, for a journey to Europe that takes three years. Equally remarkable is the fact that American and European larvae somehow find their way to their respective home waters.

The juvenile eels spend a good deal of time in the food-rich waters of estuaries where fresh and salt water meet, undergo a change in body shape, and become elvers. The majority of the males remain where they are, while the females begin to seek fresh water. They are so driven that they may actually cross miles of damp rock or land. Sexual maturity is reached after several years in fresh water, at which point they complete the astonishing cycle by migrating again to the Sargasso Sea.

The American eel, *Anguilla rostrata*, is indigenous to the fresh and salt waters of the Atlantic and Gulf coasts. (The conger eel and the sea lamprey are entirely different species.)

Eel is marketed fresh and frozen and is particularly abundant at Christmas time. Smoked eel, which is very tasty, is available all year. It makes nice appetizers and hors d'oeuvres: skin them, following the method below for fresh eel, fillet them, which is very easy, and cut the fillets in 3-inch fingers, serve with lemon wedges and cucumber rounds.

Eels live for a long time out of the water, even after decapitation, which is the easiest way to kill them. Freezing them first in a plastic bag, which is how they are handled commercially, makes things easier. An alternative is to put them in a deep container and pour enough salt over them to cover, add water to cover, and let them sit for 3–4 hours. Eels tend to be slimy; the soaking makes removing the slime easier. Scrub off the slime, wash, gut, and wash again.

To skin: Put a nail through the head into a board, thus dispatching the eel and making it easy to handle. With a razor blade or sharp knife, make a circular cut and loosen the skin about 3 inches behind the eyes. Hold the head and strip off the skin (as you would a glove) with pliers. To fillet, slice along the flesh on both sides of the backbone and lift off the meat.

Eel is good roasted, fried, charcoal-grilled, or used in a savory stew. In Italy, one of the countries that properly value this fish, large eels are threaded on a spit with bay leaves or rosemary, well salted and grilled, while being frequently basted with oil and the eels' own fat. The skin is not removed for this preparation, as it conserves the natural juices; it is removed as the eel is eaten. In Northern Italy spit-roasted eel is often served with mustard fruit *(mostarda di frutta),* which are available in cans in Italian specialty stores.

FRIED EEL

2 eels, cleaned and skinned, cut
   into 3-inch pieces
Milk to cover
Salt and freshly ground pepper

Tabasco sauce
½ cup Seasoned Flour ❁
¼ cup oil
Lemon wedges

Put the eel in a mixing bowl and add milk to cover. Season with salt, pepper, and several dashes of Tabasco, soak for 10 minutes, then drain. Dredge the eel in the seasoned flour. Heat the oil in a skillet until it is hot and almost smoking, add the eel, and cook, stirring and turning occasionally, until golden brown. Drain on paper towels. Serve at once with lemon wedges and Tartar Sauce. ❁ Serves 6.

NOTE: Deep-fried parsley is often served with this dish.

VARIATION: *Fried Eel Gremolata:* Fry the eel as directed above. Mix together ½ cup of chopped parsley, 1 tablespoon very finely minced garlic, and 1 teaspoon grated lemon peel. Pour off the excess oil in the pan, add the parsley mixture, stir over moderate heat for one minute, and spoon over the fried eel.

VARIATION: *Fried Eel and Rémoulade Sauce* ❋ . When the Danes sit down to eat fried eel, they often eat it this way and compete to see who can eat the most; each person makes an effort to make a ring of eel bones around the edge of his plate.

EEL PROVENÇAL

2 pounds eel, skinned, cut into 2-inch pieces	2 tablespoons oil
Flour	1/4 cup finely chopped shallots
Salt and freshly ground pepper	1/4 cup finely chopped parsley
3 tablespoons butter	2 cloves garlic, pressed
	3/4 cup fresh bread crumbs

Roll eel pieces in flour and season with salt and pepper. Melt the butter and oil in a heavy 10-inch skillet and when foaming add the eel, sauté over moderate heat until lightly colored. Remove to a hot platter and keep warm. Add the shallots, parsley, garlic, and bread crumbs to the pan, cook for 3 minutes. Spoon over the fish, correct the seasoning, and serve very hot. Serves 4–6.

TERRINE OF EEL À LA MARTÉGALE

This is the traditional Christmas Eve supper served in the French Martigues. It is absolutely delicious and need not be restricted to that holiday.

5 pounds eel, cleaned and skinned	2 bay leaves
3 medium-size leeks, white part only, minced	1 cup black olives, pitted (preferably the *niçoise* type)
4 cloves garlic, minced	1 1/2 cups dry white wine
1/2 cup chopped parsley	Bread crumbs
Salt and freshly ground black pepper	3 tablespoons olive oil

Preheat oven to 325°.

Select a shallow ovenproof dish large enough to hold the eels. Make a thick bed of the leeks on the bottom. Mix the garlic and parsley together and sprinkle on top of the leeks. Season well with salt and pepper. Add the bay leaves and olives. Moisten with 1/2 cup of the wine and lay the eel on this bed. Sprinkle the eel with bread crumbs, then with the olive oil. Bake for 1–1 1/2 hours, depending on the thickness of the eel, and baste from time to time with the remaining dry white wine until all of it is used. Serves 8.

EEL IN GREEN SAUCE

2 pounds eel, cleaned, skinned,
  filleted, and cut into 2-inch pieces
8 tablespoons butter
6 shallots
½ cup finely chopped parsley
1 cup finely chopped sorrel or
  spinach leaves
1 tablespoon chopped fresh sage
  or ½ teaspoon dry
1 teaspoon chopped fresh tarragon
  or ¼ teaspoon dry

1 tablespoon chopped fresh chervil
  or ½ teaspoon dry
½ teaspoon dried thyme
1½ teaspoons salt
Several grindings of pepper
3 cups dry white wine or light beer
3 egg yolks, beaten
Juice of 1 lemon

Wipe the eel, sauté quickly in 4 tablespoons of the butter. Add the remaining butter and shallots, sauté for 5 minutes more. Add the parsley, sorrel or spinach, sage, tarragon, chervil, thyme, salt, and pepper. Stir for 3 minutes, cooking until the sorrel or spinach is limp. Add the wine, cover, and simmer gently for 15 minutes.

Slowly beat some hot broth from the eels into the egg yolks. Then pour these slowly into the eel pan, beating constantly, and stir gently over low heat for 5 minutes. Do not boil. Season to taste, adding lemon juice as needed. Pour into a serving dish, cool, and chill. Serves 6.

TERRINE OF SMOKED EEL

3 smoked eels (about 1½ pounds
  total)
Freshly ground pepper
Juice of ½ lemon (about 1½
  tablespoons)
2 tablespoons dry white wine
½ pound fresh flounder or any lean
  white fish, filleted and skinned

½ cup fresh white bread crumbs
1 egg yolk
2 tablespoons melted butter
1–2 tablespoons heavy cream
Salt
1 bay leaf

Remove the skin and bones from the eels (see Index). Cut 2 of them in half the long way, then cut these pieces into finger-length pieces. Sprinkle the eel with pepper, then with the lemon juice and wine, and let marinate for about 2 hours.

Mince or pound the white fish with the remaining eel (this may be done in a food processor fitted with a steel blade). Add the bread crumbs, egg yolk, butter, and enough cream to bind. Season to taste with salt and pepper. Set aside.

Preheat oven to 325°. Pour off the marinade, stir it into the minced fish mixture, and season to taste. Put a layer of this mixture on the bottom of a buttered oval 1-quart terrine, then make a layer of the marinated eel fillets. Repeat layering until both ingredients are used, ending with the white fish mixture. Put the bay leaf on top of the terrine, cover with foil and the lid, and bake in the preheated oven in a water bath for 45 minutes.

Remove the lid, foil, and bay leaf. After the pâté has cooled, cover with a sheet of wax paper, put a 2-pound weight on top, and leave it overnight. If desired, pour a little extra melted butter on the top and let it set. Serve as a first course, sliced, with freshly made toast triangles, crusts removed, or as an hors d'oeuvre spread.

EEL ITALIAN STYLE

2½ pounds eel (large variety), skinned and cut into 4-inch pieces	1 teaspoon salt
	Several grindings of pepper
½ cup olive oil	1 cup dry white wine
1 small onion, sliced	2 cloves garlic, minced
8 anchovy fillets, chopped	3 cups shelled fresh peas
½ pound mushrooms, sliced	1 tablespoon tomato sauce
	½ cup water

Place the eels in ice water and soak for 15 minutes. Drain and pat dry.

Heat the oil in a large, heavy skillet, add the onion, and sauté until transparent. Add the anchovies, cook for 2 minutes longer. Add the eel and cook until the water from the eel evaporates. Add the mushrooms, salt, and pepper, cook for 5 minutes longer. Add the wine, garlic, and peas, cover the skillet, and cook until the wine has evaporated. Add the tomato sauce and water, continue cooking for 25–30 minutes. Add more water if needed. Serve with piping hot boiled rice. Serves 4.

FLOUNDER

Ask an American to name a fish, and chances are he or she will say flounder. It is probably the most common market and menu fish in the United States. The name encompasses more fish than is generally known—all of the so-called soles marketed in this country are really flounder, and they, together with halibut, turbot, plaice, fluke, and flounder by its own name, form the three families of flatfish, with about thirty member species, found along almost all of our coastlines.

I am fascinated by a little-known drama that takes place in the flatfish families; at a certain point in their development one eye moves up and over the head to nestle next to the other, presumably so that the flatfish, which swims with its more visible, lighter side down, can see properly. What rivets me, besides the notion of a traveling eye, is that in certain members of the species it is the *right* eye that travels and joins the left, creating *sinistral* (both eyes looking left) flatfish, while in those known as *dextral* flatfish the left eye moves, so the fish eyes are seen looking right. Winter flounders and turbot are sinistral; summer flounder (fluke) and halibut are dextral.

Winter Flounder: It is usually what you get when you just say "flounder"; whole small ones may be panfried, fillets of the sweet white meat may be broiled or sautéed. Marketed fresh and frozen.

Fluke: The market name for *summer flounder,* which is larger than the winter flounder but similar in taste and texture. It is sold whole and filleted. The bigger ones are known as "doormats" and may be sold in quarter-cut fillets. The *Southern flounder* is a close relative but much smaller.

Windowpane or Spotted Flounder: A small very thin, translucent flounder not important commercially.

Sand Dab: A miniature flounder, much prized in the West. It averages 8–10 ounces and is incredibly sweet and delicious as a panfish, whole or in fillet.

Starry Flounder: A Pacific flounder, not as tasty as the others above, and often marketed as "sole."

You may use any of the sole recipes (see Index) to prepare flounder. However, flounder may be a little coarse as a substitute for sole in very delicate sole dishes.

FLOUNDER STUFFED WITH CRAB

1 large flounder, about 3 pounds, gutted through the gills, skinned, head removed
1 recipe Crab Stuffing ✱ (see under Baked Weakfish Stuffed with Crab)

4 tablespoons butter, melted
⅓ cup white wine
2 teaspoons salt
Chopped parsley
Lemon juice

Preheat oven to 425°.

Lavishly butter a baking pan large enough to hold the fish.

Rinse the flounder and pat dry, lay it flat on a cutting board, pale side down, and make a pocket for the stuffing according to the instructions for the stuffing of flat fish (see Index). Spoon the stuffing into the "purse opening," press the edges together slightly, and put the fish in the prepared dish.

Combine the melted butter, wine, salt, and a dash of lemon juice. Pour over the fish and bake, timing according to the Canadian Theory. Serves 6.

SCANDINAVIAN DRY-BAKED FLOUNDER

An easy and absolutely delicious way to prepare fish; it emerges like velvet, gently cooked in its own natural gelatin. The subsequent flavoring is done individually, at the table, and gives a party air to a very simple dish.

A whole 4-pound flounder, cleaned
   and gutted (sole or fluke may
   also be used)
½ cup (approximately) freshly
   grated horseradish

½ cup (approximately) chopped
   parsley or dill
Coarse salt
Melted butter
Lemon wedges

Preheat oven to 200°.

Wash and dry the fish, place it in a baking dish without adding any butter, salt, or water. Bake for 1 hour. Transfer it to a heated serving platter. Discard the liquid that will have accumulated in the baking pan. Remove the skin, serve the fish with small dishes filled with the horseradish, parsley or dill, coarse salt, melted butter, lemon wedges, and a pepper mill. Serves 4.

BOMBAY-STYLE FLOUNDER

1–1½ pounds fillet of flounder,
   sole, or any other flatfish,
   skinned
1 cup yogurt

1 teaspoon paprika
1 teaspoon cumin
1 teaspoon coriander
Salt and freshly ground pepper

Put the fish in a rectangular Pyrex or earthenware dish. In a blender combine the yogurt, paprika, cumin, and coriander, blend until well mixed. Pour over the fish, cover with plastic wrap, and let marinate for a couple of hours in the refrigerator. Preheat the broiler, broil the fish for 4 minutes, turn and broil on the second side for 4 minutes more. Season with salt and pepper to taste, serve immediately with additional yogurt if desired. Serves 2.

FLOUNDER FILLETS IN BEER BATTER

1 pound fillets of flounder, skinned
   (fluke or sole may be used)
Juice of ½ lemon
2 tablespoons chopped parsley

2 tablespoons cooking oil
Salt and freshly ground pepper
1 recipe of Beer Batter with Egg ✹
Oil for deep frying

Cut the fish fillets into 2-inch pieces. Put in a bowl, add the lemon juice, parsley, the 2 tablespoons of cooking oil, salt and pepper to taste.

Heat the oil for deep frying.* Dip the pieces of fish, one at a time, into the batter and then into the hot oil. Cook, turning and submerging the pieces in the oil, until golden brown all over. Drain on paper towels. Serves 4–6.

GROUPER

There are several groupers belonging to the *Serranidae* family of the sea bass. Perhaps the best known are the red grouper, found from Virginia

*See the Index for general instructions on batter frying.

southward, and the Nassau grouper, an important market fish in Florida. Also found in Florida and Gulf waters is the largest grouper, the jewfish, which can reach 500–700 pounds in weight. The Warsaw grouper, a similar fish, ranks next in size and appears frequently in New York, where it is often sold as jewfish. Other groupers include the yellowfish and the black grouper, found mainly in the Gulf, and the red, rock, and speckled hinds.

Grouper is sold whole and in steaks and fillets, which may be used in any of the recipes in this book for sea bass (see Index) or red snapper (see Index). The skin of the grouper has a strong flavor and should be removed before cooking. Grouper meat is also good for deep-frying and poaching and excellent in chowders; the heads make superb stock.

GROUPER WITH SALSA VERDE

The Cuban *salsa verde* is quite distinct from the French *sauce verte,* which is really a green mayonnaise. There are several versions, hot and cold, and the greens may be varied with watercress, spinach, and scallions.

1 cup loosely packed parsley,
    leaves only
1 stalk celery, cut in several pieces
½ green pepper, peeled, seeded,
    and coarsely chopped
1 small onion, quartered
2 cloves garlic
2 tablespoons olive oil
¾ cup chicken stock or broth
2 tablespoons butter

1 tablespoon flour
¼ cup white wine
2 tablespoons vinegar
½ teaspoon salt or to taste
Several grindings of white pepper
1¾–2 pounds grouper fillets,
    skin on
Seasoned Flour ❋
¼ cup Clarified Butter, ❋ or half
    butter and half oil

Put the parsley, celery, green pepper, onion, and garlic in a blender or food processor. Chop briefly, scraping down sides of the container if necessary. Alternatively, you may chop these ingredients by hand until very finely minced. Add the olive oil and process again, or blend in by hand to make a paste.

Heat the stock in a saucepan. Make a *Beurre Manié* ❋ and add to the stock in small balls, whisking constantly until the sauce is thickened and smooth. Add the vegetable paste, wine, vinegar, salt, and pepper. Bring to a boil, stirring, lower heat, and simmer, uncovered, for 5 minutes. Correct the seasoning. Makes about 1½ cups of sauce. (It may be prepared early in the day, covered with plastic wrap, and refrigerated.)

Dredge the fish fillets in the seasoned flour.

Heat the clarified butter, or butter and oil, in a skillet that will accommodate the fish, sauté it over fairly high heat for 3 minutes on each side or until lightly browned. Transfer it to a heated platter. Bring the sauce to a boil, pour over the fish, and serve. Serves 4.

GROUPER IN RED SAUCE Merou à l'Algérienne

Follow the recipe for Tilefish in Red ✱ Sauce, substituting 6 grouper steaks, weighing about 2–2½ pounds, for the tilefish steaks. Serve with rice. Serves 6.

GRUNION

Where do you go fishing in the middle of the night with a gunnysack? In California, if you are a grunion fancier.

The grunion is a fascinating little smelt-like fish about six inches long whose spawning ritual is eagerly awaited by grunion lovers for three or four nights after each full moon from March to June. This is when the grunion, found only along the coast of Southern California and northern Baja California, come ashore to spawn. Since these fish leave the water to deposit their eggs, entire sections of beaches may be covered with them and they can be literally picked up while thus stranded.

To clean: Scale, remove the head with scissors, and run your fingers along the fish to squeeze the entrails out. Season and roast over a campfire (eat the bones and all—they taste like French fries) or roll them in a mixture of flour and cornmeal to which a little salt has been added, deep-fry until golden brown. Serve with tartar sauce. Alternatively, use grunions in any smelt recipe.

GRUNTS

This large family of semitropical and tropical reef fish has a delicate flesh somewhat like that of snapper (to which it is related) but not as firm. Most grunts are small, averaging just under a pound, and although they are delicious their size makes their market value limited. They can be deep-fried, sautéed, or baked, as in the following recipe for the Floridian "grits and grunts." Butterfish can also be used in this recipe.

BAKED GRUNTS

6 whole grunts, cleaned
½ cup lime juice or juice of 5 Key limes
Juice of 1 small lemon
1 small hot red pepper

Salt and freshly ground pepper
4 tablespoons softened butter
Lime slices for garnish
Avocado slices for garnish

Preheat oven to 350°.

Butter a shallow baking pan large enough to hold the fish. Add the fish, the lime and lemon juices, and the hot pepper. Cover the dish with a buttered piece of wax paper or foil, for 12–15 minutes. Transfer with a slotted spoon to a serving platter. Season to taste with salt and pepper, spread the softened butter over, and serve with lime slices and avocado slices. Delicious with hot buttered hominy grits. Serves 6.

HADDOCK

Haddock is a member of the cod family and resembles that fish greatly, though it is smaller on the average (2–5 pounds) and has a black lateral line instead of a white one. It may be used in most recipes calling for cod, although it is thought to have more flavor than cod and its flesh is a bit softer. It is sometimes served with egg sauce in New England; in Maine especially, it is popular stuffed with minced clams, onions, and buttered crackers, or simply with salt pork. Or use any good bread stuffing like the one in Jean Goddard's Stuffed Bass ❁ . Its fillets may also be baked with wine and tarragon, the sauce then enriched with cream. Follow the recipe for Trout in Tarragon Cream ❁ , and substitute haddock fillets for the trout. In addition, haddock may be substituted for cod in the recipe for Danish Boiled Cod ❁ , or poached and served cold with Rémoulade Sauce ❁ . I find broiled fresh haddock disappointing, however.

Clearly haddock's greatest gastronomic role is smoked, as finnan haddie.

HADDOCK BERCY

1¾ pounds fresh haddock fillets,
  skinned
Salt
A squeeze of lemon juice
½ cup water
6 white peppercorns
2 shallots, minced
½ cup dry white wine

2 tablespoons butter, softened
2 tablespoons flour
1 tablespoon chopped parsley
1 tablespoon heavy cream
2 ripe tomatoes, peeled, seeded,
  and cut in strips, or ⅔ cup
  canned tomatoes, seeded and
  cut in strips

Preheat oven to 350°.

Butter an ovenproof dish. Wash and dry the fillets, lay them in the baking dish, sprinkle with salt, and add the lemon juice, ½ cup of water, and peppercorns. Cover with a buttered piece of wax paper or foil, poach in the oven for 8–10 minutes.

While the fish is cooking, put the shallots in a small saucepan with the wine. Bring to a boil, lower heat, and stew the shallots until the liquid is reduced by half.

When the fish is done, remove to a heated platter and keep warm. Pour off the liquid from the pan and strain it into the wine mixture in the saucepan. Knead the butter and flour together and add in small balls to the liquid over moderate heat, whisking constantly, until the sauce is thickened and smooth. Simmer for 2–3 minutes, adjust the seasoning, add the parsley, cream, and tomatoes, and heat gently. Spoon the sauce over the fish and serve immediately. Serves 4.

NOTE: Small toast triangles fried in garlic-flavored butter may be used to garnish this dish.

FINNAN HADDIE (Smoked Haddock)

One of Scotland's great gifts to the world, Finnan Haddie—or split smoked haddock—hasn't nearly the following here that it ought to have. This fish, whose name comes from the Scottish port of Findon, where great quantities of haddock were fished, has a rich, velvety taste that satisfies and warms like few other foods I know. It is superb for breakfast or lunch, and makes a light and satisfying supper.

Occasionally smoked cod is sold in American fish markets as finnan haddie, because of the depletion of haddock in North American waters due to foreign overfishing. The more scrupulous markets call it "finnette"; others say that they can't tell the difference anyway. The flavors are quite similar, but for purists the haddock, being a smaller fish, is usually smoked as a fillet with the backbone in. A smoked crosscut, chunk, or thick center cut of fish is most likely cod. Sometimes a yellow dye is used as a part of the haddock cure, giving an improbable gold color to the fish.

POACHED: This is the easiest and, to my mind, the most delectable preparation. Allow a half pound of filleted fish per person—it is so easy to eat that one's plate empties alarmingly soon. Rinse the fish, taste a scrap, and if it seems very salty, soak it in lukewarm water for a half hour (usually this is not necessary). Poach in a mixture of half milk and half water to cover in a large covered frying pan, timing according to basic poaching instructions (see Index). Simply drain it and serve with a pat of plain butter, a knob of dill or parsley butter, and a boiled potato. Or sauce it with a Velouté Sauce ✽ made with the reduced poaching liquid. Utterly delicious and very easy. Poached finnan haddie is also superb with creamy scrambled eggs.

CREAMED FINNAN HADDIE: Poach smoked haddock as directed. Drain and reserve liquid. Make a Basic Béchamel Sauce ✽ , using 1 cup of the poaching liquid and 1 cup of light cream for the liquid requirement. Arrange individual servings of the haddock either on hot buttered toast or in pastry shells, cover with the sauce. Garnish with minced parsley. Serves 4–6.

BAKED: Preheat oven to 350°. Rinse about 2 pounds of fillets and put in a buttered shallow baking dish that accommodates the fish in one layer. Add ½ cup each of milk and cream, season with several grinds of pepper, dot with butter, and cover with foil. Bake for 20–25 minutes, basting occasionally. Transfer to a heated serving platter, spoon a little of the juice over, and serve with a knob of parsley butter if desired. Serves 4.

FINNAN HADDIE WITH HORSERADISH CREAM SAUCE

2 pounds finnan haddie
Milk for poaching
5 tablespoons butter
3 tablespoons flour
½ cup heavy cream
2 teaspoons Dijon or dark prepared
  mustard

2½–3 tablespoons freshly grated
  horseradish
Salt and white pepper
Lemon juice

Preheat the broiler and butter an appropriate sized oval gratin or serving dish.

Poach the fish, using all milk, according to directions (see Index). Measure off 1½ cups of the cooking liquid and reserve. With a slotted spatula transfer the fish to the serving dish, dot with 2 tablespoons of the butter, and cover loosely with foil.

In a heavy saucepan melt the remaining 3 tablespoons butter, add the flour, and cook, stirring, over moderate heat for 2 minutes. Remove from heat and stir in the reserved cooking liquid, cream, and mustard, simmer, stirring constantly for 3 minutes (the sauce will be quite thick). Stir in the horseradish, season to taste with salt, pepper, and lemon juice. Drain off any liquid that has accumulated around the fish into the sauce and stir in. Spoon the sauce over the fish and run under the broiler for 2 minutes or until lightly browned. Serve with steamed or parsleyed new potatoes. Serves 4.

FINNAN HADDIE SOUFFLÉ

3 tablespoons butter
3 tablespoons flour
1 cup milk, scalded
Salt and freshly ground pepper
A dash of cayenne pepper

A dash of nutmeg
½–¾ pound poached finnan haddie, flaked
4 egg yolks
4 egg whites

Preheat oven to 400°.

Butter a 1½-quart (6-cup) soufflé dish.

Melt the butter in a heavy saucepan. Stir in the flour with a wooden spoon, cook over moderate heat for 2 minutes without letting the mixture color. Remove from heat. When bubbling stops, pour in the scalded milk all at once. Beat with a wire whip until blended. Beat in the salt, pepper, cayenne, and nutmeg, return to heat, and bring to a boil, whisking for 1 minute. Remove from heat and combine with the fish. Beat in the egg yolks.

In a large bowl, beat the egg whites with a pinch of salt until stiff. Stir about ¼ of them into the sauce to lighten it, then fold in the balance. Pour the mixture into the prepared soufflé dish, put in the preheated oven, and immediately lower heat to 375°. Bake for 30–35 minutes or until well puffed and browned. Serve plain or with Mornay Sauce (see Index). Serves 4.

NOTE: This basic soufflé recipe may be used with salmon, crab, or almost any other fish.

KEDGEREE OF HADDOCK

An Indian dish designed to use leftover fish, kedgeree became popular with the British colonials and is now a traditional English breakfast dish usually made with haddock. Traditionally, it is seasoned with curry, but you may omit it if you wish. Also, it can be made with almost any other white fish.

1 cup milk	2 tablespoons butter, melted
1 cup water	3 eggs, hard-cooked
1 pound fresh or smoked haddock	Freshly ground pepper
2 teaspoons salt	½ teaspoon curry powder
4 cups cooked rice (1⅓ cups uncooked)	2 tablespoons chopped parsley

Combine the milk and water and pour over the haddock. Add the salt. Bring to a boil, cover, and simmer gently for 5 minutes. Allow the fish to cool in the cooking liquid, then lift it out, reserve the liquid, and remove the skin and bones if any. Flake the haddock, then mix with the cooked rice and melted butter in a bowl.

Shell 2 of the hard-cooked eggs, chop them finely, and stir into the rice mixture. Season with several twists of pepper and the curry powder. Moisten with a little of the cooking liquid (the mixture should be moist enough to hold together on its own yet not be soggy). Taste for seasoning. Pack lightly into a buttered 2-quart mold, cover, and keep warm. Turn out onto a serving plate and garnish with chopped parsley and the third hard-cooked egg, shelled and cut in wedges. You may also serve kedgeree mounded on a hot platter. Serves 4.

HADDOCK MONTE CARLO

2 large smoked haddock fillets, skinned, about 2½ pounds	1 cup water
	1 cup milk

¼ cup very finely minced onions
Freshly ground pepper
3 tablespooons butter
2 tablespoons flour
2 ripe tomatoes, peeled and halved

2 tablespoons heavy cream
A dash of cayenne pepper
4 poached eggs
2 tablespoons chopped parsley

Wash the haddock under running water, put it in a skillet large enough to hold it, the water, and the milk. Add more water if necessary to just cover. Add the onions and several grindings of pepper, gently bring to a boil. Lower heat and simmer for 5 minutes. Remove the fish carefully with a slotted spoon to a heated platter, strain and measure the liquid. If necessary reduce it over high heat to 2 cups and reserve.

Melt 2 tablespoons of the butter in a saucepan, add the flour. Cook for 2 minutes but do not let it color. Remove from heat and whisk in the warm fish liquid. Return to heat, bring to a boil, and simmer for several minutes, whisking constantly, until the sauce is thick and smooth. Stir in the cream, correct the seasoning, and add a dash of cayenne.

In a separate skillet melt the remaining tablespoon of butter, warm the tomato halves in it.

Drain off any liquid that has collected around the fish. Divide the fish carefully into 4 portions. Heat the sauce gently if necessary but do not boil, spoon over the fish, put a tomato half on each portion, and top each with a poached egg. Sprinkle with parsley. Serve immediately. Serves 4.

OMELET ARNOLD BENNETT

This elegant omelet was created for the writer Arnold Bennett by London's famous Savoy Hotel Grill. The hotel, which was the scene of his novel *Imperial Palace,* was also one of his favorite late supper haunts.

3 tablespoons butter
½ cup (about ¼ pound) flaked,
   poached finnan haddie
5 tablespoons heavy cream

4 eggs, at room temperature,
   separated
Salt and freshly ground pepper
¼ cup grated Parmesan cheese

Melt 1 tablespoon of the butter in a small skillet and toss with the haddock and 2 tablespoons of the cream over high heat for 2–3 minutes. Set aside.

Beat the egg yolks with 1 tablespoon of the cream, season to taste with salt and pepper. Beat the egg whites until just stiff but not dry. Add the fish to the yolk mixture, stir in, then fold in the egg whites and half the cheese.

Preheat the broiler and heat a serving platter. Melt the remaining 2 tablespoons of butter in a 10-inch skillet with an ovenproof handle. Add the egg mixture and cook over medium high heat until the underside is golden and the top fairly liquid, about 1 minute. Pour the remaining cream over, sprinkle with the remaining cheese, and brown quickly under the broiler, then slide the omelet onto the hot plate and serve at once. Serves 2.

HALIBUT

The Atlantic halibut is a species of dextral flounder (which it resembles in taste) and the largest of the flat fishes. Because of its enormous size (average 50–100 pounds) it is usually marketed in steaks or fillet segments called ''fletches.'' The vaguely sweet flesh is often compared to that of European turbot. It lends itself particularly well to poaching and may be served with any of the cold sauces you would use with salmon or bass. Halibut may be used in virtually all recipes for sole, or simply be baked or broiled. The California halibut is smaller and less desirable as a food fish.

COLD POACHED HALIBUT WITH RAVIGOTE SAUCE

Poach a thick 2½-pound piece of skinned halibut (see basic poaching directions). Put the fish on a serving dish and garnish with sliced tomatoes and cucumbers and quartered hard-cooked eggs. Serve the Ravigote Sauce ❋ separately.

POACHED HALIBUT WITH HOLLANDAISE SAUCE

Poach a thick steak (1½ to 2 inches, about 2 pounds for 4 people) in a Court-Bouillon ❋ . Serve with Hollandaise Sauce ❋ .

SEVICHE

1¾–2 pounds firm white fish such as halibut, bass, or flounder, filleted, skinned, cut into 1-inch-square pieces
⅓ cup lime juice (approximately 2 limes)
Salt and freshly ground pepper
1 medium onion, finely chopped
2 large ripe tomatoes, peeled and chopped

¼ cup minced parsley
4 serrano chili peppers, chopped (see the note p.139)
1 teaspoon oregano
1 tablespoon freshly chopped coriander or fresh parsley
½ cup olive oil

Put the fish in a glass or porcelain bowl, add the lime juice, mix well, and refrigerate overnight. Drain off and discard the juice.

Season the fish to taste with salt and pepper, add the onion, tomatoes, parsley, hot peppers, oregano, and olive oil. Mix well and refrigerate for at least 5 hours. Sprinkle with coriander or parsley before serving. Serves 6.

NOTE: *Chiles serranos* are medium-hot green peppers available in cans in the Mexican food section of many supermarkets. Fresh hot peppers may also be used.

HALIBUT WITH SHRIMP AND LEEK

1 halibut steak, 1½–1¾ pounds
Salt and freshly ground pepper
Juice of ½ lemon
6 tablespoons butter

2 leeks, well washed
1 teaspoon sweet paprika
½ pound raw medium shrimp,
   shelled and deveined

Preheat oven to 425°.

Wash and dry the fish, put in a baking dish, season with salt and pepper, and sprinkle with lemon juice. Melt 2 tablespoons of the butter and pour over the fish. Bake, timing according to the Canadian Theory, and baste once or twice.

Slice the white part of the leeks into rounds. Set aside. Cut the green part of the leeks into fine julienne and blanch for 2–3 minutes, drain, run cold water over them, and set aside.

Melt the remaining 2 tablespoons of butter in a small skillet and in it soften the leek rounds. Add the paprika and the shrimp and heat gently, stirring, until the shrimp turn pink. Add the reserved leek green to the pan and season everything with pepper.

Carefully remove the bone and skin from the fish. Spoon the shrimp-leek mixture over and serve at once in the baking dish. Serves 4.

HALIBUT MOUSSE

Making a classic fish mousse, before the advent of the blender and the food processor, required the most dedicated application of not only patience but muscle to achieve the necessary light purée. The fish first had to be pounded in a mortar or worked to a paste by hand, then puréed through a sieve. Though the texture of halibut is particularly suited to the mousse, you may use an equal amount of any firm white fish such as sole, flounder, cod, or pike.

1 pound fillet of halibut, skinned
1½ teaspoons salt
Cayenne pepper
3 egg whites
1 cup heavy cream, or more

1 teaspoon grated onion
1 tablespoon finely chopped fresh
   dill (optional)
1 tablespoon softened butter

IN A BLENDER: After processing the halibut twice through the fine blade of a food grinder (you should have about 2 cups), put the fish, salt, several dashes of cayenne, the egg whites, and 1 cup of the cream in a blender, run at high speed, stopping the motor to scrape down the sides of the jar with a rubber spatula. Continue blending until you have a smooth purée. If the blender jams, add more cream as needed, up to ½ cup.

IN A FOOD PROCESSOR: Grind the halibut to a fine pulp, using the steel blade, then proceed with the blender process above. Put the purée in a bowl, add the onion and dill. Stand this bowl in a larger one filled with cracked ice, refrigerate for 1 hour.

Preheat oven to 350°.

Butter a 1½-quart ring mold or fish mold with the softened butter. Stir the fish mixture thoroughly and spoon into the mold. Rap the mold sharply on the counter top to settle the mousse, cover with a sheet of buttered foil or wax paper, and put it into a baking pan in the lower third of the oven. Pour in enough boiling water to come halfway up the sides of the mold, bake for about 25 minutes or until firm.

Remove the mousse from the oven and discard the wax paper. Invert a serving platter on top of the mold and, holding it down tightly, invert and turn out the mousse onto the platter. Serve with Sauce Mousseline ❀ or Sauce Normande ❀ , made with shrimp. With the latter sauce, garnish the mousse with additional poached shrimp. Spoon a bit of the sauce over the mousse, allowing it to run down the sides, and pass the rest. Serves 6–8.

HERRING

Herring has played a long and involved role in the economic and gastronomic history of Europe (one of the reasons the Hanseatic League foundered is that the herring supply fell off). Though the Atlantic herring is abundant on both sides of the North Atlantic and large schools on the Pacific Coast range from Alaska to Northern California, it is rarely found fresh on the American market, perhaps because Baltic herrings are thought to be the best. The alewife, also known as "spring herring," differs from the Atlantic species in that it spawns in Atlantic coastal streams.

We see herring most commonly in a cured or pickled form, usually in bite-size pieces in a sour cream sauce, although cured whole herring fillets can be found in some good delicatessens. These are usually fat, mature or *schmaltz* (the German name) herring, or else *maatjes* herring, a Dutch name meaning "maiden." *Maatjes* herring are fat young fish from the first catch of the year and are usually lightly sugar-cured. They often have a rosy cast that comes from sandalwood added to the cure. You may also come across Bismarck herring, which are fish pickled in vinegar, salt, and sugar and flavored with onions; or rollmops, Bismarck herring rolled around onions and in a spicy sauce.

Kippers are fat herring that have been split, salted, and cold-smoked. They need only be heated, not cooked, and are best grilled lightly. Wipe them first with a damp cloth, brush with oil or dot with butter, and broil quickly, or heat in a very hot oven. Serve with scrambled eggs for a classic

British breakfast, or with mustard butter for supper. Bloaters, which are kippered, whole, older herring, should be scored before broiling.

NORWEGIAN HERRING SALAD

4 fillets pickled herring
3 medium-size all-purpose potatoes, boiled
3–4 pickled beets (see the note
   below)

½ teaspoon Dijon mustard,
   blended with 1 tablespoon vinegar from beets

Mince the herrings and potatoes finely. Mince the beets and add (the salad should be a handsome red—add more beets if required). Season to taste with the thinned mustard. The mixture should be fluffy; if it appears too stiff, add a little more of the vinegar from the beets. Serve on lettuce leaves as an appetizer with buttered brown bread. Serves 6.

NOTE: Pickled beets are available in 1-pound jars in most supermarkets.

PICKLED HERRING

6 whole herrings, heads removed,
   schmaltz or *maatjes*
2 cups water
6 tablespoons vinegar
1½ cups sugar
1½ tablespoons mayonnaise
3 tablespoons mixed pickling
   spices

1 bay leaf (optional)
3–4 stalks celery, chopped
2 dried red peppers, broken in
   pieces
2 medium carrots, sliced
3–4 onions, thinly sliced

Gut the herrings (wear rubber gloves or your hands will smell for days!) and soak for 5 hours under cold running water. Discard the water and slice the fish crosswise into miniature steaks, about 8 pieces per fish. Set aside. Blend together the 2 cups of water, vinegar, sugar, and mayonnaise. Add the pickling spices and the extra bay leaf. Put the celery, red peppers, carrots, onions, and herring pieces into a large crock or jar, pour the liquid over. Make sure the fish is covered; if not, mix in more water. Cover securely.

Let the crock stand unrefrigerated in a cool place (55°–60°) for 3 or 4 days, then refrigerate. The herring will be "ripe" in 10 days.

HERRING IN WHITE WINE

See Mackerel in White Wine ❋ .

LOVA'S HERRING APPETIZER

2–3 schmaltz herring fillets, about
   ½ pound
A 6-ounce can tomato paste
2 tablespoons vegetable oil
¼ cup lemon juice

1 medium onion, finely chopped
¼ cup chopped dill
3 teaspoons sugar or more to taste
Several grindings of fresh pepper

Wash the herring well and cut the fillets lengthwise in half. Cut each piece into bite-size pieces (about 8 or 9). Combine the tomato paste, vegetable oil, lemon juice, onion, dill, sugar, and pepper, mix with the herring. Cover and refrigerate for at least 4 hours before serving. Serve as an hors d'oeuvre or first course with buttered brown bread.

MARINATED HERRING WITH CREAM

6 fillets of miltz herring (see the
   note below)
2 medium onions, sliced
1 cup white vinegar
¼ cup water

2 teaspoons sugar
2 teaspoons pickling spice
2 bay leaves
¾ cup sour cream

Soak the herring in cold water overnight. Cut into 2-inch pieces. In a glass jar or bowl, arrange alternate layers of herring and onions. Bring the vinegar, water, sugar, pickling spice, and bay leaves to a boil. Cool slightly, blend in the sour cream, and pour over the herring. Refrigerate for at least 48 hours before serving.

NOTE: *Miltz* is the Jewish word for milt, the secretion of the male reproductive glands of fish. Miltz herring can be obtained in good delicatessens or by mail (see the Appendix: Food Shopping by Mail).

MACKEREL

The mackerel belongs to the family *Scombridae,* the same as the tuna, and because of the oiliness characteristic of the dark muscle meat of these fish is objectionable to some palates. Properly treated, however, mackerel is a natural for flavorful tomato-based sauces, for marinating, and for smoking.

There are several popular varieties including the Atlantic or Boston mackerel,* native to the northeast Atlantic, and the more delicately flavored Spanish mackerel, found all the way from Maine to Brazil. Both may be split and broiled, baked, or prepared with interesting sauces like some of

*"Boston" once was synonymous with salted mackerel, but this is no longer true.

those that follow. King mackerel, also known as kingfish, is fatter and stronger in taste and its steaks benefit from a citrus marination before oven or charcoal-broiling, as is done throughout the Caribbean. The flesh has a grayish, steely quality that may be off-putting, but it whitens after cooking.

The wahoo, the biggest mackerel, found in warm waters, resembles the king but has finer, whiter flesh and is less oily. Along with the equally delicately flavored cero mackerel, it may be treated as the Atlantic and king, and steaks may be broiled or charcoal-grilled.

The Pacific, or blue, mackerel, available in central and southern California, has a rich pronounced flavor and dark, firm meat; it is available whole and in fillets and may be treated as Atlantic or Spanish mackerel.

Chub mackerel, also known as "hardheads," is usually found smoked at market, because of its small size. It is the chub that is called Spanish mackerel in Europe. To confuse matters further, there is a sportfish called a jack mackerel that is sometimes also called Spanish mackerel. Though it resembles a mackerel, it belongs to a separate family, that of the pompano.

Tinkers are small fat school mackerel, with a maximum length of 10 inches.

MACKEREL IN WHITE WINE (Maquereau au Vin Blanc)

12 mackerel fillets, skin on (about 2 pounds)
1½ cups dry white wine
¼ cup vegetable or corn oil
½ teaspoon dried thyme or 4 sprigs of fresh
2–3 bay leaves
1 teaspoon freshly ground pepper
1 teaspoon salt or to taste

4–5 unpeeled cloves garlic, crushed
2 small onions, thinly sliced
2 medium carrots, thinly sliced
1 lemon, thinly sliced
15–18 whole peppercorns
Additional lemon slices for garnish, seeds removed

Cut away the small diagonal belly bones of the fish (leave the center bone line), as well as the thin belly flesh, if not already done. Rinse the fish and arrange in a rather deep ovenproof dish.

In an enamel pot combine the wine, oil, thyme, bay leaves, pepper, salt, garlic, onions, carrots, lemon slices, and peppercorns, simmer, covered, for about 20 minutes. Remove the broth from the fire, pour, unstrained, over the mackerel. The liquid should cover about half the fish; if it doesn't, add more white wine or water.

Bring again to a boil, cover, and keep at a slow simmer for 12 minutes, then remove from the fire, and after removing the bay leaves, let the fish cool, covered, in the liquid. Refrigerate after cooling but let it come to room temperature before serving. Transfer the fish to a porcelain or earthenware serving dish. Spoon the sauce over the fish along with some of the vegetables. Garnish with lemon slices. Serves 6.

MACKEREL IN ESCABECHE

3 tablespoons butter
¾ cup olive oil
6 small mackerel fillets, skinned
Flour
Salt and freshly ground pepper
1 medium onion, thinly sliced and
    separated into rings
1 green pepper, seeded and cut
    into thin rings

1 clove garlic, finely chopped
½ cup orange juice
Juice of 2 limes
2 green chilies, peeled and chopped
Orange slices
Lime slices
1 tablespoon grated orange rind
Chopped fresh coriander or parsley

Heat the butter and ¼ cup of the oil in a skillet large enough to hold the fish. Lightly dredge the fillets with flour, sauté them until delicately brown on both sides and tender. Season to taste with salt and pepper. Arrange them in a flat serving dish, scatter over them the onion rings, pepper rings, and garlic. Combine the remaining ½ cup oil, orange juice, lime juice, chilies, and salt and pepper to taste. Blend well and pour over the fish while it is still warm. Cover and refrigerate for 12–24 hours.

To serve, garnish with orange and lime slices, and scatter the grated orange rind and chopped coriander or parsley over the top. Serves 4 as a first course.

FRENCH BAKED MACKEREL (Maquereau au Four)

2 very fresh Spanish or Boston
    mackerel, about ¾ pound each,
    cleaned, split, and boned
Salt
¼ cup chopped shallots
½ cup chopped parsley
A sprig of thyme or ¼ teaspoon
    dried

Freshly ground pepper
2 teaspoons brandy
⅓ cup Dijon mustard
1 tablespoon lemon juice
⅔ cup dry white wine

Preheat oven to 325°.

Butter a shallow ovenproof dish large enough to hold the fish. Score the mackerel slightly and season with salt.

Mix the chopped shallots and parsley together, spread on the bottom of the baking dish. Into each fish insert a bit of thyme, one or two grindings of pepper, and a sprinkling of brandy. Mix the mustard and lemon juice together, brush the outside of each fish with it. Lay the fish on the vegetable bed, pour the white wine around, and cover the dish with a piece of buttered paper. Bake for about 20 minutes. Serves 2.

MARINATED KING MACKEREL MARTINIQUE STYLE

6 king mackerel steaks, 1½ inches
   thick (about 2½ pounds)
¼ cup lime juice
1 teaspoon dried marjoram leaves,
   crushed

2 tablespoons melted butter
1 teaspoon salt
Several grindings of fresh pepper

Wash the fish and pat dry. In a shallow dish that will hold the fish, combine the lime juice and marjoram. Add the steaks, turning to moisten on both sides with the juice. Cover and place in the refrigerator for an hour, turning once.

Preheat the broiler. Butter a 10 by 15-inch baking pan. Place the fish in a single layer in the pan, brush with the melted butter, sprinkle with salt and pepper, and broil about 4 inches from the source of heat, timing according to the Canadian Theory. The fish need not be turned during broiling. Serves 4–6.

GRAVAD MACKEREL

In Sweden, mackerel is sometimes sugar-cured the same way as salmon, producing *gravad* mackerel. The mackerel, which may be a large Boston mackerel that has been filleted, or a center cut of king mackerel, must be very fresh. Follow the instructions for *Gravlax* (see Index) and serve with *Gravlaxsås* (Mustard-Dill Sauce).

MACKEREL WITH ANCHOVY BUTTER

This is a simple Provençal way to cook mackerel: bake a split and boned mackerel in a well-oiled baking dish for 15–20 minutes in a preheated 350° oven. While it is still very hot, spread with Anchovy Butter ❋ , serve immediately.

MACKEREL WITH MAYONNAISE SAUCE

4 Spanish mackerel fillets, skin
   on (bluefish may also be used)
Salt and freshly ground pepper
½ cup mayonnaise
4 tablespoons dry vermouth

2 tablespoons chopped parsley
2 tablespoons chopped shallots or
   green onions (white part only)
Lemon wedges

Preheat oven to 425°.

Lightly oil a baking dish or line a broiler pan with foil (if it will fit in the oven) and oil. Season the fillets with salt and pepper and lay them skin side down in the pan.

Mix mayonnaise, vermouth, parsley, and shallots together. Add more vermouth if necessary to make a smooth and creamy sauce. Spread a thick ¼-inch coating of mayonnaise sauce on the fillets, bake for 15 minutes in the upper third of the oven, basting occasionally with the pan juices. If at the end of the baking time a golden brown crust has not formed, turn the heat up to broil and run the fish under the broiler until the mayonnaise dressing is brown. Serve with lemon wedges. Serves 4.

KINGFISH CREOLE

4 pounds kingfish, filleted and
    skinned (bonito may also be
    used)
2 tablespoons butter
2 tablespoons oil
1 medium onion, chopped
1 large green pepper, seeded and
    chopped

2 cloves garlic, minced
1 cup canned tomatoes, drained
    and chopped
1 bay leaf
Salt and freshly ground pepper

Preheat oven to 350°.

Heat the butter and oil in a heavy skillet. Add the onion, green pepper, and garlic, sauté until the onion is transparent. Add the tomatoes, bay leaf, salt, and pepper, stir to blend, and simmer the sauce for a few minutes. Put the fish in a baking dish, spoon the sauce over, and bake for 15 minutes. Serves 8.

WAHOO BAHAMIAN STYLE

4–5 pounds wahoo, cut into steaks
Butter
1 large green pepper, seeded and
    chopped

1 large onion, thinly sliced
1 teaspoon dried basil
1 teaspoon dried oregano
Salt and freshly ground pepper

Preheat oven to 350°.

Rub the wahoo steaks with butter, arrange on a large piece of foil. Top with the green pepper and onion, sprinkle with basil and oregano. Add salt and pepper to taste. Close the foil package well and bake for 15 minutes. Serves 8.

MULLET

There are several species of this abundant fish found along our eastern and southeastern shores, the most important being the silver or striped mullet; as a market fish, however, it is important, apparently, only in the South.

The striped mullet, sometimes called "jumping mullet" (not to be confused with the freshwater mullet), has a tender, firmly textured meat with a sweet, nutty flavor, and it is marketed whole in sizes up to 3 pounds; larger fishes are usually filleted. Small sizes can be split and broiled, the bigger ones baked. The dark portions of mullet contain a yellowish oil that make it unsuitable for long-term freezing.

The red mullet of the Mediterranean, known as *triglia* in Italian and *rouget de roche* in French, is an unusual fish that changes colors like a chameleon to match its underwater surroundings and becomes even redder after being scaled. It is not a true mullet, but a goatfish and was particularly famous and prized in antiquity. Large ones fetched enormous prices, and the ancient Greeks and Romans not only enjoyed eating them but often kept them alive for the pleasure of watching them die, an occasion to which one invited one's friends. It was considered a highly aesthetic experience to observe the subtle changes of color that took place as the fish expired, a bizarre diversion to which there are numerous references in Seneca, Pliny, and Juvenal. The name *rouget* occasionally pops up in New Orleans, but as a nickname for red snapper. We do not have a red mullet, true or otherwise.

Mullet roe* is a delicacy; ask your fish dealer for some, mix it with bread crumbs, herbs, and some lightly sautéed onion, and stuff a good-sized mullet (or other fish) with it. Mullet roe coated with seasoned cornmeal and slowly sautéed in butter and bacon drippings is popular among Florida natives. Often it is served with crisp bacon crumbled on top.

BROILED MULLETS ITALIAN STYLE

4 1-pound silver or striped mullets or	1 tablespoon chopped fresh basil leaves
2 2-pound mullets, cleaned, split, and boned	1 teaspoon chopped chives
¼ cup olive oil	½ cup cider vinegar
2 tablespoons melted butter	2 tablespoons lemon juice
1 clove garlic, minced	Salt
	Lemon wedges

---

*The dried roe of the gray mullet was the original roe used in making *taramosalata*, that addictive Greek dip now made with carp roe. Mullet roe is now a delicacy of caviar rank in Greece.

Oil and preheat the broiler pan.

Place the fish skin side down on the rack. Combine the remaining ingredients except the lemon wedges, blend well, and brush on the fish. Broil the fish about 6 inches below the flame for 10 minutes or until golden brown, brushing several times with the basting mixture. Transfer the fish to a hot platter, pour the remaining mixture over them, and serve hot with lemon wedges. Serves 4–6.

OCEAN PERCH

Ocean perch is the commercial name given to an Atlantic rockfish of the *Scorpaenidae* family. (Other names for ocean perch are: sea perch—not related to the Pacific fish below—red perch, redfish, and rosefish.) These are not generally seen at market, but are packaged in fillets and frozen.

The Pacific Ocean perch is another rockfish that is not a perch. And neither of these rockfish is to be confused with the name rockfish, which is what striped bass is called in the Maryland-Virginia area. A number of surf perches are found along the Pacific coast, one of which is called "sea perch," and these also are not related to the true perch.

POMPANO

"The renowned fish called the pompano," mused Mark Twain in *Life on the Mississippi,* "is as delicious as the less criminal forms of sin."

The silvery pompano is considered by many fish lovers to be the last word in fish, reflected in the fact that, although abundant, it is very expensive. Pompano is found from Massachusetts all the way to Brazil, but is most prolific in Southern United States waters, especially from October to May. Aided by its deeply forked tail, it has a peculiar habit of appearing to "walk" or "skate" on water. Pompano may be broiled, baked, or sautéed *meunière* and is marvelous braised in its own juices *en papillote.*

POMPANO STUFFED WITH SHRIMP

4 small pompano, about ¾ pound
   each, split and cleaned, head
   and tail intact, or 2 about 1¼
   pounds each
1 pound shrimp, cooked, shelled,
   and deveined
1 egg, well beaten

½ teaspoon salt
Freshly ground pepper
3 tablespoons sherry
1 cup heavy cream
⅓ cup white wine
Parsley clusters

Preheat oven to 350°.

Oil a shallow baking pan that will hold the fish nicely. (Tails may be removed if necessary.) Wash the fish and pat dry. Set aside.

Put the shrimp through a food grinder or mince finely in a food processor, using the metal blade. Combine with egg, salt, pepper, sherry, and ½ cup of the cream. Stuff the fish cavities loosely with the mixture. (The stuffing will expand slightly, but it is not necessary to fasten the opening.) Mix the remaining cream with the wine, pour over the fish. Bake for 35 minutes, basting occasionally. Tuck parsley clusters into the exposed gill opening of each fish and serve immediately. Serves 4.

POMPANO EN PAPILLOTE

6 small pompano fillets, skinned (about 2–2½ pounds)
6–7 ounces crab meat, fresh or canned, drained
¼ pound shrimp, cooked, shelled, and deveined
3 cups Fish Stock ✱ or water
1 teaspoon salt
2 lemon slices
1 bay leaf
¼ teaspoon dried thyme, crushed

Parchment or brown paper
Cooking oil
3 tablespoons butter
½ cup chopped shallots or green onions (white part only)
1 clove garlic, minced
3 tablespoons flour
Salt
2 egg yolks, lightly beaten
¼ cup dry white wine

Preheat oven to 400°.

Wash the fish. Pick over the crab meat. Remove the cartilage and flake the meat; set aside. Chop the shrimp; set aside.

In a 12-inch skillet, bring the stock or water, salt, lemon, bay leaf, and thyme to a boil. Add the fish, cover, reduce heat, and simmer gently for about 8 minutes or until the fish flakes easily. Carefully remove the fish. Strain the stock, reserving 1½ cups, or reduce over high heat to that amount. Remove any bones from the fish.

Cut 6 pieces of parchment or brown paper into heart shapes measuring about 12 inches long and 10 inches at the widest part. Brush the paper with cooking oil. Fold in half. Put 1 fillet on the right half of each paper heart. Set aside.

Melt the butter in a saucepan. Add the shallots or onions and garlic, cook until tender. Blend in the flour and a dash of salt. Add the reserved stock. Cook, stirring constantly, until thickened. Gradually blend a small amount of the hot mixture into the egg yolks, then add the yolks to the sauce, whisking constantly. Heat just until the mixture thickens. Stir in the wine, crab meat, and shrimp, heat briefly.

Spoon about ½ cup of the sauce over each fillet. Divide any remaining sauce among the fillets. Fold the left half of each paper heart over the fish,

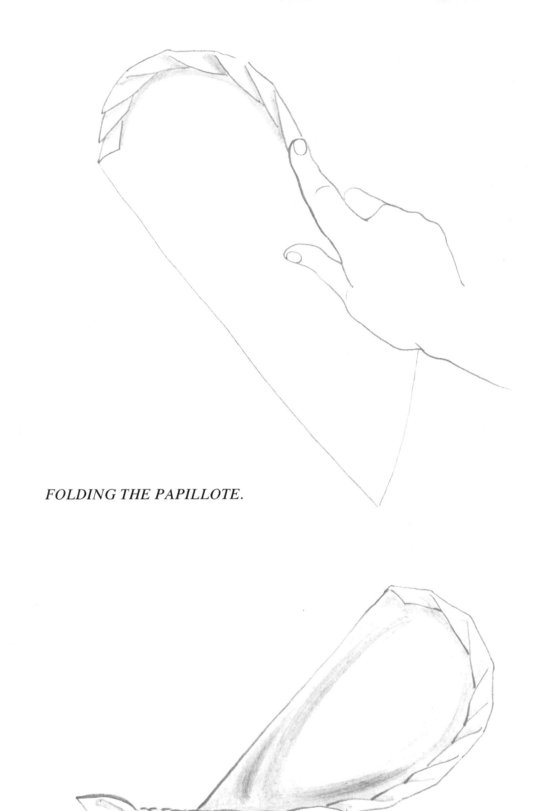

FOLDING THE PAPILLOTE.

THE FINISHED PAPILLOTE.

matching the edges. Seal the cases by starting at the top of the heart and turning the edges over in 2 or 3 narrow folds. Twist the tip of the heart to hold the case closed. Place on a baking sheet and bake for 10–15 minutes. To serve, cut the cases open by slashing a large X on top of each, then folding back each segment. Serves 6.

PORGIES

Porgies are members of a large family, the *Sparidae,* or sea bream, abundant in northern and southern Atlantic coastal waters in several varieties. The most common in the Northeast is also called scup in New England, a name derived from the Narragansett Indian word for the fish. Most porgies are small, averaging one pound, and make excellent panfish, although one variety, the jolthead, which is popular in the South, averages about two pounds and can be baked. There is a West Coast porgy as well.

Porgies have a delicate, sweet taste and slightly coarse flesh, a lot of small sharp bones, and scales that can be very tough. If you are doing the fishing, scale them as soon as possible. One old-time fisherman I know doesn't bother with scaling at all—he charcoal-grills cleaned fresh porgies and says the scales "burn off." If the porgies are large enough to fillet, skin them to begin with, and panfry the fillets. Serve with any flavored butter.

PANFRIED PORGY

4 small porgies, cleaned, whole, about ¾ pound each	1 tablespoon coarse salt
1 cup cornmeal	Several grindings of fresh pepper
	½ cup corn oil

Rinse the porgies and pat dry. Mix together the cornmeal, salt, and pepper, dredge the fish with the mixture. In one large or two medium-size skillets heat the oil until almost smoking. Fry the fish for 5 minutes on each side. Serve at once. Serves 4.

VARIATION: Wipe the skillet clean of any burned bits, melt 3 tablespoons of butter in it, and sauté ¼ cup minced shallots or scallions until soft and slightly browned. Increase heat, pour in ⅔ cup white wine, and cook until the wine is reduced to half. Swirl in 2 additional tablespoons of butter and pour over the warm fish.

RED SNAPPER

Red snapper is, hands down, my favorite fish, for its flavor, the versatility of its firm white flesh, and its beautiful color, which enhances any treatment. It is available all year round, in all parts of the country, and can be served broiled, baked, steamed, or as a component of fish soups and stews. Its handsome form and appearance make it particularly suitable to stuffing whole and presenting at an important dinner. Because of the extremely large head, consider only about 40 per cent of the total weight as edible; if you have snappers filleted, remember to ask for the head, bones, and skin for the delicious stock you can make from them.

Snappers range from ¾ pound to 30 pounds. Although relatively little is known about the life history of these members of the warm water *Lutjanidae* family, they are believed to stay in shallow water during the summer months, moving offshore again to spawn in deep water with the arrival of fall. Most red snappers for market use are caught in Florida waters and the Gulf of Mexico.

RED SNAPPER AL PESTO

1 cup *Pesto* (recipe given below)
4 red snapper steaks, skinned,
   1–1½ inches thick (about ½
   pound each)

2 ripe tomatoes
4 chopped anchovy fillets
2 tablespoons olive oil
Salt and freshly ground pepper

Make the *Pesto* according to the recipe below.

Preheat the broiler. Season the fish with salt and pepper and set aside. Peel, seed, and chop the tomatoes, put in a saucepan with the anchovies and olive oil, and cook gently over moderate heat for 5 minutes. Season to taste and set aside.

Broil the fish, timing them according to the Canadian Theory, and turning them halfway through the cooking time. Heat the tomato sauce gently while the fish is cooking; at the last minute stir the prepared *Pesto* into the sauce and pour it very hot over the steaks. Serve at once. Serves 4.

PESTO

1 cup tightly packed fresh basil
   leaves
¼ cup olive oil
¼ cup pine nuts (*pignoli*)
1–2 cloves garlic

⅓ cup grated Parmesan cheese
⅓ cup grated romano cheese
1 tablespoon softened butter
Salt

Put the basil in a blender. Add the olive oil, pine nuts, and garlic, blend to a smooth paste. Add the cheese and butter, blend again. Add salt to taste. The finished sauce should have the consistency of creamed butter. Add an extra tablespoon of oil if the sauce seems too pasty. Makes about 1 cup.

RED SNAPPER WITH LEEKS POACHED IN DRY VERMOUTH

8 tablespoons (1 stick) butter
6 shallots, minced, or an equal
   amount of scallions, white part
   only
4 red snapper fillets skin on (totaling about 2 pounds)

Salt and freshly ground pepper
5 leeks (white part only) well
   washed and cut in julienne
2 cups dry vermouth

Heat a serving platter. Select a skillet large enough to hold the fillets without overlapping. Melt 6 tablespoons of the butter in it, add the shallots or scallions. Add the fillets, skin side down. Season with salt and pepper. Add the leeks and vermouth. Bring to boil, reduce heat, and simmer, covered, for 7–8 minutes. With a slotted spatula, carefully lift the fish to the heated serving platter and keep warm.

Put the skillet containing the juices and leeks over high heat and cook, uncovered, until the sauce is reduced to about half. Swirl in the remaining 2 tablespoons of butter, pour over the fish. Serve immediately with freshly steamed potatoes. Serves 6.

RED SNAPPER LA SAMANNA

A 4–4½-pound red snapper, boned
   and split, head and tail removed
Salt and freshly ground pepper
2 cups Duxelles ❀
1 cup stale bread crumbs

1 egg, lightly beaten
⅓ cup dry white wine
⅓ cup Fish Stock ❀ or clam juice
8 tablespoons (1 stick) butter
Lemon juice

GARNISH (optional)
3 large mushrooms, stems
   removed, sliced carefully
2 shallots, finely minced

⅓ cup tomatoes, drained, seeded,
   and chopped
Minced parsley

Preheat oven to 350°.

Butter a flameproof oval *gratin* dish or a baking dish large enough to hold the fish.

Flatten the fish fillets slightly between sheets of wax paper, using a wooden mallet or the bottom of a skillet, and sprinkle them with salt and pepper.

In a bowl, combine the duxelles with the crumbs, egg, and salt and pepper to taste. Put one of the fillets in the prepared baking dish skin side down, spread with the duxelles mixture, pat it down, and top with the other fillet.

Add the wine and fish stock or clam juice to the dish, bring the liquid to a boil on top of the stove. Cover the dish with a buttered sheet of foil, bake for 25–30 minutes or until the fish flakes easily. Transfer the fish to a heated platter with a broad spatula and keep warm.

Carefully pour the liquid from the dish into a saucepan. Reduce the liquid over high heat to $\frac{1}{3}$ of its original volume (there will be only a small amount left). Lower heat and whisk in the butter, a tablespoon at a time, making sure that each piece is melted and incorporated before the next is added. (Lift the saucepan off the heat occasionally while doing this, so the sauce never gets too hot.) Continue whisking until smooth and thick. Season with a squeeze of lemon juice and salt and pepper to taste. Nap the fish with the sauce and serve as is, with a sprinkling of parsley, or with the optional garnish prepared as follows: wilt the mushroom slices in a little butter and set aside. In another pan, wilt the shallots in a small amount of additional butter. Warm the chopped tomatoes in the same pan, season, and arrange the mixture along the length of the fish down the center. Arrange the mushroom slices, slightly overlapping, in a neat row on top of the tomato bed and serve. Serves 4.

BAKED RED SNAPPER FLORENTINE

A 4–5 pound whole red snapper, cleaned, backbone removed, head and tail intact

SPINACH STUFFING
4 tablespoons butter
3 finely chopped shallots or scallions (white part only)
½ cup finely chopped, cooked fresh spinach (about ½ pound), or a 10-ounce package frozen
2½ cups fresh bread crumbs made from home-style bread (about 6 slices)

3 tablespoons heavy cream
Salt
Freshly ground pepper
Lemon juice

PREPARING THE FISH
5 tablespoons melted butter
1 cup dry white wine
2 tablespoons softened butter

Parsley sprigs
Decoratively cut lemon halves
A black olive

Preheat oven at 400°.

Wash the fish inside and out under running water, and dry it thoroughly with paper towels. Set aside.

Make the spinach stuffing: in a heavy 8-inch stainless steel or enamel skillet, melt the butter over moderate heat, sauté the shallots in it for 2 minutes or until they are soft but not brown. Squeeze the moisture out of the spinach (if you are using frozen spinach, thaw it and squeeze completely dry), add to the skillet, and cook over high heat, stirring constantly, for 2–3 minutes to evaporate most of the moisture. Transfer to a large mixing bowl, add the bread crumbs, cream, salt to taste, several grindings of pepper, and toss together gently. Season with a squeeze or two of lemon juice.

Brush 1 tablespoon of the melted butter on the bottom of a shallow baking dish that is large enough to hold the fish and that can be presented at the table.

Fill the fish with the spinach stuffing, close the opening with small skewers and string. Put the fish in the prepared dish, brush the top with another 2 tablespoons of melted butter, and season with salt and pepper. Combine the remaining 2 tablespoons of melted butter with the wine, pour it around the fish, bring to a simmer on top of the stove, then bake, uncovered, on the middle shelf of the oven. Baste the fish frequently with the pan juices. If the liquid evaporates, add up to $3/4$ cup more wine as needed. Bake for 30–40 minutes or until the fish is just firm when pressed lightly with the finger.

Remove the baking dish from the oven and spoon the juices to a small pan. Keep the fish warm.

Reduce the juices over high heat until they are syrupy, remove from heat, stir in the softened butter, and pour the sauce over the fish. Serve the fish plain or with Beurre Blanc Sauce ❀. Garnish with parsley clusters and lemon halves, and replace the eye with the black olive. Serves 6.

RED SNAPPER BAKED WITH PROSCIUTTO

$1/2$ cup olive oil
$1/2$ cup lemon juice
$1/4$ teaspoon oregano
$1/4$ teaspoon basil
$1/2$ teaspoon chopped garlic
1 cup sliced onions
A 4-pound red snapper, filleted,
    skin on

$1/2$ cup chopped prosciutto (1 slice
    $1/4$ inch thick will yield $1/2$ cup
    chopped)
$1/2$ cup fresh bread crumbs
1 tablespoon chopped parsley

Mix the olive oil, lemon juice, oregano, basil, garlic, and onions in a medium-size flat baking dish. Place the fillets skin side up in this marinade and let soak unrefrigerated for at least 1 hour. Discard the onions.

Preheat oven to 325°.

Sandwich the fillets, skin side outside, with chopped prosciutto. Bake for 30 minutes, basting two or three times with the marinade. Spoon out the liquid from the dish, mix the bread crumbs and parsley, and spread over the top of the fillets. Brown under the broiler. Cut into 4 portions. Serves 4.

RED SNAPPER WITH TURKISH ALMOND SAUCE

The butter and cream that are the basis of so many French sauces are often scarce in the regions of the Bosporus. On the other hand, fresh nuts abound, so often almonds, pine kernels, or pistachios are ground to a cream and used as a sauce base. In the famous Turkish shellfish sauce *turator,* ground green walnuts form the base. These sauces may be served hot, but more often are encountered cold, making them ideal for summer eating.

A 3-pound red snapper, cleaned, head, tail, and backbone removed (striped bass may also be used)

2 cups or more poaching broth (may be made from the head, tail, and trimmings of the above fish)

1 cup freshly blanched almonds (see the note below)

1 slice home-style white bread, crust removed

½ cup olive oil

Juice of ½ lemon

Salt and freshly ground white pepper

GARNISH (optional)

Chopped coriander leaves, Italian or regular parsley

Thin lemon slices

Poach the fish according to instructions (see Index). Allow to cool in the cooking liquid. While the fish is cooking, prepare the sauce.

Pound the almonds in a mortar or chop thoroughly in a blender until they are very fine. Work them together with the bread and enough cold water to make a creamy white paste. Add the olive oil, beating all the time, then the lemon juice and seasonings. Or process the almonds in a food processor until fine, then proceed as above. With the motor running, add the olive oil and the lemon juice, season rather highly with salt and pepper to taste. The sauce should have the consistency of thick cream. The fish and sauce may be prepared early in the day and chilled until serving time.

Garnish the cooked fish with the lemon slices and a sprinkling of chopped coriander or parsley. Pass the sauce in a bowl and serve boiled new potatoes that have been lightly dusted with paprika. Serves 6.

NOTE: The term ''blanch'' is explained in the Glossary.

BAKED STUFFED WHOLE RED SNAPPER

This recipe, with its interestingly textured stuffing, works equally well with striped bass.

A 3½–4-pound red snapper, split,
  head and tail on, backbone
  removed
Salt and freshly ground pepper
4 cups fresh bread crumbs
½ cup chopped celery
½ cup chopped green pepper

¼ cup chopped toasted almonds
1 tablespoon chopped chives or
  scallions (green part only)
1 cup dry white wine
Thin lemon slices
Parsley sprigs

Generously butter a baking pan large enough to hold the fish. Preheat oven to 350°.

Wash the fish and pat dry, rub the cavity with a little salt and pepper. Set aside.

Make the stuffing: in a bowl combine the bread crumbs with the celery, green pepper, almonds, chives or scallions, and salt and pepper to taste. Moisten with ¼ cup of the wine. Stuff the fish and skewer or sew closed with needle and thread. Put the fish in the baking pan and bake, basting frequently with additional dry white wine, for 35–40 minutes. Remove the fish to a warm serving platter. Put the baking pan over high heat and cook the pan juices until reduced by half. (If baking pan is not flameproof, pour juices into a saucepan first.) Pour over the fish and garnish with thin slices of lemon and parsley sprigs. Serve with new potatoes in Chive Butter ❋ . Serves 3–4.

YELLOWTAIL SNAPPER

When the chef of our vacation hotel in Saint Martin learned of my interest in fish, he told me that he would keep an eye out for ''a yellowtail'' at market. When he finally got one, I had eaten just about every available local fish in every local preparation anyone could think of, and I was less than enthusiastic at the thought of still another fish meal. But I was enchanted by the fresh sweet meat of the yellowtail snapper, more finely textured than that of the red or gray and very delicate. The yellowtail is found from the Florida Keys through the West Indies to South America. It must be eaten impeccably fresh and prepared simply—filleted and then broiled, perhaps dressed with butter, and accompanied by lime wedges.

SABLEFISH

Found in deep, cold Pacific waters, sablefish is a fairly neglected member of the skilfish family, a highly tasty white-fleshed fish often called ''black cod.'' However, it is not a cod and should not be prepared as such, because of its oil.

The fish, which can be as large as three feet, is marketed whole, in steaks and fillets, as well as cured. The steaks and fillets are best broiled. Smoked sablefish, sometimes called smoked Canadian black cod in the West, may be served in thin slices, as is smoked salmon. Kippered sablefish may be used in any of the finnan haddie recipes.

SHARK

Judging by the cautious appearance of mako shark at market these days, shark as a food fish is at last coming into its own in this country. It is popular in many other lands and its fins are highly prized by the Chinese, who consider the gelatinous shark fin soup a nostrum for a variety of ills. The mako, a variety fished off Long Island, is similar to swordfish,* is half the price, and, to me, tastes better. (For years a lot of "swordfish" steaks were really mako shark and few people knew the difference.) Besides its delicate flavor, it has two other advantages over swordfish: not only is it moister, but after cooking it loses the fishy edge that swordfish can have.

All of which proves that shark, heretofore only acceptable when called something else, is becoming appreciated for its own virtues: its lack of bones, firm texture, good taste, and general economy.

Shark is marketed primarily in steaks and may be prepared like any firm-fleshed fish, broiling being perhaps the most satisfactory method. Shark may be substituted in any swordfish recipe. It is particularly good for skewered dishes, as it does not break easily and fall off. Florida's blacktip shark has meat that is a little drier than mako, so care should be taken not to overcook it.

Because shark meat has poor keeping quality it should be eaten as soon as possible after buying it. Freeze in airtight wrapping if it is to be stored much longer than 24 hours.

BROILED SHARK

Follow the directions for Broiled Swordfish ❋ , substituting 1-inch-thick mako shark steaks. Serve with herb butter.

MARINATED BROILED SHARK WITH ROSEMARY

Marinate shark steaks for 1 hour in a mixture of lemon juice, chopped onion, olive oil, and rosemary. Broil in a very hot, preheated broiler about 4 inches from the flame, timing according to the Canadian Theory. Baste with the sauce. Turn the fish once or twice to brown, but do not exceed total cooking time.

*How to tell the difference: mako is pale pink, softer, and has rough, slate-colored skin; swordfish has more of a coral color, is more compact, fattier, smells stronger, and has gray-brown skin.

SKATE

Very popular in France and relatively unknown in the United States, this strangely shaped, flat, scaleless fish gets its odd kite shape from the wing-like pectoral fins and the long, rather thick tail. The name ray may be used interchangeably. Its delicate taste reflects its diet, predominantly mollusks; the flavor and texture are so similar to those of scallops that often in the past, circles were punched out of skate wings and sold or used as scallops. The difference can be discerned by the graining—scallops present a vertical bunch of muscle fibers, skate does not.

A relative of the shark, the skate is the only fish that actually gains something from not being absolutely fresh; when it is held for two or three days in the refrigerator, the texture improves and the flesh becomes less tough.

Skate is usually cooked in a simple court-bouillon before being used in various recipes. To do this, cut up the skate in chunks or divide it into the two wings. (The bone looks tough but is actually very easy to cut through.) Put the pieces, as well as the central tail part, into a pan and cover with water to which have been added vinegar (1 cup of vinegar to 1 quart of water) and salt. Bring to a boil, skim, reduce heat, and poach gently, uncovered, for 15–20 minutes until tender.

Poached skate liver, served on toast, has a certain following among connoisseurs. A *fumet* made with skate has a marvelous gelatinous quality and can be clarified to make a *velouté* for *chaud-froid,* making additional gelatin unnecessary.

SKATE BEURRE NOIR

1–2 skate wings, about 2 pounds total, cut into serving pieces

Vinegar court-bouillon (see the preceding text)

BEURRE NOIR
4 tablespoons butter
2 tablespoons capers
1 tablespoon chopped parsley

2 tablespoons wine vinegar
Salt and freshly ground pepper

Wash the wings well and cut into wedges. Cook as described in the preceding text. Drain the fish on paper towels and carefully scrape away any skin. Season and keep warm on a hot serving platter.

To make the *beurre noir,* put the butter in a small skillet and cook over high heat until it foams and begins to turn a rich golden brown. *At this exact moment* take the pan off the heat. Pour over the wings and scatter over them the capers and parsley. Add the vinegar to the same skillet and cook over high heat. As soon as it bubbles, pour over the wings and serve, still sizzling, with plain boiled potatoes. Serves 4.

SMELT

Related to the salmon, smelt are another migrating coastal fish that ascend rivers and streams to spawn. There are also lake smelt, which were introduced into the Great Lakes in 1906 as a food fish for the landlocked salmon being simultaneously stocked in Michigan. The salmon died off but the smelt proliferated. In imitation of the saltwater smelt's river run, they leave the large lake each year and throng tributary streams. During a smelt run, which may last two weeks, it is not unusual to see the banks of these streams packed with people waiting to scoop up a prize catch from the water dark with fish.

The average smelt is seven to nine inches, and anyone who fancies its distinctive sweet taste can easily put away a half dozen. If very small, smelt may be eaten crisply fried, bones and all. Otherwise, the head and backbone can be easily removed as they are eaten.

Frozen freshwater smelt are available in many supermarkets. Thaw and use as you would fresh smelt.

DEEP-FRIED SMELT

3 pounds small smelt, cleaned,   Several grindings of fresh pepper
  heads off   Seasoned flour ✳
3 eggs, lightly beaten   Fresh bread crumbs
½ cup milk   Parsley sprigs
¼ cup oil   Lemon slices
½ teaspoon salt   Tartar sauce

Rinse the smelt and dry them on paper towels. In a shallow bowl combine the eggs, milk, oil, salt, and pepper. Dust the smelt with seasoned flour, dip them in the egg mixture, then roll in the bread crumbs. Put several in the basket of the deep fryer, lower the basket into oil heated to 375°. Fry for 1 minute or until golden, then drain on paper towels. Transfer the smelt as they are cooked to racks on a shallow pan and put them in a preheated very slow oven (250°) to keep them warm.

Fry the remaining smelt in the same manner. Garnish with parsley and lemon slices, serve with tartar sauce. Serves 6.

SAUTÉED SMELT

Dip the cleaned fish in seasoned flour and sauté quickly in a combination of butter and oil until golden. Serve with tartar sauce. It is not necessary to bone the fish before cooking, it can be done by the diner; the head and backbone are easily removed. You may also dip the fish in beaten egg and then in finely rolled bread crumbs after the initial flouring.

SOLE

The writer A. J. Liebling once remarked that the foods we favor most are those with the least taste, because of a basic Puritan distrust of food.

"The reason that people who detest fish often tolerate sole," he wrote, "is that sole doesn't taste very much like fish, and that even this degree of resemblance disappears when it is submerged . . . in sauce . . ."*

On the positive side, the mild taste of sole makes it well suited to elaborate saucing, causing a body of classic preparations to have evolved rather unique to that fish. The fish cookbook of Madame Prunier† (of London's famous restaurant of that name) lists *157* distinct preparations, from *Aiglon* (white wine, mushroom, onions) to *Wilhelmine* (with potatoes, a purée of *courgettes*, oysters, and cheese sauce). The combinations in between are nothing short of mind-boggling. I won't elaborate further, but you get the idea that, once you master a few *données* of poaching and saucing illustrated in the recipes that follow and in the general discussion on poaching and saucing elsewhere in this book, you can play around with combinations dictated by your preferences and leftovers to your heart's content.

For example, you could poach sole fillets and prepare a White Wine Sauce ✻ , using the reduced poaching liquid. Arrange some asparagus tips warmed in butter around your sole fillets and cover with the white wine sauce and you have *sole Argenteuil.* Do the same thing but surround the sole fillets with shrimp, mussels, and mushrooms, cover with the wine sauce, and glaze under the broiler and you have *sole dieppoise.* And so on.

Having told you all these ways to cook it, I should also mention that practically speaking, there is no true sole in the United States. The true sole, the Dover sole, is only available frozen here (though a few fine restaurants fly it in fresh), and in that form it can never be compared to a fresh fish even of less illustrious lineage. The only real American sole is so tiny that it has no commercial value and is mentioned only in passing. All the other fish known as "sole" are really varieties of flounder. A great proportion of the fish sold or appearing on restaurant menus as "sole" is the yellowtail flounder.

Lemon Sole: the American market name for the winter flounder, found from Massachusetts to Long Island. Under three pounds, these are called "blackbacks."

Gray Sole: a market name for witch flounder.

Rex Sole: a small, delicately flavored Pacific flounder.

Petrale: a large Pacific flounder, considered the most succulent of the Western flatfish.

---

*A. J. Liebling, *Between Meals,* Simon & Schuster, New York, 1962.

†*Madame Prunier's Fish Cookery Book,* translated and edited by Ambrose Heath, Hutchinson, London, 1967.

Dover Sole: the true sole, *Solea vulgaris,* found from Scandinavia to the Mediterranean. Also the name given to a Pacific flounder, usually marketed in fillets, which has no comparison to the true Dover sole.

SOLE MEUNIÈRE

The thought of a fresh Dover sole, exquisitely filleted and sizzling in its hazelnut-colored butter sauce, makes my mouth water like nothing else. Our lemon and gray sole do not have the delicacy of real channel sole, but they make an acceptable substitute, as does a very fresh plain flounder.

Although fillets may be used, the taste is heightened when a whole fish is cooked. Besides counseling you to have nothing whatever to do with frozen Dover sole, there is an additional word of warning: since butter burns easily, to serve this dish properly, you must clarify the butter first (see Index).

4 whole sole, skinned, or 8 large   Lemon quarters
   fillets   Parsley sprigs
Seasoned flour ✳
½ pound (2 sticks) butter

Clarify one stick of the butter.

Spread the seasoned flour on a piece of wax paper, turn the fish in it until well coated, shake off the excess. Heat the clarified butter in a heavy skillet, gently sauté the fish until golden brown, turning once. Remove to a hot serving platter and garnish with the lemon quarters and parsley sprigs.

Quickly wipe out the pan with paper towels, add the remaining stick of butter to the pan, and bring it rapidly to a golden-brown foam over moderately high heat. Pour it over the fish and serve immediately. Like a soufflé, this is a dish for which the diners should be waiting. Serves 4.

VARIATION: SOLE MEUNIÈRE AMANDINE

Cook 3 or 4 ounces of thinly sliced almonds in the last 4 ounces of butter until they are golden brown. Proceed as above.

SOLE MEUNIÈRE WITH MUSSELS

6 fillets of sole (about 2 pounds),   Seasoned Flour ✳
   skinned and slightly scored   6 tablespoons butter
1 quart mussels, scrubbed and   Juice and rind of ½ lemon
   debearded   1 tablespoon chopped parsley
1 *Bouquet Garni* ✳   Freshly ground pepper
1 stalk celery   Lemon quarters for garnish
2 tablespoons melted butter in a
   small ovenproof bowl

Wash the fish and pat dry. Set aside.

Put the mussels in a large, heavy pot with the *bouquet garni* and the celery. Add ½ cup water, cover, and bring to a boil. Cook for 5–8 minutes, shaking the pot occasionally, until the mussels are open. Remove them with a slotted spoon, shell them, set aside in the 2 tablespoons of melted butter, and keep warm. Discard the broth.

Coat the fish fillets in the seasoned flour. In a heavy skillet large enough to hold the fish, melt about 2 tablespoons of the 6 tablespoons of butter. When it is foaming but not brown, add the fish, skinned side down. Cook over rather brisk heat for 3–4 minutes or until golden brown, turn carefully with a spatula, and continue to sauté on the other side. Lift the fillets onto a serving dish, overlapping them slightly. Keep warm.

To serve, wipe out the skillet, reheat, and add the remaining 4 table-spoons of butter with the lemon rind. Cook until the butter just takes on color, then add the lemon juice, mussels, parsley, and pepper to taste. Shake over the heat for a few seconds, then pour over the sole. Serve very hot, with lemon quarters. Serves 4–6.

FILLETS OF SOLE BONNE FEMME

6 whole fillets of sole or flounder
  of uniform size, skinned (about
  3–3½ pounds)
1 tablespoon butter, melted
2½ tablespoons minced fresh tarragon, or 2–3 teaspoons dried
Salt and freshly ground pepper
½ pound fresh mushrooms, stems
  removed and sliced

⅓ cup milk
2½ tablespoons butter
3½ tablespoons flour
½ cup Fish Stock ❋ or clam juice
Nutmeg
Juice of 1 lemon, strained
½–⅔ cup heavy cream

Split the fish fillets in half lengthwise, wash, and dry.

Brush a baking dish 2 by 10 by 14 inches with the melted butter. Sprinkle it with half the tarragon. Score the skin side of the fillets, season with salt and pepper, and fold each in half, scored side inside. Arrange in the pre-pared dish and set aside.

Put the mushroom slices in a skillet in one layer, cover with the milk, and set over low heat. Cook for about 10–15 minutes or until they have absorbed almost all of the milk.

Preheat the oven to 350°. Prepare a *velouté* sauce: melt the butter in a heavy enamel saucepan, stir in the flour, and cook, stirring, for a few sec-onds. Remove from heat and stir in the fish stock. Return to the fire and cook, stirring, until the sauce is smooth. Add the cooked mushrooms and any milk remaining in the pan. Season with salt and pepper, a dash of nut-meg, and the lemon juice. Add the cream and blend thoroughly over mod-erate heat but do not boil. (The dish can be prepared ahead to this point.)

Pour the sauce over the fish and bake in the preheated oven for 12–15 minutes, depending on the thickness of the fish. The tops should be nicely brown. Sprinkle with the remaining tarragon and serve. Serve in the baking dish. Serves 6.

SOLE MARGUERY

When Diamond Jim Brady mentioned to the head of the Waldorf Palm Garden that *sole Marguery* could only be had at the celebrated Marguery restaurant in Paris, restaurateur Rector sent his son to Paris and had him take a job at the Marguery to purloin the recipe. When the first American *sole Marguery* was made for Brady, he was so enchanted he ate nine orders before going into the meat course.

It could not be called a simple dish, but neither is it tricky—only time-consuming. Today there are several creditable versions—the one below is a close adaptation of the lavish, rich original.

4 large whole fillets of sole
  (prefer   ably lemon sole),
  skinned (about 1½ pounds)
Salt and freshly ground pepper
7 tablespoons butter at room
  temperature
1 teaspoon chopped shallots
1 quart mussels, debearded and
  extremely well scrubbed

½ pound shrimp, shelled and
  deveined
2 cups fish *fumet* (made with the
  bones and trimmings of the sole)
2 tablespoons flour
2 large egg yolks, lightly beaten
Lemon juice

Preheat oven to 350°.

Butter a fireproof baking dish large enough to hold the fillets when folded. Butter one side of two sheets of aluminum foil; set aside. Have a serving platter warming and ready.

Put the fillets on a flat surface and cut each lengthwise with a sharp knife along the bone line running down the center, dividing them in two. This produces 8 halves. Score the fillets lightly on their milky side, season with salt and pepper, and fold in half, scored side inside. Set aside.

Melt 1 tablespoon of the butter in the baking dish on top of the stove, cook the shallots in it for 2 minutes. Put the mussels and shrimp in the baking dish and pour the fish *fumet* around them. Bring the liquid to a simmer on top of the stove, cover loosely with a sheet of buttered foil, and poach in the preheated oven for about 10 minutes or until the mussels have opened and the shrimp are pink. Remove from the oven, shell the mussels, and set them and the shrimp aside in a warm place, covered with buttered foil.

Arrange the fillets in the baking dish, bring the liquid again to a simmer on top of the stove, cover loosely with the second sheet of buttered foil, and set in the lower third of the preheated oven for 6–8 minutes. Do not overcook. The fish is done when it loses its translucence and becomes opaquely white.

Carefully transfer the fillets, using a slotted spatula, to the serving platter, surround with a double ring of mussels and shrimp, cover loosely with the foil, and keep warm while you prepare the sauce.

Strain the liquid in the baking dish through a cheesecloth-lined sieve into a saucepan, boil it down until about 1¾ cups remain. Carefully pour off and add to the saucepan any liquid that may have accumulated in the serving platter during this time.

In a 2½–3-quart saucepan melt 3 tablespoons of the butter, stir in the flour with a wooden spoon, cook for 2 minutes without letting the mixture color, then remove from heat. Pour the hot broth into the *roux* all at once, whisking until smooth. Return to moderate heat and cook until thickened, about 5 minutes. Let the sauce cool slightly. Add a bit of the sauce to the beaten egg yolks, then return the egg mixture to the sauce and whisk in thoroughly. Over very gentle heat, whisk in the remaining butter, a tablespoon at a time. Season to taste with salt, pepper, and a dash of lemon juice. Heat the sauce but do not let it even approach a boil Nap the fish and shellfish with the sauce, evening it out if necessary with the back of a spoon, and run the dish under a hot broiler for 3 or 4 minutes to glaze lightly. Serve immediately. Serves 4.

FILLETS OF SOLE DUGLÈRÉ

4 whole fillets of sole, taken from 2 1½-pound whole soles, skinned, bones reserved
1 shallot, chopped
6 peppercorns
½ bay leaf
¼ teaspoon salt
1 cup water
1 cup dry white wine
Salt and freshly ground white pepper

2 medium ripe tomatoes, blanched and peeled, or 3 canned peeled tomatoes
3 tablespoons butter
2 tablespoons flour
½ cup heavy cream
Dash of cayenne pepper
Lemon juice
1 tablespoon chopped parsley

Make a stock by combining in a saucepan the fishbones, broken into 2 or 3 pieces, the shallot, peppercorns, bay leaf, salt, 1 cup of water, and wine. Bring to a boil, lower heat, and simmer, covered, for 20 minutes. Strain.

Preheat oven to 350°. Butter a 12-inch oval ovenproof dish. Cut the fillets in half lengthwise (you will now have 8 pieces). Score them slightly on the milky side, season with salt and pepper, fold in half, scored side inside with the pointed end on top. Arrange in the prepared dish, add the stock, bring to a simmer on top of the stove, cover with buttered foil, and poach in the preheated oven for 8–10 minutes.

Cut the tomatoes into quarters, pick out the seeds with the tip of a pointed knife, and cut each quarter into 3 lengthwise strips. Set aside.

When the fish is done, drain the cooking liquid into a 3-quart saucepan, replace the foil cover, and keep the fish warm while you prepare the sauce.

Bring the poaching liquid to a boil and cook rapidly over high heat until reduced to about 1 cup. Add any liquid that has collected in the fish dish during this time.

Melt 2 tablespoons of the butter in another saucepan, stir in the flour, and cook for 2–3 minutes without letting the mixture become more than pale blond in color. Remove from heat and whisk in the poaching liquid, stirring until smooth and thick. Return to heat, bring to a boil, and cook, stirring, for 2 minutes (the sauce will be very thick). Once more stir in any liquid that has collected in the fish dish, then stir in the cream. Season to taste with salt, pepper, a dash of cayenne, and a few drops of lemon juice. Swirl in the remaining tablespoon of butter, then fold in the tomatoes and parsley, spoon over the fish, and serve at once. Serves 6–8 as a first course, 4 as a main course.

FILLETS OF SOLE MORNAY

Poach 1½–2 pounds of skinned sole fillets in a shallow *gratin* dish, using the method described in the preceding recipe for Sole Duglère. Cover with Mornay Gratin for Poached Fillets (see Index) and proceed as directed in that recipe.

FILLETS OF SOLE FLORENTINE

Poach 1½–2 pounds skinned fillets of sole in a shallow dish, using the method described in the recipe for Sole Duglère. Arrange in a flameproof serving dish on a bed of hot, buttered chopped spinach. Nap the top with Mornay Gratin for Poached Fillets (see Index) and proceed as directed in that recipe.

FILLETS OF SOLE IN CHAMPAGNE SAUCE

8 whole fillets of sole, skinned	Juice of ½ lemon
3 shallots or 1 onion, minced	6 tablespoons butter
½ pound mushrooms, sliced	3 tablespoons flour
1 teaspoon salt	2 egg yolks
¼ teaspoon white pepper	½ cup cream
½ bottle champagne	Lemon wedges for garnish

Preheat oven to 400°. Butter a large baking dish.

Divide the fillets in half the long way and roll them. Sprinkle the shallots and mushrooms over the bottom of the prepared baking dish, place the rolled fish, cut side down, on this bed, leaving a little space for the fish to swell. Sprinkle with the salt and white pepper, add the champagne and lemon juice. Butter a large sheet of wax paper, cover the fish with it, and bake for about 20 minutes in a preheated oven or until fish flakes but is still firm. Remove to a heated serving dish and keep warm.

Bring the juices in the baking dish to a boil on top of the stove, cook to reduce a little, about 5 minutes. Meanwhile, in a small saucepan melt the butter, add the flour, and cook gently for 2 minutes without letting the mixture color. Add the pan juices and cook the sauce, stirring until thickened. Also add any liquid that has collected in the fish dish.

Beat the egg yolks and add the cream. Warm the egg-cream mixture with a little of the sauce, then add the mixture to the balance of the sauce. Cook, stirring, over a low heat until smooth and thickened. Do not boil. Correct seasoning and pour over the fish. Garnish with lemon wedges and, if desired, an empty but intact lobster shell. Serves 8.

DÉLICES DE SOLE BANNARO (with Bananas and Almonds)

1½–2 pounds fillet of lemon or
   gray sole, skinned
½ cup Seasoned Flour ✤
6 tablespoons fresh bread crumbs
4 tablespoons grated Parmesan
   cheese
1 egg, well beaten
3 tablespoons vegetable oil, or
   more

4 tablespoons butter, or more
2 large or 3 small firm ripe
   bananas, or 1 ripe plantain, cut
   diagonally into ¾-inch slices
1 tablespoon lemon juice
¼ cup blanched and slivered
   almonds

Wash and pat dry each fillet of sole. Cut 1 fillet along the dark pink line down the center, making 2 strips, then cut each strip on the diagonal into finger-like pieces about 2 inches wide. Repeat with the remaining fillets.

Spread the seasoned flour in a plate. Mix the bread crumbs and cheese together in a bowl. Roll the fish pieces in the seasoned flour, brush with the egg, then coat with the bread crumb-cheese mixture, pressing onto the fish with a spatula.

Heat the oil and 3 tablespoons of the butter in a large, heavy skillet, sauté the breaded fish fingers until crisp and golden brown. Transfer to a hot serving dish and keep warm. Depending on the size of the skillet and the number of fish fingers, this may have to be done in several batches, adding more oil and butter if necessary.

Melt the remaining tablespoon of butter in a separate 10-inch skillet, and when it foams add the banana slices, sauté quickly until brown. Add the lemon juice and the almonds and toss. Arrange the bananas and almonds around the fish and serve very hot. Serves 4–6.

CRAB-STUFFED FILLETS OF SOLE

4 tablespoons butter
1 tablespoon oil
1 small onion, minced
½ cup packaged seasoned bread stuffing
½ pound crab meat, picked over
⅔ cup chicken broth
¼ cup white wine

2 tablespoons chopped parsley
Thyme
8 small fillets of flounder or sole, skinned
Salt
¼ cup fresh bread crumbs
1 teaspoon cornstarch
Juice of ½ lemon

Preheat oven to 350°. Butter a 9 by 12-inch baking dish.

Heat 2 tablespoons of the butter and the oil in a 10-inch skillet. Sauté the onion in the mixture until transparent. Add the bread stuffing and toss until the oil is absorbed. Add the crab meat, ¼ cup of the chicken broth, the wine, parsley, and thyme, stir, bring to a boil, and cook over high heat for 1–2 minutes until the liquid is reduced slightly. Taste for seasoning. Let the mixture cool.

Wash and dry the fillets, salt them on the outside, and place them on a board, salted side down. Divide the crab mixture between the fillets placing it at the narrow end. Roll up each fillet, fasten with toothpicks if necessary, and arrange in the prepared baking dish. Sprinkle with the bread crumbs and dot with the remaining 2 tablespoons of butter.

Dissolve the cornstarch in ¼ cup of the chicken broth, then add the remaining broth, stirring until smooth. Add the lemon juice, pour the sauce around the fish, and bake for 20 minutes, basting from time to time. Serves 4–6.

TURBAN OF SOLE WITH SHRIMP MOUSSE AND SAUCE AURORE

Though long and apparently complicated, this recipe is really quite easy. The result is a light, elegant dish, ideal for lunch or as a first course at a formal dinner.

8 medium fillets of sole of uniform size, skinned (about 2–2¼ pounds)

1 tablespoon lemon juice
Salt and white pepper
1 tablespoon butter

MOUSSE FILLING
¾ pound raw shrimp, shelled and deveined, shells reserved
1 large egg white

1 scant cup heavy cream
¾ teaspoon salt
2 teaspoons tomato paste

1 tablespoon chopped parsley

2 tablespoons dry sherry

SAUCE AURORE

2 cups water
1 onion, thinly sliced
2 sprigs of parsley
6 peppercorns
2 tablespoons butter
½ teaspoon salt
2 tablespoons flour
½ cup tomato paste
½ cup heavy cream

2 egg yolks
Salt and freshly ground pepper
Cayenne pepper
½ pound fresh mushrooms
2 tablespoons butter
A good squeeze of lemon juice
1 bunch of fresh watercress or
   parsley

Butter a 5-cup ring mold 2 inches deep and about 8½ inches in diameter. Set aside.

Rinse the fillets in cold water and dry them. Sprinkle with the lemon juice, salt, and white pepper. Arrange them in U-shapes, in the mold, so that the ends of the fillets drape over the outside and inside of the mold. The light-colored side of each fillet should be face down, and the narrow end pointing to the center of the mold. Depending on the fish size, the last fillet may be cut in half lengthwise to accommodate it.

PREPARE THE MOUSSE: Cut the shrimp into chunks, place in the container of a blender or food processor, with the egg white, cream, salt, tomato paste, parsley, and sherry. Blend for several minutes, pushing the mixture down with a rubber spatula if necessary, until it is completely smooth. The mousse, which at this point is an undistinguished gray, becomes a beautiful pink when cooked. Fill the fish-lined mold with the mixture, rap it sharply on the counter top to settle, and smooth the top with the spatula. Fold the ends of the fillets over the top of the filling, lay a round of buttered wax paper over the top. (The dish may be prepared ahead to this point and refrigerated until needed.)

MAKE THE SAUCE: Make a stock by combining the reserved shrimp shells with the 2 cups of water, onion, parsley, peppercorns, and salt in a deep pot. Bring to a boil, skim, lower the heat, and simmer for 20 minutes. Strain through a cheesecloth, return to the fire, and reduce over high heat to 1 cup. (Should you have fish stock on hand, you may omit this step.)

Make a *velouté* sauce, which is the base of the *sauce aurore:* melt the butter in a heavy-bottomed saucepan, stir in the flour, and cook over low heat for 1 minute without letting the mixture take on much color. After it stops bubbling, pour in the hot fish stock, whisking constantly. Return to moderate heat, bring to a simmer, and cook for 10 minutes. You now have about 1 cup of *velouté*.

Combine the *velouté* sauce with the tomato paste. Mix the cream and egg yolks in a small bowl, warm with a little sauce, then put back into the sauce.

Stir over medium heat until smooth and thick but do not let the mixture boil. Season with salt, pepper, and several dashes of cayenne. Set the sauce aside covered with plastic wrap until serving time.

Preheat oven to 350°. Place a pan large enough to hold the ring mold in the oven on the center rack and fill it with ¾ inch of hot water. Put the mold in the pan and bake for 30 minutes.

PREPARE THE MUSHROOMS: While the *turban* is cooking, wipe the mushrooms with a damp cloth and slice thickly. Sauté in the butter until just tender and season with the lemon juice, salt, and pepper, set aside.

Put the sauce in the top of a double boiler or on an asbestos pad and warm over very gentle heat. Do not let it boil or it will curdle (see the note below).

Remove the *turban* from the oven, remove the wax paper. Invert a serving platter on top of the mold; holding the platter down tightly, tilt, and pour into a bowl the liquid that has collected inside the mold. Add to the warm sauce, turn the whole thing over, and turn out the *turban* onto the platter. Pour off any liquid that accumulates on the platter into the sauce, blend well with a whisk until smooth.

Decorate the *turban* by filling the center with the watercress or parsley. Ring the outside with the warm sautéed mushrooms. Spoon a bit of the sauce over the fish, allowing it to run down the sides, and pass the rest in a sauceboat. Serves 6.

NOTE: If, in spite of your precautions, this or any other egg yolk sauce should curdle from too much heat, beat one egg yolk in a mixing bowl and beat the curdled sauce gradually into it until it becomes smooth again.

SOLE IN ESCABECHE

3 tablespoons butter
¾ cup olive oil
6 small fillets of sole, skinned
Flour
Salt and freshly ground pepper
1 medium onion, thinly sliced and
　separated into rings
1 green pepper, seeded and cut
　into thin rings

1 clove garlic, finely chopped
½ cup orange juice
Juice of 2 limes
¼ teaspoon Tabasco sauce
Orange slices
Lime slices
1 tablespoon grated orange rind
Chopped fresh coriander or
　parsley

Heat the butter and ¼ cup of the oil in a skillet large enough to hold the fish. Lightly dredge the fillets with flour, sauté them until delicately brown on both sides and tender. Season to taste with salt and pepper.

Arrange the fillets in a flat serving dish and scatter over them the onion rings, pepper rings, and garlic. Combine the remaining ½ cup oil, orange juice, lime juice, Tabasco, and salt and pepper to taste. Blend well and pour over the fish while it is still warm. Cover and refrigerate for 12–24 hours.

To serve, garnish with orange slices, lime slices, scatter the orange rind and chopped coriander or parsley over the top (you may also top with additional green pepper rings). Serves 4 as a first course.

REX SOLE

½ cup flour
½ teaspoon salt or to taste
Several grindings of fresh pepper
½ cup milk
A 2-pound rex sole, whole, cleaned

¼ cup oil
¼ cup butter, melted
Lemon wedges
½ cup chopped parsley

Season the flour with salt and pepper, put it in a shallow dish. Put the milk in a separate shallow dish. Dip the sole first in the milk, then the flour, shake off excess.

In a heavy 12-inch skillet heat the oil over high heat until hot but not smoky. Add the sole and brown quickly, about 2–3 minutes on each side. Remove the skillet from heat, let the fish stand, covered, to keep warm for 15 minutes. Bone by slicing lengthwise along the backbone. Lift off the fillets, remove the dark skin and arrange them on heated plates. Pour melted butter over the fish, garnish with lemon wedges, and sprinkle with chopped parsley. Serves 4.

NOTE: This recipe may also be used to prepare 2 pounds of sand dabs.

SAND DABS

The smallest member of the flounder/sole family, sand dabs, like rex sole, are unique to California waters. These delicate fish have a sweet flavor enhanced by quick sautéing in clarified butter or oil (see the preceding recipe for Rex Sole). They can be baked, but the above method seems to best bring out their indescribable flavor. They also lend themselves to the subtlety of Chinese cooking, as in the recipe below.

SAND DABS ORIENTAL STYLE

3 pounds sand dabs, cleaned,
    whole
1 tablespoon peeled, grated ginger
    root
2 teaspoons salt
4 whole scallions

1 quart boiling water
⅓ cup vegetable oil, heated
⅓ cup soy sauce
6 additional scallions for garnish,
    ends fluted (optional)

Wash and dry the fish. Arrange on a heatproof platter. Sprinkle with ginger and salt. Put the whole scallions on top of the fish, place the platter on a trivet or rack inside a steamer or large roasting pan. Carefully add the boiling water. Cover and cook *over* boiling water for 5–10 minutes, depending on the size of the fish. Remove it from the steamer, discard the cooked onions, and drain off any water that accumulates on the platter. Combine the oil and soy sauce and pour the sauce over the fish; garnish with the fluted scallions. Serves 6.

SWORDFISH

Concern about high levels of mercury present in this predator fish has done little to decrease its popularity. There are a number of pros and cons regarding the implications of the mercury content of the fish; in Great Britain the feeling is that the amount of the fish any one person eats does not approach the danger potential. If you are super-cautious, on the other hand, you will want to avoid it.

Most of the swordfish on the market today is frozen; until recently most frozen swordfish came from Japan, although the fish are taken in both Atlantic and Pacific waters. It is primarily to the Japanese fish that the controversial federal ban applies, and this fish is no longer imported.

Swordfish is occasionally found fresh, in steaks and boneless chunks. Fresh swordfish, generally more expensive than frozen, is available in the West primarily from August to October; in the East, through the summer from late June on. Two pounds of fresh swordfish cut into one-inch steaks will serve 4. As frozen steaks are often thawed before being put out in fish markets, it is advisable not to freeze them for home storage unless you are absolutely sure of their freshness.

Swordfish is rich in flavor with firm, meat-like flesh that retains its firmness when cooked. The only fish comparable in texture and flavor is mako shark, which has been known to be passed off as swordfish in some markets (for reference to a discussion of the difference see the Index).

The delicate flavor of swordfish should not be masked with elaborate saucing, and generally the most popular cooking method is broiling, although it can also be barbecued, baked, and oven-fried.

MEXICAN BAKED SWORDFISH

4 swordfish steaks, 1 inch thick
   (about ½ pound each)
Salt and freshly ground pepper
6 tablespoons olive oil

½ cup sliced green onions
2 tablespoons chopped parsley
Tomato wedges for garnish
Lemon or lime wedges for garnish

Preheat oven to 350°.

Season the fish highly with salt and pepper.

Put half the olive oil in a baking dish, brush the balance thickly on both sides of the steaks. Arrange them in a baking dish and sprinkle the green onions on top. Bake, uncovered, for about 20 minutes. Transfer to a heated serving platter, sprinkle with the chopped parsley, and garnish with the tomato and citrus wedges. Serves 4.

BROILED SWORDFISH

As swordfish tends to be dry, the steaks should be at least ¾ inch thick and frequently basted while cooking. They are delicious broiled and basted with Lemon Dill Butter ✷ , Anchovy Butter ✷ , or Garlic Butter ✷ , or in the teriyaki sauce as given in Teriyaki Barbecued Albacore Steak ✷ .

TURKISH SWORDFISH WITH TOMATOES

2 pounds swordfish steaks
¼ cup olive oil
4 large fresh tomatoes, peeled, seeded, and chopped

1 teaspoon salt
Freshly ground pepper
¼ cup Fish Stock ✷ or water

Preheat oven to 350°

Heat the olive oil in a heavy saucepan, add the tomatoes and the salt, and cook for 5–6 minutes over moderate heat, stirring frequently.

Arrange half of the tomatoes on the bottom of a shallow ovenproof baking dish large enough to hold the fish. Season the fish with salt and pepper, pour the balance of the tomatoes over them. Add the fish stock or water, bake in the middle of the oven, uncovered, for 40 minutes. Serves 6.

SWORDFISH STEAKS WITH LEMON AND CAPERS, SICILIAN STYLE

6 swordfish steaks, 1 inch thick
    (about 3 pounds total)
Salt and freshly ground pepper
Flour
½ cup olive oil

Juice of 2 lemons
½ cup chopped parsley
½ cup capers, drained and
    chopped if very large

Wash and dry the steaks well with paper towels, season both sides with salt and pepper. Spread flour on a sheet of foil, dip each steak into it, coating both sides well and shaking off excess.

Select 2 heavy skillets that together will accommodate the 6 steaks without touching. Divide the olive oil between the skillets and heat. Add the steaks and cook for about 8 minutes on the first side and 6–8 minutes on the second, turning them carefully with a wide spatula, until they are golden brown and crusty on both sides. Transfer to a heated serving platter, sprinkle each with lemon juice, parsley, and capers, and serve immediately. Serves 6.

TILEFISH

The violet-tinged tilefish, with their distinctive tile-like yellow spots, made a sudden first appearance off the New England coast in 1879. Three years later they totally and mysteriously disappeared, to return just as mysteriously a decade later. Found only in very deep water just off the continental shelf, they are even now only netted occasionally, which explains their erratic market appearance in Eastern markets. The average market tilefish runs about six pounds.

The flesh is dense, sweet, moist, and well textured, not unlike that of lobster. Its unusual firmness makes it a good choice for soups and stews, although its flavor, which reflects its predominantly crustacean diet, may suggest loftier uses. It may be used in any recipe calling for cod, though its flavor is more pronounced. (I especially recommend using it in the recipe for Cod, Roman Style.) It also adapts well to highly seasoned sauces.

A Pacific tilefish, known as "ocean whitefish," occasionally appears in Western markets.

TILEFISH IN RED SAUCE

This recipe is an adaptation of an Algerian one for *merou,* or grouper, a member of the sea bass family, very prolific in North African waters. Needless to say, the method of preparation suits our own grouper as well as sea bass.

½ cup of olive oil
1 pound ripe tomatoes, peeled, seeded, and sliced, or 1 2-pound can, drained
6 cloves garlic, crushed
1 small hot red pepper, diced, or 1 dried hot red pepper, crumbled

Salt and freshly ground pepper
6 1¼-inch tilefish steaks, about 2 pounds total
2 tablespoons chopped fresh coriander leaves (or use parsley)
1 tablespoon paprika

Preheat oven to 400°.

Pour ¼ cup of the olive oil in the bottom of a shallow flameproof baking dish large enough to hold the fish steaks. Cover with half the tomato slices, the garlic, and red pepper. Season lightly. Put the fish steaks on this bed, cover with remaining tomato slices, season again, and sprinkle with the coriander. Mix the paprika together with the remaining ¼ cup of olive oil, drizzle over the fish. If it has landed in lumps, smooth over the fish with the back of a spoon. Cook over fairly high heat on top of the stove for 5 minutes, then cover with foil and bake for 20 minutes. Serves 4–6.

Cold Tilefish Roman Style

Follow the recipe for Cod Roman Style (see Index) and serve at room temperature.

TUNA

Tuna is a fish primarily associated with cans, although it can be found fresh on the West Coast during summer and fall and is caught by many Western game fishermen. Fresh tuna may be baked, broiled, or steamed but should always be skinned before cooking. Barbecued skinned tuna steaks are particularly good, and poached fresh tuna is even tastier than canned. The meat can be used any way you would use canned tuna. Occasionally fresh tuna can be found in metropolitan Eastern markets.

Tunas can weigh as much as 1,500 pounds; the Pacific albacore, or longfin tuna (generally the one available fresh), runs to 25 pounds. It is marketed fresh and canned and, as the only white meat tuna, carries a premium price. The albacore loin is delicious poached, as are the steaks, barbecued.

The yellowfin tuna (the *ahi* of Hawaii) is the backbone of the California tuna industry, with meat lighter in color than the giant Atlantic bluefin, and an important market fish in Spain, Portugal, and Italy. Another species, the dark, strong-tasting bonito, found in the Atlantic and Pacific (also known as false albacore or little tunny) is a small tuna, usually smoked or brined.

Canned tuna is put up in water, brine, cottonseed or corn oil, and is packed as follows: *fancy* means large pieces of meat; *flakes* are smaller pieces though of the same quality as fancy; Italian tuna, or *tonno*, is skipjack tuna packed in olive oil and is a darker meat; *light* tuna is usually yellowfin, skipjack, or bluefin; *white* tuna is albacore.

MARINATED TUNA, MEDITERRANEAN STYLE

6 tablespoons olive oil
½ teaspoon lemon juice
2 anchovies, mashed
½ teaspoon salt
Freshly ground pepper
Several gratings of nutmeg
1½ pounds fresh tuna in one slice
2 medium onions, chopped

3 cloves garlic, chopped
¾ cup chopped and drained
 tomatoes
½ cup white wine
½ cup chicken broth or water
2 tablespoons capers
A small handful of parsley and 2
 cloves garlic, chopped together

In a glass dish, combine the oil, lemon juice, anchovies, salt, several grindings of pepper, and the nutmeg. Add the tuna and let marinate for 2 hours.

Drain off the marinade into a skillet large enough to hold the tuna; heat and in it cook the onions and garlic until lightly browned. Stir in the tomatoes, lay the tuna on top. Cover, bring to a gentle simmer, and cook for 15–20 minutes. Remove the fish with a slotted spatula and keep warm.

Add the wine and broth or water to the skillet, mix them in, and cook, uncovered, over low heat for 30–40 minutes until the sauce is well reduced and thickened. Stir occasionally to prevent scorching.

Return the tuna to the skillet, cook, covered, over moderate heat for about 5 minutes. Transfer the fish to a heated platter and spoon the sauce over. Sprinkle with the capers and the parsley-garlic mix. Serve with piping hot rice. Serves 4.

TERIYAKI BARBECUED ALBACORE STEAK

$2/3$ cup soy sauce
$1/3$ cup medium-dry sherry
1 tablespoon sugar
1 clove garlic, crushed

2 teaspoons finely grated fresh
  ginger root or 1 tablespoon
  minced preserved ginger
A 4-pound albacore steak

In a small saucepan combine the soy sauce, sherry, sugar, garlic, and ginger. Bring to a boil over moderate heat, then strain into a shallow pan. Marinate the fish steak for about 30 minutes, turning several times. Cook on a well-oiled grill, brushing frequently with the sauce. If desired, the remaining marinade may be served in small bowls as a dipping sauce. Serves 6.

TUNA SALAD

The ubiquitous tuna salad can range from merely canned tuna mixed with mayonnaise to the following flavorful combination favored by the children at our house: to 1 can of water-packed tuna, flaked (if only oil-packed is available, rinse it in a strainer under cold running water), add 1–2 stalks of celery, chopped; 1 hard-cooked egg, chopped; 2 tablespoons of sweet pickle relish; 1 teaspoon of very finely minced onion; and enough mayonnaise to bind. Blend well and refrigerate for at least an hour before serving.

TUNA AND WHITE BEAN SALAD

12 ounces dried white kidney or
  navy beans (see the note p.177)
$1/2$ cup olive oil
2 tablespoons lemon juice
$1/2$ teaspoon salt
Freshly ground pepper
$1/4$ cup finely chopped scallions
  (white and part of the green) or
  shallots

1 7-ounce can tuna (preferably
  imported dark meat type in
  olive oil)
2 tablespoons chopped parsley
Lemon wedges

Put the dried beans in a colander, wash under cold running water until the water draining off runs clear. Put the beans in a 3- or 4-quart pot, add enough cold water to cover by about an inch. Bring the water to a boil and boil for 2 minutes. Remove from the heat and let the beans soak, uncovered, for an hour. Then bring again to a boil, lower the heat, partially cover, and simmer the beans for 1½ hours or until they are just tender but the skins have not burst. Add more water if needed during the cooking time to keep the beans covered with liquid. Drain and spread on a towel to dry.

Make the dressing by mixing the oil, lemon juice, salt, and several grindings of pepper together in a large mixing bowl. Add the still-warm beans and toss gently with a wooden spoon until they are thoroughly coated with the dressing. Stir in the scallions, set the beans aside for an hour, then taste for seasoning. It is quite likely because of their absorbent nature that they will need some salt, pepper, and lemon juice.

Drain the tuna and break it up into large pieces. Fold these gently into the beans.

To serve, mound the fish-bean mixture on individual plates and top with chopped parsley. Serve garnished with lemon wedges. Serves 4.

NOTE: 3 cups of very well-drained canned cannellini beans, which need not be cooked, may be substituted for the beans in the above recipe.

SALADE NICOISE

For best results this salad must be dressed and assembled at the last minute, although all the ingredients can be gathered and some preparation done earlier. The true *salade niçoise* does not include lettuce, but I prefer it with lettuce when served as a luncheon dish.

1 pound string beans, cooked, blanched, and at room temperature
1 cup Vinaigrette Dressing ❋ (if omitting lettuce, reduce to ¾ cup)
3 ripe tomatoes in quarters
1 head lettuce, Boston or romaine, leaves separated, washed, and dried (optional)

2 cups cold French Potato Salad ❋ (recipe given p. 178)
A 7½-ounce can tuna, drained
3 hard-cooked eggs, quartered
1 can flat anchovy fillets, drained
½ purple onion in paper thin rings
½ green pepper cut in thin rings (optional)
4 ounces small black olives, preferably cured in oil

Place the string beans in a bowl other than the salad bowl, toss with several tablespoons of the dressing. Do the same in another bowl with the tomatoes.

Place the lettuce in a salad bowl and toss with about ¼ cup of the dressing. Mound the potato salad in the center of the bowl, arrange the beans, tomatoes, tuna, and eggs in clusters or any design you wish around the potato salad. Lay the anchovies over, add the onion rings and the green pepper rings. Decorate with the black olives. Spoon the remaining dressing over all and serve. Serves 4–6.

FRENCH POTATO SALAD

5–6 medium potatoes, skins on, scrubbed
Salt

¼ cup chicken broth or stock
⅓ cup Vinaigrette Dressing ✿
3 tablespoons chopped parsley

Place the potatoes in boiling salted water to cover, cook until just tender. Do not overcook or salad will be mushy. Drain them, and when they can be handled, peel them. Cut into ¼-inch slices and immediately pour chicken broth over the still-warm slices, toss gently. Let sit a few minutes so the potatoes can absorb the broth.

Pour the vinaigrette dressing over and add the parsley. Toss again gently and serve. Serves 4 to 6.

WEAKFISH

The only thing "weak" about this curiously named fish is the tender flesh of its delicate mouth tissue, which is easily torn by hooks. Its fighting ability delights fishermen and makes it a favorite light-tackle game fish. The weakfish, also known as gray sea trout and squeteague, is a member of the drum family, closely related to the striped bass. The average size is one to three pounds, although big tide runners may weigh up to twelve.

Weakfish were so prolific in Atlantic coastal waters in the 1860s that they were netted like herring. By the turn of the century, they were unknown and appeared only occasionally during the next five decades, so one finds no references to them in cookbooks before the mid 1970s. They have recently made an astounding comeback and at the moment are again considered prolific.

Weakfish is extremely versatile and may be used in almost all recipes calling for striped bass, although I find that the flesh, which is not as white as bass, tends to look muddy when poached. However, the beautiful shape, tender flesh, and compact size make it ideal for baking and stuffing whole. Fillets are good broiled or, when dipped in egg and flour, deep-fried and served with tomato sauce.

BAKED WEAKFISH STUFFED WITH CRAB

This is my favorite way to prepare weakfish; it and crab seem to have a particularly pleasant affinity for each other.

A 3–4-pound weakfish, whole,   ½ lemon
   head and backbone removed   Salt and freshly ground pepper

CRAB STUFFING:
6 tablespoons butter   ½ cup chicken broth
1 small onion, minced   ½ cup white wine
½ cup packaged, seasoned bread   2 tablespoons chopped parsley
   stuffing   ¼ teaspoon dried thyme
½ pound crab meat, picked over   Lemon slices for garnish

Preheat oven to 375°.

Wash the fish, rub all over with the cut lemon, dry well with paper towels, and season inside and out with salt and pepper.

Prepare the stuffing: heat 2 tablespoons of the butter in a 10-inch skillet. Sauté the onion in the butter until transparent. Add the stuffing and toss. Add the crab meat, ¼ cup of the chicken broth, ¼ cup of the wine, the parsley, and thyme. Stir, bring to a boil, and cook over high heat for 1–2 minutes until liquid is reduced slightly. Season the stuffing to taste and let cool.

Stuff the cavity of the fish, sew the opening closed or secure with skewers and twine.

Line a baking pan large enough to hold the fish with heavy duty foil. Melt the remaining butter in the pan, add the fish, and bake for 15 minutes, basting once or twice with the butter. Lower oven heat to 325°, add the remaining broth and wine to the pan, baste the fish, and bake for 15 minutes more, basting frequently. Remove the fish to a heated serving platter with the aid of two spatulas. Garnish with lemon slices and serve with the pan juices. Serves 4.

MENEMSHA STUFFED WEAKFISH

A 4–5-pound weakfish, split,   4 slices bacon
   boned, head and tail removed ½ cup freshly chopped onions
1 teaspoon coarse salt   ½ cup finely chopped celery
½ teaspoon freshly ground pepper 1 tablespoon chopped parsley
2 cloves garlic, pressed   4 tablespoons butter, melted
2–3 tablespoons olive oil   ¾ cup dry white wine
2 cups fresh bread crumbs made   Lemon wedges and parsley sprigs
   from home-style white bread   for garnish

Preheat oven to 400°.

Select a baking pan large enough to hold the fish (try the broiler pan lined with foil and place the fish diagonally). Wash the fish and wipe dry. In a small bowl, mix the salt, pepper, garlic, and enough oil to make a moist paste, rub this over the inside and outside of the fish.

Put the bread crumbs in a bowl. Sauté the bacon in a skillet until crisp, drain, and crumble it into the crumbs. Pour off all but 2 tablespoons of the fat. Sauté the onions and celery over moderate heat until the onions are pale gold. Add the vegetables to the bread crumb mixture, then stir in the parsley, half the melted butter, and enough wine, say 3 tablespoons, to moisten and bind the stuffing. Toss lightly with two forks and stuff the mixture into the cavity of the fish, sew the opening, or skewer and truss.

Brush the baking pan with the remaining butter, put the fish in it, and bake for 30 minutes. Pour the remaining wine over the fish, reduce heat to 350°, and bake for about 20 minutes longer, basting several times with pan juices. Transfer the fish to a warm serving platter, garnish with lemon wedges and parsley. Serves 6.

BAKED STUFFED WHOLE WEAKFISH

Follow the recipe for Jean Goddard's Stuffed Bass ❁ , substituting a weakfish for the bass.

WEAKFISH VERACRUZANO

A whole 4–5-pound weakfish is impressive and delicious prepared with tomatoes, hot peppers, olives, and capers, following the recipe for Striped Bass Veracruzano ❁ .

WEAKFISH BAKED WITH MUSSELS AND SHRIMP IN WHITE WINE

Follow the recipe for Striped Bass Dieppoise ❁ , substituting a similar-size weakfish for the bass.

WHITEBAIT

Although these small fish were labeled as a separate species by no less an eminence than William Yarrell, the nineteenth-century ichthyologist, they are in fact simply the small fry of a number of fish, including herrings, anchovies, sand launce (or "sand eel") and silversides. Ichthyology aside, they are utterly delicious when dusted with flour and crispy fried—truly a gourmet's treat.

Because of their small size, they are marketed whole and are cooked without gutting. To cook whitebait, shake up handfuls of the fish in a paper bag containing seasoned flour, then toss in a sieve to get rid of the excess. Fry or deep-fry small amounts at a time in hot oil for a minute or so, until they are golden and crisp. Remove, drain well, sprinkle with salt, and serve garnished with fried parsley and a sprinkle of cayenne if desired. Serving them on a white napkin is a nice touch. In the South of France they are often doused with lemon juice or vinegar before flouring, then sautéed in shallow fat in which a little minced onion has been cooked.

Some people prefer to roll them in cornmeal instead of flour. On eastern Long Island they are floured, dipped in milk and then cracker dust before cooking, which I find very messy.

One rarely sees whitebait on menus here, except in a couple of famous East Coast fish restaurants. Yet they can be found for the netting in almost any saltwater bay along either of our coasts, especially in fall and winter. They range in size from 1½ inches to 4 inches, averaging about 2 inches. Enormous shoals of them are netted in England from September to April, and also in France, where they are known as *blanchailles*. If you are abroad and lucky enough to see them on a menu, order them at once. They are one of those unpredictable natural occurrences like a rainbow—to be enjoyed when you find it.

WHITING

Whiting is the market name for a member of the cod family called the silver hake, which frequents Eastern coastal waters from New England to Virginia. Perhaps because of its slightly coarse flesh it is considered an inelegant fish; a century ago, it was simply discarded and is not even listed in many older cookbooks. Its versatility makes it very important commercially; it is cheap and plentiful, generally about half the price of flounder. Its flavor is thought to be delicate to insipid, depending upon whom you are talking to. The fact that it crumbles makes simple preparations necessary; it is especially good for frying. Small whiting can be split and broiled.

What the Europeans call whiting is actually a slightly different fish, called *merlan* in French, and *merlano* in Italian. The French *merlu* is yet another hake, the equivalent of *merluza*, a hake highly esteemed in Spain. Our whiting is most similar to the Italian *merluzzo*, another hake variant.

WHITING WITH ZUCCHINI

A virtuous dish: pleasant, extremely simple to prepare, economical, and easy to digest.

4 whiting fillets, skinned, approximately 4–6 ounces each
4 tablespoons butter
Salt and freshly ground pepper
⅓ cup grated aged Parmesan cheese

3 small zucchini, washed and sliced into thin rounds
¼ cup minced parsley

Preheat oven to 375°.
Wash the fish and pat dry. Butter a shallow baking dish with 1 tablespoon

of the butter, arrange the fish fillets in it. Season with salt and pepper, sprinkle with half the cheese. Lay the zucchini rounds over the fish, sprinkle with the remaining cheese, and season again with salt and pepper. Sprinkle with the parsley and dot with the remaining butter. Bake in the upper third of the oven for 20 minutes. Baste once. Serve with hot boiled rice. Serves 4.

BROILED WHITING

2 pounds whiting fillets, skinned   Bread crumbs fried in butter
Salt and freshly ground pepper   Lemon wedges
Melted butter

Preheat the broiler.

Sprinkle the fillets with salt and pepper, brush with melted butter, and broil about 4 inches from the flame, timing according to the Canadian Theory. Halfway through, turn them, brush again with melted butter, and complete cooking. Sprinkle with fried crumbs and serve with lemon wedges. Serves 4–6.

DEEP-FRIED WHITING

1½ pounds whiting fillets, skinned   2 cups Basic Batter ✿
Lemon juice   Deep fat for frying
Seasoned Flour

Lay the fillets on a plate and sprinkle lightly with lemon juice. Refrigerate for about 1 hour. Dry with paper towels, cut each fillet into diagonal strips about 1 inch wide.

Heat the fat to 375°. Roll the fish in the seasoned flour. Put them into the batter, turn them around lightly with a slotted spatula. Lift out and lower carefully into the fat (if you are handy with chopsticks, they work well for this; otherwise try two wooden spoon handles). Fry only 6–8 pieces at a time. Lift out and drain on paper towels on a wire rack set on a piece of foil or cookie sheet. Keep warm until all are done. Serve with a tomato sauce or tartar sauce. Serves 4.

FIVE
Freshwater Fish

CARP

The credentials of the carp, largest member of the *Cyprinidae,* or minnow, family, are ancient and venerable, but methods for its preparation have not been highly developed except for one particular dish, and that one, ironically, took Italian expertise to elevate it in French cooking. The Florentine cooks of Catherine de'Medici, recently arrived at Chambord, treated the rather coarse-fleshed neighborhood carp as they did veal, larding it, stuffing it with a savory veal or whiting forcemeat, braising it in white wine, and anointing it with all manner of good things. The felicitous result, *Carpe à la Chambord,* thus became one of the glories of French cooking.

Perhaps for reasons lost in its ancient Asiatic origins, where it was the first fish to have been pond-cultured, or perhaps because it is prolific, abundant, and long-lived (up to sixty years), the carp has acquired a number of magical and symbolic connotations, and one finds it appearing and reappearing in the fables and stories of many countries.* As a foodfish it was planted in Europe as early as the eleventh century and became quickly established in America after being introduced here from Germany in the late 19th century.

In predominantly Catholic European countries it often appears on the Christmas or Lenten table, in a sweet-and-sour sauce such as in Bohemian Christmas Carp ❋ , that follows. There the fish first stands in salt, which serves to tenderize the rather coarse flesh. For baking and broiling, a dry marinade can be used for the same purpose. Mix ½ cup of coarse salt with ½ cup of grated onion, 1 tablespoon of vinegar, a liberal amount of black pepper, and several gratings of nutmeg. Pat the marinade over the fish and let stand for one hour. Then rinse the fish very well under cold running water to remove all the excess salt. Be prudent with seasonings in the subsequent preparation of the fish. Carp may be broiled in split or fillet form, stuffed and baked, poached, or rolled in flour or crumbs and fried.

Carp can be muddy and the scales difficult; it should always be skinned.

Should you have to skin one yourself, plunge the whole fish into boiling, acidulated water for a few seconds, then slip off the skin, recalcitrant scales and all.

---

* In China it was a symbol of ambition and aggressiveness, despite its sluggish mien.

BOHEMIAN CHRISTMAS CARP

A 3–4-pound carp, cleaned, head
   removed and reserved
½ cup coarse salt
3 cups water
1 carrot, sliced
1 leek, sliced
1 small onion, sliced
Several parsley sprigs
¼ cup vinegar

1 bay leaf
3 tablespoons unsulfured dark
   molasses
6 gingersnaps, crushed
⅓ cup coarsely chopped blanched
   almonds
6–8 prunes, soaked and sliced
¼ cup golden raisins, soaked
Sugar to taste

Cut the carp into 1½-inch slices, sprinkle lightly with salt, and let stand for
½ hour.

Put the 3 cups of water in a kettle, add the reserved fish head, carrot,
leek, onion, parsley, vinegar, and bay leaf. Bring to a boil and simmer for
15 minutes. Strain the stock and return to the pot.

Rinse the salt off the fish and dry, add to the stock, and simmer slowly
for 20 minutes. Remove it to a heated platter with a slotted spoon, arranging
the pieces in overlapping slices. Keep warm.

Add the molasses, gingersnaps, almonds, prunes, and raisins to the stock.
Simmer for 10 minutes until thick, stirring frequently. Season to your per-
sonal sweet-and-sour taste. Pour the sauce over the fish and serve. Serves
4–6.

ALICE B. TOKLAS' CARP STUFFED WITH CHESTNUTS

A 3-pound carp, cleaned, split,
   head and tail on
3 tablespoons butter
1 medium onion, chopped
2 slices white bread cut in small
   cubes, soaked in dry white wine
   and squeezed dry
1 tablespoon chopped parsley
2 shallots, chopped
1 clove garlic, pressed

1 teaspoon salt
Several grindings of fresh pepper
¼ teaspoon ground mace
¼ teaspoon dried thyme
12 chestnuts, boiled and peeled
   (may be canned)
1 egg
2 cups dry white wine
3 tablespoons melted butter
1 cup fine cracker crumbs

Wash the fish, pat dry, season inside and out and set aside.

Melt the butter in a skillet, sauté the onion until transparent. Add the
bread, parsley, shallots, garlic, salt, pepper, mace, thyme, and chestnuts.
Mix well and allow to cool. Blend in the egg.

Stuff the cavity and head of the fish carefully with the mixture, secure with skewers or sewing thread so that no stuffing will escape in cooking. Put the fish aside in a cool place for a couple of hours.

Preheat oven to 375°.

Put the wine into an earthenware dish or baking dish large enough to hold the fish. Bake for 20 minutes, basting once or twice. Remove from the oven, baste again, and cover the fish with a thick coating of the cracker crumbs. Drizzle the melted butter over it and return to the oven for 20 minutes more. Serve very hot with noodles. Serves 4.

NOTE: The head of the carp, which is enormous, is considered by many to be a delectable morsel.

JEWISH SWEET-AND-SOUR CARP

A 4–5-pound carp, filleted, and
  skinned
1⅓ cups olive oil
2 large onions, chopped
4 tablespoons flour
2 cups white wine
2 cups water
1 teaspoon salt

A dash of cayenne pepper
A dash of nutmeg
2 bay leaves
2 cloves garlic, crushed
2 tablespoons chopped parsley
¾ cup seedless raisins
⅓ cup wine vinegar
2 tablespoons brown sugar

Cut the fish into 2-inch slices and set aside.

Heat ½ cup of the oil in a large, heavy skillet or stewpot, add the onions, and cook until soft. Blend in the flour, stir in the wine and 2 cups of water with a wooden spoon until thickened. Season with salt, cayenne, and nutmeg, bring to a boil, and add the fish, bay leaves, and garlic. Cover and simmer gently for 20 minutes. Remove the fish with a slotted spoon and arrange on a serving dish.

Reduce the sauce over moderate heat to a third its volume. Let cool slightly, then whisk in the remaining olive oil until the sauce is smooth and thick. Stir in the parsley, raisins, vinegar, and brown sugar. Pour this sauce over the fish and chill well. Serves 6.

PAPRIKASH CARP

Although carp is most often used in this incredibly good dish from land-locked Hungary, you could easily substitute two pounds of a firm-fleshed white saltwater fish such as bass, tilefish, rockfish, redfish, red snapper, or drum.

A 4-pound carp, cleaned, filleted,
  and skinned
1 teaspoon salt
2 tablespoons vegetable oil

1 tablespoon butter
2 medium onions, minced (about
  1½ cups)

¾ cup Fish Stock ❋ , chicken
  stock, or clam juice
1 tablespoon Hungarian paprika
2 medium green peppers, seeded
  and cut into ½-inch dice (about
  2 cups)

1 medium tomato, peeled and
  diced, or 3 canned tomatoes
1 teaspoon flour
3 tablespoons sour cream

Cut the carp fillets into 12–15 pieces, season with salt.

Heat the oil and butter in a large, heavy skillet, sauté the onions until soft. Remove from the heat and stir in the stock and paprika. Add the green peppers and the tomato, return to the heat, and bring to a slow boil. Cover, lower heat, and cook for about 15 minutes.

Put the pieces of carp in the vegetable mixture, cover, and cook at a slow simmer for 5–7 minutes or until done. Transfer the fish pieces with a slotted spoon to a warm platter.

Take off 2 or 3 spoonfuls of the pan liquid and put in a bowl. Stir in the flour and the sour cream. Mix and pour into the vegetable mixture, blending well, and cook for 1 minute. Correct the seasoning. Pour over the fish and serve. Serve with hot buttered noodles. Serves 4.

GEFILTE FISH

Fish is important in Jewish cooking because it often comprises the main course of a dairy dinner. Usually Jewish recipes call for freshwater fish, the kind most available in the inland countries where these dishes originated. The fish used most often are carp, pike, and whitefish, with herring often appearing as a breakfast staple.

Gefilte fish is one of those dishes with many versions and variations. A particular family's recipe might be handed down through the generations like an heirloom, and to elicit compliments for its preparation was a great source of pride for the cook. Some like it sweet, others peppery; it can be made of all carp, pike, or whitefish, or a combination thereof; in small balls, large ovals, or as a forcemeat stuffed back into the whole carp skin and poached. For everyone it was a traditional opener to the Sabbath or holiday dinner.

1 pound carp or pike, filleted,
  heads, bone, and skin reserved
2 pounds whitefish, filleted, heads,
  bone, and skin reserved (see
  the note p. 189)
5–6 whole medium onions
3 large carrots, scraped and sliced
2 stalks celery, sliced

3 sprigs parsley
1½ tablespoons salt
1½ tablespoons sugar or to taste
3 eggs, lightly beaten
2–3 tablespoons matzoh meal
¼ cup ice water
½ teaspoon white pepper or more
  to taste

Put the fish heads, bones, and skin in a large deep pot, add 3 whole onions, the carrots, celery, parsley, 1 tablespoon each of salt and sugar, and enough water to cover well. Bring to a boil, then reduce heat so the liquid just simmers. Cover loosely and cook for ½ hour.

Meanwhile grind the fish and remaining onions together or run in a food processor in two batches until well blended but not puréed. Add the eggs, matzoh meal, and enough ice water to give the consistency of thick oatmeal, and season with the remaining salt, sugar, and the pepper. Beat vigorously with a wooden spoon to blend.

With wet hands, form the fish mixture into oval-shaped balls, using about ½ cup of the mixture for each ball. Lower carefully into the simmering fish stock, poach at below a simmer for several minutes or until the balls are opaque. Then cover and simmer gently but steadily for 2 hours. If the broth has cooked down too much, add boiling water.

Cool the fish balls to room temperature in the broth, then remove with a slotted spoon and put in a deep bowl. Strain the broth, reserving the carrots. If there is a great quantity of liquid, reduce it a bit over high heat to about 6 cups. Pour over the fish balls and chill. Broth will jell as it cools.

Garnish each serving with a little of the jellied broth and 1 or 2 carrot slices. Serve with red or white horseradish. Makes 12 pieces.

NOTE: *Buffel,* or buffalo fish, is considered a necessary component by many old-time gefilte-fish lovers. If it is available, use it in place of the whitefish, or use 1 pound of each.

TARAMASALATA

3 slices white bread, home-style,
   crusts removed
¼ cup water
5 ounces *tarama* (carp roe, available in jars)
2 tablespoons minced onion

1 egg yolk
1 cup olive oil
2 tablespoons lemon juice
2 teaspoons chopped parsley
   (optional)

Crumble the bread and soak in the ¼ cup water. Put the *tarama* and onion in a blender and process until puréed but not liquid. Squeeze out excess water from the bread and blend with the *tarama*. Add the egg yolk, blend again at medium speed.

Pour in the oil in a slow, steady stream as for mayonnaise, then add the lemon juice. If the purée seems too liquid, as occasionally happens, add another slice of crustless bread, unsoaked, and blend briefly until the bread is completely absorbed.

At serving time sprinkle with parsley. Serve as a dip with raw vegetables or with toast, sesame crackers, or Arabic flat bread. Makes about 2½ cups.

CATFISH

Catfish is one of America's most popular fish, although its popularity is concentrated in the southern and central states. Varieties include the yellow, brown, black, and flat bullheads; stonecats, blindcats, madtoms, flathead, and channel catfish. There are also two marine species, the gaff-topsail and marine catfish. Once found mainly in the warm, slow-moving waters of the Mississippi basin, catfish are now found in many parts of the country; catfish "farming," or commercial pond-culturing, is a thriving industry in ten states, and they have been introduced into California inland waters.

Catfish are omnivorous and eat all manner of living and dead things, so their taste can vary greatly according to the waters from which they are taken. Generally speaking, catfish of less than one pound are usually deep-fried. Filleting is best for those between one and six pounds. Very large catfish can be coarse in texture. Catfish are marketed fresh and frozen as steaks, fillets, and in whole dressed form. They are suitable for virtually all other cooking methods, baking, broiling, barbecuing, poaching, and—most popular—deep frying. Catfish stews with creole overtones of onions, tomatoes, and hot peppers, or with tomatoes, green peppers, garlic, and lemon, are popular in Louisiana.

HOW TO DRESS A FRESH CATFISH: All catfish must be skinned (if you are new at it, beware of the spines—they can sting). As with eels, there are several methods, the most popular being to make a cut around the nape of the neck behind the pectoral fins, then to impale the head on a heavy nail driven through a board at an angle. Using pliers, grasp the body skin and peel backward and down, then slit the belly and gut.

COUNTRY-FRIED CATFISH

6 catfish, skinned, heads and tails off (see the note p. 191)
2 teaspoons salt
Several grindings of black pepper
2 eggs

2 tablespoons milk
2 cups yellow or white cornmeal
Bacon fat, lard, or other cooking fat

Wash the fish and pat dry. Season with salt and pepper. Beat the eggs lightly and blend in the milk. Put the cornmeal on a large piece of wax paper, dip the fish in the egg mixture, then roll in the cornmeal.

In a heavy skillet, melt enough fat to give a depth of about $\frac{1}{8}$ inch. Heat until hot but not smoking. Fry the fish over moderate heat until brown on

SKINNING A CATFISH: Make a circular cut through the skin around back of head. Impale head (belly down) on heavy nail driven through board. Grasp skin with pliers and peel off with a pulling motion. If skin separates along dorsal surface, grip and pull again. Remove head, slit belly, and gut. Small catfish may be cooked whole; large ones steaked, filleted, or cut in chunks for chowder.

one side: turn carefully and brown the other side. Calculate cooking time according to the Canadian Theory. Drain on paper towels, serve immediately on a hot platter. Traditionally, fried catfish is served with Coleslaw ❀ and Hush Puppies ❀ (recipe follows) or with bacon, for breakfast. Serves 6.

NOTE: Catfish steaks may also be used in this recipe.

HUSH PUPPIES

1½ cups yellow cornmeal
½ cup sifted all-purpose flour
2½ teaspoons baking powder
½ teaspoon salt

¼ cup finely chopped onion
1 egg, beaten
½ cup milk
Fat for deep frying

Sift together the cornmeal, flour, baking powder, and salt. Add the onion, egg, and milk, stir until just blended. Heat the fat to 350°. Drop the mixture by tablespoonfuls into the deep fat, fry for 3–4 minutes or until brown. Hush puppies will rise as they are done. Drain on paper towels. Makes 18 hush puppies.

CAJUN DEEP-FRIED CATFISH

Follow the instructions for coating the fish in Country-Fried Catfish ✳ , but increase the black pepper requirement to 1 teaspoon and add 1 teaspoon of cayenne pepper. Heat the oil to 375° in a deep fryer and follow instructions for deep-frying (see Index).

PERCH

Unraveling perch terminology is one of the knottier problems in the generally confusing skein of fish nomenclature. The true perch—of the family Percidae—is the yellow perch—closely related to the yellow pike and blue pike, both walleyes, and another "pike" called the sauger. These freshwater fish, though commonly considered to be pike, are actually perch. (A close European relative spans the problem by being known as "pike perch."

Considered to have the best flavor, the yellow perch, closely related to the European perch with solid, white firm flesh, is the one found in large numbers in the Great Lakes and in sweet, cold waters from Nova Scotia to the Carolinas.

However, perch is also a market name for a number of freshwater and saltwater fish that are not percids. For example, the freshwater drum is marketed under the name "white perch." But white perch is also a name given to *Morone americana,* a small panfish belonging to a branch of the bass family and related neither to the drums *nor* the perch. Another marine drum, a small, sweet panfish found in bays and estuarine waters from New York on south, goes by the name of silver perch. Ocean perch is discussed in the section on Saltwater Fish (see the Index).

The abundant white perch is not distributed commercially, though it is a great favorite of sports fishermen. Its range is from Nova Scotia to North Carolina and inland to the Great Lakes. The firm white flesh is ideal for fish chowder or *soupe de poisson* and is delicious panfried whole or in crumb-dusted fillets.

Yellow perch is a favorite of Midwestern fishing enthusiasts who eagerly await the spring runs. It is an easy fish to fillet and may be used in almost any recipe calling for fillets of firm white fish. If the fish are small, around a half pound, they may be oven-fried or panfried, following the directions for Panfried Porgy ✳. Fillets may be cooked *meunière* (see the Index, Cooking à la Meunière) or *amandine* as in Trout Amandine.

PIKE AND PICKEREL

The northern pike and its larger version, the muskellunge, or "muskie," form a small but well-known freshwater fish family, the *Esoeidae.* The blue pike and the yellow pike share only the name; they are closely related fish belonging to another family, the *Percidae,* or perch. Yellow pike, which is actually a market name for a fish called the walleye (pickerel* is another) is used in the same way as true pike, to which it is often preferred; gefilte fish and *quenelles* recipes often specify yellow pike. One reason may be that the walleye does not have the Y-shaped intermuscular bones that the true pike shares in common with the shad, and therefore is easier to handle.

Pike, true or false, is much underrated as a food fish in the United States. Even the Indians held it in low esteem. Nor does it figure highly in the gastronomy of France; Escoffier thought that pike should be used "only in the preparation of forcemeats and quenelles," as indeed it is. There, as in England, pike is a river fish. As all the pike family are very slimy when caught, this fact, plus their bones, may be why they are not highly regarded. Also, though pike is popular as a game fish, it can be a challenge to the cook because it tends to be dry, a quality that makes it take nicely to all sorts of braising and savory stuffings, however. Since a whole pike can be inordinately long, don't hesitate to cut, stuff, and cook a center cut.

If you are dressing your own pike, scaling can be a problem because of the slime. A kettle of boiling water poured over the fish before you begin will remove a good deal of the slime yet not cook the fish.

Pike and yellow pike are marketed whole and in fresh and frozen fillets. Northern pike runs from 4–10 pounds, muskes from 10–30. The recipes that follow may be applied to pike, pickerel, or muskellunge.

PIKE AND SPINACH PÂTÉ

An elegant and different buffet item served at the fabulous New York restaurant Windows on the World.

2 pounds fillet of yellow pike, skinned
1 pound fillet of sole, skinned
Salt and white pepper
Nutmeg
3½ cups heavy cream

½ pound fresh spinach leaves, cooked, drained and finely chopped
4 egg whites
3 tablespoons butter cut in thin pats

LEMON CUCUMBER MAYONNAISE SAUCE

1½ cups mayonnaise, preferably homemade
Juice of 1 lemon
1½ tablespoons tomato paste

¼ cup finely chopped cucumbers
1 tablespoon Pernod or *pastis*
½ cup unsweetened whipped cream

* An erroneous use of the name. There is a small (2 pounds average) member of the pike family called the chain pickerel, which is primarily a sport fish. As stated, the pickerel that is called walleye pike and the closely related sauger, are not pike but perch.

Cut 1 pound of the pike fillet into ½-inch strips. Set aside. Grind well the remaining pike with the sole, then grind a second time. Alternatively, process them finely in a food processor using the steel blade. Season to taste with 1 teaspoon of salt, pepper, and several dashes of nutmeg. Put the fish mixture in an electric mixer, add the egg whites. Mix well together on medium speed. Gradually add all the heavy cream, continue mixing until the mixture has the consistency of batter. Set aside half of the mixture, and to the half remaining in the bowl add the chopped ground spinach and mix in well.

Preheat oven to 325°.

Butter a 2½-quart rectangular mold and coat it with ⅔ of the white mixture. Make a layer of the spinach mixture, approximately ½ inch thick, using ⅓ of the amount. Use two spatulas to make the layers, and handle the mixtures lightly to keep them separate. Top with half of the reserved pike strips laid widthwise. Season these with salt and pepper. Make a layer of another third of the spinach mixture, a second layer of pike strips, seasoned, and then the remaining third of the white mixture. Rap the pan sharply on the counter to settle the contents. Cut the butter pats in half and dot the top with them. Cover the mold with foil. Place it in a larger pan and put in the oven. Fill the larger pan with enough hot water to come halfway up the sides of the mold. Bake for 1¼–1½ hours or until a tester inserted 1 inch off center comes out clean.

Make the sauce: mix together the mayonnaise and the lemon juice, then beat in the tomato paste, cucumbers, and Pernod. Fold in the whipped cream and season to taste. Chill.

Remove the pâté from the oven, cool to room temperature. Refrigerate until ready to use. Unmold by running a sharp knife around the edges to loosen and then dipping the bottom of the mold briefly in hot water. Unmold on a plate or board for slicing. Serve with the sauce. Serves 14–16 as a buffet item or as a first course.

FINNISH BAKED PIKE WITH CUCUMBER RICE STUFFING

A 3–3⅓-pound pike, cleaned, backbone removed, head and tail on
1 large cucumber, peeled, seeded and coarsely chopped
Salt
8 tablespoons butter
½ cup finely chopped onion
2 hard-cooked eggs, coarsely chopped

2 cups cooked rice
½ cup finely chopped parsley
½ cup finely chopped chives
Several grindings of fresh white pepper
1–3 tablespoons heavy cream
6 tablespoons dry bread crumbs
½ cup or more hot Fish Stock ✳ or water

Wash the fish inside and out under cold running water and dry thoroughly with paper towels. Set aside.

In a small bowl, toss the chopped cucumber with ¼ teaspoon of salt. Let sit for about 15 minutes, then drain and pat dry with paper towels. In a small saucepan melt 2 tablespoons of the butter, sauté the onion and cucumber for about 6 minutes or until the onions are soft and transparent but not brown. Transfer to a large mixing bowl and add the eggs, rice, parsley, and chives. Season with 1 tablespoon of salt and the white pepper, moisten the mixture with 1 tablespoon of heavy cream, adding more if the stuffing still seems dry. Mix together lightly. Fill the fish with the cucumber-rice stuffing. (If all the stuffing does not fit into the fish cavity, it may be placed around the fish later.) Close the opening with small skewers (see illustration) and secure with string.

Preheat the oven to 350°.

In a baking dish or pan attractive enough to bring to the table and large enough to hold the fish, melt 4 tablespoons of the butter over moderate heat. When the foam dies down, place the fish in the baking dish, raise the heat, and cook for about 5 minutes or until the skin is a golden brown. With two large wooden spoons or metal spatulas, carefully turn the fish over and brown the other side. Sprinkle the top with half the bread crumbs, turn the fish over once again, and sprinkle the second side with the remaining crumbs. Dot with the remaining 2 tablespoons of butter, cut up. Carefully pour the hot stock or water around the fish and bring it to a simmer on top of the stove. Spoon any leftover stuffing around it. Bake, uncovered, in the middle of the oven, timing according to the Canadian Theory or for 30–35 minutes. (An additional ⅓ cup of stock or water may have to be added to the baking dish about halfway through cooking time if the dish appears dry.) Serve directly from the baking dish. Serves 4.

PIKE SAUCE GÉNOISE (Pike with Red Wine Sauce)

2 pike (about 1¾ pounds each) cleaned, head and tail on, or 1 pike 3½–4 pounds.
¾ cup finely chopped yellow onion
½ cup finely chopped shallots (about 6)
1 clove garlic, finely chopped
¾ cup finely chopped carrots
¼ cup minced parsley
1 bay leaf, broken into pieces

¼ teaspoon thyme
½ teaspoon freshly ground black pepper
1½ teaspoons salt
3 cups good dry red wine
4 tablespoons butter, softened
1 cup water
6 anchovy fillets, mashed, or 1½ teaspoons anchovy paste
1 teaspoon cornstarch

Preheat oven to 425°.

Select a flameproof baking pan large enough to hold the fish and about 2 inches deep, line it with heavy duty foil, and set aside. Wash the fish, pat dry, set aside.

Put the onions, shallots, garlic, carrots, parsley, bay leaf, thyme, pepper, ½ teaspoon of the salt, and the wine in a heavy porcelain-lined or stainless steel saucepan. Bring to a high boil and continue to boil for 15 minutes or until the liquid has reduced by approximately half. Strain the sauce through a fine strainer or *chinois,* pressing down on the vegetables as much as possible to extract all the flavor. Discard the vegetables.

Sprinkle the fish with the remaining salt, inside and out, and rub with 1 tablespoon of the butter. Place in the prepared baking dish, pour the wine mixture and the water over the fish. Bring to a boil on top of the stove, cover with a buttered sheet of wax paper, and place in the oven for about 15 minutes. Lift the fish to a heated serving platter and keep warm.

Pour the pan juices into a saucepan, bring to a boil over high heat and cook for 3–4 minutes or until reduced by about one third. Meanwhile, in a small bowl, combine the remaining butter, the anchovies or anchovy paste, and the cornstarch. Add to the reduced pan juices and blend in with a wooden spoon. Bring just to the boil and pour over the fish. Serve immediately, carving as necessary at the table. Serves 4.

POLISH PIKE WITH EGG SAUCE

A 3-pound pike, cleaned, head and
   tail removed
Salt
2 cups water
2 cups dry white wine
2 stalks celery, sliced
1 carrot, sliced

1 onion, sliced
3 slices lemon
2 tablespoons lemon juice
10 peppercorns
1 *bouquet garni:* 6 sprigs parsley,
   4 sprigs thyme, and 1 bay leaf

EGG SAUCE
4 tablespoons butter
8 hard-cooked eggs, finely chopped
3 tablespoons lemon juice

Salt and freshly ground white
   pepper

Sprinkle the fish all over with salt. In a small fish poacher or oval pot just large enough to hold the fish, combine the water, wine, celery, carrot, onion, lemon and lemon juice, peppercorns, *bouquet garni,* and 1 tablespoon of salt. Bring to a boil and simmer for 5 minutes. Reduce heat and add the fish. Poach, covered, for 20–25 minutes.

EGG SAUCE: Heat the butter in a large enamel skillet. Add the hard-cooked eggs and cook over a moderately low flame until they are heated through. Add the lemon juice, salt, and pepper to taste, cook the sauce, stirring, for 3 minutes longer.

Transfer the fish to a board, remove the skin and bones carefully, and arrange the fish on a heated platter. Spread the egg sauce over the fish and serve with boiled potatoes. Serves 4.

SALMON

In A.D. 77, Pliny wrote that "the river salmon is to be preferred to all the fish that swim in the sea," and appropriately the Romans announced its arrival at table with a flourish of trumpets. In France, the elaboration of its preparation kept pace with seventeenth- and eighteenth-century culinary trends until Escoffier announced that this lily needed no gilding, and served it plain. In North America it was a diet staple for the Indians long before the settlers arrived, both in its fresh form and in a dried, pulverized form called "pemmican." Cured either by salt, sugar, cold smoking, or kippering, it is sublime, the ultimate epicurean trip.

Salmon is one of the anadromous fish, those that are born in rivers but spend most of their lives in the ocean. At maturity, they return to spawn in the rivers and streams, some traveling as much as a thousand miles. After spawning they die. During the spawning run they do not feed, sustained by their considerable fat. At the end of its run, having shot its milt, or roe, the salmon is less plump, and in England there are epicures who will eat only fresh-run salmon, regarding as uneatable the "kelts," or end-run salmon.

The "parr," or small fry, emerge from the gravel of the riverbed, feeding like trout. After about two years of river life, they take on the coloration of the mature salmon and disperse to the sea. At this stage they are called "smolts."

In the early part of this century, the bulk of our commercial catch came from the Atlantic coast; sadly, overfishing has virtually eliminated this elegant fish from Eastern waters. Most fresh and all canned salmon now comes from the Pacific, from the Columbia River to Alaska.

The most esteemed of the Pacific species is the *Chinook,* or king or Columbia king, salmon, also the largest (15–20 pounds). It makes up the bulk of all salmon sold fresh, frozen, or smoked. The flesh is a deep coral, rich in oil, relatively soft, and breaks into large flakes. *Coho,* or silver salmon, is the least common, much smaller than the Chinook and a favorite of fishermen. It weighs 6–12 pounds, with deep pink flesh, lighter than the sockeye. Coho have been recently planted in the Great Lakes as a sportfish, but in general landlocked salmon do not have the quality of those fished in the sea.

Sockeye, or red salmon, runs about 3–5 pounds. The male turns a spectacular red color during spawning. Canned salmon is usually sockeye, sometimes called "blueback," and carries a premium price. *Chum,* also known as keta, dog, or calico salmon, has a somewhat coarser flesh and is less flavorsome. It averages 10 pounds. Because it is somewhat lighter in color it is the least expensive. The fine-textured *pink,* or humpback, salmon is the smallest, with a fine texture, and it figures heavily in canned salmon.

Atlantic, or *Eastern,* salmon, sometimes called "Kennebec" on menus (although few salmon of that name come from that river anymore), comes from Canada's Atlantic coast. Although Atlantic salmon may not have the deep pink we have come to regard as characteristic of that fish at its best, it has a richer taste and a firmer texture especially when used for broiling or poaching. Some restaurateurs prefer it to all the others. Although the bulk of salmon now used for smoking is from the West, old-timers feel that here, too, the Atlantic salmon is preferable.

Atlantic salmon is at its finest when it weighs between 7 and 12 pounds and is about 3 years old. It is best from June to December and is available intermittently through the rest of the year.

Cured Salmon

Lox (the name derives from the Scandinavian word for salmon [*lax*] and the German *Lachs)* is salmon mild-cured in brine, then soaked to desalinize it. Previously the salmon for lox came from Nova Scotia, but today only Western is used, mostly chinook. The final saltiness depends on the length of time of the cure and the degree of fat content of the fish.

Nova Scotia or "Nova": "Nova" is a New York term for salmon cured by cold-smoking, and although the salmon itself may have once come from Nova Scotia, today the term is used for any smoked salmon that is not Scotch and is probably Western. Elsewhere this salmon is marketed as "smoked salmon."

Scotch smoked salmon indicates cold-smoked Atlantic salmon, usually from Scotland.

Kippered salmon is cured by being brined *and* hot-smoked, which produces a drier, essentially cooked salmon. In Scotland, however, kippered salmon is produced by brining and cold-smoking.

The classic way to serve smoked salmon is as a first course, in paper-thin slices, with lemon wedges, a pepper mill, and perhaps capers. Both smoked salmon and lox are marvelous with cream cheese and bagels anytime, or with scrambled eggs for Sunday brunch.

Occasionally one receives as a gift or has an opportunity to buy a whole side of smoked salmon, which presents a problem of storage, as it is rarely consumed at once. Some people say that smoked salmon can be frozen with no deleterious effect, though I think I do find a textural change. Far better is to cut the salmon into slices as you would when serving it, and cover with vegetable or olive oil in a tightly lidded container. Salmon can be kept this way for up to six months in the refrigerator and does not absorb the oil. Pat dry before using.

BROILED SALMON STEAKS

4 salmon steaks, 1 inch thick   Salt and freshly ground pepper
   (about ¾ pounds each)   Lemon quarters
3 tablespoons butter, melted

Preheat the broiler to very hot for 15 minutes.

Dry the salmon thoroughly with paper towels. With a pastry brush spread both sides of each steak with melted butter. Arrange the steaks on the rack of the broiling pan, broil them with the top surface of the steaks 3–4 inches from the heat for 3 minutes on each side. Baste them with any remaining melted butter or with the butter from the bottom of the pan, turn them over, season, baste again, and broil, basting once, for 5–8 minutes more. With a spatula transfer the steaks to a heated serving platter and garnish with lemon quarters. Serves 4.

BROILED SALMON STEAKS WITH GARLIC AND HERB BUTTER

Prepare the salmon steaks as above. Spread with Herb Butter ❉ to which 2 cloves of garlic, pressed, have been added. Serves 4.

BROILED SALMON STEAKS WITH DILL BUTTER

Prepare the salmon steaks as above. Top each with a dollop of Dill Butter ❉ before serving. Serves 4.

SALMON SCALLOPS WITH SORREL

1½ pound center-cut piece of fresh salmon cut into very thin slices or scallops
Salt and freshly ground pepper
½ cup dry white wine
½ cup dry vermouth

½ cup *Fumet* ❉
3 tablespoons chopped shallots
1 cup heavy cream
¼ pound sorrel, cooked and drained (see the note below)
¼ cup vegetable oil

Pound the salmon scallops very lightly between sheets of wax paper, season with salt and pepper, and set aside.

Combine the wine, vermouth, *fumet,* and shallots in a saucepan. Cook over fairly high heat until the liquid is reduced to the point of becoming syrupy. Strain it through a sieve, return to the saucepan, stir in the cream, and cook again over fairly high heat until the liquid is reduced and thickened. Season to taste with salt and pepper. Stir in the well-drained sorrel.

Heat the oil in a heavy skillet and sauté the salmon scallops for a few seconds on each side; no more or they will become dry. Transfer to a warm serving dish, cover with the sorrel sauce, and serve. Serves 4.

NOTE: For instructions on cooking sorrel, see Stuffed Shad in Sorrel Sauce ❉.

SALMON STEAKS BRETAGNE (In Madeira and Cream)

4 salmon steaks, 1 inch thick
Salt and freshly ground pepper
Flour
4 tablespoons butter
6 large mushrooms, stems
   removed, thinly sliced

1 truffle, cut in julienne (optional)
¼ cup Madeira
1 cup heavy cream
A dash of cayenne pepper

Wash the salmon steaks and pat dry. Season with salt and pepper and dust them lightly with flour.

Melt the butter in a heavy skillet just large enough to hold the fish, and when it foams add the salmon steaks. Sauté them on both sides over moderate heat 5 minutes per side, until they are lightly browned. Transfer to a heated platter and keep warm.

To the butter remaining in the skillet add the sliced mushrooms and the optional truffle, cook for 3–4 minutes. Add the Madeira and simmer the sauce, stirring, for 1 minute. Stir in the heavy cream, simmer for 2 minutes to reduce slightly. Season to taste with salt, pepper, and cayenne. Pour the sauce over the salmon steaks and serve with parsleyed new potatoes. Serves 4.

NEW ENGLAND BOILED SALMON WITH EGG SAUCE

The traditional New England Fourth-of-July menu called for boiled salmon with egg sauce, boiled potatoes, and freshly picked green peas. This menu is still eaten in Maine today, although the salmon is likely to be more correctly described as "poached."

A 4-pound center-cut piece of
   salmon, or a 5-pound whole
   salmon, head and tails removed,
   skin on
1 quart Court-Bouillon
2 cups milk
1 cup light cream
8 tablespoons (1 stick) butter

½ cup flour
Salt and freshly ground white
   pepper
2 tablespoons minced fresh dill
   (optional)
5 hard-cooked eggs, peeled
Finely chopped parsley

Poach the salmon in the court-bouillon as directed in the recipe for Cold Poached Salmon ❋ . Skin and place on a serving platter, reserve the bouillon.

Prepare the egg sauce: Combine the milk and cream in a small saucepan, heat gently. In another, heavy saucepan melt the butter, add the flour, and cook, stirring, for 2–3 minutes. Add 1 cup of the reserved bouillon, add the milk mixture, stir until thick and smooth, and heat gently. Season cautiously with salt and pepper, taste it, as the amount of salt will depend on the saltiness of the bouillon. Stir in the dill.

Cut 3 or 4 slices from the center of each of two of the eggs, set aside. Chop the ends of the 3 remaining eggs, stir into the hot sauce.

Sprinkle the fish with the parsley, arrange the sliced eggs on top. Pass the sauce separately. Serves 8–10.

BETH'S BAKED SALMON

3 pounds salmon, filleted, boned, skin on
Salt and freshly ground pepper
Flour
Paprika

½ medium onion, thinly sliced
4 tablespoons butter
Several squeezes lemon juice
Fresh dill

Preheat oven to 450°.

Line a cookie sheet with foil. Place the salmon on it, skin side down, sprinkle with salt and pepper, dredge top lightly with flour, and dust with paprika. Arrange the onion slices in rings on the salmon, dot with butter, and bake, timing according to the Canadian Theory.

Slide the foil onto a serving platter, sprinkle with lemon juice and dill, and serve with parsleyed new potatoes. Serves 6.

BAKED STUFFED SALMON

A 5–6-pound salmon, boned, head and tail on
Salt and freshly ground pepper
2 tablespoons chopped green pepper
1 tablespoon minced parsley
1 teaspoon minced fresh thyme or ½ teaspoon dried thyme

¼ cup chopped mushrooms
1 cup fine dry bread crumbs
4 tablespoons (½ stick) butter, melted
2 tablespoons chopped green onion
4–6 slices bacon

Preheat oven to 400°. Line an appropriate sized baking dish or pan with foil, butter lightly, and set aside.

Wash the salmon, dry and season inside and out with salt and pepper. Mix together the green pepper, parsley, thyme, mushrooms, bread crumbs, butter, onion, and ½ teaspoon salt, stuff the fish loosely with the mixture. Fasten the opening with poultry pins and lace up (see drawings 28 and 29). Place the fish in the prepared baking dish and bake in the preheated oven for 50 minutes basting occasionally with the pan drippings. Serves 8.

KEDGEREE OF SALMON

Follow the recipe for Kedgeree of Haddock ❋ , omitting the milk and water required to poach the haddock, and substituting 1 pound cooked fresh or canned salmon for the haddock.

SOUFFLÉ OF FRESH SALMON

This is a wonderful way to extend leftover poached salmon. Follow the recipe for Finnan Haddie Soufflé ❋ and, if desired, add a tablespoon of chopped dill to the sauce before adding the egg whites.

BRAISED SALMON

1 whole salmon (4–5 pounds), dressed
½ teaspoon salt
4 tablespoons butter
2 tablespoons finely chopped shallots or onions

½ pound mushrooms, stems removed and chopped, caps reserved
⅔ cup white wine
1 cup Fish Stock ❋ or water
½ pound raw shrimp, unshelled

SAUCE
2 tablespoons butter
1 teaspoon flour
Liquid from the braising pan
2 egg yolks

¼ cup heavy cream
Freshly ground pepper
Several drops lemon juice
Chopped parsley

Wash the fish, pat dry, and season with the salt.

Melt 1 tablespoon of the butter in a shallow flameproof casserole large enough to hold the fish, add the shallots or onions, chopped mushroom stems, wine, and stock or water. Place the fish in the casserole, bring the liquid to a boil on top of the stove, and cover the fish with a piece of buttered wax paper or foil cut to fit the casserole and having a small hole in the center to allow steam to escape. Put the lid on the casserole, braise the salmon over gentle heat for 40–45 minutes, basting several times.

While the fish is cooking, melt the remaining 3 tablespoons of butter in a skillet, sauté the mushroom caps until softened. Set them aside and keep warm.

Cook the shrimp (see Index), drain, shell, and keep warm.

When the fish is done, carefully remove to a serving platter, pull off the skin with great care, using the fingers aided by a sharp knife. Garnish with the mushroom caps and shrimp. Keep the fish warm while you prepare sauce.

The sauce: Melt the butter in a heavy saucepan, stir in the flour, and cook until the *roux* takes on some color. Stir in the braising liquid and cook, stirring, until the sauce is well blended. Remove from the fire.

Beat the 2 egg yolks with the cream, add a little of the warm sauce, then add the yolk mixture to the sauce. Correct the seasoning with pepper and lemon juice, strain the sauce through a fine sieve over the hot fish and vegetables. Garnish with chopped parsley. Serves 6–8.

NOTE: Other large whole fish may be prepared this way, and you may substitute red wine for the white.

GRAVLAX

Raw salmon is cured for two days with pepper, dill, sugar, and salt in this superb Swedish specialty that is the star of every important smorgasbord. At the end the fish is actually "cooked." The fried skin is considered a delicacy in Sweden, perhaps surpassing the dish itself.

3–3¹/₂ pounds fresh salmon, center cut, split, skin on, backbone and small bones removed
1 bunch very fresh dill (10–12 branches)
¹/₄ cup coarse or kosher salt
¹/₄ cup sugar
2 tablespoons white peppercorns, crushed
Lemon wedges
1 recipe of *Gravlaxsås* (Mustard-Dill Sauce—see the following recipe)

Put half the salmon, skin side down, in a Pyrex or enamel casserole or baking dish. Wash the dill, shake dry, and remove any coarse lower stems. Chop coarsely.

In a bowl, combine the salt, sugar, and crushed peppercorns. Place half the dill on top of the salmon half, then sprinkle the salt mixture evenly over it. Top with the other salmon half, sandwich fashion, skin side up, and the remaining dill. As the two pieces will probably not be of uniform thickness, position them so one thick side is on top of one thin side. Cover the fish with foil and on this set a rectangular plate, small tray, or plank—something that is a little larger in size and will exert even pressure on the fish. Weight with several heavy cans.

Keep refrigerated for 48 hours, turning the fish every 12 hours.

To serve, remove from the marinade, scrape off the seasonings and dill, and pat dry. Place the separate halves, skin side down, on a carving board, and slice thinly with a sharp knife, slightly on the diagonal and holding the knife almost horizontal. (A thin, flexible-bladed carving knife works best.) Carefully detach the slices from the skin, arrange on a platter, and garnish with lemon wedges. Serve with mustard-dill sauce and thin slices of buttered dark bread or toast. Serves 10–12.

TO FRY THE SKIN: Dip the strips of skin in salad oil and fry them, skin side down, in a hot dry skillet. Pass these with the above dish on a separate platter.

NOTES: 1. The coho, or silver, salmon, with its fine texture, is superb for this purpose. However, you may also use sockeye, chinook, or Atlantic salmon.

2. Crush the peppercorns by placing them between 2 pieces of wax paper and rolling with a rolling pin.

GRAVLAXSÅS (Mustard-Dill Sauce)

½ cup Dijon or dark prepared
   mustard
2 teaspoons dry mustard
2–4 tablespoons sugar

¼ cup white vinegar
⅔ cup vegetable oil
⅔ cup chopped fresh dill
Salt to taste

Combine both mustards and the sugar in a small bowl. Whisk in the vinegar, then gradually add the oil, whisking constantly. Add the dill and salt to taste. Makes about 1½ cups.

MARINATED SALMON WITH GREEN PEPPERCORNS

1½ pounds salmon, tail end, in 2
   fillets, skin on
¼ cup minced onions
2 teaspoons green peppercorns,
   packed in water

½ cup lime juice
2 teaspoons snipped dill
2 teaspoons salt
¼ teaspoon paprika
¼ teaspoon sugar

Feel the salmon flesh with your fingertips for any small bones. Remove these with tweezers.

Lay one fillet, skin-side down, on a work surface. Starting at the tail end, cut thin slices of salmon, using a sharp, flexible-bladed knife (the blade points toward the tail). Use the flat of your free hand to steady the slices as you cut. Cut the larger slices again in half. Discard the skin. Repeat with the second fillet.

Arrange the slices in a shallow dish. Put the minced onions in a small tea strainer, run cold water over them, squeeze dry, set aside. Drain the peppercorns in the tea strainer, press them gently with the back of a spoon to crush them lightly.

In a small dish combine the onions, peppercorns, lime juice, dill, paprika, and sugar. Pour over the salmon slices, let marinate, covered, in the refrigerator for 3 hours. Baste with the marinade occasionally. Serve as a first course with some of the marinade and with buttered slices of toast. Serves 4.

COLD POACHED SALMON

Poach a whole fresh salmon or a 3-pound center cut piece of fresh salmon in enough Court-Bouillon ✲ to cover. Wrap the salmon first in a length of cheesecloth and lower it into the boiling liquid. Cover, lower heat, and cook for 8 minutes per pound if the fish is thick, 5–6 if it is thin. Adjust heat so the liquid just shudders—slightly less than a simmer. Let the fish cool in the liquid, unwrap it carefully, remove the skin (see Poached Striped Bass, pages 29–30), and skim off any jagged pieces.

If you wish to poach a whole fish and your fish poacher can accommodate it, by all means leave the head and tail on to make the final decorated fish look more lifelike. If at all possible, keep the salmon cool but not refrigerated, as it is most flavorful at room temperature.

The salmon—especially if you are using a whole one—may be decorated as simply or as elaborately as you wish: for suggestions, see Index, Decorating and Garnishing Fish. Serve with Green Mayonnaise ✲ or homemade mayonnaise and a cucumber salad if desired. Because of the richness and denseness of salmon, 3 pounds can serve 8–10.

SALMON MOUSSE

1 package unflavored gelatin
3 tablespoons lemon juice
½ small onion, cut up
½ cup boiling water
½ cup mayonnaise
2 cups freshly cooked salmon or a
    1-pound can, drained

¼ teaspoon paprika
1 tablespoon chopped fresh dill
1 cup heavy cream
Watercress
Thin lemon slices

Put the gelatin, lemon juice, onion, and boiling water in a blender, cover, and blend at high speed for 40 seconds. Add the mayonnaise, salmon, paprika, and dill, blend briefly. Add the cream gradually while blending for 30 seconds more. Pour into a 4-cup 12-inch diameter ring mold, chill until the mousse is set. Unmold onto a serving platter. Garnish with watercress and thin lemon slices. Serve with Salade Russe ✲ piled in the center if desired. Serves 6–8.

NEW POTATOES WITH SALMON CAVIAR

This dish is best with tiny new potatoes, the smaller the better. Scrub and bake the potatoes with skins on in a preheated 350° oven until soft, about 20 minutes. Cut in half, top each half with a dollop of sour cream, then an appropriate amount of salmon caviar and a few snipped chives on top. Arrange on a plate and pass as an hors d'oeuvre while still warm.

RILLETTES OF SALMON

Strictly speaking, there is no such thing as rillettes of salmon. The hors d'oeuvre spread known as rillettes is of pork, the word coming from *rille,* meaning a small piece of pork. The following recipe uses the same method, substituting both fresh and smoked salmon for the pork, and butter for the pork fat. If the amount of butter seems excessive, remember that it replaces the pork fat in a recipe where equal quantities of fat and meat give the pâté-like quality to the spread.

1 pound center-cut fresh salmon, skin on
1 small carrot, scraped, thinly sliced
1 small onion, quartered
2 sprigs of parsley
1 bay leaf
¼ teaspoon thyme, or 1 branch fresh thyme
Salt and freshly ground pepper

½ pound butter
1 cup chopped onions (about 2 medium onions)
½ pound smoked salmon, sliced and cut into pieces
3 anchovies, coarsely chopped
1 tablespoon oil from the anchovy can
1 tablespoon lemon juice

Put the salmon in a pot just large enough to hold it comfortably. Cover with cold water to determine the amount needed later. Remove the salmon and set aside. Add to the water the carrot, onion, parsley, bay leaf, thyme, a dash of salt, and several grinds of pepper. Bring to a boil and simmer, covered, for 20 minutes.

Add the salmon to this court-bouillon, bring again to a boil, cover, reduce heat, and simmer for 10–12 minutes or just until the fish flakes when tested with a fork. Remove the fish from the liquid and let cool.

While the salmon is cooking, melt 4 tablespoons of the butter in a small, heavy skillet. Add the onions, season lightly with salt and pepper, and cook, covered, stirring frequently, over low heat until the onions are translucent but not brown. Set aside.

When the salmon is cool enough to handle, remove the skin and bones. Flake into small pieces, chop very finely by hand or in a food processor, using the steel blade (do not use a blender). Chop the smoked salmon finely and add, or, if you are using a food processor, add to the container and blend further, along with the reserved onion mixture. Add the anchovies (chop them very finely if working by hand) and the tablespoon of oil from the can, process or beat until very smooth.

Melt the remaining butter and beat in if you are working by hand, or add gradually to the food processor with the machine running. Correct the seasoning with salt, pepper, and lemon juice. Pack into a 2-quart tureen, a crock, or a bowl, cover with plastic wrap, and refrigerate overnight. Serve with hot toast or crackers. Serves 20–30 as canapés. Can be refrigerated for up to one week.

SMOKED SALMON RISOTTO

This is an unusual way to turn a small amount of smoked salmon into a hearty dish. Do read the introduction to Risotto with Mussels ❋ for the *risotto* technique.

3 cups chicken stock or broth
½ cup dry white wine
3 tablespoons butter
¼ cup minced onion
1 cup Italian short-grain rice*

¼ pound smoked salmon, chopped
½ cup freshly grated Parmesan cheese
Freshly ground pepper

Combine the chicken broth and wine in a saucepan, bring to a boil, reduce heat, and keep the liquid at a low simmer.

In a heavy saucepan melt the butter, sauté the onion over moderate heat until transparent. Add the rice, stir for 2 minutes to coat the rice well with the butter.

Add about a half cup of the liquid to the onion mixture, cook, stirring, for 4–5 minutes or until the liquid is absorbed. Add another half cup or so of the liquid and cook, stirring, for several minutes until the liquid is absorbed. Add the salmon and another half cup of the liquid, and continue cooking, stirring and adding the liquid as each previous addition is absorbed. Take care that all the liquid does not cook away at any one time or the *risotto* will burn. It is ready when the mixture is creamy but the rice slightly chewy or *al dente*.

Stir in the cheese and a liberal amount of pepper to taste. Toss with a fork and serve at once. Serves 3–4 as a first course, or 2, with a salad, for lunch.

NOTE: The salt in the chicken broth plus the salmon should be sufficient for this dish. Taste and see if any is needed.

SMOKED SALMON STUFFED EGGS

4 ounces smoked salmon
¼ small onion
6 large eggs, hard-cooked, peeled, and halved lengthwise
2 tablespoons lemon juice
1 tablespoon drained capers

2 tablespoons mayonnaise
Several grindings of pepper
A dash of cayenne pepper
Additional capers and scallion green for garnish (optional)

---

* Italian short-grain rice, such as Arborio, is essential for making a true *risotto,* and can be found at most Italian markets.

Put the salmon and the onion in a food processor and whirl until finely chopped.

Remove the yolks from the eggs and add. Add the lemon juice, capers, mayonnaise, and red and black pepper, whirl to blend, scraping down the sides if necessary with a plastic spatula. Do not overprocess, for some flecks of salmon should be visible. (If you make the stuffing by hand, mash the yolks, grate the onion, chop the salmon and capers, and mix well with the other ingredients.) Stuff the egg white halves with the mixture, mounding it slightly into an egg shape.

If desired, garnish with "flowers" made of a caper, and "leaves and stems" cut from the scallion greens. Chill well covered with plastic wrap. Makes 12.

SHAD

As a harbinger of gastronomic spring, the appearance of shad is as eagerly awaited as that of the asparagus. These princely members of the herring family start their spawning journey up the Atlantic Coast from northern Florida in late December. Beginning in February, they are caught in Carolina waters, and later on farther up the coast as they begin to enter the major Eastern river systems to spawn. The height of their run is in March. In the Northeast, they will usually continue to appear at market until late May.

Eastern transplants are caught in the West in the Columbia River area. The season there is shorter—April to June.

Because shad has two rows of extra Y-shaped intramuscular bones, it is a more difficult fish to bone (although not very if you know how: see drawings 21 and 22) and is therefore usually sold in fillets. Those of the female shad are larger and fatter and more desirable; a whole market shad will usually be male. These may be boned for stuffing.

SHAD ROE: The roe of the female, prized for its size and delicate flavor, comes in two separate pouches, called a set, joined by a thin membrane; it may weigh as much as three quarters of a pound. Unless they are unusually large, the roe is sold in sets, and it is best not to separate the set until after cooking.

Wash the roe thoroughly, remove any veins or clots, taking care not to break the membrane. Let the roe stand in ice-cold salted water for 5 to 10 minutes before cooking, to firm it up, then sauté, bake, broil, or poach. If it is to be sautéed, gentle parboiling for 5 minutes is a good idea, as this cooks the outer membrane and prevents the eggs from breaking through. After parboiling, let it cool a bit, dredge in seasoned flour, and sauté in clarified butter over gentle heat for 4 to 5 minutes per side. Pour any butter left in the pan over the roe and serve with lemon wedges.

For baking and broiling, parboiling is not required. I do feel that sautéing is by far the most satisfactory method.

PLANKED SHAD: Put a cleaned and split 3- to 3½-pound shad on a seasoned and oiled hardwood plank, season with salt and pepper, and brush with melted butter. Bake in a preheated 400° oven for 25 minutes, remove from oven. Brush the shad with more melted butter, surround it with mounds of creamy mashed or duchesse potatoes, and return it to the oven until the potatoes are lightly browned on top. Garnish with lemon slices and parsley.

CHARCOAL-BROILED SHAD: See Index.

BAKED SHAD WITH ALMOND-STUFFED DATES

Food writer Paula Wolfert, a fabulous cook, adapted this classic recipe, which is considered "one of the great marvels of Moroccan cooking." Traditionally, it is made with the shad that run the Sebou River in winter near Fez. The shad are stuffed with large, fleshy Moroccan dates that have been stuffed with chopped almonds and spices. Lacking these, you can substitute California dates or large, fleshy prunes. Paula says that this recipe is every bit as good using carp, which can absorb a great deal of seasoning, or sea bass.

1 shad, approximately 4 pounds, cleaned, split, backbone removed, head and tail intact (or a carp or sea bass)
1 tablespoon salt
Freshly ground pepper
¾ cup water
2½ tablespoons "Cream of Rice" granulated rice
½ cup blanched almonds (about 5 ounces)

¾ teaspoon ground ginger
2–3 teaspoons sugar
6 tablespoons butter
1 pound (2 cups) pitted dates or prunes
½ cup water
2 tablespoons chopped onions
½–1 teaspoon cinnamon

Preheat oven to 350°.

Wash the fish rapidly under running water. (If you are using carp, see note p. 210). Pat the fish dry with paper towels, then rub with salt and pepper.

Bring the ¾ cup water to a boil in a small saucepan. Sprinkle with ½ teaspoon salt and quickly pour in the Cream of Rice. Boil for 30 seconds, beating well. Remove from heat and allow to stand, covered, for a few minutes until cool.

Grind the almonds, mix them with the cooled rice mixture, reserving 2 tablespoons of ground almonds for later use. Add ½ teaspoon of the ginger, the sugar, several good grindings of pepper, and 1 tablespoon of the butter to the almond-rice mixture. Blend well.

Open the dates or prunes and stuff each with about ½ teaspoon of the almond-rice mixture (if the dates are small, push two together to form a "sandwich").

Sew the opening of the fish three quarters of the way, filling the stomach cavity with as many stuffed fruits as possible. Complete the sewing.

Butter an ovenproof dish and in it place the stuffed fish on its side. Pour ½ cup water over the fish, season with salt and pepper and the remaining ¼ teaspoon of ginger. Add the chopped onions, any remaining stuffed fruit, and dot the fish with the remaining 5 tablespoons of butter, cut up. Bake for 45 minutes on the middle shelf of the oven, basting frequently.

Remove the fish from the oven, move the rack to its highest position, and raise heat to its highest setting. Carefully remove the sewing thread from the fish. Pull out the stuffed fruit from the cavity and place it around the fish. Sprinkle both fish and fruit with the ground cinnamon and the remaining ground almonds. Return the baking dish to the upper third of the oven and bake for about 15 minutes longer or until the fish is golden brown and crusty. Serve at once. Serves 6.

NOTE: If using carp, it must be soaked for about 15 minutes before proceeding with the recipe. This is not necessary with shad or bass.

A half cup of cooked rice may be substituted for the Cream of Rice, but the creamy texture of the stuffing will be affected.

BAKED SHAD STUFFED WITH SHAD ROE

2 shad fillets of equal size, skin on, totaling 1½ pounds	1 hard-cooked egg
1 pair shad roe, about 10–12 ounces	Salt and freshly ground pepper
1½ chopped shallots	1 cup fresh bread crumbs
¼ cup finely chopped parsley	½ cup milk
¼ teaspoon dried thyme	1 cup dry white wine
	3 tablespoons butter
	5 thin lemon slices for garnish

Preheat oven to 400°.

Lavishly butter a baking dish about 10 by 14 inches, set aside. Cut the roe set in half, remove and discard the membrane, chop up on a flat surface. Add the shallots, parsley, and thyme, chop briefly. Coarsely chop the egg, add, and chop all together to blend. Season to taste.

Lay 4 or 5 12-inch pieces of string across a clean work surface at roughly 2-inch intervals. In these lay one fillet, skin side down. Open the "flaps" and spoon in the roe mixture, smoothing the top with the back of the spoon. Over this lay the second fillet, skin-side up, and flaps down, thus enclosing the filling completely. Bring up the string ends and tie each with a slip knot to keep the "package" intact.

Lay the fish in the prepared baking dish, moisten the top with a table-spoon or two of wine, and dot the top with 2 tablespoons of the butter. Bake for 15 minutes. Pour the remaining wine over and around the fish, bake for an additional 15 minutes, basting frequently.

Cut off and discard the strings. Transfer the fish to a heated platter, using two spatulas. Pull off the top skin, using a sharp knife tip and your fingers.

Strain the pan liquid into a small saucepan, reduce slightly over high heat, and swirl in the remaining tablespoon of butter. Pour over the fish, garnish with lemon slices, and serve. Serves 4–5.

STUFFED SHAD WITH SORREL SAUCE

2 1-pound shad fillets, boned, or 1
    4-pound shad, cleaned, boned,
    and split
Salt and freshly ground pepper
4 tablespoons butter
2 tablespoons minced shallots
$\frac{3}{4}$ cup dry white wine

2 pairs shad roe, approximately 4
    ounces each, totaling 8 ounces
Cayenne pepper
$\frac{3}{4}$ pound fresh sorrel or $\frac{1}{2}$ cup
    canned sorrel purée
$\frac{3}{4}$ teaspoon cornstarch
1 cup heavy cream

Preheat oven to 375°.

Butter a baking dish (an oval 10 by 14-inch size works well) large enough to hold the fish, set aside.

Wash the shad, pat dry inside and out with paper towels, season with salt and pepper, and set aside.

Melt 2 tablespoons of the butter in a heavy stainless steel or enamel-lined skillet. Add the shallots, cook for a minute or two, then add the roes. Cook the roes for about 2 minutes on each side, then add the wine, cover, and simmer for 10 minutes over medium heat. Remove the roes with a slotted spoon, reserve the cooking liquid with the shallots.

Break up the roes with the edge of a spoon, season well with salt and pepper and a dash or two of cayenne, and spoon into the flap of the shad fillets. Put in the prepared baking dish, cover loosely with foil, and bake for 20 minutes in the oven.

While the fish is baking, prepare the fresh sorrel: wash the leaves well in two waters. Remove the stems by pulling backward toward the leaves. Put the sorrel in a pot of boiling salted water to cover, remove when the water returns to the boil. Drain in a colander but do not press. Melt the remaining 2 tablespoons of butter in a skillet, stew the sorrel over low heat, stirring occasionally, until all the moisture has evaporated and the sorrel is almost a purée, about 10 minutes. (If you are using canned sorrel purée, omit the stewing of the sorrel above: instead, melt the 2 tablespoons of butter and stir them into the purée.)

Reduce the reserved pan juices by a third. Dissolve the cornstarch in $\frac{1}{4}$

cup of the cream, then add to the remaining cream. Stir the mixture into the hot pan juices, simmer until smooth and thick. Add the sorrel purée, stir well, and let heat through. Correct the seasoning.

Serve the fish in the baking dish or transfer to a heated platter. Pour some of the heated sauce over and pass the rest in a sauceboat. Serves 6.

BAKED SHAD, FRENCH STYLE

1 shad, whole, cleaned, head and tail on	1 medium onion, chopped
Salt and freshly ground pepper	3 stalks celery, finely chopped
	4 tablespoons butter

Heat oven to 225°.

Wash, dry, and season the fish with salt and pepper inside and out. Combine the onion and celery, stuff the fish with the mixture. Put 2 tablespoons of the butter in small pieces inside the fish. Sew or skewer the fish opening. Rub the fish with the remaining butter, put the fish in a large, heavy brown paper bag. Secure by folding one end over several times and pinning it. Put on a baking sheet and bake for 7 hours. By this time all the small bones should be dissolved. Remove the fish to a platter and garnish with the stuffing. Serves 3–4.

COUNTRY-FRIED SHAD WITH ROE

2½ pounds shad fillets, skinned	3 tablespoons butter
2 pairs shad roe	2 slices bacon
1½ teaspoons salt	¾ cup corn oil
1 cup yellow or white cornmeal	Lemon juice
¾ teaspoon black pepper	Salt and freshly ground pepper
⅓ cup water	Minced parsley

Cut the fillets in 2 or 3 pieces, depending on their size. Put into a bowl with the roe, sprinkle the fish and roe with the salt, add cold water to cover, and let stand for 30 minutes. Drain the fish and roe, pat dry.

In a shallow dish, combine the cornmeal with the pepper. Coat the fillets with the mixture and let stand on a sheet of wax paper for 30 minutes.

Put the roe in a skillet, add the ⅓ cup of water, and cook, partially covered, over low heat until the water has evaporated. Add the butter, increase the heat, and sauté the roe for 2 minutes. Turn the roe carefully with a spatula and sauté for 6 minutes more. Keep warm in the skillet.

While the roe is cooking, sauté the bacon in a large, heavy skillet over moderate heat until crisp. Remove the bacon, add the corn oil to the bacon fat. Raise the heat until the fat is very hot but not smoking. Fry the shad in batches in the fat for 2 minutes on each side or until golden. Transfer the fish with a slotted spatula as it is fried to a platter lined with paper towels, keep warm in a low oven.

Transfer the roe to the center of the heated platter. Pour the pan butter over it, sprinkle with lemon juice, salt and pepper to taste. Arrange the shad around the roe and garnish the roe with minced parsley. Serves 6.

SHEEPSHEAD

This freshwater relative of the drum gets its name from the hump on its head. It has the flavorful white meat characteristic of crustacean-eating fish and can be used in most recipes calling for sea bass or cod. Although not a highly commercial fish, it is popular in the Midwest and South, where it appears whole or in fillets.

The California sheepshead is a wrasse, a marine fish unrelated to the freshwater sheepshead. There is also an Atlantic sheepshead, unrelated to either, whose onetime abundance gave the name to Sheepshead Bay in Brooklyn.

STURGEON

The sturgeon is the largest freshwater fish in the world, and the white sturgeon, or Pacific sturgeon (which can reach a length of 20 feet and weigh a thousand pounds) is the largest freshwater fish in North America. Along with the less desirable green sturgeon, it is taken in Pacific waters, ranging from Northern California to Alaska.

Because of the demand for their caviar, sturgeon were taken in such vast numbers at the end of the last century as to threaten their extinction. There was a total ban on sturgeon fishing from 1917 to 1954, when fishing them for sport became legal. One sees sturgeon occasionally at market, generally in steaks or boneless chunks, but it has never become very popular, although the firm hard flesh is good baked, barbecued, boiled, fried, pickled, smoked, and kippered. It is in this last form that it is primarily known and consumed in this country.

Sturgeon can be used in many of the same ways as fresh salmon; small ones (under 8 pounds) can be stuffed whole and braised or baked. Steaks may be sautéed or used like swordfish steaks.

ATLANTIC STURGEON.

SUNFISH

Sometimes called bream, sunfish belong to the same spiny-finned *Centrach-idae* family as the black bass but are found only on this continent. The bluegill is probably the best known, along with black and white crappies,* which are also sunfish. That delicately flavored crustacean eater, the rock bass, is still another sunfish.

HOW TO EAT A PANFISH: Fingers required! Pull gently up and outward on dorsal fin so that bones anchoring it come out in one piece. Detach anal fin and anchor bones in same manner; discard both pieces.

* In keeping with the maddening confusion in fish nomenclature, these are sometimes called "speckled perch."

Although not marketed commercially, sunfish are probably first in popularity with the fishermen of this country, and a lot of them are brought home for cooking. Because they tend to be small, too much is lost in trying to fillet them. The best preparation for them is simply to dip them in cornmeal seasoned with salt and pepper, and either panfry or deep-fry them. They are eaten in the manner of panfish, skin and all (indeed many think it is the best part). Hush Puppies ✹ and Coleslaw ✹ make the best accompaniment.

Bite off (and enjoy) edible meat along backbone. Leave backbone and rib bones intact, then discard.

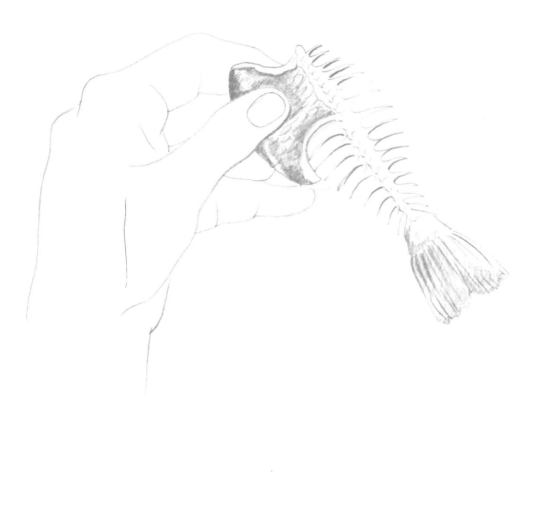

TROUT

There are numerous species of this much-loved member of the family *Sal-monidae*, all of which may be prepared more or less the same, the determining factor in the cooking of trout being the size. Generally, whole small trout up to 9 inches, including the mountain, golden, and speckled, are best pan-fried. Mountain trout are especially good dipped in cornmeal and panfried in bacon fat. Brook trout may be handled almost any way—in fillets, or butterflied and broiled. No matter what trout is used, the fish should be the freshest and the preparation simple. Trout is superb poached and a supreme delicacy smoked. Large lake trout, being salmonoids, can also be prepared as you would salmon of similar size—poached, stuffed, steaked, or sugar-cured, as *gravlax*.* The large rainbow trout known as the steelhead is good baked in foil with herb butter. Poached steelhead steaks with Lemon-Butter Sauce ❋ are simple to prepare and are worthy of a grand dinner party.

Because trout fishing is so popular, it is likely that trout is prepared over a campfire more than other fish. Nothing tastes quite as good as a trout

RAINBOW TROUT.

BROOK TROUT.

freshly caught and eaten by the stream from which it was fished. Panfrying is the most popular method; planking is another.

A freshly caught trout will ''curl'' if exposed to cooking heat within 6 to 8 hours of being caught. This makes even browning difficult and may also cause the skin to break. If very fresh trout are to be used in a formal meal, plan to dust them with seasoned flour and refrigerate overnight.

Trout is marketed whole, alive in tanks, flash frozen, and in breaded fillets.

Smoked Trout

Smoked trout, available whole and in fillets in fine specialty shops, is a great delicacy ranking with caviar and Scotch smoked salmon. It is formally served in fillet, usually with Horseradish Cream Sauce ✸ its only accompaniment. Puréed, it makes an interesting and different hors d'oeuvre.

SMOKED TROUT CANAPÉS

3 smoked trout
⅓ cup heavy cream
Juice of ½ lemon
2 tablespoons olive oil

12 slices buttered toast, crusts
    removed, cut diagonally into
    two triangles
Minced radishes

Remove the skin and bones from the trout, purée the fillets in a blender or food processor fitted with the steel blade. Add the cream, lemon juice, olive oil, and process in the blender. Spread on toast triangles and garnish each with a sprinkle of minced radish. Makes about 2 cups of purée, enough for 24 canapés.

VARIATION: For a delicious low-calorie hors d'oeuvre, spread this purée on sliced cucumber rounds. Makes about 30.

TRUITE AU BLEU

This preparation will afford you an indescribable pleasure, the sublime essence of trout, but can only be done with freshly caught trout or those taken live from a tank. Several small trout or one larger trout may be used.

The first thing to know is that, although your inclinations dictate otherwise, the slime, or natural waterproofing of the fish, must be kept on, as it is this coating, composed of microscopic scales, that makes *truite au bleu* blue. In order to keep the coating intact, do not wash the fish, and handle it as little as possible; certainly do not freeze it. The other characteristic of the dish, the curled position of the trout at the end of the cooking, is dictated by the muscles and nerves of a trout fresh from the water.

The live trout should be stunned by a sharp blow on the back of the head, then quickly gutted, gills removed, and the back and side fins cut off with kitchen scissors.

Here is a *truc* if the trout is not quite as fresh as it should be: curl it by threading a trussing needle with a long string and passing it through both eyes and then through the tail. Tie the head and tail together.

Put the trout in the bottom of a large pot. Have ready 2 quarts or so of boiling court-bouillon. Bring ¼ cup white vinegar to the boil and sprinkle it over the trout. Then add the court-bouillon, return to a boil, remove the pot from the heat, and let stand for 15–20 minutes. Remove the fish, drain, and serve with hot melted butter or Beurre Blanc Sauce ❋ or Hollandaise Sauce ❋, parsleyed new potatoes, and a salad. If you have tied the trout, remove the string.

Another way to do this dish is to prepare a simple court-bouillon of 1 cup vinegar, 4 quarts water, 1 bay leaf, salt, and some peppercorns, and after that simmers for 10 minutes or so, drop the trout in and simmer for 5 minutes longer. But this gives a more pronounced vinegar flavor preferred by some. I am not among them.

TROUT WITH ALMONDS

6 tablespoons butter	1 cup Seasoned Flour ❋
1 cup blanched slivered almonds	¾ cup Clarified Butter ❋
Juice of ½ lemon	Lemon wedges
4 12-ounce trout, whole, cleaned	

Melt the 6 tablespoons of butter in a small skillet, let cook for a minute or two until it takes on some color. Sauté the almonds in the butter over low heat until the butter becomes hazelnut brown. Remove from heat, sprinkle with lemon juice, and when the foam subsides return pan to low heat for a minute. Stir to coat nuts evenly, set aside and keep warm.

Wash and flour the trout as for Trout Meunière ❋. In a heavy skillet melt the clarified butter and fry the fish, 2 at a time, for 4 minutes per side or until golden brown. Shake the pan from time to time to prevent sticking.

Transfer the fish to a heated platter, spoon the almonds over, letting a few fall to each side, and serve, garnished with lemon wedges. Serves 4.

TROUT WITH PINE NUTS: Reduce the initial butter to 4 tablespoons and, following the recipe above, substitute ⅓–½ cup pine nuts for the almonds. Omit the lemon juice.

CAMP TROUT FRY

This is a hearty, filling dish that can be easily cooked over a camp charcoal fire as well as on the home stove. Just don't forget to take along the other ingredients!

4 trout, 8–12 ounces, cleaned,
head and tail on
Salt and freshly ground pepper
Flour

⅓ cup vegetable oil
3 medium potatoes, unpeeled,
parboiled for 10 minutes
1 small onion, sliced

Prepare a charcoal fire as required.

Season the trout with salt and pepper and dust lightly with flour.

Peel the potatoes, sliced in ¼-inch slices, and set aside.

When the fire is very hot, heat the oil in a large iron skillet until it is very hot but not smoking. (Or heat it on the stove.) Cook the fish until crisp and golden, 4–5 minutes per side, depending on the fish size.

As the fish cook, push them to one side, add the potato and onion slices. Season lightly. If the fish are done before the potatoes and onions, remove them from the pan and wrap in a double thickness of foil to keep them warm. Serves 4.

TROUT MEUNIÈRE

6 trout, 8 ounces, or 4 trout, 12
ounces, whole, cleaned
½ cup Seasoned Flour ❁
Vegetable oil
8 tablespoons (1 stick) sweet butter

Juice of ½ lemon
1 tablespoon finely chopped
parsley
Lemon wedges

Wash the trout under cold running water, drain, but do not dry. Dredge each fish completely with seasoned flour. Shake off excess.

In a heavy skillet pour oil to a depth of ¼ inch, heat until hot but not smoking. Fry the trout, 2 or 3 at a time, until golden. The smaller trout will take 3 minutes per side, the larger trout 4 minutes. Drain on paper towels and keep warm on a heated serving platter.

Pour off excess oil from the skillet and wipe it out. Melt the butter and let cook until it is golden brown (see Sautéing à la Meunière in the Index). Add the lemon juice and pour over the fish, sprinkle with chopped parsley, and serve with lemon wedges. Serves 4–6.

TROUT GRENOBLOISE

Follow the recipe for Trout Meunière (above), using the 12-ounce trout. To the melted butter add the pulp of 1 lemon, cut into tiny cubes, and 1 tablespoon of capers for each fish.

TROUT STUFFED WITH CRAB

4 12-ounce trout, split (see the
note p. 220) and boned
Salt and freshly ground pepper

8 tablespoons (1 stick) butter
½ cup finely chopped celery
½ cup finely chopped onions

½ cup finely chopped green pepper

1½ cups fresh crab, lump or backfin preferred

½ cup fresh bread crumbs

2 egg yolks

2 tablespoons finely chopped
   parsley

⅓ cup Fish Stock ✲ or clam juice

¼ cup dry white wine or vermouth

¾ cup heavy cream

1 teaspoon Dijon or dark prepared
   mustard

1 tablespoon sherry

Preheat oven to 400°.

Butter a baking dish large enough to hold the trout. Rinse the trout, pat dry, and sprinkle inside and out with salt and pepper.

Prepare the stuffing: heat 4 tablespoons of the butter in a skillet, add the celery, onions, and green pepper, and sautè until the onions are wilted. Remove from heat, stir in the crab meat, bread crumbs, parsley, and one beaten egg yolk. Mix gently but well and season to taste.

Stuff the trout with the crab mixture, arrange them on their sides in the prepared baking dish. Dot with the remaining 4 tablespoons of butter, cut up. Pour the fish stock and the wine around them, bake for 20 minutes, basting frequently.

Remove from oven, carefully pour off the liquid from the baking pan into a small saucepan, and bring it to a boil.

With your fingers, remove the skin from both sides of the fish, leaving it intact on the heads and tails. Transfer the fish to a heated serving platter and keep warm.

Add the cream to the saucepan and bring the mixture to a boil. Put the remaining egg yolk in a small bowl, add a bit of the hot sauce to it, blend, then pour the yolk mixture into the saucepan. Return to the heat and stir in the mustard and sherry. Correct seasoning but do not boil. Serves 4.

NOTE: For this recipe the fish should actually be "kited," or split along the top and joined by the belly skin.

TROUT IN TARRAGON CREAM

8 small trout, cleaned and drawn,
   tail end and fins removed

Salt and white pepper

3 tablespoons clarified butter or
   vegetable oil

8 small branches fresh tarragon
   (dried may not be substituted)

⅓ cup Fish Stock ✲ or clam juice

⅓ cup dry vermouth

1 teaspoon cornstarch

1¼ cups heavy cream

1 cup fresh soft bread crumbs

¼ cup butter, melted

2 tablespoons fresh tarragon
   leaves, minced

Preheat oven to 350°.

Wash and dry the trout thoroughly. Sprinkle on all sides with salt and pepper. Heat the butter or oil in a heavy 12-inch skillet, raise heat slightly, and brown trout on both sides, approximately 3–5 minutes.

Place the trout in a single layer in a shallow 9 by 13-inch baking dish. Place a branch of tarragon inside each, pour the stock and vermouth around them. Bring to just below a simmer on top of the stove, cover the baking dish with a lid or foil, and bake for 20 minutes. Baste occasionally.

Carefully pour off the pan juices into a small saucepan and bring to a boil. Cook until reduced by half. Keep the fish warm, covered with foil.

Dissolve the cornstarch in ¼ cup of the cream, blend into the rest of the cream, and whisk into the pan juices. Cook, stirring constantly, for 2 minutes, then cover and let simmer for 5 minutes. Pour over the fish, cover with the bread crumbs, drizzle melted butter over the bread crumbs, and place under the hot broiler for 3–5 minutes or until the crumbs are lightly browned. Garnish with the minced tarragon and serve at once. Serves 8.

SALMON TROUT

This trout, with a pink flesh that the French call *truite saumonée,* is a brown trout whose diet of crustaceans has produced a sweet pale pink flesh. It runs from 1½ to 4 pounds is expensive and impressive when served whole, hot or cold; decorated and glazed the salmon trout is the *ne plus ultra* of the buffet table. All preparations, hot and cold, that apply to salmon of similar size are applicable to salmon trout.

My favorite way to enjoy this delicacy is to simply season and enclose it in a buttered foil case on a bed of *mirepoix,* with some additional *mirepoix* and butter on top, and bake it according to the Canadian Theory. Noisette potatoes accompany nicely.

In England, it should be noted, salmon trout is sometimes called sea trout, not to be confused with our weakfish, also known as sea trout, an unrelated fish.

SALMON TROUT WITH SAUCE MOUSSELINE

Poach a whole dressed salmon trout that has the head and skin left on. Then carefully peel off the skin on one side, arrange on a serving plate surrounded by a continuous border of halved lemon slices with parsley clusters tucked into each point where the slices meet. Serve at room temperature with *Sauce Mousseline* ✽

BRAISED SALMON TROUT

Use a 4–5-pound salmon trout in the recipe for Braised Salmon.

WHITEFISH

The sweet-meated whitefish is found in the Great Lakes as well as many small lakes all over the country. Members of the *Salmonidae* (the same family as the salmon and trout), they are especially delicious poached and served cold; garnish as you would salmon.

The whitefish, which weighs from 2 to 6 pounds, is usually available at market, whole or in fillet. The fillets may be broiled or oven-fried, and the whole fish is delicious stuffed. For anglers, planking is a popular treatment. The roe is a delicacy and may be cooked as shad roe. Because of its low salt content whitefish is popular with people on low-sodium diets.

Smoked whitefish is a great delicacy and is especially popular as a Sunday brunch item with those of Middle-European or Jewish background. Frequently, a small whitefish, called cisco or chub, is served along with a variety of other smoked fishes such as salmon and sturgeon, and garnished with onion and cucumber slices and lemon wedges.

HUNGARIAN BAKED WHITEFISH WITH POTATOES

2 2-pound whitefish, cleaned,
  heads off, backbones removed
Salt and freshly ground pepper
8 tablespoons (1 stick) butter,
  softened
1 tablespoon minced scallions,
  white part only
1 tablespoon snipped dill
4 large potatoes, sliced $\frac{1}{8}$ inch
  thick

$2\frac{1}{4}$ teaspoons sweet Hungarian
  paprika
1 medium Spanish onion, thinly
  sliced
$\frac{1}{4}$ cup flour
A pinch of thyme
$\frac{2}{3}$ cup heavy cream
2 tablespoons minced parsley

Preheat oven to 450°.

Butter a baking dish or pan large enough to hold both fish. Season the fish well, inside and out, with salt and pepper, make 5 diagonal slits in one side of each fish. Lay them on a large sheet of foil, set aside.

In a small bowl, work together 4 tablespoons of the butter with the scallions and dill, using the back of a wooden spoon. Fill each slit with some of the mixture.

In a small saucepan, melt the remaining 4 tablespoons of butter. Spread the potato slices in the prepared baking dish, brush them with half the melted butter, and sprinkle them with salt and $\frac{1}{4}$ teaspoon of the paprika. Top the potatoes with the sliced onion and brush them with the remaining butter.

Mix the remaining 2 teaspoons paprika with the flour and thyme, dredge the fish with the mixture. Lay the fish on the onion-potato bed, bake in the upper third of the oven for 10 minutes, basting with a little of the cream. Reduce heat to 350°, continue baking for 25–30 minutes more, basting the fish frequently with the cream until the entire amount is used. When done, the fish should flake easily and the potatoes should be soft.

Transfer the fish to a heated platter, arrange the potatoes and onions around it, and sprinkle the fish with the parsley. Serve with a cucumber salad if desired. Serves 8–10.

WHITEFISH STUFFED WITH SALMON MOUSSE

A 2-pound whitefish, cleaned, boned through the back, head and tail removed
Salt and freshly ground pepper
1 pound fresh salmon steak
1 egg white, unbeaten
1 tablespoon lemon juice
3/4 cup heavy cream

1 tablespoon minced onion
4 tablespoons (1/2 stick) butter, melted
1/4 cup dry white wine
8 medium raw shrimp, peeled and butterflied
Parsley sprigs

Preheat oven to 300°.

Wash the whitefish, pat dry, and spread open, skin-side down, on a work surface. Run your fingers over it to locate any bones that remain and remove these one by one, preferably with large tweezers. Season the whitefish lightly with salt and pepper, set aside. Lightly butter a shallow baking dish of suitable size and set aside.

Prepare the salmon mousse: remove the skin and gray edge from the salmon steak, cut the flesh away from the center bone, scraping it free from the fine rib bones. Make sure that all bones are removed before cutting up the flesh in chunks. Put in a food processor, add the egg white, lemon juice, cream, onion, 1 teaspoon salt, and pepper to taste. Process until puréed, then taste and correct seasoning.

Using a rubber spatula, scoop out the salmon mixture and spread evenly on one side of the whitefish, about one inch thick. Fold over the other half of the fish, press down lightly, and with the tip of a sharp knife make several diagonal slashes on the side of the fish. (The recipe may be prepared ahead to this point and refrigerated; let the fish come to room temperature before proceeding.) Pour the melted butter over the fish, sprinkle with the wine, and bake for 30 minutes, basting occasionally.

At the end of 15 minutes, remove the fish from oven, arrange the shrimp on top, baste them with the pan juices, and return to oven to complete cooking. When the fish is done, garnish with parsley and serve immediately. Serves 4.

SIX

Shellfish, Mollusks, and Bivalves

ABALONE

A univalve mollusk found clinging to rocks along the California coast, the abalone consists of a large single shell and a strong foot-like muscle that grasps the rock. The tough foot (the edible portion) must be pounded to tenderize it before eating. Fresh abalone is becoming a rare sight in California fish markets; skin divers are reluctant to go for them, because strict state laws regulate the daily take as well as the seasons during which they may be gathered. Abalone colonies are also decimated by the sea otter, who adores them. It is now forbidden by law to ship abalone taken from California waters to other states.

Abalone was not always prized by the Californians—indeed at the beginning of the century it was a subject of almost complete indifference and prized only by Chinese immigrants who, knowing a good thing, dried them and shipped them back to China in great quantities.

Abalone is available in cans, and frozen abalone "steaks" from Mexican and Japanese waters are ready for cooking after thawing.

TO SHUCK AND PREPARE LIVE ABALONE: Force a heavy wooden wedge or tire iron tip between the meat and the shell, move it around until the muscle falls from the shell. Cut off the stomach on the side that was attached to the shell, taking care not to break the sack. Wash the meat in cold water. With a sharp knife trim off the dark mantle around the edges, and the dark skin from the bottom of the foot. (These trimmings may be minced and used for chowders or fritters.) Hold the meat down firmly on a board and with a thin sharp knife cut *across* the grain into slices about ⅜ inch thick. To tenderize, pound each slice with a wooden mallet, using a light rhythmical motion, pounding evenly until it is limp and velvety. An alternative to pounding is mincing the meat through a food chopper.

CANNED ABALONE: After draining, these may be used in any recipe calling for abalone. Reserve the liquid for soups. To store abalone, rinse it with cold water and put into a jar with fresh cold water to cover and cap tightly. Refrigerate and change the water every other day if not used immediately. It will keep for about a week.

ABALONE STEAKS

Abalone steaks can be either great or terrible. It's all in the cooking, assuming that the meat is already tenderized, and overcooking even by a few seconds toughens them. San Franciscans eat abalone steaks with a fork only; they feel that if it is not tender enough to be cut thus and consumed, it is not tender enough to eat.

Slice abalone as described in the preceding section or buy precut steaks, allowing one or two per person. You may slash the edges to prevent curling, although this is not really necessary. Dip the slices in an egg beaten with a tablespoon of water, then in very fine bread crumbs, and panfry for *a maximum of 50 seconds per side* in hot butter. Time precisely by the clock; don't leave it to chance; additional cooking will make it rubbery. The cooked color of both sides should be pale gold. Serve at once with lemon wedges.

CLAMS

There are three species of this popular mollusk along the Atlantic Coast. The largest member of the hard clam species *(Venus mercenaria)* is known variously as "quahog"* (its Indian name), "mahogany clam," or "black quahog" because of its dark shell. Because the quahog's strong clam flavor enhances chowders, it is often referred to simply as "chowder clam." "Cherrystone" and "littleneck" are market names indicating two sizes of quahogs, littlenecks being the smaller and cherrystones the larger. Any clam larger than a cherrystone (maximum: 3 inches in diameter) is referred to as a chowder clam.

The second species, *Mya arenaria,* the soft-shell clam, has a thin, elongated shell and a "neck," or siphon, that extends beyond the shell. These

STEAMER CLAM.

* Pronounced kwo-hog.

are popularly known as "steamers" and in the Chesapeake Bay area as "maninose."

The surf clam *(Spisula solidissima)*, also known as the "skimmer," "sea," or "bar clam," is the third species and makes up the largest volume of clams caught along the Atlantic Coast, although it is not so valuable as the hard and soft-shell clams. Canned clams are mostly surf clams.

In general, the best of the hard-shell clams have fine-textured, concrete gray shells that when tapped sound full and solid. Coarse-grained shells streaked with yellow look and are softer. The clam inside will be flatter, less firm, slightly yellow and have less of that characteristic deep-sea taste. Live clams should be tightly closed, although those varieties with the protruding neck are not as tightly closed as the others.

WHITE SAND CLAM.

The Pacific Coast has a number of varieties including the geoduck (pronounced gooeyduck), the razor clam, so called because its shape resembles an old-fashioned folding razor, and the small, sweet butter clams, usually eaten on the half-shell. These are sometimes called "moneyshells," as the Indians of the Pacific Northwest used them as wampum. There is also a Pacific littleneck, unrelated to the Eastern bivalve of the same name.

STOUT RAZOR CLAMS.

One of the choicest—and scarcest—of the Pacific clams is the Pismo, named for the beach where it was first found. It is a large clam (only those 5 inches or more across may be gathered), and one usually eats the tender adductor muscle on the half shell and uses the body meat hashed, minced, fried, or in chowders.

Some people think that the geoduck clam, which is mostly neck, tastes like abalone but sweeter. The average geoduck weighs about 3 pounds, about half of which is meat; it lives beneath several feet of hard-packed sand or gravel and must be harvested by diving rather than dredging or surf-digging as with the other clams. Canned, they are available minced or smoked.

The oval mud clam is found along the Northern California and Pacific coasts. Only its white flesh is eaten. The white sand clam, sometimes called the giant Macoma and its relative, the bent-nose clam, are other favorites of do-it-yourself clammers. Both can be used in any clam recipe after being purged of the considerable mud that characterizes both.

Clams from both coasts are sold live and in the shell, either by the dozen, the count, or the pound. Shucked, they are sold by the pint and the quart, which usually includes the liquor. East Coast varieties are available the year round, which is also true of varieties harvested in the Pacific Northwest. The season in California is shorter, roughly November through April. There, in the spring and summer, microscopic organisms are present in the sea, known as the "red tide," which make clams and certain other shellfish poisonous. Beaches where they are gathered are quarantined during this time.

Quick-frozen clams are available shucked and minced. In the West, the geoduck is available commercially frozen, in steaks, or in chunks. To cook frozen clams, allow them to thaw completely in the refrigerator, then prepare as you would fresh. Cook them immediately and never refreeze.

Canned clams, which are available whole or minced, are already cooked and need only be heated.

TO CLEAN: Scrub clams well and rinse one by one under cold running water or put in a large soup kettle and cover with fresh, cold sea water or salted water* (1 teaspoon to 1 quart) and let stand in a cold place for several hours then rinse in cool water. Discard any that are open.

TO OPEN CLAMS: To facilitate opening, put them in a bowl with ice cubes and water to cover for a half hour. Hopefully this will cause the muscle to relax enough to permit insertion of the knife without a major battle. When

---

*Fresh clean sea water is the ideal medium to purge clams. It can be prepared artificially from sea salt available in pet shops handling saltwater aquarium fish. If placed in fresh water, most saltwater clams will close tightly and will not purge themselves of sand and other material. Those that cannot close their shells tightly will expire in a relatively short time, because the salt balance in their tissues will be upset. Soft-shell clams can survive in waters of lower salinity. A cup of cornmeal added to the water will help clams expel sand.

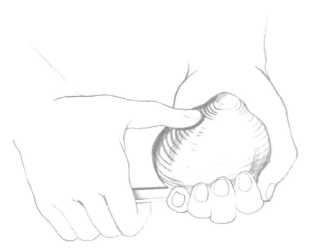

TO OPEN CLAMS: Hold clam flat side down in palm of left hand. Using blunt-ended clam-shucking knife, position knife edge along groove between shells at hinge or thick end of clam. Curl middle three fingers of left hand over blade and try to push or squeeze it into crack without wiggling it, which may cause shell to crack.

Once knife is inserted, sever hinge or adductor muscle, which holds shells shut, with a quick slightly twisting motion. Make a quick run of knife blade around inside of shells.

Cut clam free of shell and remove any grit or bits of shell.

opening clams, work over a large bowl, so you don't lose any of the clam juice.

Shucked clams may be stored in the coldest part of your refrigerator for up to five days.

Fresh clams can also be steamed open (frowned on by purists) by pouring a little boiling water over them and letting them stand for a few minutes until the muscle relaxes. The clams must then be promptly removed from the hot water, plunged into cold, and opened. Another method is to put the clams in the freezer for about an hour, which will cause the muscle and the hinge ligament to relax. Complete extraction with a knife as described above. Knife shucking, however, is by far the most popular method, and really very simple once you master the firm, quick motion. The clams may then be served on the half shell or the clam meat removed and used as required. If the clams are not to be served raw, they may be opened by placing in a preheated 450° oven for 3–5 minutes, in one layer in a baking pan. Discard any unopened ones.

Razor clams: Use any of the above methods to open the razor clam, then snap off the neck with scissors. Remove the dark parts, which are the gills, and the digestive tract.

Geoduck clams: Plunge into boiling water until the shells open. Sever the adductor muscle, discard the skin and stomach, and rinse well in cold water. It is possible to cut three steaks from one geoduck (one from the breast and two from the neck). These may be breaded and fried and the remaining meat minced and used for chowder.

Pismo clams: Undisturbed clams often open their shells a fraction of an inch; a swift knife insertion will cut one of the adductor muscles so the clam cannot close tightly. Then the other muscle can be severed. At this point the clam should have all its sand washed out under running water. Any attempt to rinse them before the muscles are cut will cause them to "clam up" the minute water hits. Open clams over some vessel to collect the juices, which you can then drink, use in soups or in fish cookery.

Having removed the adductor muscles (called "buttons"), trim off the siphons, mantle, and gills. The liver, a dark, ball-shaped mass, can be flicked out. This leaves the foot, which may have one hard, dark side from digging—this can also be trimmed. Often the outer portions of the foot are darker than the pink center; this is normal and may be eaten.

All parts of the clam may be used; the buttons in a seafood cocktail, the trimmings ground or chopped for chowder or clam stuffing, and finally, the foot, which may be sliced into two discs, pounded (as abalone) and fried. (Slicing this way reveals the intestine, which can be picked out and discarded.) Or the meat may be minced for chowder or hash.

STEAMERS

Soft-shell clams are traditional for this dish, though there is no reason that hard clams, or butter clams cannot be steamed. Plan on 18–24 clams per person, depending on size and appetites.

If you have dug the clams yourself, soak them in at least 2 changes of water for 15 minutes each time to get rid of excess sand, or soak for 1 hour in cold water to which ¼ cup of cornmeal has been added. Then scrub each clam well and rinse under running water. If you have a special clam steamer, put them in the top with 2 inches of salted cold water in the bottom. Otherwise put this amount of water in a large kettle with a secure lid and add the clams. Cover; after the water comes to a rolling boil, steam just until the clams open, 3–5 minutes. Do not overcook the clams or they will be tough and rubbery. Discard any that remain closed. Drain off the broth and serve in bowls along with bowls of melted butter. To eat, dip each clam first in broth (this washes off any stubborn sand and seasons the clam as well), then in the melted butter. Often the clam juice is drunk at the end of the meal.

CLAMS ON THE HALF SHELL

Allow 6–8 cherrystone, littleneck, or butter clams for each serving. If possible, have the fish market open them and discard the top shells. Otherwise follow the directions for cleaning and opening. Open as close to serving time as possible. Serve on crushed ice garnished with lemon wedges and pass a pepper mill.

CLAM DIP

An 8-ounce can minced clams or 1 cup fresh clams, minced
3-ounce package cream cheese

1½ teaspoons chopped scallion or onion
½ teaspoon Worcestershire sauce

Drain the clams, reserving 1 tablespoon of the juice. Soften the cream cheese by beating it with the juice. Add the scallion or onion and the Worcestershire sauce, mix well, then mix in the clams. Serve with crackers, chips, or raw vegetables. Makes 1–1½ cups.

PAN-FRIED CLAMS

Pat shucked clams dry on paper towels. Dredge in flour that has been seasoned with salt and pepper, sauté in butter (about 3 tablespoons for each pint of clams) for about 3 minutes over moderate heat, turning once, until the clams are lightly browned. Serve with lemon wedges.

VARIATION *Clam Pan Roast:* Pat the clams dry but do not flour. Sauté in butter (about 4 tablespoons to 1 pint clams) for 2–3 minutes just until the clams plump up and are heated through. Serve with lemon wedges.

VARIATION *Breaded Fried Clams:* Pat the clams dry and dredge in flour lightly seasoned with salt, pepper, and a dash of cayenne. Dip in a mixture of beaten egg and milk (2 tablespoons for each egg) and roll in cracker meal or a half-and-half mixture of flour and cornmeal. Sauté as above until golden and drain on paper towels before serving.

TO DEEP-FAT-FRY: Flour the shucked clams as above. Heat the cooking oil in a deep fat fryer to 375°. Place a single layer of clams in the basket, lower into the fat, and fry for 1–2 minutes or until golden brown. Drain on paper towels and serve with lemon.

GAGE AND TOLLNER'S SOFT CLAM BELLY BROIL

Allow about 15 steamers per person. Open the clams, trim away the muscle, and cut off the siphon. Roll the clam "bellies" in cracker meal and refrigerate for a half hour. Broil by the handful on a fine-meshed grill set over red-hot charcoal for about 5 minutes with the rack set as close to the flame as possible. As soon as the crumbs take on color, remove from fire. Do not overcook, as the delicate belly can toughen. If they are being done in batches, keep them warm until all are done. Place on whole wheat toast, brush bellies with melted butter and serve as an appetizer.

CLAMS CASINO

24 cherrystone clams on the half
   shell
4 slices bacon, cut into 6 squares
   each
4 tablespoons butter, softened
2 teaspoons anchovy paste

¼ cup finely chopped parsley
¼ cup minced green pepper
¼ cup minced pimiento
Several dashes of Tabasco sauce
Lemon wedges

Preheat oven to 450°.

Make a bed of rock salt in a jelly-roll pan or on several pie plates, dampen it slightly, and heat, uncovered, in the oven for 5 minutes. Arrange the clams on the half shell on the hot rock salt.

Partially fry the bacon in a skillet, drain, and set aside.

Blend the butter with the anchovy paste, spoon about ½ teaspoon of the mixture *under* each clam, sprinkle the tops with the parsley, green pepper, and pimiento, and season each with a dash of Tabasco. Top each with a piece of bacon. Bake until the bacon is crisp and the butter has melted, or broil for about 5 minutes. Serve with lemon wedges. Serves 4.

ITALIAN-STYLE STUFFED CLAMS

If stuffed clams consisting largely of flavored bread crumbs leave you cold, these will be a pleasant treat; the flavor is very special. They may be prepared early in the day and baked just before serving.

36–48 littleneck clams on the half
  shell
6 shallots, peeled
4 cloves garlic, peeled and cut in
  half
½ cup loosely packed fresh basil
  leaves (optional)
½ cup loosely packed fresh parsley
  leaves
1 small tomato, quartered, or 2
  canned tomatoes, peeled

¾ cup freshly grated Parmesan
  cheese
2 slices lean bacon, cut into pieces
Salt and freshly ground pepper
¼ teaspoon red pepper flakes or
  more to taste (optional)
¼ cup olive oil
½ cup dry white wine

Preheat oven to 400°.

Loosen the clams on the shells and arrange them on a baking sheet with a rim.

Combine the shallots, garlic, basil, parsley, tomato, ½ cup of the cheese, bacon, and salt and pepper to taste (not too much salt because clams are salty). Grind or chop in a food processor until only very small pieces of the ingredients are visible. Stir in the red pepper flakes.

Spoon the mixture over the clams, dividing equally, and smooth the tops with the back of a spoon. Sprinkle with small pinches of the remaining cheese. (They may be prepared ahead to this point and refrigerated, covered with plastic wrap.)

Drizzle the oil and wine over the tops and bake for 15 minutes or until piping hot. Run briefly under the broiler to brown the tops slightly. Serves 6–8 as a first course.

BAKED STUFFED CLAMS ORIGANATA

36 littleneck clams in the shell
2 cups fresh bread crumbs made
  from home-style white bread
1 cup freshly grated Parmesan
  cheese (about 4 ounces)
1 handful parsley sprigs, minced
  (about 2 tablespoons)
¼ teaspoon minced garlic

1 teaspoon dried oregano
½ teaspoon dried thyme
½ teaspoon dried basil
½ cup dry sherry
Freshly ground pepper
½ cup olive oil
½ cup white wine

Open the clams or have your fish dealer do it for you. Reserve ¾ cup of the clam juice, set aside the remainder for another use. Free each clam from the shell. Discard the shallower shell halves, wash, dry, and reserve the deeper halves.

Place the shells with a clam in each in a baking pan (or two) and refrigerate while preparing the stuffing.

Combine the reserved clam juice with the bread crumbs, cheese, parsley, garlic, oregano, thyme, basil, and sherry. Season with several good twists of pepper. Do not use salt; the clam juice contains enough.

Remove 2 tablespoons of the olive oil, set aside. Combine the remainder with the bread crumb mixture and mix very well.

Preheat oven to 450°.

Remove the clams from the refrigerator, top each with some of the crumb mixture, dividing it equally (they can be prepared ahead to this point and refrigerated). Arranged the filled shells in the pan, spoon a drop of the reserved olive oil over each. Pour the wine into the pan (or pans), taking care not to wet the stuffing. Add more if the bottom of the pan is not covered.

Bake in the upper third of the oven until well browned and crusty, 10–15 minutes. If you like them a little browner, run under a hot broiler for a minute or two. Just before serving, spoon a little of the pan juices over each clam. Allow 6 per person as a first course. Serves 6.

CLAMS MARINARA

Follow the recipe for Mussels Marinara ✱ but substitute 3 dozen littleneck clams, cleaned, for the mussels.

AMÊIJOAS NA CATAPLANA

A *cataplana* is an ingenious hinged copper cooking pot used in Portugal's Algarve Province for stove-top cookery. It functions like a very tightly sealed casserole. You can substitute a shallow heavy pot with a tightly fitting lid to make this tasty dish of clams, sausages, tomatoes, and onions.

36–40 littleneck or cherrystone
  clams
3 tablespoons olive oil
1½ cups thinly sliced onions
1 teaspoon paprika
1 teaspoon crushed, dried hot red
  pepper
1 chorizo, chopped (see the note
  p. 237)

3 tablespoons chopped prosciutto
  or plain ham
2 tomatoes, peeled and seeded
1 bay leaf
2 cloves garlic, minced
1 tablespoon chopped parsley
½ cup white wine

Scrub the clams and set aside.

Heat the oil in a medium-size heavy pot and in it sauté the onions until translucent. Add the paprika, red pepper, chorizo, and prosciutto, mix well. Add the tomatoes, bay leaf, garlic, parsley, and wine, cook over medium heat until liquid is reduced by a third. Lay the clams on the vegetable bed, cover the pot tightly, and reduce heat. Cook for 8–10 minutes or until the clams open. Discard any that remain closed. Serve them in their shells in heated soup plates, with some of the sauce spooned over. Serves 4.

NOTE: The chorizo, or Spanish pork sausage, is available in specialty food shops and Latin markets.

CLAM HASH

3 slices bacon
¼ cup finely minced onions
1½ cups finely diced cooked
    potatoes
1½ cups minced clams, or a 10½-
    ounce can, drained

3 eggs, lightly beaten
¼ cup light cream or milk
1 teaspoon salt
Several grindings of fresh pepper
A dash of nutmeg

Fry the bacon in a skillet over moderate heat until crisp, drain on paper towels, crumble, and reserve.

Add the onions to the drippings in the pan, cook over low heat until just transparent. Add the potatoes and the clams, press them down with a spatula to form a large pancake, and cook over moderate heat for 7–10 minutes. As a crust forms on the bottom, stir it in with a fork. Finally press down and let cook without stirring.

Mix the eggs with the cream or milk, salt, pepper, and nutmeg, pour over the clams, and cook just until the eggs are set, tilting the pan as needed to let the uncooked portion run underneath. Sprinkle with the reserved bacon and cut in wedges as pie. Serves 4.

CLAM FRITTERS

1½ cups flour
½ teaspoon salt
6 tablespoons butter
3 eggs, separated
¾ cup beer
24 fresh cherrystone clams,
    shucked, drained, and finely
    chopped

1 tablespoon finely chopped
    parsley
1 tablespoon snipped chives
2 tablespoons vegetable oil
Lemon wedges (optional)
Parsley sprigs (optional)

Sift the flour and salt into a mixing bowl. Melt 4 tablespoons of the butter and stir in. Beat the egg yolks lightly and add. Gradually blend in the beer, let this batter stand in a warm place for about 1 hour.

Add the clams, parsley, and chives to the batter. Beat the egg whites until stiff, stir a small amount into the batter, then fold in the rest.

Heat the remaining 2 tablespoons of butter with the oil in a heavy skillet. When hot, drop the batter in by the tablespoonfuls. Brown the fritters lightly on both sides and drain on paper towels. Serve hot, as an hors d'oeuvre or as a first course, garnished with lemon wedges and parsley. Makes about 36 2½-inch fritters.

CLAM PIE

Clam pie is particularly indigenous to New York's eastern Long Island. Like clam chowder, its variations have passionate exponents. Some use all quahogs or hard clams. Others use both hard and soft clams. Additional flourishes can include diced cooked bacon, grated green pepper, or chopped celery.

The pie can have one crust or two, or it can be enriched by adding egg and cream. One old recipe directs that the pie be served with hot chicken gravy. The old recipes are uniform in omitting salt, but you may add some if you wish. However they are made, clam pies are a special treat.

2 cups clams, drained and cut up
   (18–24 cherrystones or 1 dozen
   chowder clams)
1 medium onion, cut up
1 medium potato, peeled and
cut up
1 egg

¼ cup heavy cream
¾ teaspoon poultry seasoning
Freshly ground pepper
2 tablespoons chopped parsley
1 recipe Rich Pastry Dough ❋ for a
   2-crust pie
2 tablespoons butter

Preheat oven to 400°.

Put the clams, onion, and potato through a meat grinder or chop coarsely in a food processor. Beat the egg with the cream, add to the clam mixture along with the poultry seasoning, pepper, and parsley, and refrigerate mixture while you prepare the pastry.

Line a 9-inch pie pan with the bottom pastry, fill with the clam mixture, dot with butter, and add the pastry top. Crimp the edges and make a few slits to let steam escape. Bake for 10 minutes, then lower oven heat to 350° and bake for 30–35 minutes more. Serve piping hot. Serves 4 as a main course (Coleslaw ❋ is the traditional accompaniment) or 6 as a first course.

CONCH AND SCUNGILLI

Conch (pronounced "conk") is a marine gastropod or ocean snail with an interesting flavor rather like that of a strong, exotic clam. Because of its tough muscle fiber and rubbery texture, it must be treated in some way to tenderize it: in the Antilles it is usually pounded with a mallet; in the Bahamas it is allowed to stand with salt for 15 minutes, beaten with the edge of a shell for 5 minutes, then washed. Unless it is to be subjected to long stewing, it requires parboiling before using. Initial preparation is as follows: scrub the shell under cold running water, put in a large, heavy kettle with boiling water to cover, and add 1 tablespoon salt and the juice of a half lemon. Cover, bring to a second boil, and boil for 3 minutes. Drain and let cool or run cold water over the shells until they can be handled. Knock out the meat or pry out of the shell with a skewer, cut off the hard black foot and the curled tip. Rinse in cold water. The meat is now ready to be simmered, ground, parboiled, or tenderized by beating or pounding.

TO PARBOIL CONCH: Put in a pot with water to cover and 1 tablespoon lemon juice for each 2 cups of water. Simmer, covered, for 2–4 hours until tender. Cooking time can be reduced by half by first slicing the meat rather thinly. Drain and proceed with recipe.

TO FRY CONCH: Thin slices of parboiled conch may be panfried with onions that have been wilted in butter. Dry the conch slices well first.

Conch is available fresh in Florida* and on the Gulf Coast, and canned and frozen in some localities. The latter need not be thawed before cooking.

Scungilli, though often translated as conch, is actually a smaller, stronger-flavored conch relative, the whelk, much loved by Italians. In this country it can be found along the northeast coast, especially in New Jersey coastal waters. It is more like a large snail and does not require the lengthy tenderizing of the semitropical conch.

CONCH SALAD

1 pound conch meat
1 large onion, finely chopped
⅓ cup lime juice
¼ cup wine vinegar
4 tablespoons olive oil
1½ teaspoons Worcestershire
    sauce

2 hot red peppers, finely chopped,
    or ¼ teaspoon hot pepper sauce
1 large green or red pepper,
    seeded and chopped
2 stalks celery, coarsely chopped
Salt and freshly ground pepper

Put the conch meat through the coarse blade of a food grinder, combine with the onion, lime juice, vinegar, olive oil, and Worcestershire sauce in the bowl. Mix well and refrigerate for several hours or overnight.

Add the peppers or pepper sauce, green or red pepper, and celery, season to taste. Mix thoroughly and chill for at least an hour. Serves 4–6.

NOTE: Chopped tomatoes may be added for color.

FLORIDA CONCH SOUP

1 pound conch steak
¼ pound salt pork
1 large onion, coarsely chopped
1 sweet pepper, seeded and
    coarsely chopped

½ cup pearl barley, cooked
    according to directions and
    dried
1 quart water
2 tablespoons salt

*Native-born Key Westers are often called "conchs."

Pound the conch, salt it, and let stand for 15 minutes. Rinse, cover with water and bring to a boil. Drain, wash again, then put through the finest blade of a meat grinder or chop finely in a food processor.

In a heavy soup kettle render the salt pork, add the onion and pepper, and cook until the onions are transparent. Add the conch, the barley, 1 quart of water, and salt, bring to a simmer, cover, and simmer for 1½–2 hours until the conch is very tender. Add more water as needed to keep the soup from getting too thick. Serves 4–5.

SCUNGILLI MARINARA

1 pound scungilli, thinly sliced
3 tablespoons olive oil
2 cloves garlic, pressed
1 medium onion, thinly sliced
⅓ cup finely chopped celery
2 cups Italian plum tomatoes, undrained
⅓ cup tomato paste
¼ cup dry red wine

1 teaspoon salt
Freshly ground pepper
1 teaspoon dried oregano
1 teaspoon fresh basil, chopped, or ½ teaspoon dried
1 bay leaf
¼ teaspoon hot pepper flakes (optional)

Parboil the scungilli for 15 minutes and drain.

Heat the oil in a large, heavy skillet, add the scungilli, garlic, onions, and celery, brown well. Add the tomatoes, tomato paste, wine, salt and pepper to taste, bring to a simmer, cover, and cook slowly for about 5 minutes. Add the oregano, basil, bay leaf, and pepper flakes, uncover, and cook for 5 minutes longer. If the liquid in the pan is too thin, raise the heat and cook for 5 minutes more to reduce. Discard the bay leaf. Serves 4.

CRAB

Crab in its various forms ranks with lobster, shrimp, and perhaps even caviar as the ultimate gift of the sea to the palate. The taste for it may run to passion, whether one's preference is for soft-shell crabs or velvety crab meat, with its elusive, haunting sea taste.

HARD-SHELL ATLANTIC BLUE CRAB (also known in the South as sea crab): *Callinectes sapidus,* whose males are called "Jimmies" and females "sooks," are found in salt and brackish water all along the Atlantic and Gulf coasts. The best come from the Chesapeake Bay area. The season for blue crabs is mid-March or April until November, with the best crabbing in late July to September, when the crabs frequent shallow water. They are especially abundant in mouths of streams and rivers around eel grass.

SOFT OR SOFT-SHELL CRAB: There is an impression that the hard-shell Atlantic blue crab and the soft-shell variety are two separate species.

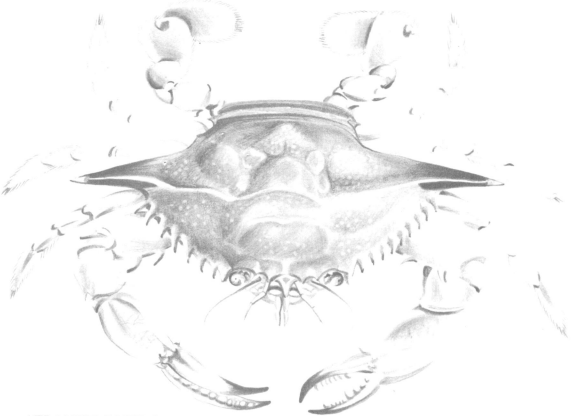

ATLANTIC BLUE CRAB.

Actually the latter are simply blue crabs that have molted or shed their shell, something the average crab does three times a year as part of its growth process. The season for soft crabs is Memorial Day to Labor Day, with the peak in June and July. In Louisiana, where crabs are a way of life, it is not uncommon to gather one's own "green"* crabs (those within a day of shedding), take them home, and peel off the shell, or wait for the crabs to burst out themselves. In the latter case the crabs are then known as "busters," in the former, "peelers." Soft-shell crabs may be deep-fried (the preferred method if they are very small) or sautéed meunière. The smaller soft-shells are thought to be the choicer; allow 2–3 per person, or more for big appetites. They can also be broiled, though I can't think why anyone would. In any event, they should be alive when you buy them.

To clean live soft-shell crabs, peel back the triangular "apron" or flap that folds under the rear of the body. With a small sharp knife, scrape out the stomach and intestines, found behind the eyes. Turn the crab and cut off the "face" at a point just behind the eyes. Lift each point at the sides with the fingers, clean out the feathery gills, or "dead man's fingers." Squeeze the body so the sand sac pops out of the head opening, and wash under cold running water.

*Not to be confused with the bellicose green crab *(Carcinus maenas)* found in great numbers along tide lines from Cape Cod to Long Island.

TO COOK LIVE BLUE CRABS: Boil in lightly salted water, and when the crab is cool, remove the back and spongy parts under the shell. Split the body and remove meat. Crack the claws and dig out the meat.

DUNGENESS CRAB: the prince of crabs, the Dungeness *(Cancer magister)*, gets its name from that region in Washington State, but it is found from Alaska to Southern California. It is one of the largest crabs. To eat a freshly dressed Dungeness crab is a gastronomic high, not at all the same as eating the precooked, frozen version available in Eastern markets. My fondest memories of San Francisco revolve around a feast of freshly boiled Dungeness crab at an oilcloth-covered table in the back room of Swann's Oyster Depot, the tasty morsels dipped into either fresh mayonnaise, Louis dressing or the incredibly rich and unctuous roe, or "crab butter" itself, everything washed down with great drafts of California Colombard. Some people feel that the Dungeness tastes better if cleaned *after* cooking—others do it routinely before.

TO CLEAN DUNGENESS CRAB: Lay the crab on its back on a cutting board, put a sharp knife along the midline, and whack it with a mallet. As with lobster, this will kill the crab instantly. If you are cleaning it before cooking, twist off the front claws where they join the body. Do the same with the legs. Scrub well and reserve. Pry off the shell, using a knife if needed, and scrape out the spongy gills. Then crack each claw and leg segment, split the crab body along midline, then divide each half in half.

TO CLEAN AND CRACK A LIVE DUNGENESS CRAB: Grasp crab from rear and, holding onto two legs, place shell down on board. (You may want to wear rubber gloves.)

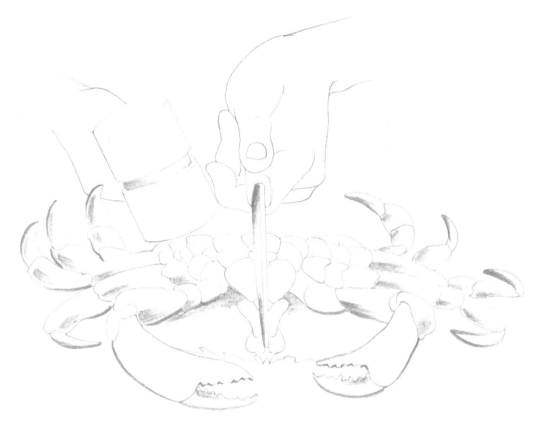

Lay cutting edge of heavy knife along midsection of crab, between legs; hit knife hard with mallet or similar object; this will kill crab instantly.

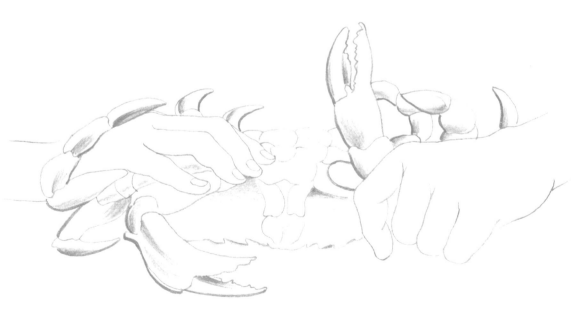

Grasp one front claw firmly and twist off at body juncture point. Repeat with other claw and each leg.

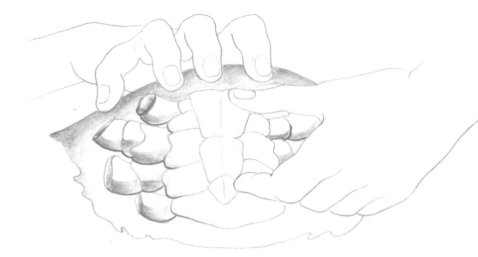

Pry up and pull off top shell; remove gills and spongy lungs and discard; remove and reserve creamy crab "butter."

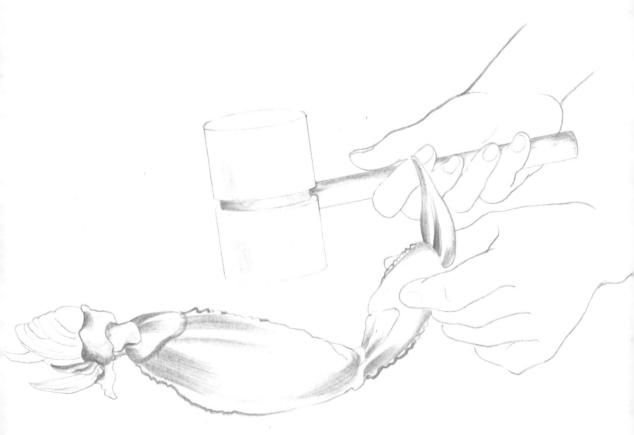

Position claws on edge as shown; crack each section with mallet or hammer.

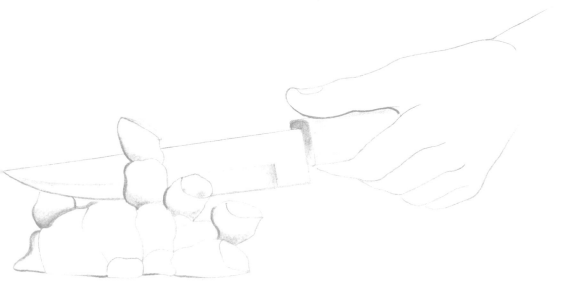

Cut body cavity in half. Cut each half into several pieces to facilitate removal of meat.

TO COOK DUNGENESS CRAB: Drop into a large kettle of lightly salted boiling water. When the second boil is reached, cover and simmer for 10–12 minutes. If the crab is being boiled whole, simmer for 15–20 minutes, then clean and crack as described above before serving. In either event be sure to save the "crab butter." Serve with mayonnaise, Louis dressing, or melted butter.

STONE CRAB: The Southern or Florida stone crab is another hard-shell variety, and since only the claws are eaten, little cleaning is required. Twist off the claws, scrub well, and cook, covered, in lightly salted water to cover for 15 minutes. Serve hot with melted butter or at room temperature with Mustard and Mayonnaise ❀

Lump crab meat is the most highly prized meat, very expensive, available fresh and pasteurized in cans. The best lump comes from Chesapeake Bay (although there are those who say that Florida lump is whiter, if that means anything) and may contain bits of flavorsome roe and fat that you should not discard. It is very expensive, because extracting it from the shell is totally a hand operation, but worth it, as there is no waste.

Backfin is another term you will come across in connection with lump crab meat; lump and backfin are taken from the same chambers of the crab's body, "lump" being merely the larger pieces, and backfin the smaller or broken bits. For salads, the choicest lump is required, but regardless of use good lump should be handled as little as possible to avoid breaking it up. Pick it over judiciously for bits of shell, but be gentle. Use only your hands, never a fork for this.

FROZEN CRAB: If only frozen crab meat is available to you, try to get the precooked Alaska king crab legs, which can be broiled and served with melted butter. The meat is as sweet as, if a bit more fibrous than, the lump. The Alaska snow crab is less expensive and less velvety than good Eastern lump, but it can be used in a variety of dishes where texture is not of paramount importance.

TO BROIL KING CRAB LEGS: If necessary, peel away enough of the shell so the meat can be basted. Brush the meat with melted butter and broil only until heated through, as the meat is already cooked. Serve with lemon wedges and more melted butter.

PASTEURIZED CRAB: At market one often sees "fresh" crab that is pasteurized. This is a most acceptable middle-ground technique for extending the shelf life of a highly perishable food while retaining its characteristic flavor and texture. It means that the meat has been heated in a hermetically sealed can to a temperature lower than that used in canning but high enough to kill most bacteria associated with spoilage. Pasteurized seafood must be refrigerated.

STEAMED SPICED CRABS

1 quart cider vinegar
⅓ cup salt
1 stalk celery
¼ cup powdered mustard
¼ cup whole cloves
3 tablespoons cayenne pepper

2 tablespoons powdered ginger
1 tablespoon mace
1–2 gallons boiling water
12–24 medium-size hard-shell
    crabs, preferably blue

Place all ingredients except the crabs in a 3-gallon enamel or stainless steel kettle, bring to a boil, cover, and simmer for 5 minutes. Have the top handy to keep the crabs from escaping. Add the crabs, cover, and simmer for 15 minutes. Let cool, uncovered, in the pot. Drain and serve warm or cool, or chill and serve with lobster crackers and picks. Serves 4–6. See the note below on how to eat crab.

The crabs are done when they turn bright red and the apron is loose.

If you have a choice between small heavy crabs and large light ones, choose the former.

NOTE: If you were not born and bred in Maryland or the South, where eating blue crabs is a way of life, then any recipe for making spiced or steamed crabs can only be half the story. For example, one Maryland cookbook advised in a postcript: "Spread newspapers, put on a bathing suit, collect some cold beer or dry ginger ale, and pitch in. If you don't know how to eat hot steamed crabs, get someone to show you.''

If there is no ''someone,'' here's how:

Rip off the large claws by pulling laterally, and set aside.

Lift the ''apron,'' the flap ending in a little point on the bottom, tear off, and discard.

Working from the end where the apron was, pry up and tear off the hard shell, using both fingers. Reserve and pick over the shells, because there are edible portions buried in both sides of the shell tips.

Cut off and discard the antennae between the crab's eyes and cut or pull off and discard the spongy lungs. Then break the crab in half.

Pull off the small claws, or feelers. Maybe a large morsel of crab meat will come along with it.

Using a knife, cut the crab down the center to reveal the chambers, pry the meat out. Crack the claws at pincer ends and pull on a pincer to extract the meat. Treat the legs like soda straws, sucking one end to get out bits of meat.

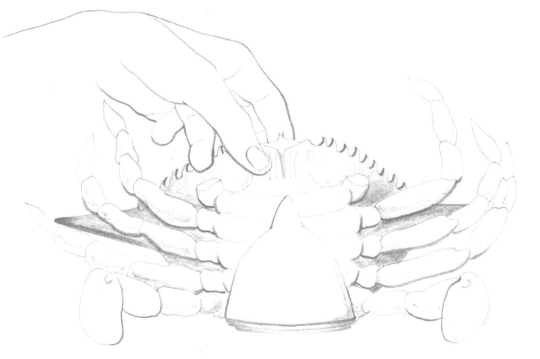

Underside of blue crab, showing pointed ''skirt.''

Blue crab with shell removed.

CRAB MEAT RAVIGOTE

Prepare a Ravigote Sauce, ❋ .

Mix ¾ cup of the sauce with 1 pound of fresh lump or backfin crab meat, correct the seasoning with salt, and pile the mixture into individual serving shells or ramekins. Coat the crab meat with the remaining sauce and serve with lemon wedges. Serves 6.

CRAB MEAT RÉMOULADE

Prepare a Rémoulade Sauce ❋. Follow the instructions for Crab Meat Ravigote (preceding recipe), substituting *rémoulade* sauce for the *ravigote* sauce.

CRAB PUFFS

½ pound crab meat, canned or
   fresh
2 cups flour
½ teaspoon salt
Several dashes of cayenne pepper

3 teaspoons baking powder
1 egg, well beaten
1 cup milk
2 cups peanut oil for frying

Pick over the crab meat if necessary, set aside.

In a large mixing bowl, sift together the flour, salt, cayenne, and baking powder. In another bowl, blend together the egg and milk, stir in the crab meat. Add this to the flour mixture and mix well.

Heat the peanut oil in a large skillet until hot but not smoking, or in an electric fryer set at 365°. Drop the crab mixture by rounded tablespoonfuls into the hot oil, fry 3 minutes or until golden. Don't crowd the pan. Drain on paper towels and keep warm until all are done. Serve piping hot as an appetizer or a first course with tartar sauce. Makes about 24 puffs.

CRAB WITH CAPERS

1 pound backfin crab meat
¾ cup homemade Mayonnaise ✳
1 tablespoon or more capers to
   taste

Crisp lettuce leaves
8 thin slices of country ham
   (optional)

Pick over the crab to remove shell and cartilage. Combine the mayonnaise with the capers, gently blend with the crab. Serve on lettuce leaves. Garnish each portion with 2 slices of ham if desired. Serves 4.

CRAB LOUIS

1 cup Mayonnaise ✳
2 tablespoons grated onion
¼ cup chili sauce
8–10 sprigs parsley, minced
A dash of cayenne pepper
⅓ cup heavy cream, whipped

1 pound lump crab meat, picked
   over
Shredded lettuce
Ripe tomatoes, quartered, hard-
   cooked eggs, and black olives
   for garnish

Mix together the mayonnaise, onion, chili sauce (this is for color), parsley, and cayenne. Allow the mixture to stand, covered, for an hour or so to mellow, then fold in the whipped cream. Arrange the crab on a bed of shredded lettuce and dress with sauce. Garnish with the tomato quarters, hard-cooked eggs, and black olives. Serves 4.

CRAB SAUTÉ

1 pound best quality lump crab
    meat
4 tablespoons butter
Salt
4–6 slices thin toast

Chopped herbs: parsley, tarragon,
    chives, chervil, any or all
Freshly ground pepper
Lemon wedges

Pick over the crab meat to remove shell and cartilage.

Melt the butter in a skillet, and when it starts to sizzle add the crab. Cook, stirring as gently as possible, until the crab is piping hot (the crab lumps should remain as whole and firm as possible). Season with salt to taste.

Put a slice of toast on a plate for each diner. Spoon the crab onto the toast, sprinkle with chopped herbs. Serve with a pepper mill and lemon wedges. Serves 4–6.

BAKED CRAB MORNAY

1 pound fresh lump or backfin crab
    meat, picked over
1¾ cups Mornay Sauce ❀

¼ cup finely grated Gruyère or
    Parmesan cheese

Preheat oven to 375°.

Gently toss the crab meat with the Mornay sauce to blend, spoon into an ungreased 10-inch *gratin* dish or other shallow baking dish. Sprinkle the cheese over the top and bake, uncovered, for 15–20 minutes, then run quickly under the broiler to brown the top. Serves 4.

CRAB IMPERIAL

3 pounds deluxe backfin or lump
    crab meat
1 green pepper, finely diced
⅓ cup chopped canned pimiento
1 tablespoon dry English mustard
1 tablespoon salt
½ teaspoon white pepper

Several dashes of cayenne pepper
2 eggs
1 teaspoon Worcestershire sauce
1 cup mayonnaise (preferably
    homemade)
Paprika

Preheat oven to 350°.

Butter 9 shells or individual *gratin* dishes.

Pick over the crab meat with your fingers to remove any bits of shell, but take care not to break the large lumps. Set aside. Combine the green pepper, pimiento, mustard, salt, pepper, cayenne, eggs, and Worcestershire sauce with ¾ cup of the mayonnaise. Combine the crab with the mayonnaise mixture, using the hands or by tossing back and forth from one bowl to the other several times; again, avoid breaking the crab lumps.

Divide the mixture among the shells or dishes, mask lightly with the reserved ¼ cup of mayonnaise and sprinkle with paprika. Bake for 15 minutes or until the mayonnaise browns. Serve hot or cold. Serves 9 as a main course, and 12 as a first course.

NOTE: This recipe may be halved.

DEEP-FRIED SOFT-SHELL CRABS

4 large or 8 small soft-shell crabs,
   cleaned
1 cup milk
2 cups flour
1 teaspoon salt

Several grindings of fresh pepper
Several dashes of cayenne pepper
Oil for deep frying
Lemon wedges
Tartar Sauce ❋ (optional)

Rinse the crabs under cold running water and pat dry with paper towels. Put them in a shallow dish in one layer and add the milk. Let soak for 10–15 minutes, turning them in the milk once or twice. Combine the flour, salt, pepper, and cayenne, put in a large shallow dish.

Preheat the oil to 375°.

Remove the crabs from the milk, let drain, then coat thoroughly with the flour on both sides, placing them on a large sheet of wax paper as you do. Fry the crabs in the hot oil 1 or 2 at a time, depending on size, turning as necessary until crisp and golden brown (this will take from 6–10 minutes, depending on the size of the crabs). Drain on paper towels and keep warm until all are cooked. Serve hot with lemon wedges and tartar sauce. Serves 4.

SOFT-SHELL CRABS AMANDINE

16 small to medium soft-shell
   crabs
Milk to cover
½ cup sliced blanched almonds
7 tablespoons butter
1 tablespoon oil

Flour for dredging
8 tablespoons Clarified Butter ❋
2 tablespoons lemon juice
Salt and freshly ground pepper
Lemon wedges
Parsley sprigs

In a large, deep dish cover the crabs with milk, let them stand for 30 minutes.

In a skillet, sauté the almonds in 1 tablespoon of the butter and the oil over moderately high heat, shaking the pan occasionally until they are golden. Transfer the almonds with a slotted spoon to paper towels to drain, sprinkle them with salt. Discard the cooking oil.

Transfer the crabs with a slotted spoon to paper towels to drain, sprinkle them lightly on both sides with salt and pepper, and dredge them in flour.

Heat all of the clarified butter in a heavy skillet large enough to accommodate all the crabs (or divide the clarified butter between 2 smaller heavy skillets). Add the crabs, shell side down, and sauté them over moderately high heat for 3 minutes. Turn them and cook for 3 minutes more.

In a small saucepan cook the remaining 6 tablespoons of unclarified butter over moderately high heat until it is golden brown. Arrange the crabs in rows on a heated platter and sprinkle them with the lemon juice, salt, and pepper. Add any pan butter to the melted butter and pour the mixture over the crabs. Top with the almonds and garnish the dish with lemon wedges and parsley sprigs. Serves 4.

DEVILED CRAB I

1 pound lump or backfin crab
   meat, picked over
1 tablespoon butter
2 tablespoons flour
1 cup heavy cream
1 teaspoon salt
½ teaspoon dry mustard

Worcestershire sauce
Cayenne pepper
2 hard-cooked eggs, chopped
   finely
½ cup or more buttered bread
   crumbs

Preheat oven to 425°.

Butter 4 or 5 individual baking shells or crab-shaped ramekins.

Melt the butter in a saucepan, stir in the flour over low heat. Off heat, add the cream, stir until smooth, and cook over moderate heat for 5 minutes. Add the salt, mustard, Worcestershire sauce, and enough cayenne pepper to make the sauce spicily hot according to your taste. Gently fold in the crab meat and chopped eggs. Fill the prepared shells, top with the crumbs, and bake for about 20 minutes or until the crumbs are brown. Serves 4–5.

DEVILED CRAB II

1 pound crab meat (need not be
   best quality lump)
4 tablespoons butter
½ cup finely chopped onion
½ cup plus 4 teaspoons bread
   crumbs
1 cup heavy cream

½ teaspoon dry mustard
¼ teaspoon cayenne pepper
Tabasco sauce
2 egg yolks, beaten
Salt
Chopped parsley for garnish

Preheat oven to 375°.

Pick over the crab meat to remove shell and cartilage. Butter 4 ramekins or shells.

Melt 2 tablespoons of the butter in a skillet, sauté the onions until wilted.

Add ½ cup of the bread crumbs, the cream, mustard, cayenne, and Tabasco to taste, eggs, and salt to taste. Gently mix with the crab meat.

Spoon the mixture into the ramekins or shells, dot with the remaining butter. Sprinkle with the rest of the bread crumbs. Bake until golden brown, about 20 minutes. Garnish with parsley. Serves 4.

CRAB CAKES

2 cups backfin crab meat	2 eggs, well beaten
¼ cup milk	1 teaspoon Worcestershire sauce
2 tablespoons finely chopped	4 tablespoons butter
parsley	Lemon wedges
Salt	Tartar Sauce ❋
½ cup fresh bread crumbs	

Pick over the crab to remove shell and cartilage. Blend it with the milk, parsley, salt to taste, bread crumbs, eggs, and Worcestershire sauce. Shape into 4–6 cakes, fry in butter on both sides until golden brown. Serve with lemon wedges and tartar sauce. Makes 4–6 crab cakes.

CRAB "CHOPS"

This is a very rich crab cake shaped to look like a breaded pork chop and is believed to have been designed by Louisiana cooks as a special dish for Lenten days. You can shape it as a regular crab cake, also.

1 pound crab meat, fresh or frozen	¼ cup chopped green onion, white
8 tablespoons (1 stick) butter	part only
¾ cup flour	2 eggs, beaten
½ teaspoon salt	2 cups soft bread crumbs
¼ teaspoon cayenne pepper	¼ cup cooking oil
1 cup milk	Lemon wedges
¼ cup chopped parsley	Tartar sauce

Pick over the crab meat to remove any shell or cartilage. In a small saucepan, melt 4 tablespoons of the butter, blend in ¼ cup of the flour, the salt, and cayenne. Gradually stir in the milk, cook and stir until thickened. Gently fold in the crab meat, parsley, and green onion. Cover and refrigerate for 2 hours.

Divide the crab mixture into 6 equal portions. Pat and shape each portion into a "chop" about 5 inches long and ½ inch thick. Spread the remaining ½ cup flour in a dish, coat both sides of each chop with it. Then dip each chop into the egg, then turn in the bread crumbs to coat evenly. You will have to rinse your hands before you make the next "chop." Refrigerate for at least 30 minutes to firm the coating.

In a heavy 12-inch skillet, heat the remaining butter and the cooking oil until hot but not smoking. Carefully place each chop in the skillet with a pancake turner, sauté over moderate heat until delicately browned on both sides, 4–5 minutes on each side. Serve with lemon wedges and tartar sauce. Makes 6 servings.

GRATIN OF CRAB

½ pound lump or backfin crab
  meat
3 tablespoons butter
2 tablespoons minced shallots
Salt and freshly ground pepper
¼ teaspoon dried tarragon
⅓ cup dry white wine

1 tablespoon cornstarch
½ cup heavy cream
½ teaspoon tomato paste
Lemon juice
2 tablespoons finely grated Gruyère
  or Parmesan cheese

Preheat oven to 400°.

Butter 4 scallop shells, crab-shaped ramekins, or one 8-inch oval *gratin* dish.

Remove any bits of shell or cartilage from the crab meat.

Melt 2 tablespoons of the butter in an 8-inch enamel skillet over moderate heat, stir in the shallots, and cook for 1 minute. Stir in the crab, season with salt, pepper, and the tarragon, cook, stirring, for a minute or two. Add the wine, raise the heat, and boil, stirring, until the liquid has almost evaporated. Remove from heat.

Put the cornstarch in a small mixing bowl and beat in 2–3 tablespoons of the cream to make a smooth paste. Gradually beat in the balance of the cream and the tomato paste. Add to the crab mixture, bring to a simmer over moderate heat, stirring, for 2–3 minutes to cook the cornstarch. If the sauce is too thick, add a tablespoon or two of cream. Correct the seasoning with salt and pepper and a dash of lemon juice.

Spoon the crab into the prepared containers, sprinkle the tops with the grated cheese and the remaining tablespoon of butter, melted. (The recipe may be prepared ahead to this point and refrigerated; bring to room temperature before baking.)

Place in the upper third of the oven for about 15 minutes, or for 5–7 minutes under a moderately low broiler flame, until the cheese is lightly browned. Serve with hot French bread. Serves 4.

NOTE: This recipe can easily be doubled.

CRAYFISH OR CRAWFISH

Along with crabs, crayfish, as they are spelled and pronounced by the upper crust, or crawfish (or even "crawdads") as in southwestern Louisiana, are

adored in that state—the spicier the better. These small 6-inch-long crustaceans seem to be either a subject of indifference (though they can be found,
in addition to the Louisiana bayous, in upper New York State and in Connecticut, in creeks around Lake Michigan and in the Pacific Northwest) or
passionate involvement, witness the French and the Scandinavians. The
latter have made a yearly national ritual out of their consumption.

Louisiana harvests more crayfish than any other area its size in the
world—about twenty million pounds a year. The season for crayfish varies,
but usually peaks in mid- or late summer. They are sometimes shipped fresh
into metropolitan areas in other parts of the country; the displaced or the
nostalgic can order them flown in (see the Index for Food Shopping by
Mail).

After the first Friday in August, when it becomes legal to catch crayfish
(a smaller variety) in Scandinavia, those Finns and Swedes who are not
arguing with each other as to whose national dish it is are busy cutting open,
sucking, and washing down crayfish with great slugs of aquavit with beer
chasers or of vodka. Impromptu groups gather outdoors in the evenings to
demolish prodigious amounts of them by the festive light of paper lanterns.
Songs are sung, the sillier the better, and people of otherwise serious mien
wear absurd paper hats.

The spicy court-bouillon of our Creole kitchen is replaced by one in which
the dominant note is dill. In Finland, dill and dill crowns as well are used to
flavor a sugared vinegar and beer court-bouillon. Tradition dictates a skål,
or toast of aquavit, with each claw, and two with every crayfish tail—which
gives you some idea of the jocular nature of this feast at its height, especially
since ten is an absolute minimum and fifteen to twenty a more likely number
per person.

HOW TO EAT CRAYFISH: Bibs, newspapers, or paper cloths first. Finger
bowls. Then, holding the crayfish, belly side up, noisily (if you are doing

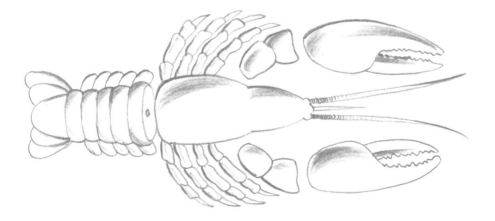

*HOW TO EAT CRAYFISH: The parts of a crayfish when dissected for
eating.*

Detach claws, cut off pointed tips and small movable part. Cut through claw shell with sharp knife to loosen meat, which can then be sucked from claw.

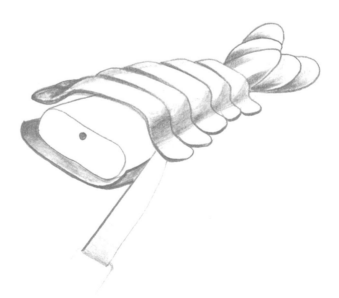

Detach tail from body. (Suck juices from body cavity before discarding.) Cut open tail shell along line where top and bottom shells meet. Remove digestive tract (a black string similar to those seen in shrimp) before eating.

this in Scandinavia, prudently elsewhere) suck up the juice from the feelers and claws. Bite open small ones, cut larger ones open with a knife (Scandinavians have a special one for this purpose), chop off the claw, and dispatch that heavenly morsel. In America, some like to dip it into melted butter. Finally, the tail meat is taken out and eaten after removing the string-like digestive tract.

SCANDINAVIAN DILL-FLAVORED CRAYFISH

3 quarts cold water
¼ cup salt
3 tablespoons dill seed

3 large bunches fresh dill
30 live freshwater crayfish

GARNISH

1 bunch fresh dill, or dill crowns if available
Toasted white bread

Caraway-flavored cheese—*Kryddost*—(optional)

Combine the water, salt, dill seed, and 2 of the bunches of fresh dill, tied with a string, in a 6- to 8-quart kettle. Bring to a boil over high heat, boil briskly, uncovered, for 10 minutes.

Wash the crayfish carefully under cold water, making sure that all are alive. Drop them, a few at a time, into the rapidly boiling water. When all the crayfish have been added, cover the kettle tightly, boil for 6–7 minutes. Stir them so the bottom ones end up on top.

Line a 3- to 4-quart bowl with the third bunch of fresh dill. Remove the crayfish from the kettle with a slotted spoon and arrange them in the bowl over the dill. Strain the stock through a fine sieve over the crayfish, let them rest in the liquid until they have reached room temperature. Then cover the bowl loosely with plastic wrap, refrigerate for at least 12 hours (they may marinate for as long as 2 days).

To serve, drain the crayfish of their liquid, pile them high on a platter, and garnish with the fresh dill. They are best served at room temperature. Serve with toast and cheese. Chilled vodka is highly recommended. Serves 3–4.

SPICED CRAWFISH

2 quarts red wine
1 quart water
3 bay leaves
4 cloves garlic
¼ teaspoon Tabasco sauce
2 tablespoons salt

3 sprigs of parsley
6–8 whole allspice
1 teaspoon dried tarragon or 1 tablespoon chopped fresh tarragon
6–8 dozen crawfish

Bring the wine, water, bay leaves, garlic, Tabasco, salt, parsley, allspice, and tarragon to a boil in a deep pot. Lower the heat, simmer for 10 minutes. Add the crawfish and cook for 8–10 minutes or until they are just done but not mushy. Drain (save the bouillon, it makes a fine bisque base).

Allow 12–16 crawfish per person, serve chilled with small picks or forks to extract the meat. They are best without sauce, but a bowl of French dressing or mayonnaise for dunking may be added if desired.

LOBSTER

If shrimp is America's most popular shellfish, lobster is surely its most luxurious and coveted. Its elevated price is one of the fine ironies of gastronomy; in colonial days lobsters were so plentiful and easily come by that they were considered fit eating only for those too poor to afford anything better, and lobster meat was often used as bait in cod fishing. In his *Eating in America,* Waverley Root relates: "When there was a storm in Plymouth, lobsters piled up in windrows 2 feet high on the beach . . . in 1622, when a group of new colonists arrived in Plymouth, Governor William Bradford was deeply humiliated because his colony was so short of food that the only dish they could present was lobster. . . ."*

In general, the colder the water, the tastier and more succulent the flesh, which is why Maine lobsters are more highly prized than the spiny Florida and Pacific lobsters. The spiny, or rock, lobster, which does not have the large anterior claws, resembles the Mediterranean *langouste,* while *homard,* with its large meaty claws, is the equivalent of the Maine type. Lobster tails, which are available frozen, are usually from South African or Australian rock lobsters.

A miniature variety of lobster, called *langoustine* or *langostino,* has recently begun to appear at market. Long residents of Gulf waters, but only recently fished commercially, these are marketed as *rock shrimp,* although they neither taste like nor have the texture of shrimp. This is to get around the fact that any lobster under one pound is not legal prey. About the size of a medium shrimp, they are available frozen, peeled or unpeeled, and can be used in salads or other dishes where cooked or canned lobster meat would be used.

Northeastern lobsters are available in some West Coast specialty fish markets as well as from companies that will airmail them to you, live, packed in seaweed.† They can probably be gotten live by special order elsewhere. In buying lobsters remember that large lobsters tend to toughness.

---

*Waverley Root and Richard de Rochemont: *Eating in America,* William Morrow & Company, 1976, New York.
†See the Index for Food Shopping by Mail.

Calculate roughly one third of the weight as edible; because of its richness, a lobster of one and a quarter pounds can be ample for one person.

If, as I do, you seek out female lobsters for the coral, or undeveloped roe, they can be identified in two ways: first by the greater width of their tail, and then by the last pair of swimmerets on the underside where chest and tail meet. Those of the female are soft, hairy, and crossed; the male's are hard, pointed, and straight. On rare occasions during the spawning season, you may encounter a female about to lay eggs (the French have a special name—*paquette*—for such a female). Then the roe looks like dark greenish-black caviar and is even more delicious. Connoisseurs regard the *paquette* as the most succulent of lobsters.

FROZEN: Frozen lobster forms are: the tails (uncooked) and whole lobsters, usually cooked before freezing. The latter needs to be only heated through for hot dishes, and can be used after thawing in salads and such. In no way can frozen lobster meat compare in sweetness and tenderness with that from a lobster alive until cooked.

TO PREPARE LIVE LOBSTERS: Lobster is at its very best when cooked live. The cooking method may be boiling, steaming, broiling, or baking. Baking and broiling require that the lobster first be killed, then split and cleaned. If this troubles you, stick to steaming or boiling. Many markets will boil them for you, and perhaps split them, too. For easier handling, the spiny lobster is best boiled first, and then split and cleaned for broiling or baking. In this case, care should be exercised in the second cooking to just heat the meat through without further cooking it.

TO KILL A LIVE LOBSTER: Lay the lobster, stomach side down, on a firm work surface such as a wooden board and plunge the tip of a sharp knife through the segment where the tail section and the body section meet. This will sever the spinal cord and kill the lobster instantly. (Stay calm during any subsequent movements that may occur: this is pure muscle reflex and not the creature thrashing about in pain.)

TO SPLIT A LOBSTER: Lay the uncooked lobster on its back and slit the undershell down the middle. Then, using a heavy knife, start at the head and split the lobster from end to end. A wooden mallet or hammer is useful to add force to the knife in making a clean break through the hard shell back, which is now on the bottom. Remove and discard the small sac inside the lobster near the eyes. A cooked lobster may be split the same way. Just behind the eye you will see a milky-colored sac—the stomach. Remove it, along with the attached intestinal vein running down the tail section near the back shell. Do not discard the greenish-yellow liver or tomalley, nor the coral (if you are so fortunate to have a female). They are both incredibly delicious and add much to the beauty of the finished dish if you are doing a stuffed lobster. Crack the claws. Spiny lobster legs should be twisted off.

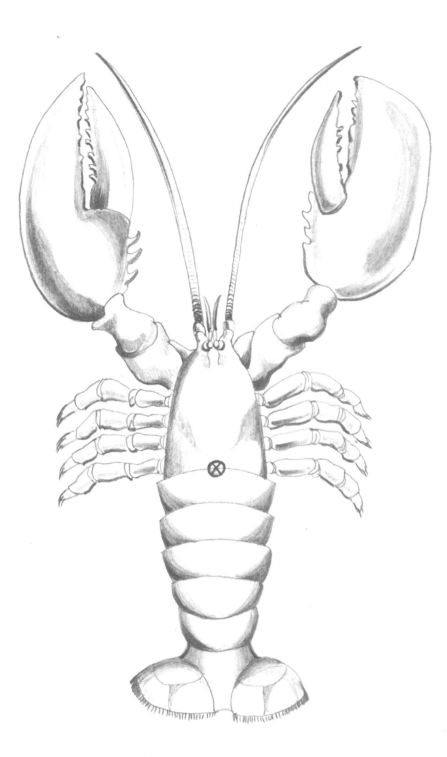

AMERICAN LOBSTER: "X" indicates point at which knife is inserted to kill.

TO BOIL LOBSTER: Hold lobster firmly behind head and put into pot head-first.

TO BOIL: Lobsters taste best cooked in sea water; next best is well-salted water, about 1 tablespoon for each quart. Bring the water (about 6 quarts for 2 1-pound lobsters) to a full rolling boil, grasp the lobster firmly behind the head,* and plunge it head first into the boiling water. Cover loosely and begin timing when the second boil is reached. A 1-pound lobster will cook in about 7–8 minutes, turning a beautiful intense scarlet. Add 2 minutes for each additional *half* pound. Remove from the water with tongs, letting excess water drain back into the pot. Plunge briefly into cold water to facilitate handling. Split the lobster, crack the claws, and serve hot with melted butter and lemon wedges.

TO STEAM: According to Down Easters, who tend to be fanatical purists about their lobsters, this is the only way to prepare them: in a lobster pot or any large, heavy kettle, pour in about 1 inch of sea or salted water. Add a branch or two of seaweed if available. Bring to a boil, add the live lobsters to the kettle (or the top section of a lobster pot), and steam over moderately high heat for 15 minutes. Serve as boiled lobster.

TO BROIL: Kill the lobster, split and clean as directed above, and crack the claws. Preheat the broiler. Brush the exposed flesh with melted butter and broil, flesh side up, about 4 inches from the flame for 10–15 minutes, depending on size. Baste once or twice with more melted butter. Season to taste with salt and pepper and serve immediately with additional melted butter, lemon wedges, and French-fried potatoes. Do not overcook or the meat will be tough and dry.

TO BROIL PRECOOKED LOBSTER: Broil as above, for about 4 minutes, or just until the lobster is heated through and edges of the flesh char slightly.

TO CHARCOAL GRILL: See Chapter VII, Barbecuing and Grilling.

Lobster Tails

These are usually frozen uncooked and should be completely thawed before cooking. They may be either boiled or broiled, stuffed, or served with any of the flavored butters.

TO PREPARE LOBSTER TAILS FOR BROILING: Use kitchen scissors to cut along both sides of the thin undershell. Peel back and discard. Clip off the fins along the edges. Bend the tails backward until they crack and lie flat, to prevent curling during broiling.

TO BROIL: Arrange prepared tails on a foil-lined broiler pan, shell side down. Sprinkle with lemon juice and brush liberally with melted butter.

*Gloves may be useful in handling spiny lobsters.

Broil 4 to 5 inches from the heat, brushing with additional butter if desired, for 10 to 15 minutes, depending on size, or until lightly browned. Sprinkle with pepper and serve with lemon wedges and additional melted butter.

NOTE: If large tails are unavailable, use smaller ones and adjust cooking times as follows: for 3- to 5-ounce tails, 5 to 6 minutes; for 6- to 8-ounce tails, 7 to 9 minutes.

VARIATION: Low-calorie rock lobster tails: Using the 8-ounce tails, broil as directed and substitute a low-calorie herb salad dressing for the butter.

TO BOIL: Plunge the thawed tails into several quarts of boiling salted water, 1 tablespoon for each quart. After the second boil is reached, cover and simmer for about 5 minutes for 4-ounce tails, adding 1 minute for each additional ounce. Remove and drain.

COLD CURRIED LOBSTER SALAD

1½ pounds cooked lobster meat, well picked over and cut in bite-size chunks
⅔ cup mayonnaise
⅓ cup sour cream
2 tablespoons minced parsley
2 tablespoons minced fresh dill
2 tablespoons capers
1 tablespoon curry powder
2 tablespoons grated onion
Juice of ½ lemon
3–4 dashes of Tabasco sauce

Put the lobster in a large bowl. Mix the remaining ingredients until well blended, pour over the lobster, and toss to coat well. Cover and refrigerate for several hours. Serve in avocado halves or on a bed of shredded lettuce. Serves 4–6.

LOBSTER SALAD RÉMOULADE

Follow the recipe for Shrimp Rémoulade ✹ , substituting for the shrimp 1½ pounds of cooked lobster meat, well picked over and cut into bite-size chunks. Serves 4 as a luncheon dish, 6 as a first course.

VARIATION: Add 1 cup blanched, julienned celery root to the lobster salad.

LOBSTER À l'AMÉRICAINE

The origin of this dish has always been a subject of discussion among gastronomes; sautéing in oil and using tomatoes are characteristic of Mediterranean cooking (indeed, tomatoes were little used anywhere else before the nineteenth century), yet the name itself is regarded by many as a corruption of *armoricaine,* from Armorica, the ancient name for Brittany. In the classic recipe a fish *fumet* is used as well as wine, and the sauce enrichment comes from blending butter together with the lobster coral, with more butter added at the end.

3 live lobsters, about 1¼ pounds
  each
¼ cup olive oil
3 tablespoons butter
3 tablespoons finely chopped
  shallot
1 small onion, finely chopped
1 teaspoon finely minced garlic
2 cups chopped fresh tomatoes,
  peeled and seeded, or drained
  canned tomatoes
2 tablespoons tomato purée

½ teaspoon dried tarragon, or 1
  tablespoon minced fresh
  tarragon
½ teaspoon dried thyme, or 1 sprig
  of fresh thyme
1½ cups dry white wine
1 tablespoon chopped parsley
Salt
Several dashes of cayenne pepper
½ cup cognac
Chopped fresh parsley and
  tarragon

Follow the directions for killing a live lobster (see Index). Break off each tail, cut into 2 pieces crosswise, and set aside in a large bowl. Break off the large claws and the small feeler claws, add to the bowl. Scoop out and reserve the tomalley and coral, if any. Discard the stomach sac behind the eyes, discard the intestinal veins, and split the body sections in half lengthwise.

Heat the oil in a deep, heavy skillet or porcelain-lined cast-iron pot large enough to accommodate all the lobster pieces. When the oil is very hot, add the lobster and cook, stirring, for about 5 minutes, until the shells turn red and the meat is lightly browned. Remove the lobster pieces to a warmed platter.

Add the butter to the skillet and in it sauté the shallot and onion until the onion takes on a little color. Add the garlic and cook for 1 minute longer. Add the tomatoes, tarragon, thyme, wine, parsley, salt, and cayenne to taste, and cook, stirring, over high heat for 15 minutes. Pour the cognac over the tails and claws, ignite, and let the flames die away. Add to the tomato sauce, cover, and simmer for about 15 minutes. Remove lobster and keep warm.

Simmer tomato sauce, uncovered, over high heat for 8–10 minutes to reduce the sauce. Mix in the reserved tomalley and chopped coral, heat for 1–2 minutes longer.

While the sauce is cooking, when the tails and claws are cool enough to handle, break or crack them and remove the meat. Add the meat to the sauce along with any accumulated juices. Sprinkle with parsley and tarragon. Serve with hot steamed rice or rice pilaf. Serves 6–8.

STUFFED LOBSTER

1 live lobster, 1½–2 pounds
3 tablespoons olive oil

6 tablespoons butter
2 cloves garlic, minced

2 tablespoons chopped parsley
½ teaspoon dried oregano or dried
   tarragon or 1 tablespoon chopped
   fresh tarragon

½ cup fine homemade bread
   crumbs
Salt and freshly ground pepper

Preheat oven to 400°.

Split the lobster and clean, reserving the green tomalley and coral, if any. Brush the shell and flesh with olive oil, place in a baking dish, set aside.

Melt 3 tablespoons of the butter in a skillet, sauté the garlic, parsley, and chosen herb for 2 minutes. Add the bread crumbs, reserved tomalley and roe, and salt and pepper to taste, cook for a minute more.

Spread this paste over the lobster halves, dot with the remaining butter (cut up), and bake for 20 minutes. If desired, run under the broiler briefly to brown. Serves 2.

STUFFED LOBSTER WITH ESCARGOT BUTTER

This dish was extremely popular at New York's old Café Chauveron. Roger Chauveron has now retired to Florida and the restaurant has moved there; Chef Marcel Challamel has kindly shared the recipe with us for this book.

A 2½ pound live Maine lobster
2 ounces crab meat (see the note
   p. 266)
2 tablespoons butter, softened
1 teaspoon Dijon or dark prepared
   mustard

½ cup fine fresh white bread
   crumbs
Reserved tomalley and coral from
   the lobster
Salt and freshly ground pepper

ESCARGOT BUTTER
8 tablespoons butter (1 stick)
½ teaspoon finely minced garlic
½ teaspoon finely minced shallot
2 tablespoons chopped parsley

Salt
Freshly ground black pepper
Lemon wedges

Preheat oven to 350°.

Rinse the lobster thoroughly in cold water.

Chop off the claws and the legs; discard the legs.

Crack the large claws, leaving the meat intact. Place the lobster on a chopping board, split in half, and remove and discard the stomach sac and intestinal vein. Scoop out and save the tomalley and coral if any. Set the halves aside.

Prepare the stuffing: Combine the crab meat, butter, mustard, tomalley, and coral with the bread crumbs into a pasty consistency. Lightly season to taste. Fill the lobster shells with the mixture, using a fork to smooth it. Place on a baking dish along with the claws and bake in the upper third of the oven for approximately 25 minutes or until the filling is golden brown.

While the lobster is baking, prepare the escargot butter: Melt the butter in a saucepan and add the garlic, shallot, parsley, and salt and pepper to taste. Simmer for 2–3 minutes without letting the shallot brown. Serve the lobster at once either from the baking dish or on a separate platter. Spoon the escargot butter over it and garnish with lemon wedges. Pass additional escargot butter if desired. Rice is a nice accompaniment. Serves 2.

NOTE: The original recipe calls for cleaned Maryland backfin crab meat; however, if this is difficult to obtain, substitute canned or frozen Alaska king crab or snow crab meat. If you use canned crab, wash it and watch the salt when seasoning, as the crabs may be packed in brine.

BAKED LOBSTER WITH HERB BUTTER

2 1½-pound live lobsters
1 teaspoon olive oil
Salt and white pepper
4 tablespoons (½ stick) butter, softened

1 tablespoon finely chopped shallot
1 tablespoon finely chopped parsley
1 teaspoon finely chopped fresh tarragon or ½ teaspoon dried

Preheat oven to 450°.

Follow the directions given at the beginning of this section for killing, splitting, and cleaning live lobsters.

Arrange the lobster halves, split side up, in a baking dish, brush with oil. Sprinkle with salt and pepper. Bake for 15 minutes.

Combine the butter with the shallot, parsley, and tarragon. At the end of the baking time, remove the lobster from the oven. Using a fork, lift up the tail sections from each shell, spoon a teaspoon or so of the butter into the shell, and replace the tail. Spread the remaining butter on top of each lobster half. Return to the oven for 5 minutes or until butter melts. Serve immediately with piping hot rice or baked potatoes. Serves 4.

LOBSTER THERMIDOR

This famous dish made its debut at the Café de Paris in Paris. Essentially it is cooked lobster meat, diced and mixed with a savory stuffing, put back in the shell, and baked with a cheese topping. There are many variations, from the original, which uses a *béchamel* sauce as a binder, to a quick American version, which is nothing more than lobster in cream sauce liberally laced with sherry. The original recipe gets its distinctive bite from dry mustard; I prefer the tang of Tabasco and the dominant sherry-cognac taste in the recipe below. It is not difficult to make and is a dish to serve to one's dearest food-loving friends—showy, messy (if you savor the last delectable drops in the shell), and totally satisfying.

4 live lobsters, 1½ pounds each
8 tablespoons (1 stick) butter
1 cup chopped mushrooms
Salt and freshly ground pepper
½ cup soft bread crumbs
1 tablespoon Worcestershire sauce
Tabasco sauce

4 teaspoons chopped parsley
¾ cup dry sherry
¼ cup cognac
1¾ cups heavy cream
4 egg yolks
½ cup grated Parmesan cheese
Paprika

Using your largest pot, bring 3–4 quarts salted (1 tablespoon for each quart) water to a boil. Unless your pot is absolutely enormous, cook the lobsters two at a time. When the water has reached a rolling boil, grasp each lobster behind the head and plunge it head first into the water. Cover and cook for 8–9 minutes, timing from the second boil. Remove the lobsters from the water when done.

Place a lobster on its back, twist off the claws, reserving the small claws for garnish. Slit the tail section and cut away the thin undershell with a kitchen shears. Grasping the lobster firmly in both hands, bend it back until it lies flat and open. Remove the stomach and intestinal vein. Using a spoon, carefully remove the tomalley, or green liver, and any coral or roe. Reserve. Remove the meat from the body and cut into small pieces. Crack the large claws, remove the meat, and cube. Reserve the shell. Repeat this procedure with the other 3 lobsters.

Preheat oven to 350°.

Heat 4 tablespoons of the butter in a skillet, add the mushrooms, and cook for 3 minutes. Season with salt and pepper. Add the lobster meat, crumbs, Worcestershire sauce, several dashes of Tabasco, the parsley, sherry, cognac, heavy cream, and egg yolks. Mix well. Carefully stir in the tomalley and coral.

Fill the lobster shells with the mixture and sprinkle with the cheese. Dot with the remaining butter and sprinkle with paprika. Place in a shallow pan or two baking dishes and bake for 15 minutes. Serve immediately with hot buttered rice. Serves 4.

LOBSTER NEWBURG

1 cooked lobster, 1½–2 pounds
¼ cup butter
½ cup dry sherry
Several grains cayenne pepper

Salt and freshly ground pepper
½ cup heavy cream
2 egg yolks, lightly beaten

Split the lobster and lift out the meat. Cut it across the grain into slices about ⅓ inch thick. Crack the claws, remove the flesh, and slice.

Melt the butter in a skillet, add the lobster meat, and poach gently for 3–4 minutes, turning once.

Warm the sherry and pour over the lobster, which should almost be covered; if not, add more sherry as required. Gently simmer over the heat, shaking the pan until the liquid is reduced to about half. Add the cayenne and salt and pepper to taste. Add all but 2 tablespoons of the cream, bring again to a simmer over moderate heat, shaking the pan.

Beat the remaining cream and the egg yolks together, mix a little of the hot sauce into the egg mixture, return the egg mixture to the pan, and heat, stirring, for 2–3 minutes or until slightly thickened. Spoon over piping hot boiled rice. Serves 4.

COLD LOBSTER TAILS WITH DILLED MUSTARD SAUCE

8 frozen lobster tails, defrosted   3 tablespoons chopped dill
1 recipe of Dilled Mustard Sauce ❀   Several sprigs of watercress
3 cucumbers, peeled and sliced   Lemon quarters for garnish

Set the lobster tails on a rack over 2 inches of boiling water in a deep pot, steam them, covered, for 20 minutes. Remove with tongs and let them cool. With kitchen shears slit the soft underside of the shells along the sides, remove the meat in one piece from the shells. Reserve the shells.

Put the lobster tails on a cutting board, white meat side down. Make a series of deep cuts through the meat at about 1-inch intervals; do not cut all the way through. In a wide shallow dish toss the lobster tails in 1 cup of the dilled mustard sauce, chill them for at least 4 hours.

Arrange the reserved shells on a large round serving platter. Insert a slice of cucumber in each cut of the lobster tails and set each tail in a shell. Garnish each with a thin line of minced dill down the center, and decorate the platter with sprigs of watercress and the lemon quarters. Serve additional dilled mustard sauce separately if desired. Serves 8.

MUSSELS

A mollusk found clinging to rocks along both East and West coasts, the crescent-shaped edible blue mussel is one of the most delicious and neglected of our seafoods. It is also one of the most nutritious, its protein content being almost the same as steak (which has four times as many calories and eighteen times more fat).

It is generally thought that the best mussels come from Maine—they are larger, firmer, and more flavorsome than others, and are distinguished by the vertical grain on the shell (others have more horizontal lines). Although mussels are gathered the year round, the best time for them is from the end of February to late April. Late August is another good time.

On the Pacific coast, it may be dangerous to eat mussels gathered between May and October. During this time, beaches where they abound are quarantined and posted with warning signs.

Mussels may be sold by the quart or the pound. Depending on size, one can calculate 16 to 20 in a pound. About 1½ pounds, or 32 to 40 mussels, equals a quart. You can tell if a mussel is fresh by pinching it between the thumb and forefinger and then trying to spread the shells. If it closes tightly, it is alive. Your fingertips will also tell you if it is filled with black mud, as sometimes happens. If so, it should be discarded, as well as any that are not tightly shut.

Mussels may be found along coastal rock outcroppings that are exposed to a pounding surf. Look for them at low tide and take along a screwdriver to pry them off. Shun the open ones; they are dead.

Canned mussels may be used in any recipe where the broth collected from steaming open fresh ones is not a requirement. If you see any sand in the bottom of the can, soak the mussels in several changes of cold water. Canned mussels can be quite salty, so bite into one and check before adding salt to your recipe.

CLEANING: Cleaning mussels is a relatively long and involved process and must be done with a lot of care. The object is to remove the sand from the interiors, and the slime, dirt, and the byssus, or "beard," from the exteriors. This latter, which looks like a piece of tough dried grass, is the means by which the mussel attaches itself to rocks.

First, scrub each mussel with a strong brush, such as a wire one, under running water. Scrape off any crusted material with a small knife. Then drop them into a pan or bucket of cold fresh water and let soak for an hour or two so they can throw off sand and salt.

TO DRAIN: Do not pour the water off, rather scoop the mussels out, leaving undisturbed any sand that has collected at the bottom. Wash once again until the water runs clear, and discard any that are not tightly shut.

TO STEAM OPEN: Raw mussels can be opened with a knife, but by far the easiest way is to steam them open. One of the simplest methods is to put them in a large, heavy pot with a half inch of water, cover, and steam them open over high heat for about 5 minutes. Or, using no liquid, lay over them a clean tea towel that has been dipped in hot water and wrung out. Set them in the pot, covered, over high heat for 5 to 8 minutes, shaking the pot two or three times, until all the mussels are open. Again, discard any that remain closed. If your recipe requires the mussels to be removed from the shell, use an empty shell half to scoop them out.

By steaming them open in wine and aromatic vegetables you get the bonus of a delicious broth to use on its own or as a soup base. When the broth is to be used in the further preparation of the dish, or in a fish soup or stew, it is a good idea to let the pot in which the mussels were steamed sit for a few minutes after removing the mussels. This allows any sand to settle to the bottom. Disturb it as little as possible when pouring off the broth.

TO STEAM OPEN MUSSELS IN WINE: For 4 quarts of mussels: in a large kettle bring 1½ cups of wine to a boil with ⅓ cup finely minced onion, several parsley sprigs, half a bay leaf, a pinch of thyme, and several grindings of pepper. Boil for 2 to 3 minutes, then add the mussels, cover, and cook over high heat for 5 minutes or until the shells open. Give the kettle one or two shakes during the cooking time. Remove the mussels with a slotted spoon, and after the broth has settled strain it through a sieve lined with 4 layers of cheesecloth. Remove the mussels from the shells. They are now ready to be sauced or used as indicated in a specific recipe.

MUSSELS RÉMOULADE

Steam open 2 quarts of scrubbed and debearded mussels as described on previous page. Discard any that remain closed. Remove the rest from the shells, reserving half the shells. Let the mussels cool.

Make a Rémoulade Sauce ✱ but omit the anchovy paste, add instead 2 teaspoons dry mustard. Season to taste with salt, pepper, and a dash or two of Tabasco. Stir the mussels into the sauce to coat well, put one back into each shell with a little of the sauce. Chill until serving time. Pass as an hors d'oeuvre or serve on a bed of shredded lettuce as a first course. Serves 6.

MOULES FRANCILLON

The original version of this salad, also called *salade Dumas,* originated with Dumas Fils. It called for several whole truffles to be gently simmered in champagne and then slivered into the salad. Few people can afford this flourish, however, so it usually appears as follows.

1 quart mussels, scrubbed and
  debearded
4–5 medium potatoes, unpeeled
2 cups chicken broth
2 tablespoons wine vinegar
½ cup dry white wine

½ teaspoon salt
Freshly ground pepper
½ teaspoon dried tarragon or 1
  tablespoon fresh tarragon
6 tablespoons olive oil

Steam the mussels open according to instructions given on previous page. Remove from the shells and set aside.

Scrub the potatoes, simmer in the chicken broth until tender, about 20 minutes. Peel and slice into a bowl. Add the reserved mussels.

Combine the wine vinegar and the wine. Beat in the salt, pepper to taste, tarragon, and olive oil. Pour over the potato-mussel mixture and toss gently. Chill for 2–3 hours. Serves 4–6 as a first course.

MUSSELS VINAIGRETTE (Salade de Moules)

4½ pounds (3 quarts) small mus-
    sels, scrubbed and debearded
½ cup white vinegar
2 sprigs fresh thyme or ½ teaspoon
    dried
1 bay leaf

¾ cup minced red onion
⅓ cup chopped parsley
½ cup vegetable or corn oil
Salt and freshly ground pepper
Lettuce leaves

Put the mussels in a kettle and add ¼ cup of the vinegar, the thyme, and the
bay leaf. Cover and steam until the mussels open, 5–8 minutes. Drain and
discard the broth.

Remove the mussels from their shells, drain again, and place them while
still warm in a large serving dish or bowl. Toss with the onion, parsley, oil,
the remaining ¼ cup vinegar, and salt and pepper to taste. Serve on lettuce
leaves. Serves 8–10 as a first course.

MOULES FÉCAMPOISE (Mussel Salad with Celery Root)

Fécamp is a town in Normandy famed for Benedictine, the liquor invented
by a monk of that order, the recipe for which is a closely guarded secret.
Happily, the seafood dishes for which the town is also known are public
domain.

2 pounds mussels, scrubbed and
    debearded
1 pound celery root, peeled and
    cut in julienne
2 teaspoons salt
1½ teaspoons lemon juice
6 tablespoons olive oil

2 tablespoons wine vinegar
Freshly ground pepper
1 cup mayonnaise ✳ , preferably
    homemade, with mustard added
2–3 tablespoons chopped parsley
    or mixed green herbs

Steam open the mussels as directed on page 269. Remove them with a slotted spoon. Shell and pull off the black membrane from each. Set aside.
Strain and reserve the broth into a small saucepan.

Using two forks, toss the celery root in a bowl with the 1½ teaspoons of
the salt and the lemon juice, let steep for 30 minutes, then rinse, drain, and
pat dry. In a small bowl, make a vinaigrette sauce by whisking the olive oil
into the vinegar, and adding the remaining half teaspoon of salt and pepper
to taste. Toss the dressing with the celery root and arrange it in a serving
dish.

Set the reserved mussel broth over high heat, cook until very much reduced and slightly syrupy. Thin the mayonnaise with some of the reduced broth, mask the mussels with it, arrange on the celery root, and sprinkle with chopped parsley or herbs. Serves 4.

COLD STUFFED MUSSELS, GREEK STYLE

3 dozen fresh mussels
Coarse salt
1½ cups water
½ cup white wine
2 large onions, chopped
¼ cup olive oil
¾ cup raw rice

½ teaspoon cinnamon
½ teaspoon allspice
⅓ cup pignoli nuts
⅓ cup currants
3 tablespoons chopped parsley
Freshly ground pepper
Lemon wedges for garnish

Clean and debeard the mussels and scrub well with a stiff brush under cold running water. Put in a kettle with the salt, water, and wine. Cover and steam for 8–10 minutes or until the shells open. Discard any that remain closed. Remove from heat and cool. Strain and reserve liquid.

In a skillet, sauté the onions in the olive oil until soft. Add the rice, cook for a few minutes longer, stirring constantly. Add 1½ cups of the reserved mussel broth, stir in the cinnamon, allspice, pignoli, currants, parsley, and several twists of pepper. Cover, bring to a boil, and cook for 15 minutes or until the rice is tender and liquid absorbed.

Remove the mussels from their shells and stir them into the rice. Fill the shells with the mixture, allowing 1 mussel per shell. Chill and serve, garnished with lemon wedges.

FRIED MUSSELS

2 quarts large mussels, scrubbed
  and debearded
Flour
1 egg

½ cup fresh bread crumbs
Oil or fat for deep frying
1 lemon or 2 cups Tomato Sauce,
  fresh or canned

Follow directions for steaming open mussels in wine, given on page 269. Remove them from the shells, strain and reserve the liquid. Wash the cooked mussels in cool fresh water, drain, and dry on paper towels.

Roll each mussel first in flour, then in the beaten egg, and finally in the bread crumbs. Fry 6–8 at a time in deep fat until golden. Drain on paper towels.

Fried mussels may be served either with lemon quarters or with tomato sauce served separately. If you use tomato sauce, mix in some of the strained mussel broth. Serves 4.

MOULES MARINIÈRE

2 cups dry white wine
½ cup finely minced onion
6 tablespoons butter
Several parsley sprigs
1 small bay leaf

¼ teaspoon thyme
Several grindings of pepper
6 quarts mussels, scrubbed and
  soaked
½ cup chopped parsley

Put the wine, onion, butter, parsley sprigs, bay leaf, thyme, and pepper in
a large kettle with a cover, bring to a boil. Boil for 2–3 minutes, then add
the mussels, cover, and cook over high heat for 5 minutes or until the shells
open. Give the kettle several vigorous shakes during the cooking period.
Dish out the mussels into deep soup plates, spoon the liquid over, sprinkle
with the chopped parsley, and serve. Serves 6–8.

MOULES POULETTE

3 quarts mussels, cleaned and
  debearded
1 large yellow onion, chopped
1 clove garlic, minced
4–5 parsley sprigs
1 bay leaf
6–8 peppercorns
2 cups dry white wine

8 tablespoons (1 stick) butter
3 tablespoons flour
½ cup heavy cream
2 egg yolks
Lemon juice
Salt and white pepper
Chopped parsley for garnish

Put the mussels in a large heavy pot, add the onion, garlic, parsley, bay leaf,
peppercorns, wine, and 3 tablespoons of the butter. Cover the pot, bring the
liquid to a boil over high heat, and cook for 5–8 minutes or until mussels
open, shaking the pot once or twice.

Lift the mussels from the broth with a slotted spoon. Discard any that
have not opened. Remove the empty halves of the mussel shells, discard
them, and put the mussels on the half shell in a serving dish. Keep warm,
covered with buttered foil.

Strain the broth through a double layer of cheesecloth or towel-lined sieve
into a clean pot, taking care not to disturb any sand that may have settled in
the bottom of the cooking pot. Discard the vegetables.

Work the remaining 5 tablespoons of butter together with the flour to
make a *beurre manié*. Add it to the broth in small balls over low heat,
whisking constantly until smooth. Bring the mixture to a boil, lower heat,
and cook slowly, uncovered, for 8–10 minutes. Slowly stir in ¼ cup of the
cream, bring to a boil, and remove from heat.

Beat the egg yolks with the remaining cream in a small bowl. Pour a bit
of the hot broth mixture into them, stirring, and gradually whip this mixture

into the remainder of the broth in the pot. Bring almost to a boil but do not let it boil or it will curdle. Correct the seasoning with a good squeeze of lemon juice, several grindings of white pepper, and if needed a small amount of salt. Pour the sauce over the mussels, sprinkle with parsley, and serve immediately in heated soup plates. Serve as is for a first course, or with hot rice for a main course. Serves 6.

MUSSELS MARINARA

This dish is a specialty of Le Marche region in Southern Italy.

MARINARA SAUCE
¼ cup olive oil
1 clove garlic, minced
1 medium onion, minced
15-ounce can plum tomatoes,
    drained and chopped

Salt and freshly ground pepper
1 tablespoon chopped parsley

3 dozen mussels, scrubbed and
    washed
½ cup water
1 small onion, chopped

½ bay leaf
½ teaspoon thyme
3 sprigs parsley

Prepare the sauce: Heat the olive oil in a medium-size saucepan, and sauté the garlic and onion until lightly colored. Add the tomatoes, season to taste, bring to a boil, cover, and simmer for 15 minutes. Add the parsley, cook for 3 minutes longer, stir occasionally.

Put the mussels, the ½ cup of water, onion, bay leaf, thyme, and parsley in a large kettle. Cover tightly and steam for 5–8 minutes or until the shells open. Remove from heat and scoop out the mussels with a slotted spoon. Strain the broth and save for another use. Add the mussels to the marinara sauce, simmer for 10 minutes. Serve the mussels in the shell in soup bowls. Serves 3–4.

PORTUGUESE MUSSELS WITH PORK

6 boneless pork shoulder chops, ¾
    inch thick, untrimmed of fat
1 tablespoon butter
1 tablespoon oil
2 large onions, chopped
4–6 tomatoes, peeled, seeded, and
    chopped
3 cloves garlic, minced

1 green and 1 red pepper, seeded
    and cut in julienne
Bouquet garni ❋
Salt and freshly ground pepper
6 quarts mussels, scrubbed and
    debearded
½ cup white wine

In a large, heavy skillet, sauté the pork chops gently in the butter and oil. When brown, remove them with a slotted spoon and keep warm. Discard some of the fat in the skillet, keeping just enough to brown the onions, cook them gently over moderate heat until wilted. Add the tomatoes, garlic, peppers, *bouquet garni,* and salt and pepper to taste, cook gently, uncovered, for 7–10 minutes. Reserve.

In a heavy pot with a lid, heat the mussels until they open without adding any liquid. Shake the pot occasionally. Remove them from pot with a slotted spoon, shell half of them. Detach a half shell from each of the remaining mussels, reserve both batches.

Strain the liquid in the mussel pot through a cheesecloth, add it to the tomato sauce along with the white wine. Cover and cook over medium heat for 30 minutes. Correct the seasoning.

Stir in the shelled mussels and let them heat through. To serve, put a chop and some of the mussel-tomato sauce on each of 6 heated plates. Divide the mussels on the half shell among the plates as a garnish. Serve with hot rice and a green salad. Serves 6.

MUSSELS WITH ESCARGOT BUTTER
(Mouclade à la Provençale)

48 uniform-size, extra-large
   mussels, scrubbed and soaked
12 tablespoons (1½ sticks) softened
   butter
3 tablespoons finely minced shallot

2–3 cloves garlic
¼ cup minced parsley
½ cup fine white bread crumbs
Freshly ground pepper

Steam the mussels open as directed on page 269, or open them with a knife. Discard a half shell from each, arrange the full half shells in one layer in a large, shallow ovenproof dish (individual ovenproof dishes may also be used).

To make the escargot butter: Beat the butter until light and fluffy. Beat in the shallots. Put the garlic through a press, add, and beat it in along with the parsley, bread crumbs, and pepper to taste (salt has been omitted from this recipe, as mussels are usually quite salty, but you may want to add some). Divide and spread the butter mixture over each of the mussels. (The dish may be prepared ahead to this point, covered with plastic wrap, and refrigerated.)

Heat the broiler, and just before serving time run the mussels under the flame until the butter bubbles and the crumbs are light brown. Serve at once with plenty of crusty French bread. Serves 4–6.

VARIATION: MOULES CHARENTAISES
Follow the above procedure but omit the garlic.

BAKED MUSSELS AU GRATIN

2 quarts mussels, scrubbed and
   debearded
3 cups minced mushrooms
5 tablespoons butter
¼ cup minced shallots or scallions

1 tablespoon minced parsley
Salt and freshly ground pepper
½ cup fresh bread crumbs
2 tablespoons freshly grated Parmesan cheese

Preheat oven to 425°. Steam open the mussels as directed on page 269, shell them, and remove the black rims. Arrange them in a well-buttered oval *gratin* dish. In a skillet sauté the minced mushrooms in 3 tablespoons of the butter for 3–4 minutes or until the moisture has evaporated.

In a separate saucepan melt the remaining 2 tablespoons of butter, set aside. In a small bowl combine the mushrooms with the shallots or scallions, the parsley, and salt and pepper to taste. Spread the mixture over the mussels. Sprinkle the top with the bread crumbs, the Parmesan cheese, and the melted butter, bake the mussels for 10 minutes or until the bread crumbs are browned. Serves 6 as a first course.

TOURTE BRETONNE

This savory pie is a meal in itself, a kind of super-quiche.

1 recipe of Rich Pastry Dough ✻
1 shell, fully baked, in a shallow,
   false-bottomed 9-inch pan (see
   Index)
1 pint (about 20) mussels, scrubbed
   and debearded
1 cup heavy cream
½ cup light cream
4 eggs
1 additional egg yolk
Several dashes of cayenne pepper

Salt and freshly ground pepper
¼ cup minced onion
2 tablespoons butter
1 tablespoon tomato paste
¼ cup dry white wine
½ pound raw shrimp, shelled,
   deveined, cut into 1-inch pieces
¼ pound crab meat, picked over
2 tablespoons minced parsley
2 tablespoons snipped chives

Preheat oven to 375°.

Steam open the mussels as described elsewhere (see Index) and shell them.

In a bowl combine the heavy and light cream, the eggs and extra egg yolk, cayenne, and salt and pepper to taste. Set aside.

In a skillet sauté the onion in the butter until soft but barely colored, stir in the tomato paste. Add the wine, reduce it over high heat to 2 tablespoons. Add the shrimp, toss in the wine mixture for a few seconds or until they just begin to turn pink. Remove the pan from the heat, add the crab meat, mussels, parsley, and chives, season to taste.

Distribute the seafood mixture in the pastry shell. Stir the custard and pour it over the seafood. Bake the quiche in the upper third of the oven for 35–40 minutes or until it is well puffed and golden. Remove it from the pan, transfer it to a rack, and let it cool for 10 minutes before serving. Serves 6.

GRATIN DE FRUITS DE MER

16–20 mussels (about 1 pound), scrubbed and debearded
2 cups dry white wine
1½ pounds bay scallops
¾ pound raw shrimp, unshelled
1 pound mushrooms, stemmed and sliced

Salt and freshly ground pepper
6 tablespoons butter
4 tablespoons flour
1 cup heavy cream
Lemon juice
¾ cup fresh bread crumbs

Preheat oven to 350°. Butter an 11 by 14-inch oval baking dish or 8–10 individual *gratin* dishes.

In a 3–4 quart heavy enamel-lined or stainless steel pot, steam open the mussels as directed elsewhere (see Index); discard the shells. Scoop out the mussels with a slotted spoon and set aside in a bowl. Strain the broth through a cheesecloth-lined sieve and return to the pot.

Add the wine to the broth, bring the liquid to a simmer, and add the scallops and unshelled shrimp. Lower heat and poach them gently, uncovered, for 3 minutes or just until the shrimp turn pink. Stir once or twice to redistribute them. Do not boil. Remove with a slotted spoon and add them to the reserved mussels. Then poach the mushrooms in the same liquid for 8–9 minutes. While the mushrooms cook, shell and devein the shrimp.

Remove the mushrooms with a slotted spoon and add to the reserved shellfish. Measure the liquid (taking care when you pour it off not to disturb any sand or gut that may have settled in the bottom of the pot). There should be 3 cups. If there is more, reduce over high heat to that amount, and season with salt and pepper.

In a heavy 1½ or 2-quart saucepan make a *roux* with 4 tablespoons of the butter and the flour, remove from heat, and pour in the hot broth all at once, whisking until smooth. Return the sauce to moderate heat, cook for 1 minute, stirring until smooth, then allow it to cool for a few minutes.

Whisk in the heavy cream a bit at a time, correct the seasoning, and add a few drops (up to 1 tablespoon) of lemon juice to taste. Drain the reserved seafood of any liquid that may have accumulated and gently combine this sauce with the seafood. (The dish may be prepared ahead to this point; cool, cover with plastic wrap and refrigerate until proceeding.)

Put the seafood mixture in the prepared baking dish(es). Melt the remaining 2 tablespoons of butter, mix thoroughly with the bread crumbs, and sprinkle on top of the seafood. Bake in the upper third of the oven for 15–20 minutes or until the crumbs are brown. Serves 8–10 as a first course or 4 as a luncheon main course.

CURRIED MUSSEL AND RICE SALAD

Rice and mussels have a particular affinity and are economical as well.

4 quarts mussels, scrubbed and
    debearded
3 teaspoons curry powder, or
    more to taste
½ cup Vinaigrette Dressing ✽
2⅔ cups water
Cooking oil

1⅓ cups raw long-grain rice
Salt
1 cup cooked green peas
⅓ cup mayonnaise, preferably
    homemade
Freshly ground pepper

Open the mussels by steaming in wine as directed at the beginning of this section. Transfer them to a bowl with a slotted spoon, strain the broth into another bowl. Refrigerate or freeze the broth for another use.

Shell the mussels and pull off and discard the black rims. Add 1 teaspoon of the curry powder to the vinaigrette dressing and beat in. Toss the mussels in a bowl with half of the dressing to coat them lightly. Reserve the remainder of the vinaigrette and set aside the mussels.

Bring the water to a boil in a 2- or 2½-quart saucepan. Add a drop of cooking oil to the water. Add the rice, 1 teaspoon of salt, bring to a second boil, cover, and cook over moderate heat for 18 minutes. Put a clean folded tea towel over the rice, replace the lid, and let sit in a very slow oven for 10–15 minutes. Put the rice in a large salad bowl and toss with two forks. Add the mussels, peas, and, using two rubber spatulas, carefully toss with the remaining vinaigrette.

In a small bowl, combine the mayonnaise with the remaining 2 teaspoons of curry powder, fold into the rice mixture, and add salt and pepper to taste. Cover the salad with plastic wrap and chill for 1 hour. Serves 6.

RISOTTO WITH MUSSELS

Risotto is not just the Italian word for rice cooked in broth; it is a very special rice-cooking technique that requires a good deal of attention for half an hour or so, but one that is very rewarding in its unique result. A *risotto* is stirred frequently, generally a no-no for rice cooking. The length of time required for cooking and the amount of liquid needed cannot be stated precisely—the *risotto* is done when the rice is tender yet *al dente*—firm to the bite. The result should be creamier than regular rice but neither too soupy nor too dry. It is important to add the liquid a little at a time, so it has a chance to be absorbed into the swelling grains. Freshly grated, authentic, aged Italian Parmesan cheese is the crowning touch and is worth going out of your way to obtain.

1½ quarts mussels, scrubbed and debearded
¾ cup finely chopped onion
3 tablespoons butter
3 tablespoons olive oil
2 cloves garlic, minced
¼ cup chopped parsley
½ cup dry white wine

Freshly ground pepper
2½ cups chicken broth (homemade, or 1 cup canned mixed with 1½ cups water)
1½ cups imported Italian rice, such as Avorio or Arborio
Freshly grated Parmesan cheese

Put the mussels in a large, heavy pot with a lid. Wring out a tea towel in hot water and lay it on top. Cover the pot and put over high heat, shaking occasionally until the mussels open, 8–10 minutes. Discard the shells and reserve the mussels. Let the liquid settle, then strain through another thin tea towel or 4 layers of cheesecloth. Reserve the liquid, which should be about 2 cups (if there is less, increase the chicken broth accordingly).

In a heavy 2½–3-quart saucepan, melt the butter in the olive oil, sauté the onion until lightly golden. Add the garlic, parsley, wine, and several gratings of pepper, simmer, uncovered, for 5 minutes.

Combine the mussel broth and chicken broth in a small saucepan, bring to a boil, and keep at a gentle simmer while the *risotto* cooks.

Stir in about ¾ cup of the mussel-chicken broth to the onion mixture and bring to a boil. Lower the flame, add the rice, and cook, stirring frequently, until all the liquid is absorbed (watch so that at no time does all the liquid cook away at any one time, or it will burn). Continue adding liquid by small ladlefuls until the rice reaches the desired doneness, which ideally is slightly chewy and yet moist.

Shortly before the rice completes cooking, add the mussels, stir in gently. Serve with Parmesan cheese passed separately.

NOTE: The salt in the chicken broth should be enough to season this dish. If you use unsalted broth, add salt to the rice to taste.

OYSTERS

"Oysters are the usual opening to a winter breakfast," says the *Almanach des Gourmands* in 1803, "indeed they are almost indispensable." And certainly oysters have been a gourmet's delight since ancient times. The Greeks served them at banquets to whet the appetite, and the Romans imported them all the way from Britain, packed in snow, and discussed their merits, compared to Italian ones, as we might debate the merits of Chincoteagues vs. Lynnhavens. Ancient shell middens, or refuse heaps, tell us that the American Indians ate them, and the early colonists quickly learned to do the same. In fact oysters were an important source of food for Eastern seaboard dwellers in pre-Revolutionary days. In the nineteenth century oysters were the rage, and those from Louisiana were as famous as the Long Islands, Chincoteagues, and Olympias became later.

There is great variety in this bivalve—some are salty, some have a coppery aftertaste, some are flattish, others plump. Many feel that the small Olympia has the most distinctive taste. Whatever the variety, they are rich in vitamins and minerals, contain more phosphorus—"brain food"—than any other food, and they help to prevent goiter.* Indeed the phenomenon of "oyster hunger"—well known in such great oyster towns as Philadelphia, Baltimore, and New Orleans, where a person is suddenly possessed with the need to down several dozen raw oysters—may be an instinctive iodine hunger. Compared to other foods, they were eaten by our forebears with curious gusto and abandon. Brillat-Savarin recalls that any banquet of note always began with oysters, and that it was not unusual for a guest to down a gross at a sitting. Robert Courtine cites a dinner at which Balzac put away a hundred "just for starters"!

The species of American oysters are: Eastern or native; Olympia; and Western or Pacific. The Eastern oyster, gathered all along the Atlantic seaboard from Massachusetts to the Gulf Coast, comprises the overwhelming majority of the country's supply. These are known by name origin—Bluepoints, Lynnhavens, Robbins Island, and Gardiners Island (all Long Island) and Chincoteagues.

The only native Western oyster is the costly Olympia, once found growing all along the Pacific coast and now grown commercially primarily in the Puget Sound area. The other Western oysters are Japanese, including those seeded in the Pacific Northwest in the 1920s, and there is a large variety called Kumamoto, now being raised experimentally. Eastern oysters are occasionally imported to the West Coast, and they are expensive. Western oysters are graded by size rather than name. Extra-small ones are sometimes called petits-points.

Eastern oysters are sold live and in the shell, by the dozen, the pint, or the quart. A quart averages 36 medium oysters. Western oysters are also available in bottles and cans.

Despite the old "R" caveat, oysters *are* edible in months without that letter (that is, spring and summer); the notion has more to do with the summer breeding habits of the oyster than with health. They simply are not in their prime after spawning, being watery and less succulent. Also, as oysters were shipped great distances, transporting such a perishable in hot weather must have been a questionable practice in earlier days. European oysters, however, besides being gritty when breeding, are, unlike ours, subject to a summer disease and there the rule should be followed.

---

*Louis XI made it obligatory for his group of advisers to eat a certain number every day. Presumably to keep them in peak mental form.

The only cooking rule for oysters is—hardly at all. Never boil, which shrinks and toughens them. For eating on the half shell, purists prefer lemon juice and pepper and eschew all spicy tomato sauces. The only sauce that does not annihilate them is the delicate *mignonette* (see p. 282), with which they used to be served at Les Halles in Paris. Ideally they should be bought as near to serving time as practical, and eaten as soon as they are opened.

OPENING, OR SHUCKING, OYSTERS: Hold oyster firmly in one hand with hinge part resting in palm. Push blade of oyster knife between shells at a point near hinge and work it around circumference until you feel it cut the muscle holding the shells together.

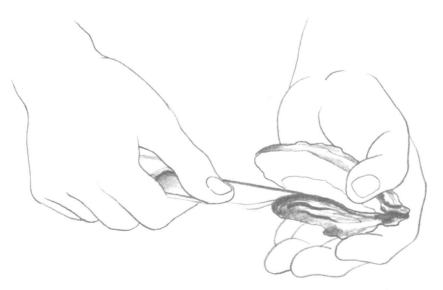

Flip up top shell with knife, aided by thumb. (To save liquor, do this over a bowl, but be sure to strain liquor before using to remove any bits of shell and debris.)

TO SERVE ON THE HALF SHELL: allow at least 6 per person. Have your fish dealer prepare them on the half shell or follow the illustrations offered here. Serve them on crushed ice with lemon wedges, a pepper mill, and buttered black bread if desired.

TO POACH OYSTERS: Oysters to be fried or breaded should be poached first to remove the slippery coating. This is a simple procedure: Remove them from their shells, put them in a saucepan with their own juices, bring the liquid to a boil, remove from heat, and let stand for several minutes. Then drain thoroughly. Be sure to reserve the juice or liquor to use as part of the liquid measurement if you are doing a sauced dish.

SAUTÉED OYSTERS: Poach them briefly as directed, drain, and pat dry. Dredge them in seasoned flour, and sauté them in butter, allowing about 3 tablespoons for 1 pint of oysters. Sauté them over moderate heat just until they are golden brown and plump. Serve with lemon wedges.

FRIED BREADED OYSTERS: Poach them as directed, pat dry, dredge in seasoned flour, dip in a mixture of egg beaten with a teaspoon of cold water, then coat with fine dry bread crumbs or cracker meal. Arrange them in a single layer in the deep-fryer basket and fry at 375° until golden. Drain them on paper towels and keep each batch warm, uncovered, until all are done.

Breaded oysters may also be done in a skillet—browned in butter and turned once, then drained and served with lemon wedges.

BATTER-FRIED OYSTERS (OYSTER FRITTERS): Poach them briefly as directed, drain, and pat dry. Sprinkle them with lemon juice and coat with Beer Batter ❋ . Heat the cooking oil to 375°. Place oysters in the deep-fryer basket and fry until golden, no more than 6–8 at a time. Serve with lemon wedges and tartar sauce.

MIGNONETTE SAUCE

½ cup mild wine vinegar
2 tablespoons finely minced shallot
Salt

2 teaspoons crushed or coarsely
   ground black pepper

Combine all ingredients in a small bowl. Serve in a small side dish with oysters on the half shell.

ANGELS ON HORSEBACK—SKEWERED OYSTERS

24 oysters
12 slices bacon

Melted butter
4 slices toast

Maître d'Hôtel Butter ✻ (optional)   Lemon wedges
Parsley sprigs

Preheat broiler.

Poach the oysters as described on page 282. Drain, pat dry, and roll each one in a half slice of bacon. Secure with toothpicks and sprinkle with a little melted butter. Broil lightly, turning often, about 3 inches below the flame. Serve on toast with a knob of maître d'hôtel butter. Garnish each plate with a parsley sprig and a lemon wedge. Serves 4 as a first course.

VARIATION: May also be served as an hors d'oeuvre without the toast and maître d'hôtel butter.

DEVILED OYSTERS

1 quart medium oysters, liquor   1 egg beaten with 1 tablespoon
  reserved   salad oil
¼ cup Dijon or dark prepared   2 cups fresh bread crumbs
  mustard   6 tablespoons melted butter

Mix the oyster liquor with the mustard, whisking until smooth. Poach the oysters in this mixture for 2 minutes, stirring very gently. Drain them and cool. Dip them, one at a time, in the beaten egg, then coat with bread crumbs. Refrigerate for at least an hour.

Preheat broiler to 400°. Put the oysters in a buttered pan. Dribble the melted butter over the tops, broil for 4–5 minutes on each side. Serve as a first course or on toothpicks as an hors d'oeuvre.

COTTON PATCH OYSTERS

It is an old Maryland custom to serve these oysters as a side dish with chicken salad.

1 pint shucked oysters, drained   2 eggs, well beaten
1 cup flour   Cracker crumbs
1 heaping teaspoon baking powder   Vegetable oil
A dash of salt

Pat the oysters dry with paper towels. Sift together the flour, baking powder, and salt. Dip the oysters, one at a time, first in the flour mixture, then the egg, then the cracker crumbs. Pat the crumbs gently in place and set the oysters aside.

Just before serving time, heat about ¾ inch of oil in a skillet, fry the oysters over medium heat, no more than 8 at a time (they should not touch), until golden brown on each side. Remove with a slotted spoon and keep warm until all have been fried. Serves 4–6.

STEAMED OYSTERS, BALTIMORE STYLE

The White House Cook Book, 1887, offers this simple preparation: "Wash select, fresh shucked oysters by dipping them in their own liquor, and drain. Put them in a shallow pan and place in a steamer over boiling water; cover and steam just until they are plump and the edges curl, but no longer. Transfer to a heated dish with butter, pepper and salt. Serve immediately."

OYSTER PAN ROAST

8 tablespoons (1 stick) butter
1 pint shucked oysters, drained
1 tablespoon Worcestershire sauce
A dash of cayenne pepper

Salt and freshly ground pepper
Lemon juice
4 pieces toast or fried bread

Melt the butter in a skillet. Do not let it brown, as you should poach the oysters, not fry them. Add the oysters, Worcestershire sauce, cayenne, salt and pepper to taste, and a big squeeze of lemon juice, cook them gently over moderate heat, stirring constantly until the oysters plump and puff up, 1–2 minutes. Place them on toast. Serves 4.

VARIATION: PEPPER PAN ROAST   Sauté ¼ cup each minced yellow onion and green pepper in 3 tablespoons of the above butter for 3–5 minutes. Add the rest of the butter and proceed as above.

PANNED OYSTERS AND HAM

4 slices bread, crusts removed
4 slices thin ham, country-style or
   regular
1 pint shucked oysters, drained

½ cup heavy cream
2 egg yolks
Salt and freshly ground pepper
3 tablespoons butter

Preheat oven to 300°.
   Toast the bread slices, butter them, transfer to 4 heated plates, and keep warm. Trim the ham slices to the size of the toast, set aside.
   In a small bowl whisk together the heavy cream and the egg yolks, season to taste. In a skillet melt 2 tablespoons of the butter over moderately low heat, add the oysters, and cook for 2–3 minutes or until the edges curl. Reduce the heat to low, stir in the egg yolk mixture, and cook, stirring constantly, until the sauce thickens but do not let it boil.

Melt the remaining tablespoon of butter in a skillet and warm the ham slices in it on both sides. Top each piece of toast with a ham slice and spoon the panned oysters over each. Serves 4.

SCALLOPED OYSTERS

24 shucked oysters (about 1½ pints)
3 tablespoons butter, melted
3 tablespoons chopped shallot
1½ cups cracker crumbs

Several grindings of pepper
½ teaspoon salt
1 cup heavy cream, or half milk, half cream

Preheat oven to 375°.

Butter a shallow 1-quart baking dish. Drain the oysters and discard their liquid.

Sauté the shallots in half the melted butter, add with the rest of the butter to the crumbs, and mix well. Spread half the crumb mixture in the baking dish, arrange the oysters over them, and season to taste. Pour the cream over them, top with the remaining crumbs. Bake until the crumbs are nicely browned, 20–25 minutes. Serves 4.

CREAMED OYSTERS AND SWEETBREADS

2 pairs sweetbreads, 16–18 ounces each
2 tablespoons vinegar
1 stalk celery, cut up
Several parsley sprigs
Salt
4 tablespoons butter
4 tablespoons flour

1 cup heavy cream, heated
1 pint shucked oysters and their liquor
White pepper
A dash of cayenne pepper
A dash of nutmeg
¼ cup dry sherry
Fresh toast

Soak the sweetbreads in cold salted water in a large bowl for 4 hours or overnight. Drain them and put in a heavy saucepan. Add the vinegar, celery, parsley, and 1 tablespoon of salt. Bring to a boil, remove from heat, let stand for 10 minutes, drain, and plunge immediately into ice water to blanch. When cold, trim off the tubes, cartilage, and sinews.

Press the sweetbreads to give them a firm texture: Put them on a tray or plate that is covered by a tea towel, then cover with another towel and a second flat plate or tray. Weight with about 3 pounds of cans, stones, or what have you. Let stand for 4 hours. Transfer them to a board and cut into ¾-inch slices. Melt the butter in a skillet, coat the slices with flour, and sauté until golden. Add the cream, cook over low heat, stirring constantly, until the consistency is smooth and thick.

In a saucepan heat the oysters in their liquor until the edges begin to curl. Combine with the sweetbreads. Season with white pepper, several dashes each of cayenne and nutmeg, and the sherry. Serve on toast. Serves 6.

NOTE: Both the sweetbreads and sauce may be prepared the day before. This dish can also be served over rice or in puff pastry shells.

OYSTER-SWEETBREAD PIE: Preheat the oven to 425°. Pour the complete ingredients into a deep pie dish and cover with *Pâte Brisée* (see Index). Trim the edges, paint with an egg wash, and bake for 20 minutes or until the crust is golden brown.

PICKLED OYSTERS

3 pints shucked oysters
¾ tablespoon salt
8 cloves
1 teaspoon mace
1 teaspoon allspice

1 teaspoon white peppercorns
1½ cups white wine vinegar
Lettuce leaves
Lemon slices

Drain the oysters of their liquor, put the liquor in a saucepan with salt, and bring to a boil. Make a *bouquet garni* of the cloves, mace, allspice, and white peppercorns, add to the liquor. Then add the oysters. Bring to the boil, remove from heat, and let sit until the oysters begin to curl around the edges and appear plump. Remove them from the liquid immediately with a slotted spoon, place in cold water to stop further cooking. Add the vinegar to the spiced oyster juices, bring to a boil once again, strain, and cool. Replace the oysters in the liquid and serve on individual plates garnished with a lettuce leaf and a lemon slice as an appetizer. Serves 6–8.

OYSTERS CASINO

Rock salt
24 oysters in the shell
4 slices bacon, cut into 6 pieces
  each
8 tablespoons (1 stick) butter at
  room temperature

⅓ cup finely chopped shallot
¼ cup finely chopped parsley
¼ cup finely chopped green pepper
A few drops of Tabasco sauce
Lemon wedges

Preheat oven to 450°.
  Make a bed of rock salt in a jelly-roll pan or on several pie plates, dampen slightly with water, and heat, uncovered, in the oven for 5 minutes.
  Open each oyster and reserve the deeper of the two half shells for each one. Arrange the oysters on the half shell on the hot rock salt.

Partially fry the bacon in a skillet, drain, and set aside.

Blend the butter, shallot, parsley, and green pepper, season with Tabasco. Put a spoonful on top of each oyster. Top each with a piece of bacon. Bake until the bacon is crisp and the butter melted, or place under the broiler for about 5 minutes. Serve with lemon wedges. Serves 4.

OYSTERS REMICK

Rock salt
6 slices bacon
24 oysters on the half shell
¾ cup mayonnaise
3 tablespoons chili sauce

1 teaspoon Dijon or dark prepared
  mustard
Several dashes of cayenne pepper
1 teaspoon lemon juice

Preheat oven to 450°.

Make beds of rock salt in 4 pie tins, dampen slightly with water, heat the tins, uncovered, in the oven for several minutes.

Meanwhile, cut each bacon strip into 4 equal pieces, partially fry over moderate heat, drain on paper towels, and reserve. Arrange 6 oysters in their shells in each pie tin, pushing the shells down in the rock salt so they won't tip. Blend the mayonnaise, chili sauce, mustard, cayenne, and lemon juice, cover each oyster with a heaping teaspoon. Top with a piece of bacon, bake, uncovered, for 6–7 minutes until the bacon is crisp. Serve in the tins as a first course. Serves 4.

OYSTERS ROCKEFELLER

Created in 1899 at New Orleans' renowned Antoine's and handed down from one member of the Alciatore family to the other, this is a famous "secret" recipe, with numerous interpretations. The one below is among the tastier.

1 pound fresh spinach, or 2 10-
  ounce packages frozen
6 tablespoons butter
½ cup chopped shallots or green
  onions, tails and tips
⅓ cup chopped celery
⅓ cup finely chopped parsley

½ teaspoon dried tarragon
⅓ cup fine bread crumbs
2 tablespoons Pernod or anisette
Several drops of Tabasco sauce
Salt
36 oysters on the half shell
Rock salt

Preheat oven to 450°.

Rinse the spinach, pick it over, and remove the tough leaves. If you are using frozen spinach, defrost it and drain. Set aside.

Melt 4 tablespoons of the butter in a saucepan. Sauté the shallots or onions, celery, parsley, and tarragon for several minutes. Add the spinach, cover, and let it wilt over low heat. Pour the spinach mixture in a blender or food processor with the bread crumbs, the Pernod or anisette, and the remaining 2 tablespoons of butter. Purée and season to taste with Tabasco and salt.

Layer rock salt in pie tins, dampen it a bit. Put the oysters in their shells on top. Put a heaping teaspoon of the spinach mixture on each, bake for about 20 minutes or until the topping is lightly browned. Serve immediately. Serves 6.

OYSTER LOAF—LA MÉDIATRICE

In turn-of-the-century New Orleans, a prudent husband returning home after an all-night binge stopped to buy a *médiatrice* (as the oyster loaf was called) to assuage his angry wife. In San Francisco, it had a similar function and there was known as "the squarer." The oyster loaf was popular throughout the country in the nineteenth century, whether as a peacemaker or just for good eating. In Connecticut, it was simply known as "boxed oysters."

1 loaf French bread, 12 inches long, or a small round Italian loaf	1 pint shucked oysters, drained
⅓ cup melted butter	Tabasco sauce
	Hot heavy cream (optional)

Preheat oven to 425°.

Cut off the top of the bread lengthwise, scoop out most of the bread of the bottom half, leaving a shell about ¾ inch thick. Brush the inside of the bottom and the cut side of the top with melted butter. Put the loaf and "lid," cut sides up, on an ungreased baking sheet, bake until toasted golden brown, about 20 minutes (the lid will be done first; check that it does not overcook).

Meanwhile, sauté the oysters (see Index) in hot butter until plump. Add salt, pepper, a dash of Tabasco, and, if desired, a little hot cream. Fill the loaf with the hot fried oysters and put the lid on top. Heat for 10 minutes or until ready to serve. Cut in thick slices if the loaf is long, or in wedges if it is round. Serves 4–6.

NOTE: Individual rolls can also be used: allow about 3 oysters for each one. The amount of oysters required for this recipe varies according to the size of the oysters and the size of the loaf of bread. In any case the bread "basket" should be filled to the top with oysters.

HANGTOWN FRY

One legend says that this dish, a kind of oyster-egg pancake, was created during the California Gold Rush when a miner came into Hangtown (now Placerville) loaded with nuggets and asked for the most expensive food on the menu, which at that time was oysters and eggs. Another story says that a desperado, about to be hanged there for stealing gold dust, requested it as his last meal. It was originally made with small Olympia oysters.

1 dozen medium oysters, shucked   Cracker meal
⅓ cup flour   Butter
Salt and freshly ground pepper   ¼ cup heavy cream (optional)
9 eggs

Drain the oysters on paper towels. Season the flour on a plate with salt and pepper. Beat one of the eggs well in a small bowl. Put cracker meal in another bowl. Dip each oyster first in the seasoned flour, then the egg, then the cracker meal. Sauté them gently in butter until browned on both sides. Add more butter if necessary but do not let it burn.

Beat the remaining eggs with the cream, season to taste. Pour over the oysters, cook over medium heat until firm on the bottom. Turn with a spatula or slide out and flip over. Cook the second side for a minute or two longer. Serves 4.

OYSTER STUFFING FOR TURKEY

An old American tradition, oyster stuffings for the holiday bird range from layers of buttered slices of toast, alternated with raw oysters, to the following:

1 cup chopped celery   6–7 cups coarse bread crumbs
8 tablespoons (1 stick) butter   1 egg
¼ cup chopped parsley   Salt and freshly ground pepper
½ cup grated onion   Several dashes of cayenne pepper
4 tablespoons chopped chives   1 pint shucked oysters, drained

Sauté the celery in 4 tablespoons of the butter until soft. Add the parsley, onion, and chives, toss with the bread crumbs in a large bowl. Add the egg and mix well. Season to taste with salt, pepper, and cayenne.

Melt the remaining 4 tablespoons of butter in a saucepan. Cut the oysters in halves or quarters, poach for 2 minutes in the butter. Toss lightly with the stuffing. Allow the mixture to sit for a while at room temperature to develop the flavor before stuffing the bird. Makes enough for a 10- to 14-pound turkey.

OYSTER SOUFFLÉ

36 medium oysters or 24 large   3 tablespoons butter
    oysters, shucked, cut in half,   3 tablespoons flour
    liquor reserved   ¾ cup hot milk

¾ cup hot oyster liquor   4 egg yolks
Salt and white pepper   5 egg whites
A dash of cayenne pepper

Preheat oven to 400°.

Butter a 1½-quart (6-cup) soufflé dish.

Melt the butter in a heavy saucepan, stir in the flour with a wooden spoon, and cook over moderate heat for 2 minutes without letting the mixture color. Remove from heat. When the bubbling stops, pour in the hot milk and oyster liquor all at once, whisk vigorously until blended. Beat in the salt, pepper, and cayenne, return to heat, and bring to a boil, whisking for 2 minutes. Remove from heat and beat in the egg yolks. Gently stir in the oysters.

In a large bowl, beat the egg whites with a pinch of salt until stiff. Stir about ¼ of them into the sauce to lighten it, fold in the balance. Pour the soufflé mixture into the prepared mold, put into the oven, and immediately lower heat to 375°. Bake for 30–35 minutes or until the soufflé is well puffed and browned. Serves 4.

SCALLOPS

As a religious symbol, the scallop shell is closely associated with St. James, who, according to legend, wandered through Spain for seven years, converting heathens, until he was beheaded by order of King Herod, thus becoming the first of Jesus' disciples to become a martyr. Another part of this legend tells how the Apostle James rescued a bridegroom and his horse from the sea, both of whom emerged covered with scallop shells. Buried in Spain, James is said to have risen again in 844 to lead Christian soldiers to victory against the Moors. In the twelfth century, a cathedral was built in his honor in the little Spanish town of Compostela. The figure of Santiago, or St. James, dressed as a pilgrim, can be seen there today, on the Romanesque façade of the church, a scallop shell ornamenting his wide-brimmed hat.

Pilgrims to Santiago de Compostela were given a scallop shell to signify having completed the journey. A number of the pilgrims were French and the association is fixed forever in the French language, whose name for scallop is *coquille Saint-Jacques*.

As the scallop lacks the siphons of most similar bivalves, it swims by compressing its shell valves open and shut, forcing the water backward in jets and itself forward. This movement develops a muscle or "eye," which is the part we in America eat. In Europe, the entire scallop, including the mass that surrounds the muscle, and the roe, if present, is eaten. Many people who have eaten this crescent-shaped coral delicacy in France wonder why it has not developed a following here. The main reason is that the roe never gets to market. Since scallops cannot close their shells tightly and lose body moisture quickly, they die soon after being removed from the water. Therefore, it is customary here to shuck and trim them on board the fishing boats and the roe is habitually discarded as part of that operation.

AVAILABILITY: The tiny delicately flavored bay scallops are available in the autumn and winter months; the larger sea scallops, slightly less tender than bays, have a longer season and are around until April. In the summer months some Eastern markets carry bay scallops from Florida, but the best flavored ones come from the cold inshore waters of Long Island.

The freshness of both varieties can be judged by sight and smell. Scallops should gleam wetly yet not be swimming in liquid, and they should smell mild and sweet. Beware of those that are too opaquely white—this may be an indication that they have been soaked in water to increase the weight.

In addition to buying them fresh, sea scallops may be bought freshly frozen, breaded and frozen, or breaded, precooked, and frozen. (Bay scallops are almost never available frozen; there simply aren't enough of them.) Thaw frozen scallops in the refrigerator, then cook them as you would the fresh. Cook breaded ones according to package directions.

TO OPEN: If you have gathered scallops yourself, simply insert a sharp knife between the shells and cut the single adductor muscle, then cut away the flesh and cut out the eye. If you are adventurous, eat the flesh, which is discarded for commercial purposes—it is superb with a squeeze of lemon and a twist of black pepper.

TO COOK: Bay scallops are so delicate they can easily be eaten raw, with a twist of black pepper and a squeeze of lemon juice—nothing more. Cooking (quick sautéing is best) should be done as briefly as possible, lest they toughen and lose their sweet flavor. The scallops should be carefully dried and the pan very hot, so that browning will take place almost immediately before vital juices are lost. Sea scallops can be most simply broiled, plain or breaded. Preheat the broiler and arrange in a single layer in a baking pan. Broil 3–4 inches from the heat until lightly browned. Turning is not necessary. Season with salt and pepper and serve with lemon wedges.

BROILED BREADED SCALLOPS: Dip the scallops in melted butter, roll them in fine dry bread crumbs or cracker meal. Broil as above, but turn them once so they brown evenly.

DEEP-FRIED BREADED SCALLOPS

1 pound sea scallops
1 egg
2 tablespoons milk
Salt

Flour for dredging
1 cup fine bread crumbs
Oil for deep frying
Lemon wedges

Rinse the scallops, drain, and pat dry. Combine the egg with the milk and salt to taste in a shallow dish.

Put the scallops on a plate and dredge them with flour (either use a dredger or sprinkle the flour on them through a large strainer). Dump the scallops into the same large strainer over the sink to get rid of excess flour. Discard the flour in the dish.

Put the floured scallops into the egg-milk mixture, turn them carefully with a large metal spoon to coat evenly. Then turn them into the same large strainer over the sink and let the excess liquid drain off.

Spread out the bread crumb mixture on the same plate you used for the flour. Turn the scallops out of the strainer onto the crumbs and turn them about gently with another dry spoon. Arrange on a plate or rack so they do not touch. (These may be prepared an hour ahead to this point and refrigerated.)

Heat cooking oil or shortening in a deep-fat fryer to 375°. Place a single layer of scallops in the basket, lower into the fat, and fry for 2–3 minutes until golden brown. Drain on paper towels and serve with lemon wedges. Serves 3–4.

VARIATION: "OVEN-FRIED" SCALLOPS   Preheat oven to 500°. Mix ½ teaspoon paprika in with the bread crumbs. Prepare the scallops as above, arrange in a single layer in a buttered shallow baking pan, drizzle with melted butter, and bake, uncovered, without turning or basting for 7–9 minutes or until golden. Serve with tartar sauce and lemon wedges.

SAUTÉED SCALLOPS

The best and simplest way to cook fresh bay scallops, but you can also use sea scallops, cut in half.

2 pounds bay scallops   Salt and freshly ground pepper
8 tablespoons (1 stick) butter   Lemon wedges

Wash the scallops well in cold water, remove any bits of shell and grit, and dry well.

As scallops will brown faster if they are not too crowded in the pan, it is a good idea to do them in two batches. Melt 4 tablespoons of the butter in a large, heavy skillet, sauté half the scallops over moderately high heat for no more than for 4–5 minutes until the edges are lightly browned. Keep these warm while you cook the remainder. Melt the rest of the butter, sauté the second batch of scallops. Sprinkle with salt and pepper, serve at once with lemon wedges. Serves 4–6.

VARIATION: SCALLOPS MEUNIÈRE   Dip the scallops first in milk, then in lightly seasoned flour. Sauté as directed above, transfer to a hot platter, and sprinkle with lemon juice and handful of minced parsley. Turn the skillet, add 1–2 tablespoons additional butter, heat until light brown, pour over the scallops, and serve.

RAW SCALLOPS LE DUC

2 pounds very fresh sea scallops
⅓ cup olive oil
2 small onions, peeled and thinly sliced

4 whole cloves
¼ teaspoon cognac
Freshly ground pepper

With a long, very sharp thin knife, cut the scallops into the thinnest possible slices, approximately ⅛ inch thick. As the slices are cut, arrange them in a slightly overlapping flower petal pattern on 8 small plates.

Combine the olive oil, onions, cloves, and cognac, set aside. When ready to serve, drain off the onions and cloves, discard, and brush the scallop slices very lightly with the oil (the best way to do this is to dip a large spoon into it and gently smear the fish with the spoon back). Season with several good grindings of fresh pepper. Serves 8.

MARINATED SCALLOPS

1 pound bay or sea scallops
Juice of 2 limes

2 tablespoons chopped dill

Marinate the scallops in the lime juice and chopped dill for 3–4 hours in the refrigerator. Serve with toothpicks.

SEVICHE OF SCALLOPS

2 pounds bay scallops
½ cup lime juice (about 4 limes)
2 cloves garlic, minced
¼ cup chopped pickled hot green chilies (optional; see the note below)
¼ cup chopped sweet red pepper or pimiento

¼ cup chopped parsley
¼ cup chopped shallots or green onions
1 teaspoon salt
1 tablespoon chopped fresh coriander leaves
½ cup olive oil

Wash the scallops and pat dry. Toss lightly with the lime juice, refrigerate for 2–3 hours. Drain, toss well with the remaining ingredients, and let stand another hour. Serve on lettuce as a first course or with toothpicks as an hors d'oeuvre. Serves 8.

NOTE: Pickled green chilies are available in many supermarkets in the section where Mexican food is sold. You may also use 1 or 2 fresh green chilies if available.

SEVICHE OF SCALLOPS, PERUVIAN STYLE

In Peru, this *seviche* is eaten together with cold cooked sweet potatoes and cold cooked corn on the cob. The play of flavors and textures is exquisite; under no circumstances be tempted to serve the corn hot or with butter!

2 pounds sea scallops
¾ cup lime juice (4–6 limes)
1 large red onion, thickly sliced
3 small hot green pickled chili
    peppers, or more to taste (see
    note below)

½ cup chopped parsley
¼ cup chopped fresh coriander
    leaves
¾ cup olive oil
Salt and freshly ground pepper

Put the scallops in a colander and wash them by letting *hot* water run over them briefly. Cut them in quarters or, if very large, into sixths. Put them into a pottery or glass bowl, add the lime juice, stir to make sure that all pieces are coated, cover with plastic wrap, and refrigerate for 4 hours. Drain the scallops and discard the juice.

Put the onion, chili peppers, parsley, coriander into a blender or food processor, whirl until finely chopped. Add oil and whirl again to blend. Pour the oil mixture over the scallops, season to taste with salt and pepper, and chill. Serves 6 as a first course, 4 as a main course.

NOTE: See note at end of preceding recipe.

COQUILLES SAINT-JACQUES à LA PARISIENNE (Scallops and Mushrooms in Wine Sauce)

When one speaks of *coquilles Saint-Jacques* in this country, one is usually referring to the recipe below, scallops in *sauce parisienne, coquilles Saint-Jacques* being merely the French term for scallops. The dish may be prepared ahead and gratinéed at the last minute.

1½ cups dry white wine
3 tablespoons minced shallot
1 bay leaf
1 parsley sprig
½ teaspoon salt
Freshly ground white pepper
1½ pounds bay or sea scallops,
    washed
½ pound mushrooms, wiped clean
    and minced

4 tablespoons (½ stick) butter
5 tablespoons flour
⅔ cup heavy cream
2 egg yolks, lightly beaten
Lemon juice
½ cup grated Swiss or Gruyère
    cheese
2 tablespoons butter

Butter 6–8 large scallop shells or individual *gratin* dishes, set aside.

Put the wine, shallot, bay leaf, parsley, salt, and several grindings of white pepper in an enamel or stainless steel saucepan. Bring to the boil, lower heat, and simmer for 5 minutes, uncovered. Add the scallops and mushrooms to the wine mixture, pour in enough water to just cover. Bring again to a simmer, cover, and simmer slowly for 4–5 minutes until the scallops turn milky white. Remove the scallops and mushrooms with a slotted spoon, set aside.

Return the saucepan to high heat and boil the liquid rapidly, covered, until reduced to about 1 cup. Strain and set aside.

Prepare the sauce: Melt the 4 tablespoons of butter in a small, heavy saucepan, blend in the flour. Cook both together slowly for 2 minutes. Remove from heat, blend in the hot cooking liquid. Return to moderate heat, stirring constantly, until thickened and smooth, about 1 minute.

Combine the egg yolks and cream in a bowl, spoon a little of the hot sauce into the yolks, beat in, then beat in the balance of the sauce slowly. Pour the sauce into the pan, set over low heat, and cook, stirring, for 1 minute. Do not boil. Thin with more cream if necessary. Season to taste with salt, pepper, and lemon juice.

Blend about ⅔ of the sauce with the reserved scallops and mushrooms. Divide the mixture equally among the buttered shells and spoon the balance of the sauce over the tops. Sprinkle with the cheese and dot with butter. Arrange the shells on a broiling pan (the recipe may be prepared ahead to this point, covered with plastic wrap, and refrigerated until serving time).

Preheat the broiler, then broil the scallops about 5 inches from the heat for 4–5 minutes until bubbly and lightly brown. If the dish has been prepared ahead and refrigerated, set the broiler shelf on the lowest rack and broil the scallops for 5–6 minutes to warm them, then move the rack up to 5 inches from the heat and broil an additional 3–4 minutes until the top is bubbly and brown. Serves 8 as a first course.

NOTE: If you are using sea scallops, cut them horizontally into pieces about ⅛ inch thick.

COQUILLES SAINT-JACQUES à LA PROVENÇALE (Scallops with Wine, Garlic, and Herbs)

Like the above recipe, this one may be totally prepared in advance and gratinéed just before serving. It may be served with rice as a light lunch or as a first course at dinner.

1½ pounds bay or sea scallops
¾ cup unsifted flour
Salt and freshly ground pepper
⅓ minced yellow onion
5 tablespoons butter

2 tablespoons minced shallots or
   green onions (white part only)
1 clove garlic, minced
1 tablespoon olive oil
⅔ cup dry white wine

1 small bay leaf   ¼ cup grated Swiss or Gruyère
A pinch of thyme   cheese

Butter 6 scallop shells or a 2-cup oval *gratin* or baking dish.

Wash the scallops and pat dry with paper towels. Combine the flour with salt and pepper to taste in a plastic or brown paper bag. Add the scallops, a handful at a time, and shake gently to coat evenly with the flour. Turn out into a colander or strainer and shake off the excess flour.

Melt 1 tablespoon of the butter in a small saucepan, sauté the onions for 4–5 minutes until translucent but not brown. Add the shallots or green onions and garlic, cook slowly for a minute or two more. Set aside.

Heat 2 tablespoons of the butter with the olive oil in a heavy skillet, sauté the floured scallops very quickly over high heat for 2 minutes to brown them lightly. (Depending on the size of the skillet, this may have to be done in two batches. Return the first batch to the skillet before proceeding.)

Add the wine to the skillet along with the bay leaf, thyme, and the onion mixture. Raise the heat, cover the skillet, and simmer for 5 minutes. Uncover, and if necessary boil for a minute or two longer until the sauce is slightly thickened. Correct the seasoning and discard the bay leaf.

Spoon the scallops and the sauce into the prepared shells or baking dish. Sprinkle with the cheese and dot with the remaining 2 tablespoons of butter cut into small pieces. (The recipe may be prepared ahead to this point, covered with plastic wrap, and refrigerated.)

Preheat the broiler, then set the filled scallop shells or baking dish about 5 inches from the heat for 4–5 minutes until bubbly and browned. If the dish has been refrigerated, set the broiler rack in its lowest position and broil the scallops for 5–6 minutes, then move up and broil 5 inches from the heat for 3–4 minutes until bubbly and brown. Serves 6.

NOTE: If you are using sea scallops, cut them crosswise into pieces about ⅛-inch thick.

SEA URCHIN

The sea urchin is a spiny-skinned echinoderm, a marine animal with a globular shell, or "test," found around the world in various forms and valued as food in almost every country except this one. (If Americans know them at all, it is most likely because of having stepped on one—the spines are very painful.) In Barbados, for example, where they are known as sea eggs, they are so prized that the gathering of them is regulated by law.

There are about five hundred species of sea urchins throughout the world; the largest and most widely used in American waters *Strongylocentrotus franciscanus,* is found along the West Coast, a giant reddish brown or deep purple creature with a test that measures 5 inches in diameter and has 2-

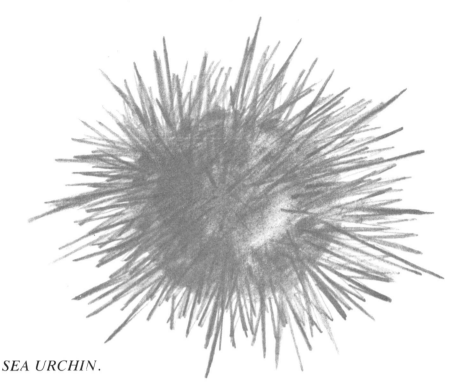

SEA URCHIN.

inch spines. The most common is its relative, the smaller Pacific purple urchin, *S. purpuratus*. Other species include the green sea urchin, a rare brown urchin found on both coasts, and the Atlantic purple urchin, slightly smaller than the green, with round-tipped spines.

The edible portions of the mature urchin are the male and female gonads. These roe or sperm sacs may range in color from white to deep orange and, if removed as a piece, look like a small starfish, to which the sea urchin is related. The sac is housed in a fascinating five-plate construction that is interspersed with five of another design. The roe has a delicious, delicate flavor that one writer has described as ''sea with a hint of melon.'' The darker the roe, the more pronounced the flavor.

Sea urchins rarely appear at market, although the purple urchin can usually be bought in California, and I am told that Maine urchins are available at the Fulton Fish Market in New York City at Christmas time. Gathering them is primarily a seasonal do-it-yourself operation, and it helps to know their habits. They tend to be found in tide pools and along shallow rocky shores at low tide, especially in shaded areas under overhanging rocks.

TO OPEN: The bottom, or mouth side, of the sea urchin is slightly flattened; you can cut a section out of this side with a knife or scissors and dump the roe out. Or put the urchin on a solid surface, mouth side up, and crack the test in half by tapping all around with a rock or hammer. Free each of the five points and release the roe. Or scoop it out with a spoon. I have gathered them in Italy and eaten them immediately this way, a squeeze of lemon the only accompaniment. The roe can also be spread on thin crackers or toast; six to twelve urchins will be needed for one decent portion.

The people of Marseilles eat the roe by dipping buttered sippets of bread into it. The whole urchin can also be boiled like an egg: cook it in a good amount of boiling salted water, drain, open by cutting the mouth side with scissors, and eat it with toast or buttered bread. If you have a plenitude of roe, you might try the following recipe for *crème d'oursins,* which is essentially the mashed sea urchin roe mixed with hollandaise sauce. The French serve it traditionally with *daurade,* a sea bream, but it could be served with poached snapper or sea bass as well.

SEA URCHIN CREAM FOR POACHED FISH (Crème d'Oursins)

1 sea bass or other firm-fleshed white fish, about 1½ pounds, cleaned, head and tail on	6–7 peppercorns
	Salt
	Juice of 2 lemons
1 onion	¾ cup sea urchin roe, about 20–24 sea urchins
1 carrot	
A sprig of thyme	1 teaspoon olive oil
1 bay leaf	¾ cup Hollandaise Sauce ✿

Put the fish in a fish poacher, cover with cold water, and add the onion, carrot, thyme, bay leaf, peppercorns, salt to taste, and lemon juice. Bring to a boil over high heat, cover, lower heat, and simmer for 10–15 minutes. Remove from the broth and keep warm.

While the fish is cooking, mash the sea urchin roe with the olive oil. Blend thoroughly into the hollandaise sauce, pour over the fish and serve. Serves 2.

SHRIMP

Shrimp, ancient Greek table delicacy, a featured item on the menu at the coronation banquet of Henry V, are still going strong as America's number one shellfish love. What we see in our markets are the creatures minus their heads, which are usually discarded as soon as they are caught. All the available sizes belong to the same variety of Crustacea. They may be purchased in a fishmarket raw (or "green," as they are called in some areas), raw and shelled, cooked in the shell, or cooked, shelled, and deveined. They are also available in 4½- to 5-ounce cans. If you buy them raw, look for firm, springy, moist meat. Connoisseurs feel that shrimp cooked in the shell generally have more flavor than those peeled before cooking, but this is a matter of degree and depends on how they are to be used. It is a good idea

never to cook shrimp before adding them to a cooking sauce, or they will
be overdone.

Shrimp are sold according to count, the size also determining the price.
The very largest size is sometimes called a prawn, and in England all shrimp
regardless of size are called prawns, but actually a prawn is a crayfish and
this is a misnomer. In Eastern markets, the following rules usually prevail:

> Colossal 10 and under = 1 pound
> Jumbo 10–15 = 1 pound
> Large 16–20 = 1 pound
> Medium 21–30 = 1 pound
> Small 31–35 = 1 pound
> Tiny ocean shrimp 150–180 = 1 pound (only sold shelled and cooked)

One pound of raw shrimp will yield, on the average, $\frac{1}{2}$–$\frac{3}{4}$ pound of
cooked shelled meat. This is calculated by an approximate $\frac{1}{4}$ pound loss per
gross pound in shelling and up to another $\frac{1}{4}$ pound for shrinkage through
cooking. This is an important but often overlooked fact to keep in mind
when calculating how much to buy. Also keep in mind that, while a half
pound per person might be a good rule of thumb for a main course, a thick
sauce and/or other ingredients in the dish might stretch a pound to serve 3.

FROZEN: Shrimp are sold frozen in block packages, raw in the shell, and
also shelled and deveined in blocks and bags (the advantage of the latter
being that you can take out and thaw just what you need, it is also the most
expensive way to buy them). Always defrost frozen raw shrimp before
cooking them. (Frozen uncooked breaded shrimp are the one exception.)
Defrost in the refrigerator or under cold running water. Never refreeze.

CANNED: These are fully cooked and shelled and must be rinsed and thoroughly drained before using. Add to the dish being made just long enough
to heat them; to cook them longer would destroy their texture.

TO SHELL: Shell in two motions: Hold the tail in your left hand, slip your
right thumb under the shell between feelers. Lift off 2 or 3 shell segments at
once, then, still holding onto the tail, pull the shrimp itself out of the rest of
the shell. Another quick way is to use kitchen shears. Cut from the front
back toward the tail, following the outer back curve. This will also expose
the dark vein, which can be removed under cold running water at the same
time the shell is peeled off. Drain and pat dry with paper towels.

TO CLEAN: A subject of some controversy. The French don't; we generally do. Sometimes in larger shrimp the black intestinal vein can be sandy
or gritty, but primarily the vein is removed for aesthetic reasons. They can
be deveined as described under "To Shell" (above) or by making a shallow
cut along the back with the point of a sharp knife and then lifting out the
vein before or after shelling, or, if you have a particular reason for not wish-

ing the shrimp to show a cut down the back, you may insert a slender sharp skewer underneath the vein at the middle of the back curve. Lift out the vein carefully in one piece. If it should break, make a second insert and repeat the process.

TO BUTTERFLY: Deepen the cut where the shrimp was deveined and cut almost through, so shrimp opens like a book. Pat dry. For deep-frying, they

A BUTTERFLIED SHRIMP.

may be flattened slightly by placing between sheets of wax paper and pounding lightly.

TO COOK: Allow one quart of water for each pound of raw shrimp. Add 2 tablespoons of salt if the shrimp are unshelled, 1 tablespoon if shelled. Bring the water to a boil, add the shrimp, bring the water to a second boil, cover, and immediately remove from heat. Let sit for 5–8 minutes (depending on size of the shrimp) or until they turn bright pink. Drain and cool immediately under cold running water. Let stand for 5 minutes before handling. Of course a court-bouillon may also be used and definitely should be used instead of salted water, to cook shellfish that are to be served cold, or in aspic. Let the court-bouillon cook for 10 minutes before adding the shrimp, to heighten its flavor. A court-bouillon is not required when shrimp are to be served with a highly flavored sauce.

SHRIMP PASTE

Shrimp paste was a traditional breakfast item in Charleston, South Carolina. Although it is now used as a cocktail accompaniment, I can personally vouch for the pleasure of starting the day with some, spread on toast!

1 pound shrimp, cooked, shelled, and deveined
An 8-ounce package cream cheese
3 tablespoons chili sauce
2 tablespoons grated onion

1 teaspoon Worcestershire sauce
1 tablespoon lemon juice
Milk
2 teaspoons chopped parsley (optional)

Chop the shrimp finely, mash the cream cheese with a fork and whip until very smooth. Blend together the chopped shrimp, cream cheese, chili sauce, onion, Worcestershire sauce, and lemon juice. If the mixture seems too stiff, beat in some milk, a teaspoon at a time, until a pleasing consistency is reached.

IN A FOOD PROCESSOR: With the steel blade in place, chop the shrimp very finely, remove to a bowl. Cut the cream cheese block in several pieces and whip with the steel blade until smooth and creamy. Add the shrimp and blend in, then blend in the rest of the ingredients as above.

Pack the shrimp mixture into a serving bowl or crock and chill. Just before serving, sprinkle parsley on top. Serve with crackers for spreading.

ORIENTAL SHRIMP TOAST

½ pound medium-size shrimp, cooked	1 tablespoon cornstarch
4 water chestnuts, finely chopped	1 egg, lightly beaten
1 teaspoon salt	6 slices firm, slightly stale white bread
½ teaspoon sugar	2 cups vegetable oil

Shell and devein the shrimp, wash under a stream of cold water, dry, then mince very fine by hand or in a food processor.

Chop the water chestnuts finely by hand or in a food processor. Mix the shrimp, chestnuts, salt, sugar, cornstarch, and egg thoroughly. Trim the crust off each bread slice, cut each slice into 4 triangles. Spread a teaspoon of the shrimp mixture smoothly over each triangle.

Heat the oil to 375° in a heavy skillet. Carefully place the bread on a wide spatula, *shrimp side down,* and slide into the hot oil a few at a time. After 1 minute, turn and fry for a few more seconds or until golden brown. Drain on paper towels. Serve immediately as an hors d'oeuvre. Serves 6–8.

SCANDINAVIAN SHRIMP TOAST (Toast Skagern)

1 pound shrimp, cooked, shelled, and deveined*	Oil
4 teaspoons mayonnaise	10 slices home-style white bread, crusts removed
2 teaspoons whipped cream	A 4-ounce can salmon roe caviar
Curry powder	2 branches of dill
Butter	Lemon wedges

Chop the shrimp coarsely. Mix together the mayonnaise, whipped cream, and curry powder, fold in the shrimp, set aside.

*Canned shrimp or frozen Alaska shrimp may be used in this recipe.

Melt the butter in the oil, gently sauté the bread slices until crisp and golden brown. Drain on paper towels.

Pile the shrimp mixture on the toast, dividing it equally. Heap a teaspoon or so of salmon caviar on each toast, decorate with a feather of dill and serve each with a lemon wedge. Serves 10 as a first course.

NOTE: The toast may be sliced in half diagonally and served as a drink accompaniment. Makes 20 hors d'oeuvres.

SHRIMP WITH MELON IN KIRSCH

This recipe is an old European one that originally called for lobster instead of shrimp. A friend began making it with shrimp in the days when the price difference between the two was significant; we liked it so much we have been eating it that way ever since as a first course in the summer.

20 medium shrimp, cooked, shelled, and deveined
½ ripe medium-size melon, preferably Spanish, cassava, or honeydew
2 inside stalks celery, diced

1 cup mayonnaise, preferably homemade
1 tablespoon chili sauce
Tabasco sauce
2 tablespoons kirsch
Salt

Cut the shrimp crosswise into 3 pieces each. Cut the melon in cubes of a size compatible with the shrimp. Drain off as much of the melon juice as you can, reserve it in a cup. Combine the shrimp and melon with the celery in a bowl and set aside.

Put the mayonnaise in a small bowl. Beat in the chili sauce, several dashes of Tabasco, the kirsch, and salt to taste. Thin the sauce to a pleasing consistency with some of the reserved melon juice. Pour the sauce over the shrimp mixture, cover, and allow to mellow for at least an hour in the refrigerator. Serves 4.

INSALATA ALLA PESCATORI (Fishermen's Salad)

1 cup sliced onions
2 cups dry white wine
4 cups water
½ bay leaf
1 small stalk celery, cut up
1 pound raw medium shrimp in the shell
1½ pounds small squid, cleaned (see Index)

2 dozen cherrystone clams, scrubbed and rinsed
3 pounds mussels, scrubbed and debearded
1 cup olive oil
⅓ cup wine vinegar
4 tablespoons Dijon or dark prepared mustard
2 teaspoons chopped garlic

1 teaspoon salt
2 tablespoons chopped parsley
2 tablespoons capers, rinsed
¼ teaspoon white pepper

½ cup very thin, diagonally cut
  celery slices
Lemon wedges for garnish
Parsley for garnish (optional)

In a 4–5-quart saucepan simmer the onions, uncovered, with the white wine, water, bay leaf, and celery for 40 minutes. Add the shrimp, simmer for 7 minutes, lift out, cool, shell, and devein. Add the squid, simmer, uncovered, for 15 minutes, lift out, cool, and cut into ¼-inch slices. Add the clams, cook, uncovered, until the shells open (about 5 minutes), lift out, remove and discard the shells. Add the mussels, cook, uncovered, until the shells open (about 7 minutes), lift out, remove and discard the shells. Discard the cooking liquid.

MAKE THE MARINADE: In a bowl mix together the olive oil, wine vinegar, mustard, the garlic, crushed together with the salt, the chopped parsley, capers, and white pepper. Toss with the seafood and celery slices. Let marinate for 8–12 hours in the refrigerator, stir well once or twice. Serve with lemon wedges and additional chopped parsley if desired, to 6–8 as a first course, or to 4 for lunch.

SHRIMP PONTCHARTRAIN

2 tablespoons very finely minced
  heart of celery
1 teaspoon anchovy paste
1 clove garlic, very finely minced
1 tablespoon paprika
1 tablespoon minced shallots or
  scallions
1 tablespoon minced parsley
2 tablespoons wine vinegar
7 tablespoons olive oil

Salt and freshly ground pepper
1 tablespoon Dijon, dark prepared,
  or hot mustard
Several dashes of hot pepper
  sauce (optional)
2 teaspoons grated white
  horseradish
24 medium shrimp, cooked,
  shelled, deveined, and chilled

Combine all the ingredients except the shrimp. Whip with a wire whisk or fork until well blended. Pour the mixture over the shrimp, chill until ready to use. Serve if desired over shredded lettuce. Serves 4 as a first course.

MARINATED SHRIMP I

¾ cup olive oil
3 cloves garlic, minced
1 small onion, minced
2 pounds raw shrimp, shelled and
  deveined

6 scallions, minced, tails and tips
½ cup white wine vinegar
1 teaspoon salt
1 teaspoon dry mustard
¼ teaspoon cayenne pepper

Heat ¼ cup of the oil in a large, heavy skillet: Sauté the garlic and onion over moderate heat until transparent, stirring constantly, 8–10 minutes. Add the shrimp, raise heat a bit, and cook for 5–7 minutes, always stirring, until they turn pink. Remove from heat and cool.

Make a marinade of the remaining oil, the scallions, vinegar, salt, mustard, and cayenne in a large bowl. Add the shrimp, toss thoroughly, and chill for several hours or overnight. Stir them up occasionally.

Serve in a bowl placed in a larger one filled with cracked ice. Mask the ice with bunches of parsley. This recipe may be easily doubled. Serves 8 with drinks, or 4 as a first course.

MARINATED SHRIMP II (Soused Shrimp)

3 pounds shelled shrimp, cooked
3 medium onions, thinly sliced
4 slices lemon
½ cup chopped parsley
Salt and freshly ground white
   pepper

Tabasco sauce
Olive oil
3 bay leaves

Make several layers of the shrimp, onions, lemon, and parsley in a casserole or serving dish. Add salt and pepper to each layer, several dashes of Tabasco, then enough good olive oil to cover. Top with the bay leaves. Marinate for 6–8 hours in a cool place, then serve straight from the dish in which the shrimp were marinated. This dish is a nice addition to a buffet table and also makes a good and easy outdoor dining dish in summer. Serves 6 as a main course.

PUERTO RICAN MARINATED SHRIMP WITH AVOCADO

3 pounds raw medium shrimp in
   the shell
1 carrot, scraped and cut into
   several pieces
1 stalk celery including leaves,
   cut up
1 bay leaf
1 small dried hot red pepper
10 peppercorns
1 teaspoon salt

½ cup very thinly sliced onion
1½ cups salad oil
¾ cup vinegar
2 cloves garlic, finely minced
3 medium tomatoes, peeled,
   seeded, and chopped
Freshly ground pepper
⅓ cup chopped parsley
1 ripe avocado, peeled and cubed

Put enough water to eventually cover the shrimp in a 3½–4-quart saucepan, add the carrot, celery, bay leaf, red pepper, peppercorns, and salt. Bring to the boil, simmer for 10 minutes. Add the shrimp and cook for 5 minutes after the second boil, let them cool in the broth.

Drain the shrimp and shell them. In a large bowl combine the onion, oil, vinegar, garlic, tomatoes, and salt to taste. Stir in the shrimp, chill for 12 hours. Just before serving, add a goodly amount of pepper, the parsley, and the avocado. Serves 6–8 as a first course, 4–6 as a main luncheon course. This is also an ideal dish for picnics.

SHRIMP RÉMOULADE

Make a Rémoulade Sauce ❋ , refrigerating it for an hour or so as directed. Coat the shrimp well with the sauce and arrange on a bed of lettuce. Garnish with hard-cooked egg quarters if desired. Serves 4 as a luncheon dish, 6 as a first course.

SHRIMP WITH DILLED MUSTARD SAUCE

2 pounds raw shrimp in the shell
1 bay leaf
12 whole allspice
6 parsley sprigs
1 rib celery with leaves, quartered

Salt
10 peppercorns, crushed
1¼ cups Dilled Mustard Sauce
  (given below)

Combine the shrimp, bay leaf, allspice, parsley, celery, water to cover, salt to taste, and peppercorns in a saucepan, bring to a boil, cover, and turn off heat. Let the shrimp remain for 10 minutes in the cooking liquid, then drain, and chill. Shell and devein the shrimp, serve with the dilled mustard sauce. Serves 6 as a first course.

DILLED MUSTARD SAUCE

1 egg yolk
1 teaspoon wine vinegar
3 tablespoons Dijon or dark prepared mustard
Several drops Tabasco sauce

Salt and freshly ground pepper
1 cup oil (half olive oil, half vegetable oil)
Lemon juice
¼ cup finely chopped fresh dill

Place the egg yolk in a mixing bowl, add the vinegar, 1 tablespoon of the mustard, the Tabasco, and salt and pepper to taste, beat vigorously for a second or two with a whisk. Start adding the oil gradually, beating continuously with the whisk. Continue in this manner until all the oil is used. Taste the sauce, add more salt to taste and a few drops of lemon juice if desired. Beat in the remaining mustard and the dill. Yields 1¼ cups.

NOTE: The sauce may be made in a blender or food processor.

HORSERADISH SHRIMP SANDWICHES

1 pound cooked shrimp, shelled
   and deveined
1 teaspoon Dijon or dark prepared
   mustard
1 tablespoon mayonnaise
2 teaspoons prepared horseradish,
   or more to taste

1 tablespoon chopped chives
Lemon juice
Whipped cream
Salt and freshly ground pepper
16 thin slices home-style white
   bread

Put the shrimp through the medium blade of a meat grinder or chop very finely. Blend in the mustard, mayonnaise, horseradish, chives, and a few drops of lemon juice. Add enough whipped cream to bind and give a good spreading consistency. Mix again briefly, season to taste with salt and pepper.

Remove the crusts from the bread and make sandwiches with the shrimp filling. Cut each into 4 triangles.

IN A FOOD PROCESSOR: Chop the shrimp finely, using the steel blade. Blend in the remaining ingredients. Proceed as above. Makes about 32 small sandwiches for hors d'oeuvres or tea.

SHRIMP AND CUCUMBERS IN TOMATO ASPIC RING

ASPIC

1 cup chicken stock
½ medium onion, sliced
1 stalk celery, cut up coarsely
2–3 sprigs parsley
½ teaspoon sugar
½ teaspoon salt
A dash of cayenne pepper
A 14-ounce can peeled tomatoes,
   or 1 pound fresh, peeled

½ bay leaf
5 peppercorns
1 tablespoon (one envelope) unflavored gelatin
½ cup liquid from the above tomatoes, or the same amount of
   water

FILLING

20 medium shrimp (about 1 pound),
   cooked, shelled, and deveined
1 cucumber, peeled and diced
¼ cup heavy cream
1 tablespoon olive oil

1 teaspoon lemon juice
Salt and freshly ground pepper
A dash of cayenne pepper
½ teaspoon dried tarragon or 1
   tablespoon snipped fresh dill

Chill an 8½-inch (5½-quart) ring mold.

Put the chicken stock, onion, celery, parsley, sugar, salt, cayenne, and tomatoes into a saucepan. Tie the bay leaf and peppercorns in a piece of cheesecloth and add. Bring to a boil, cook over a medium heat until thickened and reduced to 1½–2 cups. Let cool slightly.

While the tomato mixture is cooking, sprinkle the gelatin over the tomato liquid in a small saucepan, stir constantly over low heat until the gelatin dissolves, about 3 minutes. Remove the cheesecloth bag from the tomato mixture, combine the mixture with the gelatin and purée in a blender or food processor.

Remove the mold from the refrigerator, rinse quickly in cold water, and pour in the tomato-gelatin mixture. Refrigerate for at least 3 hours or until firm.

Cut the shrimp in half crosswise, add the cucumber. Whisk together the cream, oil, lemon juice, salt and pepper to taste, cayenne, and tarragon. Combine with the shrimp and cucumbers, refrigerate.

Unmold the tomato ring by dipping it in warm water to the depth of the aspic for 30 seconds. Put a serving plate on top and invert quickly. Fill the center with the shrimp mixture, and serve. Serves 4.

VARIATION: Instead of shrimp, cold leftover cooked white fish, bound together with mayonnaise and seasoned, may also be used to fill the ring.

SHRIMP QUENELLES IN THE FOOD PROCESSOR

1½ pounds raw shrimp, shelled
¾ pound sole or flounder fillets, all bones removed, cut in 1-inch cubes
2 eggs
Salt and freshly ground pepper

2 cups heavy cream
Cayenne pepper
A dash of nutmeg
1 recipe of Beurre Blanc Sauce ✻
A pot of boiling salted water
Chopped parsley for garnish

Chop the shrimp and fish in a food processor fitted with the steel blade, turning on and off until the mixture is smooth. Add the eggs, salt and pepper, heavy cream, several dashes of cayenne pepper, and nutmeg, blend until thoroughly smooth. Spoon the mousse into a mixing bowl.

Butter one or two skillets large enough to accommodate the *quenelles* when they are shaped. Have two large soup spoons and a bowl of water ready. Scoop up a rounded mass of the fish mousse in one spoon. Dip the other spoon in the bowl of hot water and smooth the top of the *quenelle*. Scoop it out of the spoon, making a neat egg shape in the second spoon, and lay it in the skillet. Continue making *quenelles,* placing them close together in the skillet(s). Ladle some of the boiling salted water over them to barely cover, then cover tightly with a piece of wax paper cut to fit the inside of the cooking utensil. Bring to a boil, lower heat, and simmer for 3 minutes. Do not boil.

Lift the paper and gently turn each *quenelle* with a rubber spatula.

Remove the pan from the heat and let stand for a few minutes. Drain the *quenelles* on paper towels, arrange them on a heated serving dish, and spoon *beurre blanc* sauce over each. Garnish the center of each with a pinch of chopped parsley. Pass the remaining sauce when serving. Makes about 20 *quenelles,* serving 6 people for lunch or as a first course.

NOTE: These *quenelles* may be prepared in advance, refrigerated, and reheated in a 350° oven. Reheat for 10 minutes (not in liquid).

GAMBAS AL AJILLO (Shrimp in Hot Sauce)

Salt
1 pound or 12–15 raw jumbo
   shrimp, shelled
4 tablespoons olive oil

4 small cloves garlic, peeled and
   sliced
1 dried hot red pepper, cut into 1-
   inch pieces

Salt the shrimp. Heat the olive oil in 1 large or 4 small flameproof casseroles. Add the garlic and hot pepper, sauté until the garlic is light brown. Add the shrimp, and cook over high heat briefly, moving the shrimp about and turning them over with a wooden spoon until they are pink. Serve hot. Serves 4.

SHRIMP NEWBURG

Follow the directions for Lobster Newburg ❋ , substituting 2 pounds of large shrimp in the shell.

SHRIMP DE JONGHE

Like oysters Rockefeller, the original recipe for this dish is said to be a family "secret" of the De Jonghe family who originated it in their Chicago restaurant. Easy to prepare, it is very popular throughout the Midwest and in the South, varying basically in the herb combinations that are used.

2 cloves garlic, minced
1 tablespoon chopped parsley
1 tablespoon chopped shallot
1 tablespoon chopped chives
½ teaspoon dried tarragon
½ teaspoon dried thyme
¼ pound (1 stick) butter at room
   temperature

1½ cups bread crumbs
½ cup dry sherry
Several gratings of nutmeg
A dash of powdered mace
Salt and freshly ground pepper
2 pounds raw shrimp in the shell

Mix together the garlic, parsley, shallot, chives, tarragon, and thyme, work these into the butter. Combine with the bread crumbs, sherry, nutmeg, and mace. Add salt and pepper to taste. Let the mixture mellow for a half hour or so.

Preheat oven to 400°.

Shell the shrimp, cook in boiling salted water for 3 minutes, drain. Butter 6 individual baking dishes or one oval *gratin* dish. Put half the crumb mixture on the bottom of the dish(es), arrange the shrimp over it, pressing them into the crumbs lightly, then top with the remaining crumb mixture. (The dish may be prepared ahead to this point and refrigerated, then let it come to room temperature before putting it in the oven.)

Bake for 10 minutes, then place under the broiler for several minutes until the tops brown. Serves 6.

IN A FOOD PROCESSOR: With the metal blade in place, mince the garlic, parsley, shallot, and chives. Add the tarragon, thyme, butter, nutmeg, mace, and salt and black pepper and process briefly. Add the crumbs and sherry, process briefly again, and proceed as above.

SCALLOP-STUFFED SHRIMP

1 dozen raw jumbo shrimp
6 ounces scallops, minced
¼ cup fresh bread crumbs
¼ cup grated Parmesan cheese
Paprika for garnish

1 clove garlic
3 tablespoons melted butter
¼ cup dry white wine or dry
   sherry (optional)

Preheat oven to 350°.

Shell the shrimp, leaving the tails intact. Devein and butterfly them according to instructions on pages 299 and 300. Stuff each with ½ teaspoon of chopped scallops, arrange in a buttered baking dish. Combine the bread crumbs and cheese, sprinkle over the scallop stuffing. Top each with a light dash of paprika. Put the garlic clove through a press, add to the melted butter, and drizzle over the shrimp. Bake for 15 minutes. Baste with white wine or sherry. Serves 2 as an entree or 4 as an appetizer.

VIETNAMESE SHRIMP CAKES

2 cups water
1½ cups flour
3 eggs
1 pound raw small shrimp, shelled,
   deveined, and minced
4 scallions, including some of the
   green, cut diagonally into 1-
   inch lengths

2 small carrots, finely julienned
⅓ cup minced celery
2 teaspoons salt
1½ teaspoons ground coriander
¼ teaspoon ground cumin
1 clove garlic, finely minced
White pepper
Oil for deep frying

Make a batter by whisking together the 2 cups of water, flour, and eggs in a large bowl until smooth. Add the shrimp, scallions, carrots, celery, salt, coriander, cumin, garlic, and pepper, combine well. Let stand for 20 minutes or so.

Heat 1½ inches of vegetable oil in a deep fryer to almost smoking, 425°. Half-fill a ⅓-cup measuring cup with the shrimp batter, carefully pour into the oil. Make 3 or 4 cakes at a time in this manner—no more—lifting them from the bottom of the fryer with a slotted spoon. Fry for 2 minutes on each side or until they are golden. Transfer the cakes to paper towels to drain. Makes about 24 cakes, which can be served alone, as hors d'oeuvres, or as a first course on Boston lettuce leaves. In either case, provide Vietnamese *noc manh* sauce (available in Oriental markets) or plain light soy sauce for dipping. The traditional way to present these cakes is to roll each in a lettuce leaf and serve.

SZECHWAN PRAWNS

Szechwan is a fertile inland province of China and is noted for its spicy cuisine.

2 pounds raw large shrimp, shelled
   and deveined
½ cup cornstarch
2⅓ cups corn oil
1 clove garlic, peeled and crushed
2 scallions, white and part of green,
   cut diagonally into 1-inch pieces
4 hot red or green chili peppers or
   Tabasco sauce, or Chinese
   pepper sauce to taste

3 thin slices ginger root, cut in
   finest possible julienne, or ½
   teaspoon powdered ginger
1½ tablespoons soy sauce
2 tablespoons dry sherry or dry
   white wine
½ teaspoon salt
¼ teaspoon MSG (optional)

Dredge the shrimp lightly with cornstarch.

Heat 2 cups of the oil to 365° in a deep-fat fryer, fry the shrimp, a few at a time, for exactly 2 minutes. Remove with a slotted spoon, drain on paper towels, and keep warm. Place the remaining ⅓ cup corn oil in a heavy skillet or wok, in it stir-fry the garlic, scallions, chili peppers, and ginger root for 3–4 minutes or until the scallions turn bright green. (If you use Tabasco or Chinese pepper sauce instead of chili peppers, add to the following soy sauce-wine mixture.) Add the soy sauce, wine, salt, and optional MSG, bring to a boil. Add the shrimp and heat. Serves 6.

SHRIMP TEMPURA

3 pounds raw large shrimp
Corn oil
Tempura Batter ❀

Dipping Sauce for Tempura (given
   p. 311)
½ cup sifted flour

Shell the shrimp, leaving the tails intact, and reserve the shells for the tempura sauce. Devein and butterfly the shrimp according to instructions on pages 299 and 300. Rinse, pat dry, and refrigerate for a few hours.

About ½ hour before serving, begin heating the oil in a deep-fat fryer. Prepare the tempura batter and sauce.

When the oil reaches 380°, quickly dredge the shrimp in the flour. Holding them by the tail, dip in the batter and fry them, 5 or 6 at a time, for 3–5 minutes or until golden. Drain on paper towels and keep warm, uncovered, in a slow oven. Remove any crumbs of batter from the oil with a slotted spoon as these will burn and appear as black flecks on subsequent shrimp. Keep the oil temperature as nearly constant as possible. Serve immediately with the tempura sauce as a dip. Serves 8 as an entree, 12 as an hors d'oeuvre.

NOTE: In addition to shrimp, you may make tempura using cauliflower flowerets, small pieces of broccoli, cubed eggplant, strips of seeded green pepper, small fingers of zucchini, clusters of parsley, wedges of onion, bite-size chunks of almost any white fish, clams, and mussels. In addition, grated white radish may be served separately, to be added to the dipping sauce to taste.

DIPPING SAUCE FOR TEMPURA

Reserved shells from the shrimp in
   the recipe above
1 cup water
⅓ cup Japanese soy sauce
1 cup hot beef broth

1½ teaspoons sugar
2 tablespoons dry sherry
½ teaspoon finely grated peeled
   fresh ginger root

In a saucepan combine the reserved shrimp shells with the 1 cup water, bring to a boil, boil for a minute, strain into another saucepan, and discard the shells. Add the rest of the ingredients, bring to a boil over moderate heat, and cook, stirring, until the sugar is dissolved. Serve at room temperature. Serves 4.

BUTTERFLY SHRIMP

2 pounds raw large shrimp, shelled
   and deveined
½ cup olive oil

1½ teaspoons salt
½ teaspoon freshly ground pepper
¾ cup dry bread crumbs

SAUCE
2 tablespoons olive oil
½ cup chopped onion
1½ tablespoons dry mustard

⅓ cup wine vinegar
1 cup beef broth
1 cup tomato sauce

Preheat the broiler. Line the broiler pan with foil.

Wash and dry the shrimp, butterfly them (see instructions on page 300). Dip them in the olive oil, season with salt and pepper, and roll in the bread crumbs. Place on the broiler pan, broil 3 inches from heat for 3–5 minutes on each side. To serve, arrange on a plate and put the sauce in a dish in the center.

TO PREPARE THE SAUCE: Heat the oil in a small skillet, sauté the onion until lightly golden. Blend in the mustard, broth, and vinegar, bring to a boil, and simmer for 5 minutes. Stir in the tomato sauce, cook over low heat for 10 minutes longer. Serves 4–6.

HERBED SHRIMP IN GARLIC BUTTER

36 raw large shrimp, shelled, deveined, tails intact
1 tablespoon salt
1 teaspoon oregano
1 teaspoon thyme

12 tablespoons (1½ sticks) butter at room temperature
4 cloves garlic, peeled
1 tablespoon minced parsley
¼ pound mushrooms, sliced

Toss the shrimp with the salt, oregano, and thyme, chill, covered for a half hour.

Preheat the oven to 375°.

Butter a shallow baking dish large enough to hold the shrimp and mushrooms, preferably one that can go to the table. In a bowl, cream 8 tablespoons of the softened butter with the garlic pressed, and the minced parsley. Set aside.

Melt the remaining 4 tablespoons of butter in a skillet, sauté the mushrooms for 3–4 minutes until wilted. Arrange the shrimp in the baking dish, cover with the mushrooms, and dot the garlic butter over the top. Bake for 12–15 minutes. Serve with wild rice. Serves 6.

SHRIMP "SCAMPI"

A very popular item appearing on countless menus across the country, "shrimp scampi" is actually a confusing term. Strictly speaking, scampi are giant prawns found only in the Mediterranean and the Adriatic. Prawns are close relatives of shrimp but are crayfish, sometimes also known as Dublin Bay prawns. In the United States the name is usually interpreted to mean broiled shrimp with garlic and oil.

12 jumbo shrimp, shelled, deveined, tails intact
1 cup olive oil
3 tablespoons Marsala or dry white wine

2 tablespoons minced parsley
2 cloves garlic, crushed
1 teaspoon salt
Several grindings of fresh pepper

Rinse the shrimp in cool water, pat dry. Mix the olive oil, wine, parsley, garlic, salt, and pepper to taste, pour over the shrimp in a shallow dish. Cover and chill for 2–3 hours in the refrigerator, turning the shrimp once or twice in the marinade.

Preheat the broiler. Put the shrimp on a foil-lined broiler pan, brush with the marinade, and broil about 6 inches from the heat, 3 minutes to a side, basting with the marinade. Serve immediately with piping hot rice. Serves 2.

SWEET-AND-SOUR SHRIMP

¼ cup brown sugar
2 tablespoons cornstarch
½ teaspoon salt
¼ cup vinegar
1 tablespoon soy sauce
¼ teaspoon ground ginger
A 1-pound 4-ounce can pineapple
  chunks, drained (reserve syrup)

1 green pepper, seeded and cut
  into thin strips
2 small onions, cut in thin rings
1 pound shrimp, cooked and
  shelled

Mix the sugar, cornstarch, and salt in a saucepan. Add the vinegar, soy sauce, ginger, and the reserved pineapple syrup, cook slowly until slightly thickened, stirring constantly. Add the green pepper, onions, and pineapple chunks, simmer for 2 minutes, add the shrimp, and bring to a boil. Serve immediately with hot rice. Serves 2–4.

ITALIAN BAKED SHRIMP WITH PROSCIUTTO

2½ pounds raw medium shrimp
¼ cup olive oil
2 cloves garlic
¼ pound prosciutto, cut in fine
  julienne
½ cup red wine

1 can tomato paste
1 teaspoon dry mustard
1 teaspoon dried oregano,
  crumbled
Several grindings of pepper
¼ cup chopped parsley

Shell and devein the shrimp, leaving the tails intact. Put them in an oven-proof serving dish and set aside.

Heat the oil in a medium-size saucepan. Put the garlic through a press, add, and cook for 2–3 minutes until softened but not brown. Add the prosciutto and cook for 2 minutes. Add the red wine, tomato paste, mustard, oregano, and pepper, stir to blend, and let the mixture cook for a few minutes. Pour over the shrimp in the serving dish, let them marinate in the refrigerator for 3–4 hours.

Remove the dish from the refrigerator and allow to come to room temperature. Preheat the oven to 350°, bake the shrimp for 20 minutes, uncovered, then run under the broiler for 3–4 minutes to char the tails slightly. Sprinkle with chopped parsley and serve with a big salad, garlic bread, and wine. Serves 4–6.

SHRIMP WITH FETA CHEESE

¾ cup olive oil
2 large onions, finely chopped
3 cloves garlic
A 6-ounce can tomato paste
2 8-ounce cans whole pimientos, drained and cut in julienne
A 2-pound 3-ounce can Italian whole tomatoes, drained
Freshly ground pepper
1 teaspoon dried basil

1 teaspoon dried marjoram
Several dashes of Tabasco sauce
Salt
¾ pound feta cheese, drained and crumbled
4 pounds raw medium shrimp, shelled and deveined
Juice of one small lemon
2 tablespoons chopped dill or parsley

Heat the olive oil in a large skillet, cook the onions until transparent. Put the garlic through a press and add. Blend in the tomato paste, add the pimiento, tomatoes, several grindings of pepper, the basil, marjoram, Tabasco, and salt to taste. Simmer gently for ½ hour. Remove from heat and stir in the cheese, cover, and let stand for 5 minutes. (The recipe may be prepared ahead to this point.) Let stand in a cool place until needed.

Bring the sauce to a simmer, add the shrimp and lemon juice, and cook gently until the shrimp turn pink, about 5 minutes. Correct the seasoning. Sprinkle with the dill or parsley. Serves 6–8.

BAKED SHRIMP IN MUSTARD SAUCE

2 pounds raw shrimp, shelled and deveined
5 tablespoons butter
4 tablespoons flour
2 cups milk
Salt and freshly ground pepper
Cayenne pepper
3 tablespoons finely chopped shallot

½ cup dry white wine
¼ cup finely chopped parsley
1 egg yolk, lightly beaten
3 tablespoons Dijon or dark prepared mustard
¼ cup freshly grated Parmesan cheese

Preheat oven to 450°.

Cut each shrimp in half crosswise. Set aside.

In a heavy saucepan melt 3 tablespoons of the butter, stir in the flour, using a wire whisk. Add the milk, stirring rapidly. Season with salt, pepper, and a dash of cayenne. Bring to a boil, lower heat, and simmer, stirring occasionally, for 5 minutes.

In another, smaller saucepan combine the shallot, wine, and parsley, cook over high heat until the wine has almost totally evaporated, 3–5 minutes. Add the white sauce and cook, stirring occasionally, for 5 minutes. Add the egg yolk to the sauce, stirring rapidly. Stir in the mustard, set aside.

Heat the remaining 2 tablespoons of butter in a skillet, add the shrimp, and cook, stirring constantly, just until the shrimp turn pink, 4–5 minutes. Off heat add ⅓ of the white sauce to the shrimp, stir to coat them well.

Spoon the shrimp into 6 individual ramekins or large scallop shells. Spoon an equal amount of the sauce over each. (The recipe may be prepared ahead to this point and refrigerated; bring the dishes to room temperature before baking.) Sprinkle the tops with the cheese, bake for 10–15 minutes or until hot. Serves 8.

PAELLA

There are many versions of paella, with additions and variations made according to locally available items. In Valencia, Spain, where it originated, paella contains chicken, pork (in the form of sausages or fat pork), olive oil, garlic, tomatoes, and seafood or shellfish. It may be cooked in a deep, good-sized skillet, but for best results it should be made in a special pan called a *paellera*. Paella is a great party dish, and if you are going to cook it from time to time, it's worth investing in the pan, available now in most good cookware shops.

½ cup olive oil
2 small chickens, cut in 8 pieces each or 8 legs and 8 thighs
Flour
½ pound medium squid, cleaned (optional)
1 *chorizo* (pork sausage) or 6 Italian hot or sweet sausages
12–18 mussels (optional)
1 cup chopped onion
3 cloves garlic, minced
1 medium green pepper, seeded and cut in strips
3 cups uncooked long-grain rice
12–16 large shrimp, peeled and deveined

3 large fresh tomatoes, peeled, seeded, and chopped, or 1½ cups canned tomatoes, drained and chopped
½ teaspoon powdered saffron
6½ cups liquid: a combination of heated chicken broth and water or mussel broth
Salt and freshly ground pepper
Lemon wedges
½ cup cooked green peas
3 canned pimientos, drained, dried, and cut in strips

Heat 3–4 tablespoons of the olive oil in a large, heavy skillet or a paella pan, dredge the chicken pieces with flour, and gently sauté them until they are golden brown on all sides. Set aside and keep warm while preparing the other ingredients.

If you are using squid, cut them into ½-inch rings, and in a small skillet sauté in 2 tablespoons of the olive oil, set aside.

If you are using Italian sausages, cover with cold water in a shallow skillet, bring to a boil, and cook over high heat, uncovered, until the water boils away. Prick them occasionally to release fat, then turn heat down and fry until brown. Drain and cut into 2-inch pieces. If you are using *chorizo,* it is not necessary to cook it first.

Scrub the mussels and steam them open. Remove them from the shells and reserve. Keep as many of the best shell halves as you have mussels. Strain the broth and set aside.

Add the remaining 2 tablespoons of olive oil to the pan, sauté the onion and garlic until transparent. Add the pepper strips, cook for 10 minutes longer. Add the rice and cook slowly in the oil for about 5 minutes, stirring constantly, until most of the grains have become opaquely white. Do not let them scorch or brown.

Stir in the shrimp and tomatoes. Dissolve the saffron in a teaspoon of boiling water, stir into the chicken broth-water or mussel liquid mixture. Add 6 cups of it to the pan. Season to taste with salt and pepper, bring to a boil, and continue cooking over medium high heat, stirring occasionally, until the liquid in the pan is almost completely absorbed and the rice is tender but the grains are separate (if the mixture looks too dry before the rice is cooked, add the remaining liquid; if it looks too moist, increase the heat). Turn off the heat and cover the pan with a clean folded tea towel to absorb excess moisture.

To assemble: Distribute the chicken pieces over the top of the rice. Put the mussels in the reserved shells and arrange these and the squid rings around the chicken, interspersed with lemon wedges, sprinklings of peas, and the pimiento strips. Serve with warm, crusty bread, a salad, and a rough country wine. Serves 8–10.

NOTE: Spanish *chorizos* are available in fancy grocery stores, packed in 11-ounce cans or preserved in fat.

Other ingredients often added to paella are: small pieces of fried pork, pieces of cooked lobster, tiny clams, or mushrooms. You can also use more rice, always keeping the proportion of 2 cups of liquid to 1 cup of rice.

CREOLE SHRIMP

This is a purposely large recipe; it makes an ideal party dish because it can be prepared almost completely ahead of time. The recipe can be easily halved, however.

9 slices bacon
Olive oil
3 cups chopped onions (about 10 medium)
6 green peppers, seeded and chopped

4 quarts canned whole tomatoes, drained, lightly chopped, liquid reserved
3 6-ounce cans tomato paste
4 cups finely diced celery
6–8 cloves garlic

5 teaspoons sugar
10 teaspoons salt
5 teaspoons dried thyme
3 teaspoons Tabasco sauce

4 bay leaves
10 pounds shrimp, shelled and
  deveined

Cut the bacon roughly into half-inch squares with kitchen scissors. Fry in a large skillet until crisp. Remove with slotted spoon and reserve. Add an appropriate amount of olive oil to the bacon drippings in the pan, sauté the onions until wilted. Add the peppers, cook gently for a few minutes more. Add the tomatoes, tomato paste, and celery, press in the garlic, and bring to a boil. Reduce heat. Add the sugar, salt, thyme, Tabasco, and bay leaves, simmer, uncovered, for about a half hour. Correct the seasoning. (The recipe may be prepared ahead to this point.)

If the sauce appears too thick, thin to desired consistency with some of the reserved tomato liquid. Add the shrimp, bring to a simmer, and cook for 8–10 minutes or until the shrimp just turn pink. It is very important not to overcook the shrimp or they will become mealy. Top with the reserved bacon, crumbled. Serve immediately with hot steamed rice. Serves 25.

JAMBALAYA

Jambalaya is the Spanish contribution to the rich and varied cuisine of New Orleans. It derives from *jamón*—the Spanish word for ham, with which it was made. Creole cooks, drawing on the riches of the Gulf waters, later embellished it with shrimp and oysters.

4 tablespoons bacon fat, or
  rendered ham fat, or 2 tablespoons
  oil and 2 tablespoons butter
½ pound ham, cut into ½-inch
  cubes (see Note 1 p. 318)
2 medium onions, chopped
1 tablespoon flour
A 16-ounce can tomatoes, drained
  and chopped
1½ cups uncooked long-grain rice
2 cloves garlic, minced
3 cups chicken stock (see Note 2
  p. 318)

1 small dried hot red pepper,
  crumbled, or ¼ teaspoon cayenne pepper
½ teaspoon dried thyme
1 medium green pepper, diced
2 tablespoons minced parsley
1½ pounds raw shrimp, peeled
1½ pints shucked oysters, juice
  reserved
Salt and freshly ground pepper

Melt the bacon fat in a heavy pot with a tight-fitting lid, add the ham, and cook for 5 minutes. Add the onions, more fat if needed, and stir over medium heat until the ham is lightly browned and the onions translucent. Add the flour, stir for a minute until the flour has taken on a golden color. Stir in the tomatoes, cover tightly, and simmer over low heat for about 20 minutes. Stir once or twice.

Add the rice, garlic, chicken stock, red pepper, thyme, green pepper, and parsley, bring to a simmer. Lower flame, cover, and continue simmering over a very low heat until the rice is cooked but still firm, about 40 minutes. Do not stir at this time or the rice will get lumpy. Stir in the shrimp with a fork, cook for 5 minutes or until they are uniformly pink. Stir in the oysters, cook for 3 minutes more. Taste, and season with salt and black pepper. (The amount of salt required will depend on the kind of ham used.) Serves 6.

NOTE 1: Have the ham cut in ¼-inch slices so it can be diced. Paper-thin slices won't do for this dish. And if you can get country ham, so much the better—but then watch the amount of salt you add later. Prosciutto may also be used.

NOTE 2: Part of the stock requirement may be made by the oyster liquid; in which case reduce the amount of chicken stock accordingly.

SPANISH SHRIMP AND RICE

1½ pounds raw medium shrimp in the shell
2 tablespoons vinegar
1 tablespoon salt
Several dashes of cayenne pepper
2 medium onions, coarsely chopped

3 tablespoons olive oil
2 cloves garlic, finely minced
1 cup tomato sauce
1 teaspoon dried oregano
Freshly ground pepper
1⅓ cups uncooked long-grain rice

Measure enough water to cover the shrimp, bring it to a boil in a saucepan. Add the vinegar, salt, cayenne, and the shrimp, cover, and cook for 3–5 minutes or until the shrimp turn pink. Skim off any scum that has formed, drain off the liquid, and reserve. When shrimp are cool enough to handle, shell and devein them, set aside.

Sauté the onions in the olive oil until translucent. Add the garlic, sauté for 5 minutes longer. Stir in the tomato sauce, oregano, and pepper, cover, and simmer on a low flame for 10 minutes. Add the rice, stir to make sure it is well coated, then add 2½ cups of the reserved shrimp liquid, bring to a boil. Cover tightly, lower heat, and cook until the rice is tender but firm, each grain separate. Do not stir during this time. Add the shrimp, toss the rice gently with a fork, and cook for 3–5 minutes more over low heat. Correct the seasoning and serve. Serves 4.

SHRIMP QUICHE

1 baked Rich Pastry ❋ shell
¾ cup heavy cream

¾ cup milk
4 egg yolks

½ teaspoon salt
Freshly ground pepper
Nutmeg
¼ pound bacon (preferably slab type)

¼ pound Gruyère or Swiss cheese, grated
½ pound medium shrimp, cooked, shelled, and deveined

Preheat oven to 375°.

In a bowl combine the cream and milk, beat with the egg yolks until the mixture is thick. Stir in the salt, pepper, and several gratings of nutmeg.

Dice the bacon and sauté in a skillet until crisp. Drain on paper towels and reserve.

Sprinkle the pastry shell with the grated cheese, the reserved bacon, and arrange the shrimp on top. Carefully pour the custard mixture over, bake in the upper third of the oven for 30 minutes or until the custard is set. Let stand for 10 minutes before serving.

Serves 6 as a first course or 4 as a luncheon dish with a green salad.

SHRIMP CURRY

½ cup finely chopped onion
2 cloves garlic, minced
4 tablespoons butter
¼ cup flour
2 tablespoons curry powder or more to taste
½ teaspoon powdered ginger

1 teaspoon salt
2 cups chicken broth
1 cup light cream
3 cups cooked and peeled shrimp (1½ pounds uncooked small shrimp)
2 tablespoons lemon juice

Sauté the onion and garlic in the butter over low heat until wilted. Stir in the flour, curry powder, ginger, and salt. Add the chicken broth and cream, blend, and cook until thickened, stirring occasionally. Add the shrimp and lemon juice, continue cooking until the shrimp are heated through. Do not allow the mixture to boil. Correct the seasonings, add more curry powder if you like it hot.

Serve over hot rice with any or all of the curry garnishes listed at the end of the next recipe. Serves 4 as a main course, 6–8 as a buffet dish.

SHRIMP CURRY WITH TOMATOES

2 pounds ripe tomatoes, or 3 cups canned tomatoes, drained
4 tablespoons olive oil
2 medium onions, chopped
2 cloves garlic, minced
A 6-ounce can tomato paste

Salt
2 tablespoons or more of curry powder
½ cup dry white wine or dry sherry
2 pounds raw shrimp, shelled and deveined

Peel the tomatoes, seed them, and chop very finely. If you use canned tomatoes, chop them. In a saucepan heat the olive oil, add the onions and garlic, and cook until soft but not brown. Add the tomatoes, cover, and simmer gently over very low heat for about 40 minutes. Add the tomato paste and salt to taste, cover again, and simmer gently for another 10–15 minutes. Add the curry powder, cook to blend for a minute or two, then put through a strainer.

Return the sauce to the stove, thin down if necessary to a desired consistency with the white wine or sherry, and heat to the boiling point. Add the shrimp, simmer gently for about 5 minutes or until the shrimp turn pink. Serve with hot rice and any of the curry garnishes listed below. Serves 4.

CURRY GARNISHES—Provide the following garnishes in individual bowls, a spoon for each:

> Chopped, roasted, salted peanuts
> Raisins (plumped in sherry and drained)
> Grated coconut (fresh or packaged)
> Diced bananas
> Diced unpeeled apples
> Crumbled fried bacon
> Chutney
> Cucumbers in yogurt
> Hard-boiled eggs (white and yolk separate)

CRÊPES AUX FRUITS DE MER (Shrimp-filled Crepes)

This recipe is long and must be followed accurately, but it is not as involved as it seems, and it has the virtue of being able to be prepared ahead completely and then baked for a short time before serving.

SAUCE

4 tablespoons (½ stick) butter
6 tablespoons flour
2½ cups milk, scalded
½ cup heavy cream

¾ teaspoon salt
Freshly ground white pepper
¼ teaspoon lemon juice

FILLING

1 pound raw medium shrimp, shelled and deveined
2 tablespoons butter
1 tablespoon chopped shallots or scallions (white part only)
1 tablespoon finely chopped fresh dill

¾ teaspoon salt
Freshly ground white pepper
¼ teaspoon lemon juice
12 7-inch crepes (see Basic Crepe Recipe in the Index)

TOPPING

1 tablespoon bread crumbs   1 tablespoon butter
1 tablespoon grated Swiss cheese

SAUCE: Melt the butter in a 2-quart enameled cast-iron or stainless steel saucepan. Remove the pan from heat. Add the flour, stirring with a wooden spoon until the mixture is smooth. Pour in 2 cups of the milk all at once, whisk the flour mixture and milk together until blended. Return the pan to high heat and, whisking constantly, bring to a boil, cook for 2 minutes (the sauce will be very thick at this point). Pour ¾ cup of the sauce into a medium-size mixing bowl (to be used later for the shrimp filling) and set aside.

Pour the remaining ½ cup milk and the cream into the sauce in the saucepan. Add the salt, several grindings of white pepper, and lemon juice, whisk until smooth. Taste for seasoning.

FILLING: Cut the shrimp into ¼-inch slices. Melt the butter in a medium-size sauté pan set over moderate heat. When the butter begins to foam, add the chopped shallots or scallions, sauté for about a minute, stirring constantly. Add the shrimp pieces and, still stirring, sauté for about 2 minutes or until they are pink and firm. Transfer the contents to the bowl of sauce. Add the dill, salt, several grindings of white pepper, and lemon juice, gently mix all the ingredients together with a wooden spoon. Taste for seasoning.

The crepes may be filled at this point or the filling refrigerated for an hour, in which case it will become firmer and easier to handle.

TO ASSEMBLE: Lay the 12 crepes side by side on a long strip of waxed paper, the brown side up. With a tablespoon, divide the filling equally among the crepes, placing it on the lower third of each crepe but leaving the edge bare. Lift up the bare edge and bring it over the filling. Then carefully roll up the crepes but do not tuck in the sides.

Preheat the oven to 375°. Put the pan of cream sauce over moderate heat, heat it for 2–3 minutes or until it is lukewarm, stirring constantly. Pour about ¼ cup of the sauce into an ovenproof baking dish large enough to hold the crepes in a single layer. Tip the baking dish from side to side to coat the bottom lightly and evenly with sauce; if necessary add a little more sauce. Place the crepes in a row, touching, seam side down. Spoon the balance of the sauce over them. Make the topping by combining the bread crumbs, Swiss cheese, and the butter, cut into bits. Sprinkle the topping over the crepes. (The dish may be prepared ahead to this point, covered with plastic wrap, and refrigerated; allow it to come to room temperature before baking.)

Bake in the preheated oven, with the oven rack in its highest position, for 15 minutes or until the top is brown and bubbly. If you find it necessary, you may slide the dish under the broiler for a minute to complete the browning. Serve immediately. Serves 4.

SQUID AND OCTOPUS

Sometimes referred to as *inkfish*, these tentacled creatures are not fish at all, but mollusks, named by the Greeks *cephalopods* because the feet (podos) literally grow out of the *kephale* (head). They are the most highly evolved of the mollusks, being the only ones to have a centralized nervous

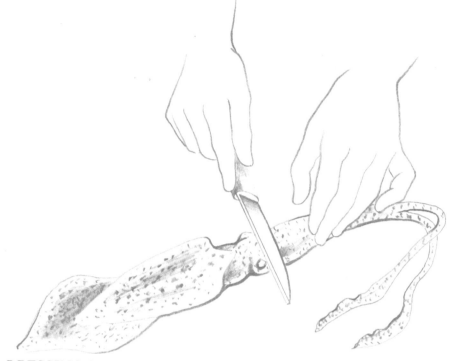

DRESSING SQUID: Cut through the arms and tentacles near the eyes. With thumb and forefinger squeeze out the inedible beak located near the cut.

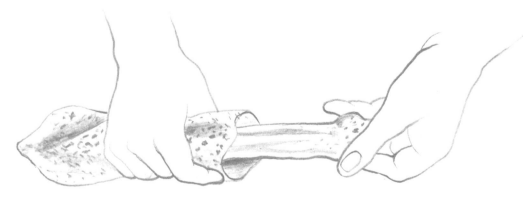

Feel inside mantle for chitinous "pen." Firmly grasp pen and attached viscera and pull from mantle. Pull off any brown skin. Wash mantle thoroughly and drain. Mantle is now ready to be stuffed or cut crosswise into rings.

To make bite-size pieces: lay mantle flat and cut down center from top to tail. Spread open and wash well.

Then cut into 1-inch pieces. (Arms and tentacles can be chopped or left whole.)

SQUID.

system. They are a favorite in many cuisines of the world, although Americans, perhaps unduly influenced by Jules Verne, tend to avoid them.

The ten-armed squid has the capacity to eject a cloud of ink roughly the same size and shape as its body and then to shoot away from its attacker. The Spaniards are fond of stewing squid in this ink and eating it with rice in a dish called *calamares en su tinta*.

In this country, squid is caught along the East Coast from the Carolinas to New England, from midsummer until early fall. The Atlantic long-finned squid, a pretty light red, pink, and purple creature, can be found from Nova Scotia to Florida. Squid are available fresh all year round in California; frozen squid from that state is always available in the East. Squid are sold whole and dressed by weight.

TO DRESS SQUID: Large squid are cut into bite-size pieces before cooking; very tiny squid may be left whole.

The octopus has eight tentacles, each lined with a twin row of suction cups that help it capture the shellfish that are its major diet. Though they do paralyze their prey by a toxic secretion in the beak, they do not, contrary to belief, bite people. Without the protective shell of their cousins the bivalves, they are vulnerable fellows who prefer flight to fight.

The Pacific octopus is found among offshore rocks from Alaska to Lower California; the Atlantic variety from New England to the Gulf.

TO DRESS OCTOPUS: Octopus is market fresh and frozen and always dressed, but should you have one of your own to clean, lay it flat, tentacles extended, cut down the center to expose the cuttlebone or "celluloid," pull this out and discard. Then turn the octopus inside out like a glove, taking care not to rupture the ink sac. Discard all the internal organs.

Some people feel that octopus must be beaten or pounded to tenderize it. In Spain our cook never did this, but just dipped it twice into boiling water for about 10 seconds each time, then simmered it for an hour in a covered pot.

OCTOPUS.

SQUID AND MUSSEL SALAD

2 pounds squid, dressed
1½ pounds mussels, scrubbed and
   debearded
¼ cup lemon juice

¼ cup olive oil
Salt and freshly ground pepper
1 teaspoon finely minced garlic
3 tablespoons finely minced parsley

Wash the squid well in several changes of cold water to remove any lingering traces of sand.

Bring 3 quarts of salted water to a boil, add the squid, and when the water returns to a boil cover loosely and simmer for 20–30 minutes, testing the squid for tenderness after 20 minutes by using the tip of a sharp knife. Do not overcook or the squid will be rubbery. Drain and, when cool enough to handle, cut the bodies into rings, about ⅜-inch wide. Cut off the tentacle clusters, leaving them whole, and set all aside.

While the squid cooks, steam open the mussels as directed elsewhere (see Index). Remove from their shells and put into a large bowl.

Add the squid, lemon juice, and oil to the mussels, mix thoroughly. Season to taste with salt and pepper, add the garlic and parsley, and toss well. Cover with plastic wrap and refrigerate for at least 3 hours or overnight. Allow the salad to stand at room temperature for half an hour before serving. Place on individual lettuce leaves. Serves 4–6 as a first course.

SQUID AND SHRIMP SALAD

1¼ pounds squid, dressed
½ pound raw shrimp
¼ cup minced parsley
¼ cup chopped chives

3 tablespoons olive oil
1 tablespoon wine vinegar
2 tablespoons lemon juice
Salt and freshly ground pepper

Wash the squid well in several changes of water. Cook in boiling water to cover for 20 minutes, drain. Chop up the tentacles, slice the body into ½-inch rings.

Bring 3 cups of salted water to a boil. Add the shrimp, bring to a second boil, cover, remove from heat, and let stand for 5 minutes or until pink. Drain and run cold water over, shell, and devein.

Combine the squid and shrimp with the parsley, chives, oil, vinegar, lemon juice, and season to taste. Chill, then serve on lettuce leaves. Serves 6.

RICHARD OLNEY'S SQUID AND LEEKS IN RED WINE

An astoundingly good dish!

2 pounds medium-size dressed
    squid
2 pounds leeks, white and pale
    green parts, well rinsed and cut
    into 2-inch lengths
¼ cup olive oil
Salt
2 tablespoons flour
Dash of cayenne pepper

½ teaspoon crumbled dried thyme
½ teaspoon crumbled dried
    oregano
1 bay leaf
8 cloves garlic, sliced paper-thin
About 2 cups red wine
About 1 cup water
Croutons (see the note p. 327)
Chopped parsley

Wash the squid well in several changes of water. Cut off and reserve the tentacles, slice the mantles into ½-inch widths, set aside.

In a heavy skillet or a large, low-sided earthenware casserole large enough to hold the squid and leeks gently packed in a single layer, stew the leeks, salted, in the olive oil for 10 minutes or so, turning them carefully with wooden spoons so as not to damage them. Remove them from the pan and set aside.

Raise the heat, add the squid, salt well, and sauté in the same oil for several minutes, until the liquid exuded is almost entirely evaporated. Sprinkle them with the flour, stir and cook for another minute or so. Add the cayenne, thyme, oregano, bay leaf, and garlic. Slowly add the red wine, stirring constantly, then the water, and bring to a boil. Gently replace the leek sections in the pan, one by one, easing each into place between the squid pieces. Cover and cook at a simmer for about 1½ hours—the squid and leeks should be absolutely tender but still intact. Sprinkle with the croutons and chopped parsley, serve immediately in the cooking vessel. Serves 4.

NOTE: To make croutons: Cut several slices of home-style white bread into ⅜-inch dice, dry out in a slow oven. Melt some butter in a skillet and toss the croutons in it until lightly brown and crisp. Season with salt and pepper.

STUFFED SQUID PROVENÇALE

5 small squid (about 2 pounds) dressed
3 tablespoons olive oil
1 cup chopped onions (about 2 medium)
4 tomatoes, peeled, seeded, and chopped (fresh or canned)
½ cup soft bread crumbs
1 tablespoon chopped parsley

2 cloves garlic
Pinch of thyme
Salt and freshly ground pepper
Dash of cayenne pepper
Dry white wine
1 egg, beaten
½ bay leaf
1 tablespoon flour

Wash the squid well. Remove and chop the tentacles, set aside.

Heat 2 tablespoons of the olive oil in a heavy skillet, add half the onions, and sauté until golden brown. Add the reserved tentacles, 3 of the tomatoes, the bread crumbs, parsley, garlic, thyme, salt, pepper, and a dash of cayenne to taste. Sauté for 5 minutes, then stir in the beaten egg. Moisten with enough wine to bind the mixture. Stuff each squid (not too full, to allow for expansion) and tack it closed with 2 stitches of thread or with toothpicks (messy). Transfer the stuffed squid to a casserole.

Heat the remaining oil in the skillet, add the remaining tomato and onion and the bay leaf, sauté for 5 minutes.

In another skillet, brown the flour slightly and stir it into the tomato mixture. Add 1 tablespoon of wine, season highly with salt and pepper. Pour the sauce over and around the squid. Bring to a simmer, cover, and cook for 25 minutes or until the squid yields to the touch. Remove the thread or toothpicks. Serves 4.

TAKO —Japanese-Hawaiian Squid

1 pound squid, dressed
½ cup white wine or *sake*
3 tablespoons *miso* (see the note p. 328)

1–2 teaspoons sugar
1 teaspoon vinegar
1 teaspoon water

Wash the squid well. Put them in a pot with the wine or *sake*. Cover, bring to a boil, lower the heat, and simmer until the squid just begins to turn from translucent to opaque. Drain squid and set aside.

In a small bowl combine the *miso*, sugar, vinegar, and water. Slice the squid into ½-inch pieces, coat with the sauce. Serve with toothpicks as an hors d'oeuvre or as part of an Oriental meal.

NOTE: *Miso*, or fermented soybean paste, is available in Oriental grocery stores. See Food Shopping by Mail.

SQUID CACCIATORE

Follow the recipe for Squid Cacciatore with Linguine (see Index) but serve over hot rice, accompanied by a green salad and garlic bread.

PULPO A LA GALLEGA (Spanish Octopus in Red Sauce)

2 pounds octopus, dressed
1 tablespoon paprika, sweet or
  semi-hot

3 cloves garlic
½ cup olive oil
Salt and freshly ground pepper

Wash the octopus well, remove and discard the ink sac if present, and bang the octopus several times on a hard surface to tenderize.

Bring 2–3 quarts of water to a boil in a deep pot, dip the octopus into it 3 times. Then leave the octopus in the water, bring it to a boil, cover, and simmer over moderate heat for 3 hours or until tender. Remove and, when cool enough to handle, cut into ½-inch pieces.

Meanwhile, in a blender or mortar, blend the paprika, garlic, oil, and salt and pepper to taste. Pour over the octopus pieces and serve hot, warm, or cold. Serves 4–6.

GREEK OCTOPUS IN WINE SAUCE

2 pounds fresh octopus, dressed,
  well pounded
½ cup olive oil
2 medium onions, finely chopped

1 bay leaf
Salt and freshly ground pepper
1 cup red wine

Wash the octopus well, remove and discard the ink sac if present. Cut the octopus into bite-size pieces. Heat the olive oil in a skillet, sauté the onion until soft and golden. Add the octopus, bay leaf, and salt and pepper to taste, the wine, and enough water to cover. Bring to a boil, cover, and simmer for about an hour or until the octopus is tender. In Greece this is served as a hot hors d'oeuvre, but it may also be served as a main dish with rice. Serves 4.

SEVEN

Barbecuing and Grilling

OUTDOOR FISH COOKERY

No matter how sophisticated indoor cooking equipment becomes, there is still a special satisfaction to outdoor cooking, compounded of the tantalizing smell, the simplicity and primitiveness of the procedure, and the conviviality that goes with it. It is one of summer's special pleasures.

Start your fire according to the manufacturer's instructions for the type of cooker you have. Make sure that the grill is absolutely clean. I have found that especially in cooking foil-wrapped fish, sharp charred bits of food from previous grillings can pierce the foil and cause you to lose not only heat but succulent juices. Make a solid layer of charcoal or briquets, slightly wider than the area covered by the food to be cooked on the grill; start the fire with paper and kindling at least a half hour before cooking time, and let the flames die down. Cooking should be done over the intense heat of glowing coals rather than flames. Hardwood, if you have access to it, makes the best fire for outdoor cookery. If you use a fluid starter, make sure it is odorless; paint thinner is good for this. When the charcoal or briquet surface is covered with a gray ash, spread the coals evenly and begin cooking.

Burning wood chips add a delightful smoky flavor to outdoor-grilled fish. Most used are fruitwood chips (apple or cherry), or oak, maple, hickory, or alder. Soak the chips in water for at least an hour before kindling, so they will give maximum smoke and not burn too rapidly. On a charcoal grill put them on the fire early and add a few more at a time while cooking. On a gas grill, scatter the wet chips directly on the ceramic bricks, or, for more subtle flavor, wrap them in perforated foil first.

There are other ways to flavor fish subtly while grilling; in France one often sees grapevine cuttings together with a handful of herbs tossed on the coals. A cook I know uses orange peel. Italians use branches of bay leaves. Use whatever smells good to you.

If you prefer to use a hinged iron grill to hold the fish during cooking, remember that it, too, should be hot—hot enough to mark the fish as soon as it is put on. Both fish and grill should be well oiled, and the fish can be

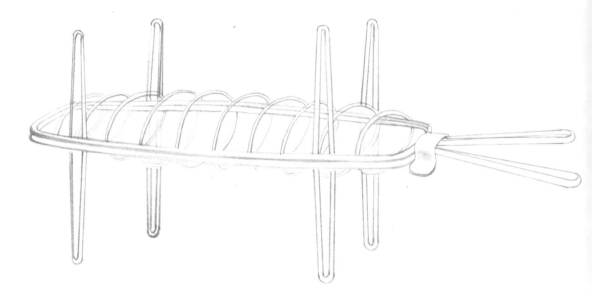

CLASSIC FISH-SHAPED GRILL.

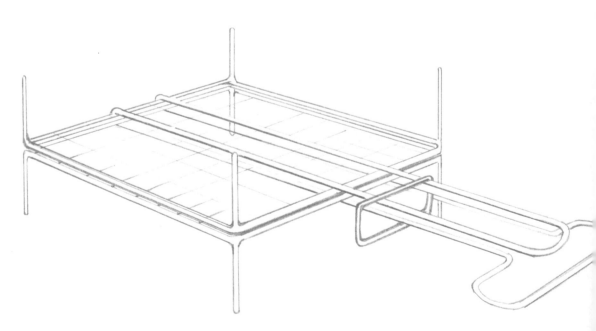

HINGED GRILL FOR BUTTERFLIED FILLETED AND SMALL FISH.

lightly floured in addition. Leave the fins on. Brush the fish with extra oil, or marinade, if one is used, during the cooking. If you are not following a specific recipe, use the Canadian technique to calculate cooking time, but remember that timing can be affected by certain variables such as the thickness of the fish, the distance from the coals, and the wind if any. So don't wander away, and do test the fish when you think it is cooked. It is done when there is no trace of red and clear juices ooze. If the fish is actually flaky, it is usually overcooked. A 3-pound fish will take about 25–35 minutes; a 4–5-pound fish 35–40 minutes. To test a fish for doneness: open the foil and pull the fin bone back; if it comes out clean with no flesh attached, it is done; if the meat is still attached to the bone, cook for an additional 10 minutes.

You can leave the scales on whole fish to be barbecued—they actually strengthen the skin and keep the juices in. Skin and those scales that have not burned off are removed before eating.

The recipes that follow can serve as a general guide for cooking many types of fish and are not necessarily limited to the fish specified.

CHARCOAL-BROILED FISH

6 small whole fish (1–1½ pounds each) washed, cleaned, and heads removed, or 6 fish steaks about ¾ inch thick

Vegetable oil
Salt and freshly ground pepper
Lemon wedges

Dry the fish well, rub oil into all the exposed surfaces. Season to taste. Oil a hinged fish grill or heavy wire hamburger turner, put the fish on it. Cook over a hot charcoal fire for 7–8 minutes on each side or until the skin is brown and crisp and the flesh is cooked through. A total cooking time of 15 minutes is usually enough, but you can check by sticking a knife or fork through to the bone to make sure the fish is tender all the way through. Be careful not to overcook or it will be dry. Serve with lemon wedges. Serves 6.

PROVENÇAL GRILLED FISH

Use this old method for any whole fish, including freshwater fish such as whitefish or trout: make several diagonal slashes at 1- or 2-inch intervals along the sides of a cleaned and scaled whole fish. In each incision place a branch of fennel fern or little branches of fresh rosemary or thyme. Make a small bundle of the herb you are using, dip one end in olive oil, and use to baste the fish as it cooks on an oiled grill over a moderately hot charcoal fire.

GRILLED FISH WITH BASIL

A 3-pound red snapper or sea
　bass, boned and butterflied (see
　the note below)
3–4 sprigs fresh basil, washed and
　dried

Salt and freshly ground pepper
Olive oil
1 recipe Beurre Blanc Sauce ❋

Wash the fish and pat dry with paper towels. Be sure to remove all pieces of gills and scales. Season the inside with ½ teaspoon of salt and a few grindings of pepper. Bring the two halves of the fish together, stuff with basil. Brush the outside with oil, wrap tightly in aluminum foil. Refrigerate for 4 hours.

Prepare the fire, take the fish out of the refrigerator 30 minutes before cooking time. Grill the foil-wrapped fish for 15 minutes on one side, then turn it over and grill for 10 minutes more. Open the foil and test to see if fish is done. If not, cook a little longer. Open the foil, discard the basil, and serve fish with *beurre blanc* sauce on the side. Serves 4–6.

NOTE: A butterflied fish is one that is boned and split, with the skin left on to join the two fillets like a hinge. The head and tail are removed.

CAUCASIAN BARBECUED FISH

2 pounds thick fillets of firm-fleshed
　white fish, such as sea bass,
　cod, tilefish, blackfish, halibut,
　or haddock (salmon and shark
　may also be used)
Salt
¼ cup sour cream or yogurt
¼ cup freshly squeezed and
　strained lemon juice

2 tablespoons butter, melted
1 bunch scallions, finely chopped,
　including 2 inches of the green
　tops
¼ cup finely chopped parsley
2 fresh medium-size tomatoes, cut
　into eighths
Lemon wedges

Wash the fish well under cold running water, dry thoroughly with paper towels. Cut it into 1½-inch cubes. Sprinkle with salt.

Combine the sour cream or yogurt and lemon juice, mix well. Coat the fish cubes thoroughly with the mixture. Thread them close together on skewers, leaving a few inches bare at each end. Broil, preferably over charcoal fire, 3–4 inches from the heat, about 10 minutes or until tender, basting occasionally with the melted butter and the remaining sour cream mixture. Turn the skewers several times to allow the fish to brown evenly on all sides. Serve immediately sprinkled with the scallions and parsley and garnished with the tomatoes and lemon wedges. Serves 6.

CHARCOAL-GRILLED WHOLE STRIPED BASS OR SEA BASS

A 3–5-pound whole striped or sea
  bass, cleaned and split, fins on
Salt and freshly ground pepper
6 tablespoons butter
1 teaspoon dried tarragon or 1
  tablespoon minced fresh

½ teaspoon dried thyme or 2 teaspoons fresh
2 tablespoons minced shallot
2 small cloves garlic, finely minced
¼ cup white wine

Prepare a moderately hot charcoal fire.

Wash the fish inside and out, pat dry with paper towels. Salt and pepper
the fish inside and out.

Melt 2 tablespoons of the butter and brush the fish with it. Mix the tarragon, thyme, shallot, and garlic together in a small bowl, rub this mixture all
over the fish. Place on a large, double thickness of heavy duty foil with the
remaining 4 tablespoons of butter cut up, sprinkle with the white wine.
Close the foil securely, cook the fish over the fire about 4 inches from the
coals, turning from time to time. Test for doneness as described at the
beginning of this chapter.

CHARCOAL-BROILED CHERRYSTONE CLAMS WITH GARLIC

For each person put 12 cherrystone clams on a large square of heavy duty
aluminum foil. In a small bowl put enough salt to equal about ¼ teaspoon
per person, a generous amount of freshly ground pepper, and a small piece
of garlic per person, put through a press. Mix this seasoning well and sprinkle over the clams. Add a good lump of butter. Bring the foil up over the
clams and twist to make a tight bundle. Put on a medium-hot charcoal fire,
cook for 8–10 minutes, shaking the packages once or twice. Open a package
to test: the clams should be removed from the fire the minute they are
opened. Serve each person a clam bundle with hot French bread to dunk in
the tasty sauce.

CHARCOAL-GRILLED EEL

2 pounds eel, skinned and cut into
  2-inch pieces
½ cup milk
2 cups fine bread crumbs made
  from home-style white bread

Salt
Dilled Mustard Sauce ❋ or Tartar
  Sauce ❋

Dip the eel pieces into the milk, then into the crumbs, putting each piece on a cookie sheet. Refrigerate for 10 minutes or so. Cook on a hot oiled grill over a charcoal fire for about 15 minutes. Salt them halfway through cooking time. Serve with either of the suggested sauces. Serves 4.

CHARCOAL-GRILLED LOBSTER WITH LEMON BUTTER SAUCE

Kill, split, and clean two lobsters, each 1½–2 pounds, as directed (see Index). Crack the claws. Carefully remove the coral and tomalley to two small dishes and reserve.

Prepare the fire and preheat the grill for at least 20 minutes. Grill the lobster halves, cut side down, for 10 minutes. During this time, prepare a double recipe of Lemon Butter Sauce ❀ . Turn the lobsters, replace the coral and tomalley, and baste them and the meat liberally with the sauce (let some run down under the tail meat if you can). Cook for about 10 minutes on the second side. Serve with small ramekins of the remaining sauce, claw crackers, and picks. Serves 2–4.

BLUEFISH BAKED IN FOIL

3 pounds bluefish fillets
1 medium onion, chopped
2 tablespoons chopped parsley
½ teaspoon dried thyme
3 tablespoons white wine
6 tablespoons olive oil

Salt and freshly ground pepper
2 large ripe tomatoes, sliced
1 bay leaf, crushed
Juice of ½ lemon
6 lemon wedges

Wash the fish and pat dry. In a small bowl, combine the onion, parsley, thyme, wine, oil, and salt and pepper to taste. Cut a piece of wide, heavy duty aluminum baking foil that will accommodate all the fish in one layer, tightly wrapped. (You will need a piece of foil at least 40 inches long.) Spread half the onion mixture on the foil, lay the fillets over it in one layer, and cover them with the tomato slices. Sprinkle with the crushed bay leaf and lemon juice. Bring up the sides of the foil and spoon the remaining onion-wine mixture over the fish. Wrap and seal well, bake over a charcoal grill for about 25 minutes or until the fish flakes easily. It is not necessary to turn. Check toward the end to prevent overcooking.

Open the foil carefully to prevent the fillets from breaking. Serve with lemon wedges. Serves 6.

NOTE: This dish may also be prepared in the oven, preheated to 350°; bake for approximately the same amount of time.

CHARCOAL-BROILED BLUEFISH FILLETS: Leave the skin on. Make several shallow slashes in the skin to prevent drawing, and oil the skin. Follow the instructions for charcoal-broiling fish at the beginning of this chapter, cook for 8 minutes per side. Serve with lemon butter or Maître d'Hotel Butter❋.

CHARCOAL-BROILED SWORDFISH STEAK WITH SHALLOT BUTTER SAUCE

A 7–8-pound swordfish steak, 4 inches thick (without flank if possible)
2 tablespoons oil

Salt and freshly ground pepper
Juice of 1 lemon
1 teaspoon powdered ginger

SAUCE
4 tablespoons (½ stick) butter
2 tablespoons chopped shallot
2 tablespoons lemon juice

Salt and freshly ground pepper
¼ cup chopped parsley

Preheat oven to 350°.

Coat both sides of the steak with oil, sprinkle with salt and pepper. Put the fish on a hinged wire grill with a handle. Position the grill about 6 inches from moderately hot coals, cook for a total of about 10 minutes per side or until each side is well browned. Transfer the fish to an ovenproof dish, sprinkle with the lemon juice and ginger, and bake for 20 minutes.

While the fish is cooking, prepare the sauce: In a saucepan, melt the butter—it should be warm, not hot—add the shallot, lemon juice, salt, and pepper. Keep warm. Just before serving sprinkle in the parsley, pour over the fish. Serves 6–8.

TERIYAKI BARBECUED SWORDFISH STEAK

Follow the recipe for Teriyaki Barbecued Albacore Steak❋, substituting one or two large swordfish steaks (totaling about 5 pounds) for the albacore.

SKEWERED SWORDFISH, TURKISH STYLE

2 pounds swordfish steak
Juice of 1 lemon
½ cup olive oil
2 tablespoons grated onion
Salt and freshly ground pepper

4 ripe medium tomatoes
3 medium Spanish onions
18–20 bay leaves, cut in half (see the note p. 338)
Lemon wedges

Cut the swordfish steak into 1-inch cubes. Marinate them for 2 hours in a mixture of the lemon juice, oil, grated onion, salt, and pepper. Reserve the marinade.

Cut the tomatoes into chunks and the onions into wedges. Thread the fish cubes onto skewers, alternating with pieces of tomato, wedges of onion, and bay leaf (there should be a bay leaf between every 2 pieces of fish). Brush with the reserved marinade, broil over hot charcoal or in a preheated broiler. Turn frequently, brushing with the marinade, and broil until the fish is golden brown on all sides—about 15 minutes. Serve with lemon wedges. Serves 4–6.

NOTE: The bay leaf flavor is not at all overwhelming in spite of the number used.

SKEWERED TROUT

4 medium trout, cleaned, *not split,*
  and drawn as described below
Salt and freshly ground pepper

Melted butter
Fresh tarragon leaves or fresh
  parsley

Draw the fish (remove the entrails) as follows: Cut down through the throat of each fish just behind the gills. With a long-handled spoon, scoop out and discard the entrails. Wash the fish inside and out, dry with paper towels.

Carefully make several parallel diagonal gashes on the outside of each fish with a sharp knife. Sprinkle the fish inside and out with salt and pepper to taste. Put long skewers lengthwise through the fish, grill over charcoal, brushing the fish with melted butter and turning from time to time until golden brown and cooked through. Slide the fish off the skewers onto a heated serving platter, pour additional melted butter over them. Serve garnished with fresh tarragon leaves or parsley. Serves 4.

GRILLED HERBED WEAKFISH

A 3½-pound weakfish, head and
  tail on, completely split (head
  too)
Coarse salt and freshly ground
  pepper
Olive oil

½ cup mixed minced fresh herbs:
  parsley, thyme, tarragon,
  chives, or other
1½ cups coarse dry bread crumbs
  (see the note p. 339)

Do this operation on a piece of foil or waxed paper.

Sprinkle the fish (opened and flat) with salt and pepper to taste, brush with oil, then, using your hands, press a coating of the herbs and then of bread crumbs firmly into the flesh on both sides—skin sides and insides. Carefully transfer the fish to an oiled, hinged grill and when in place drizzle a little more oil over. Grill over hot coals for about 12 minutes or until the crumbs are a crusty brown on one side. Turn carefully and cook on the other side for the same amount of time. Serves 4.

NOTE: Of course you would never use those dreadful crumbs in cans, but for this recipe, not only must you use crumbs from home-style bread or French bread, you should dry them out slightly in a 250° oven for, say, a half hour. If you have stale bread, this is not necessary.

EIGHT

Seafood Sauces
for Pasta

Surrounded as it is by waters thronging with fish and shellfish of every description, pasta-loving Italy has made an art of developing seafood sauces for its favorite foodstuff. The recipes in this chapter are some of my favorite examples of this happy gastronomic marriage.

SALSA PUTTANESCA

The story of this sauce is that it was presumably created by Italian prostitutes because it could be made very quickly, "between jobs."

2 tablespoons olive oil
2 cloves garlic, minced
8 flat anchovy fillets, cut in pieces
4½ cups (a 2-pound 3-ounce can)
   Italian plum tomatoes, put
   through a food mill or a coarse
   sieve

8 pitted black olives, sliced
1 teaspoon capers
1 teaspoon dried sweet basil or 1
   tablespoon chopped fresh
¼ teaspoon crumbled dried red
   pepper

Heat the oil in a skillet, sauté the garlic until soft, then add the anchovies. When they have broken apart, add the tomatoes, simmer for 10 minutes. Stir in the olives, capers, basil, and red pepper. Simmer, uncovered, for 20 minutes or until the sauce has thickened. Serve on linguine or spaghettini. Makes about 4 cups.

SHRIMP AND ANCHOVY SAUCE FOR PASTA

1½ pounds raw medium shrimp
4 tablespoons olive oil
2 teaspoons finely minced garlic
4 cups canned plum tomatoes
1 teaspoon dried basil or 2 tablespoons finely chopped fresh basil
Salt and freshly ground pepper

2 tablespoons anchovy paste, or 6
   fillets, finely chopped
¼ pound mushrooms, thinly sliced
1 dried small hot red pepper,
   crushed
¼ cup drained capers
1 pound linguine or spaghetti

Peel and devein the shrimp. Rinse and pat dry. Set aside.

Heat 2 tablespoons of the olive oil in a small skillet, add half the garlic, cook briefly, but do not let it brown. Add the tomatoes, half the basil, and salt and pepper to taste. Simmer, uncovered, for about a half hour, stirring frequently, then stir in the anchovy paste or chopped anchovies.

In a 12-inch skillet, heat the remaining oil, add the shrimp, remaining garlic, remaining basil, and the mushrooms. Cook, stirring constantly, until the shrimp turn bright pink, about 1 minute. Add this mixture to the tomato-anchovy sauce. Add the hot pepper, capers, and salt and pepper to taste, bring to a boil, and serve immediately on the cooked pasta. Serves 6 as a first course, 4 as a main course.

PENNONI AL TONNO ALLA PAVAROTTI

The great opera tenor Luciano Pavarotti loves to cook as well as eat. This is a dish he often prepares for friends. It can be relied upon to bail you out of any food emergency, as all the ingredients may be kept on your kitchen shelf.

¼ cup olive oil	A 6-ounce can tomato paste
½ cup chopped onion	A 12-ounce can tomato juice
3 7-ounce cans imported tuna (Italian or Spanish), packed in olive oil	1–2 cloves garlic, pressed
	1 pound pennone, penne, or other tubular pasta, cooked
A 2-ounce can flat anchovies, drained and chopped	1½ cups grated Parmesan cheese

Heat the oil in a skillet, cook the onion until transparent. Add the tuna and anchovies, stir for 2–3 minutes. Add the tomato paste, tomato juice, and garlic, stir well, and simmer, uncovered, for 15 minutes. Put the cooked and drained pasta in a warm bowl, add the sauce, and stir well. Add the grated cheese, toss, and serve in heated dishes. This must be served and eaten immediately. Serves 6.

NOTE: Part of the olive oil may be made up by the oil drained from the tuna.

MUSSELS IN CREAM—A Sauce for Pasta

3½–4 pounds fresh mussels, scrubbed and debearded	3 tablespoons flour
3½ tablespoons butter	½ cup heavy cream
¼ cup chopped shallot	¼ teaspoon salt or more to taste
1½ cups dry white wine	White pepper
	Several dashes of cayenne pepper

³/₄–1 pound linguine or spaghetti   2 tablespoons chopped parsley
4 tablespoons butter for the pasta

Steam the mussels open according to directions given elsewhere (see
Index). Pour off the mussel liquor, let it settle for a few minutes, then strain
it carefully and reserve (see the note below). Shell the mussels and set aside.

In a small saucepan melt 1 tablespoon of the butter, cook the shallot without letting it color for 1–2 minutes. Add the wine, reduce over high heat to
1 cup. Pour off 1 cup of the reserved mussel liquor, add it to the wine. Keep
the mixture warm.

Melt the remaining 2½ tablespoons of the butter in a heavy saucepan,
make a *roux* with the flour. Remove the pan from the heat and pour in the
hot wine mixture all at once, beating vigorously with a wire whip. Set the
saucepan over high heat and stir until it comes to a boil. Lower heat to a
simmer and beat in the cream until the sauce is thick and smooth. Season to
taste with salt, pepper, and cayenne. Fold in the reserved mussels. Keep
the sauce warm.

Cook the pasta.

Put the 4 tablespoons of butter in a warmed large bowl, let it melt at the
back of the stove while the pasta is cooking. Test the pasta frequently, and
when it is just done fork it directly from the cooking pot into the bowl,
letting each forkful drain off as you do so. Toss the pasta quickly with two
forks to coat with the butter. Divide it among heated serving plates, top
each with a large spoonful of the sauce and a sprinkling of chopped parsley,
and serve immediately. Serves 4.

NOTE: The sand content of mussels varies greatly, depending on where
they were taken. Based on this, mussel liquid may have to be strained as
many as four times in order that the sauce in which it is used not be gray in
color and gritty to the tongue.

SPAGHETTI WITH MUSSELS MARINARA

Prepare mussels as in the recipe for Mussels Marinara ❋ , remove them
from the shells and stir into the sauce. Mix half the sauce with a pound of
spaghetti cooked *al dente,* divide among 4 heated plates, and top each with
the remaining sauce. Serves 4.

SQUID CACCIATORE WITH LINGUINE

2 pounds whole squid   1 clove garlic, finely chopped
¼ cup olive oil   ½ teaspoon dried oregano
1 cup finely chopped onion   1 tablespoon freshly chopped basil
1 small green pepper, seeded, cut   (optional)
   into thin strips   ½ teaspoon salt or more to taste

Several grindings of pepper

1 dried hot red pepper, crumbled,
  or ¼ teaspoon hot pepper flakes

1½ cups canned plum tomatoes,
  partially drained and crushed

¼ cup dry red wine

½ pound freshly cooked linguine

If the squid has not been already dressed, do so as directed on pages 322–323. Wash the mantle thoroughly, lay it flat, cut down the center from top to tail, spread it open, and cut into bite-size pieces crosswise. Cut the tentacles into manageable lengths. Rinse the pieces well in a sieve to remove any traces of sand, dry with paper towels.

Heat the oil in a large, heavy skillet, add the squid, and cook over moderate heat for 3–4 minutes. The squid will give off some liquid. Add the onion, green pepper, garlic, oregano, basil, salt, pepper, and hot pepper, cook for an additional 3–4 minutes. Add the tomatoes and wine, bring to a boil, cover, lower heat, and simmer for 10 minutes. Do not overcook or the squid will be rubbery. Correct the seasoning.

Serve with the freshly cooked, well-drained linguine. Grind more black pepper over the top just before serving. Serves 4 as a first course.

ADDI'S CAPELLI D'ANGELI WITH CRAB

One of the most elegant and different ways to serve pasta that I have come across. If you can find green (spinach-flavored) homemade *capelli d'angeli,* or angel hair pasta, the dish is sublime, and visually, a knockout!

2 tablespoons olive oil

2 tablespoons minced shallot

2 leaves fresh basil

4 tablespoons (½ stick) butter, cut
  in thin pats

½ cup chicken broth

½ pound lump or backfin crab
  meat, picked over

Salt and freshly ground pepper

4–5 canned Italian plum tomatoes,
  drained

½ pound *capelli d'angeli,* preferably homemade

3 tablespoons freshly grated, aged
  Parmesan cheese

1 tablespoon chopped parsley

Heat the olive oil in a heavy 10- or 12-inch skillet, add the shallot, and cook over moderate heat until wilted, 2–3 minutes. Add the basil and butter and as the butter melts stir in the chicken broth. Add the crab and season to taste with salt and pepper. Be careful not to break up or shred the crab. Add the tomatoes, break them up lightly with the side of a wooden spoon, and cook the mixture over moderate heat for a few minutes. At this same time cook the pasta in a large pot of boiling salted water that you have gotten ready, as it takes only two minutes to complete.

Drain the pasta, pour the crab mixture over it, add the cheese, parsley, and numerous grindings of pepper, toss well, and serve at once on heated plates. Serves 4 as a first course.

COQUILLES SAINT-JACQUES CARLIER

The French have never hesitated in elaborating on the best that Italy has to offer. The recipe below originally called for a tablespoon of finely julienned truffle to be mixed with the ham and tongue.

¾–1 pound fettuccine or spaghetti	Lemon juice
1 pound bay scallops	¼ pound cooked ham, cut in
Flour	julienne (see the note below)
7 tablespoons butter	¼ pound tongue, cut in julienne
2 tablespoons cooking oil	Chopped parsley for garnish
Salt and freshly ground pepper	

Cook the fettuccine or spaghetti, drain, and keep warm.

Wash and dry the scallops, roll them in the flour.

Heat 2 tablespoons of the butter and the cooking oil in a skillet. Add the scallops, sauté quickly over high heat until pale gold, 3–4 minutes, no longer (overcooking results in tough scallops and a loss of flavor). Turn into a serving dish, season with salt, pepper, and a dash or two of lemon juice, and keep warm.

Pour off the fat from the pan in which the scallops were cooked. Make noisette butter: add 3 tablespoons of the butter and cook it until it is light brown, set aside.

In a separate skillet, melt the remaining 2 tablespoons of butter, briefly heat the ham and tongue. Toss the cooked pasta with them, mound on a heated serving platter, and top with the scallops. Pour the noisette butter over and garnish with chopped parsley. Serve immediately. Serves 4.

NOTE: Buy the ham and tongue in thick slices. The usual paper-thin ones cannot be successfully cut into julienne.

LINGUINE WITH WHITE CLAM SAUCE

⅓ cup olive oil	A large pinch of dried oregano
2 cloves garlic, put through a press	12 cherrystone clams, shucked,
½ cup clam juice, bottled,	minced, juice reserved, or a
reserved from fresh clams, or a	10½-ounce can minced clams
combination of both	2 tablespoons chopped parsley,
¼ teaspoon salt	preferably Italian type
Freshly ground pepper	1 pound linguine

Heat the oil in a heavy skillet, sauté the garlic until pale gold. Add the clam juice, salt, several grindings of pepper, and the oregano, simmer, covered, for 5 minutes. Stir in the clams and their juice, cook, uncovered, for about 10 minutes or until the liquid is reduced slightly. Stir in the parsley.

Cook the linguine *al dente,* drain, and put in a heated large bowl, add half the clam sauce, and toss well. Serve in heated soup bowls with the remaining sauce spooned on top. Serves 4–6.

LINGUINE WITH RED CLAM SAUCE

1/4 cup olive oil
2 medium yellow onions, chopped
2 cloves garlic, minced
4 cups (a 2-pound 3-ounce can) Italian plum tomatoes, drained
3/4 teaspoon salt
Freshly ground pepper
1 small dried red pepper, crumbled, or 1/2 teaspoon red pepper flakes
1 teaspoon dried oregano

4 anchovy fillets, chopped
15 cherrystone clams, shucked (juice reserved) and coarsely chopped, or a 10 1/2-ounce can minced clams
3/4 cup clam juice, reserved from the clams, bottled, or a combination of both
1 pound linguine

Heat the oil in a large, heavy skillet or saucepan with a cover, sauté the onions and garlic until soft. Break up the tomatoes, stir into the onion mixture, and simmer, uncovered, for 5 minutes. Add the salt, black and red pepper, oregano, and anchovies, cover, and simmer gently for 15 minutes. Stir once or twice. Add the clams and their juice, stir well, add more black pepper, and simmer, uncovered, for 3–4 minutes, stirring frequently.

Cook the linguine *al dente,* drain, and put in a heated large bowl. Add half the clam sauce, toss well, dish out into heated soup bowls, and top with the remaining sauce. No cheese with this, please. Serves 4–6.

NINE

*A Miscellany
of Techniques
and Cooking Terms*

FISH CAKES

1½ cups cooked, cold, flaked fish,
  skin and bones removed
1½ cups highly seasoned mashed
  potatoes
1 tablespoon grated onion

2 tablespoons minced parsley
1 egg, lightly beaten
Salt and freshly ground pepper
Butter or fresh bacon fat

Combine the fish, potatoes, onion, parsley, and egg, season to taste. Form into cakes about 3 inches in diameter and about 1½ inches thick. Sauté them in butter or bacon fat until golden brown. Serve with tartar sauce or tomato sauce if desired.

FISH CROQUETTES

1½ cups boned, cooked, skinned
  fish (any kind)
2 tablespoons butter
3 tablespoons flour
1 cup hot milk
¼ teaspoon salt
White pepper
1 tablespoon Worcestershire sauce

¼ teaspoon thyme
1 cup soft white bread crumbs
1 tablespoon lemon juice
1 egg yolk, lightly beaten
Oil for deep-fat frying
French Fried Parsley ❀ for garnish (optional)

CRUMB COATING
1 egg, lightly beaten

1 cup fine dry bread crumbs or
  cracker meal

Grind the fish in a food processor or put through a grinder, set aside.

Melt the butter in a 2½-quart saucepan over moderate heat, blend in the flour, and cook for 2 minutes, stirring. Off heat, whisk in the milk, stirring until thickened. Add the salt and pepper to taste, the Worcestershire sauce, thyme, bread crumbs, fish, and lemon juice. Blend in the egg yolk. Taste and adjust seasoning if necessary. Cover and chill the mixture for 3 hours.

Start heating the fat to 375° in a deep fryer.

Shape the mixture into 12 sausage-shaped rolls. If you are a perfectionist, round the ends nicely with a sandwich spreader or palette knife. To coat the croquettes, dip them in the beaten egg and roll in the crumbs. As each is made, place it on a wire rack; do not let them touch. Let them stand at room temperature for 10 minutes or so.

When the fat reaches the proper temperature, put 3 or 4 croquettes in the fryer basket and lower into the hot fat. Fry for 2–3 minutes until golden brown and crisp, drain on paper towels, and keep warm until all are made. Garnish with fried parsley. Serve hot with tartar sauce or tomato sauce. Serves 4.

RICH PASTRY DOUGH (Pâte Brisée)

Proportions are for an 8-inch or 10-inch single-crust pie or quiche shell. Proportions for a 2-crust pie follow this recipe.

1½ cups all-purpose flour
¼ teaspoon salt
5 tablespoons cold butter, cut into
    5 or 6 pieces

2 tablespoons stick margarine, soft
    margarine, Crisco, or lard
¼–⅓ cup ice water

IN A FOOD PROCESSOR: With the metal blade in place, combine the flour, salt, and butter. Process briefly, turning on and off quickly, until the butter is cut into the flour (3–5 seconds) and the flour resembles coarse cornmeal. Do not overprocess or the butter will get too soft. The mixture should be light and dry. Then, with the machine running, add the ice water in drops through the feeder tube. In about 15–20 seconds the dough should begin to form a ball on the blade. If it seems too soft, sprinkle 1–2 additional tablespoons of flour over the dough and process briefly again. If it is too firm, add another tablespoon or two of water. Remove, press into a large round cake, flour lightly, wrap well in plastic wrap, and refrigerate for 1–2 hours or put in the freezer for 45 minutes. Then roll it out on a lightly floured board.

NOTE: This cannot be done successfully in a regular blender.

BY HAND: Sift the flour and salt together. Work the butter into the flour with your fingertips or a pastry blender until it resembles coarse cornmeal. Then add only enough water to make a cohesive mass. Turn it out onto a lightly floured board and knead briefly, using the heel of the hand in a pushing-out-and-smearing motion, to evenly blend the butter and flour. Chill as above.

Made either way, this dough when wrapped, may be kept frozen for future use.

PROPORTIONS FOR A 2-CRUST PIE:

2 cups flour
½ teaspoon salt
8 tablespoons (1 stick) butter

3 tablespoons vegetable shortening
⅓ cup ice water or more as needed

Use the same food processor or hand procedure as described above.

CREPES

1¼ cups flour
3 large eggs
1 cup milk

¼ cup water
¼ teaspoon salt
Peanut or corn oil

Put all the ingredients except the oil in a jar, blend at top speed for about a minute. If you are making the recipe by hand, whisk the combined ingredients until smooth. Strain the batter if lumps or flour specks remain, refrigerate for at least 2 hours. If the batter appears too thick at the end of this time, thin with a few drops of cold water. Ideally, it should be the consistency of heavy cream.

Stir the batter before using. Have a plate handy on which to stack the crepes, and squares of wax paper to separate them.

Put a seasoned 7-inch crepe pan over moderately high heat and brush it with a little of the oil. If a drop or two of water dances and disappears on the pan, it is hot enough to begin making the crepes. Pour a small quantity of batter (equivalent to about 2 tablespoons) into the center of the pan. Immediately tip the pan rapidly in all directions to spread the batter evenly. Cook for 1 minute. Bubbles should have appeared on the crepe almost immediately, and it should be very thin. Flip it over by turning with a spatula and your fingers, cook the second side for about a half minute. This side browns only in spots, but this will be the ''wrong'' side, or inside, of the crepe and no one will see it. The first crepe may look a bit anemic, but never mind—as the pan gets to the right temperature and your hand becomes surer, they will get better. Stack them on the plate as you make them, with a piece of wax paper in between so they do not stick.

If you make them ahead, they can be covered and refrigerated, and will keep for 2 days. Makes about 15 7-inch crepes.

CRÈME FRAÎCHE

Put 1 cup of heavy cream in a small bowl, stir in 1 teaspoon of buttermilk. Cover it with plastic wrap and let it stand in a warm place for 12–24 hours or until the cream is about twice as thick as before. Use it for thickening sauces and as a topping for fresh fruit desserts. It will keep, refrigerated, for about 2 weeks. Makes about 1 cup.

HOT MUSTARD

Combine 6 tablespoons of powdered mustard in a mixing bowl with 3 tablespoons of beer or water. Add salt to taste. Let stand for 20 minutes to develop flavor. Makes about ⅓ cup.

DUXELLES

A mixture of finely chopped, cooked mushrooms and shallots or onions, used in sauces or fillings.

1 pound mushrooms	4 tablespoons (½ stick) butter
2 shallots, peeled and quartered	1 teaspoon salt

Wipe the mushrooms with a damp cloth, cut them in quarters, and chop very finely by hand. Mince the shallots.

In a food processor: Place the mushrooms and shallots in the bowl and whirl for 5–6 seconds or until finely chopped.

Heat the butter in a skillet, cook the mixture slowly until all the moisture has evaporated (about 30 minutes), season with salt. Makes about 2 cups.

FRENCH-FRIED PARSLEY

This is a simple and wonderful garnish for fried fish or fish croquettes. After you have fried your fish or croquettes in the deep fryer, turn the heat off or lower the setting so the oil cools a little. Put a bunch of washed and well-dried parsley in the basket and lower very gently into the oil. Don't immerse it completely until the sputtering stops. Fry for 2 minutes or until the bubbling stops.

LEEKS

To clean: Cut off the coarse green tops and save for stock or soup. Cut off the roots but leave the base intact. Set on a board and make a lengthwise cut through the center to within 1½ inches of the base. Make a half turn and repeat the cut—the leek is now quartered but held together at the base. Clean under cold running water, spreading the leaves slightly.

SALAD ACCOMPANIMENTS AND SALAD DRESSINGS

PEPPER HASH (With thanks to Julie Dannenbaum)

Anyone who knows what pepper hash is most certainly comes from either Philadelphia or Baltimore, where it is always served with fried oysters. The recipe is simple enough but appears only in obscure local cookery books (this one is adapted from the) *Philadelphia Cook Book,* by Anne Wetherill). It is included here for the adventuresome.

1 cup minced green pepper
½ cup minced sweet red pepper
4 cups minced cabbage
1 cup minced celery

2 tablespoons salt
2 tablespoons mustard seed
2 tablespoons brown sugar
½ cup vinegar

Combine the green and red peppers, cabbage, celery, and salt, let stand overnight. Drain thoroughly and put in an earthenware crock or glass jar, set aside. Combine the mustard seed, brown sugar, and vinegar in an enamel or stainless steel saucepan, bring to a boil. Pour over the drained vegetables, let cool, and refrigerate. This is best if served within 3 days. Makes about 1 quart.

SALADE RUSSE —A Cold Vegetable Salad

A 10-ounce package frozen peas, partially defrosted
½ pound fresh string beans, ends removed, cut into inch-long pieces
1 tablespoon lemon juice
½ teaspoon salt

⅓ cup mayonnaise
Several grindings of white pepper
2 teaspoons sugar
2–3 carrots, cut in medium dice
2 tablespoons finely minced shallots or onions
¼ cup finely chopped dill

Bring a cup of salted water to a boil in a large pot, add the peas, and when the water returns to a boil, lower the fire and cook for 7 minutes. Drain in a colander and run cold water over. While the peas are cooking, bring 2–3 quarts of salted water to a boil in another pot, add the string beans, a handful at a time so the water does not stop boiling. Cook these for 5–6 minutes, drain in a colander, and run cold water over. Allow the vegetables to cool while you make the dressing.

Beat the lemon juice into the mayonnaise with the salt, pepper to taste, and sugar. Put the cooled peas and string beans in a large mixing bowl. Add the diced carrots and the shallots or onions. Pour the dressing over the vegetables, stir gently to coat them. Add the dill and mix again. Cover tightly with plastic wrap and refrigerate. Serves 5–6.

COLESLAW

1 medium head firm green cabbage	2 carrots, peeled
1 small onion	½ green pepper

DRESSING

6 tablespoons mayonnaise	2 teaspoons sugar
3 tablespoons cider vinegar	2 teaspoons celery seeds
1 tablespoon salt	Heavy cream (optional)

Cut the cabbage in quarters, remove the hearts, and shred on a slaw grater or with a knife. Grate the onion, carrots, and green pepper over the cabbage, mix thoroughly with your hands. Combine the dressing ingredients, thin with a little heavy cream if desired, pour over, mix thoroughly, and refrigerate for several hours before serving. Good with any fried fish or shellfish. Serves 8.

HOT ANCHOVY DRESSING FOR SALAD

Heat ¼ cup olive oil over a low flame. Stir in 2 teaspoons anchovy paste until well blended, add pepper to taste. In a salad bowl arrange romaine lettuce, watercress, chicory, and cucumbers. Sprinkle with 3 tablespoons regular vinaigrette dressing, toss well, then sprinkle on ¼ cup grated romano cheese. Pour the hot anchovy sauce over the greens and serve.

GREEN GODDESS SALAD DRESSING

Cut up very finely 1 bunch of scallions (including the green tops) and 1 small bunch of parsley. Chop 1 small can of anchovies and add to the chopped greens. Add the oil, add lemon juice and mayonnaise to taste, and pour over shredded romaine and shredded head lettuce.

SARDINE DRESSING FOR SALAD

In a blender put one can sardines (3½–4 ounces boneless and skinless) and the oil, the juice of one or two lemons (depending on size), and the grated rind of ¼–½ lemon. Add several grindings of black pepper and oil until smooth. Serve with romaine lettuce and red onion rings.

VINAIGRETTE DRESSING

2 tablespoons wine vinegar
½ teaspoon Dijon or dark prepared
  mustard
1 teaspoon salt

Freshly ground black pepper
⅓ cup olive oil

Put vinegar in a small bowl. Add the mustard, salt and pepper to taste and beat with a wire whisk. Continue whisking while you add the oil in a slow steady stream. Makes about ½ cup dressing.

TOMATOES

TO SKIN: Put ripe tomatoes in a bowl, pour boiling water over them, count to twelve, then pour off the hot water and replace it with cold. The skin may then be peeled off easily.

TO SEED: Cut a slice from the top (not the stem end) of each tomato and reserve the slices. Hold a tomato in the hollow of your hand, flick out the seeds with the handle of a teaspoon, using the bowl of the spoon to detach the core. If the spoon is thin and has slightly sharp edges, so much the better.

TO REMOVE JUICE AND SEEDS: Cut a tomato in half crosswise (not through the stem end), hold each tomato half in the palm of your hand and gently squeeze over the sink to remove the juice and seeds. At the same time augment seed removal with the tip of a teaspoon. The flesh is now ready to be roughly chopped, sliced, or diced as a recipe indicates.

TOMATO FONDUE: This is tomato pulp diced and sautéed for several minutes in butter or olive oil with minced shallots or garlic plus herbs and seasoning. It may be used to garnish fish dishes. See the recipe for Stuffed Red Snapper La Samanna as an example of how tomato fondue is used for this purpose.

BASIC TOMATO SAUCE

3 tablespoons olive or vegetable
  oil
1 large clove garlic, chopped
½ cup finely chopped onion
¼ cup finely chopped celery
A 28-ounce can Italian tomatoes,
  drained and coarsely chopped

1 tablespoon chopped parsley
1 tablespoon butter
½ teaspoon salt, or to taste
½ teaspoon sugar, or to taste
Several grindings of fresh pepper
½ teaspoon oregano

Heat the oil in a heavy enameled cast-iron pot, sauté the garlic, onion, and celery until the onions are soft but have not taken on any color. Add the tomatoes, parsley, and butter, simmer, loosely covered, for 30 minutes, stirring frequently. Add the salt, sugar, pepper, and oregano, cook for 10 minutes more. Strain the sauce and purée through a sieve, food mill, or in a food processor. Makes about 1½ cups of sauce.

A SHORT GLOSSARY OF COOKING TERMS

BEURRE MANIÉ: A paste of flour and uncooked butter used for thickening sauces.

BLANCH: To plunge food into boiling water for the purpose of softening, partially cooking or precooking, or to remove unwanted flavor (as the smoky taste in bacon or pork).

To blanch almonds: Drop in boiling water for a few seconds. Rub between thumb and index finger while they are still warm; skins will slip off. If the nuts are to be pulverized, dry them first for 5–10 minutes in a low oven.

BOUQUET GARNI: A combination of herbs, tied together, usually in a cheesecloth bag, cooked with a dish to flavor it, and removed before serving. The usual combination is parsley, thyme, and bay leaf, but other herbs may be added or used in place of these.

DREDGE: To coat lightly and evenly with flour.

FRUITS DE MER: Literally "fruits of the sea." Crustaceans and shellfish served or used together, raw or cooked.

GLAZE (FISH): To cover with a white sauce and run under the broiler until the sauce takes on some color.

JULIENNE: To cut food or vegetables into small, matchstick-size strips about ⅛ inch by 1½ to 2 inches.

MIREPOIX: Finely diced carrots, celery, onions, and sometimes ham, cooked slowly in butter with seasonings and used as a flavoring for sauces, stews, and braised dishes.

PURÉE: To sieve or grind to a fine pulp.

REDUCE: In cooking, to lessen the quantity of a liquid by boiling, hence to concentrate its flavor.

REFRESH: To plunge vegetables into cold water from boiling water to stop the cooking process; to chill anything, especially fruits, by icing or refrigerating.

SCORE: To make shallow, diagonal slashes on the surface membrane of a fish fillet to prevent curling while cooking.

SEASONED FLOUR: Flour to which salt and pepper have been added.

Appendixes

SEA ROBIN.

SUGGESTIONS
FOR MENUS

About the recipes: Since this cookbook is not organized like most others by the categories into which the recipes fall, but rather by the alphabetical order of the fish themselves, the following list is included as an aid in menu planning. This is not to say that the dishes listed can be served *only* in the category in which they appear, nor does the list include all the recipes in the book; the outline is intended as a quick reference only, and I urge you to experiment freely and make your own additions to the list.

HORS D'OEUVRES OR APPETIZERS (some may also be used as first courses)

Anchoiade
Angels on Horseback
Barbadian Codfish Fritters
Clam Dip
Clam Fritters
Crab Puffs
Deviled Oysters
Greek Cold Stuffed Mussels
Horseradish Shrimp Sandwiches
Little Provençal Pastries
Lova's Herring Appetizer
Marinated Salmon with Green Peppercorns
Marinated Shrimp 1 and 2
New Potatoes with Salmon Caviar
Pickled Herring Salad
Rillettes of Salmon
Salmon Cru le Duc
Shrimp Paste with Crackers
Smoked Eel
Smoked Salmon-Stuffed Eggs
Smoked Trout Canapés
Swedish Shrimp Toast
Tapenade with Crudités
Taramasalata, with Crudités or with Toast
Terrine of Smoked Eel

FIRST COURSES—HOT

Baked Crab Mornay
Baked Mussels au Gratin
Baked Stuffed Clams Oreganata
Brandade de Morue
Clams Casino
Coquilles Saint-Jacques à la Parisienne
Coquilles Saint-Jacques à la Provençale
Crab Imperial (hot)
Creamed Oysters and Sweetbreads
Gefilte Fish
Gratin de Fruits de Mer
Gratin of Crab
Halibut Mousse
Italian-Style Stuffed Clams
Linguine with Mussels in Cream
Moules Poulette
Mussels with Escargot Butter
Oysters Casino
Oyster Soufflé
Oysters Rockefeller
Pike and Spinach Pâté
Scalloped Oysters
Scallop-Stuffed Shrimp
Shrimp de Jonghe
Shrimp in Mustard Sauce
Shrimp Quenelles
Shrimp Quiche
Soufflé of Salmon
Turban of Sole and Shrimp Mousse Sauce Aurore

SOUPS

Billi-Bi
Charleston Crab Soup
Lobster Bisque
Oyster Bisque
Soupe aux Moules
Soupe de Poisson
Zuppa di Vongole

FIRST COURSES—COLD

Cold Halibut Ravigote
Cold Poached Bass with Cucumber Sauce

Cold Poached Salmon, Sauce Verte
Cold Smoked Trout Fillets with Horseradish Cream Sauce
Crab Louis
Crab with Capers
Gravlax with Mustard Sauce
Halibut Mousse with Shrimp Sauce
Insalata alla Pescatori
Mackerel in White Wine
Marinated Salmon with Green Peppercorns
Moules Fécampoise
Mousse of Salmon
Mussels Ravigote
Pike and Spinach Pâté
Raw Scallops le Duc
Raw Scallops with Lemon and Black Pepper
Salade Niçoise
Salmon Mayonnaise with Salade Russe
Seviche of Sole
Shrimp Rémoulade
Shrimp with Melon in Kirsch
Smoked Eel
Tomatoes with Anchovies and Mozzarella
Tuna and White Bean Salad

LUNCHEON DISHES—HOT

Bouillabaisse
Brandade de Morue
Charleston Crab Soup
Clam Pie
Coquilles Saint-Jacques à la Provençale
Coquilles Saint-Jacques Carlier
Crêpes aux Fruits de Mer
Finnan Haddie with Horseradish Cream Sauce
Finnan Haddie Soufflé
Grand Central Oyster Pan Roast
Gratin de Fruits de Mer
Kedgeree
Kedgeree of Haddock
Lobster Soufflé
New England Clam Chowder
Omelet Arnold Bennett
Salmon Soufflé
Scalloped Haddock au gratin
Scalloped Oysters

Scallops Sautéed Provençal
Shrimp de Jonghe
Shrimp Quiche
Smoked Cod with Potatoes and Onions
Smoked Salmon Risotto
Tourte Bretonne
Turban of Sole and Shrimp Mousse with Sauce Aurore

LUNCHEON DISHES—COLD

Cold Lobster Tails with Dilled Mustard Sauce
Cold Poached Halibut Ravigote
Cold Poached Bass
Cold Poached Salmon, Sauce Verte
Cold Smoked Trout Fillets with Horseradish Cream
Crab Louis
Crab Meat Ravigote
Crab Meat Rémoulade
Crab with Russian Dressing
Curried Mussel and Rice Salad
Haddock Salad
Halibut Mousse
Gravlax with Mustard Sauce
Insalata alla Pescatore
Kedgeree
Lobster Salad
Lobster Thermidor
Marinated Shrimp 1 and 2
Moules Fécampoise
Moules Francillon (Salade Dumas)
Mousse of Salmon
Pan Bania
Puerto Rican Marinated Shrimp with Avocado
Red Snapper with Turkish-Style Almond Sauce
Salade Dumas (Moules Francillon)
Salade Nicoise
Seviche
Seviche of Scallops
Shrimp in Tomato Aspic Ring
Shrimp Ponchartrain
Shrimp Rémoulade
Squid and Mussel Salad
Squid and Shrimp Salad

Tuna Salad
White Bean and Tuna Salad

DINNER MAIN COURSES—HOT

Baked Bluefish with Potatoes
Baked Lobster with Herb Butter
Baked Marinated Fillets of Red Snapper with Prosciutto
Baked Red Snapper Florentine
Baked Shad with Almond-Stuffed Dates
Baked Steaks al Pesto
Baked Stuffed Whole Salmon
Beth's Baked Salmon
Bohemian Christmas Carp
Bouillabaisse
Braised Fish in White Wine
Braised Salmon
Broiled Salmon Steaks with Dill Butter or Garlic-Herb Butter
Broiled Striped Bass Niçoise
Carp Stuffed with Chestnuts
Catfish Stew
Cioppino with Red Wine
Cod Roman Style
Crab Stew
Creole Shrimp
Danish Boiled Cod with Mustard-Dill Sauce
Eel in Green Sauce
Eel Provençal
Finnish Baked Pike with Cucumber and Rice
Flounder Stuffed with Crab
Haddock Bercy
Halibut with Shrimp and Leek
Jean Goddard's Stuffed Bass
Lobster à l'Americaine
Mariscada al Marinero
Matelote Marinière
Paprikash Carp
Poached Halibut with Hollandaise Sauce
Poached Striped Bass with Beurre Blanc Sauce
Pompano en Papillote
Pompano Stuffed with Shrimp
Portuguese Seafood Stew
Red Snapper Baked with Prosciutto
Red Snapper La Samanna
Rhode Island Oyster-Stuffed Cod
Risotto with Mussels

Romeo Salta's Butterfly Shrimp
Salmon Scallops with Sorrel
Scallop-Stuffed Shrimp
Seafood Gumbo and Variations
Shad Stuffed with Dates
Shad Stuffed with Roe
Shrimp Curry
Shrimp Curry with Tomatoes
Soft-Shell Crabs Amandine
Sole Bannaro
Sole Bonne Femme
Sole Duglèré
Sole Florentine
Sole Marguery
Sole Mornay
Steamed Sea Bass with Ginger
Striped Bass Dieppoise
Striped Bass Fermière
Striped Bass Marechiare
Striped Bass Veracruzano
Stuffed Lobster with Escargot Butter
Stuffed Striped Bass Middle Eastern Style
Stuffed Striped Bass Parmentier
Terrine of Eels à la Martégale
Trout with Almonds
Trout in Tarragon Cream
Trout Meunière
Whitefish Stuffed with Salmon Mousse

MAIN COURSES—COLD

Cold Poached Salmon
Crab Imperial
Crab Salad Orientale
Halibut Mousse with Shrimp Sauce
Le Grand Aioli
Red Snapper with Turkish-Style Almond Sauce
Seviche of Scallops, Peruvian Style
Shrimp with Dilled Mustard Sauce

BUFFETS—HOT

Bagna Cauda
Cod Baked with Tomatoes
Crab Stew
Creole Shrimp

Jansson's Temptation
Paella
Portuguese Seafood Stew
Risotto with Mussels
Shrimp with Feta Cheese
Spanish Shrimp with Rice

BUFFETS—COLD

Cold Poached Bass
Cold Poached Salmon, Sauce Verte
Cold Poached Salmon with Salade Russe
Cold Stuffed Mussels
Gravlax with Mustard Sauce
Halibut Mousse with Cucumber-Mustard Sauce
Marinated Shrimp 2
Mussels Vinaigrette
Pike and Spinach Pâté
Salade Niçoise
Salmon Mousse
Seviche
Squid and Mussel Salad
Squid and Shrimp Salad
Tomatoes with Anchovies and Mozzarella
Tuna and White Bean Salad

HEARTY ONE-DISH MEALS

Aioli
Bob Thomas' Fish Chowder
Cioppino
Cod Baked with Tomatoes
Crab Stew
Creole Shrimp
Finnish Salmon Soup
Jambalaya
Jansson's Temptation
New England Clam Chowder
Paella
Portuguese Seafood Stew
Shrimp with Feta Cheese
Solianka
Spanish Shrimp with Rice
Squid and Leeks in Red Wine
Squid Cacciatori with Linguine
Zuppa de Pesce

SPECIALIZED KITCHEN EQUIPMENT FOR COOKING FISH

Poacher: Used on top of the stove, the poacher is a long, narrow container with a lid and an inside rack that allows a fish to be cooked in liquid over direct heat, yet protects the fish from the heat and facilitates its removal when cooked. Poachers range in size from 16 to 36 inches; the larger ones can be used over two burners. They are usually made of tinned steel. Cheaper models in aluminum should be avoided, as this metal can discolor the cooking liquid.

Oval sauté pan: Not found in many American home kitchens but found in France, the oval skillet is usually made of copper lined with tin. Its two advantages over the conventional round pan in fish cookery are: it accommodates well to the shape of a whole or filleted fish without the corresponding "bare" area in which butter can burn; and it is attractive enough to be used for serving. It is made of medium-gauge copper, with a brass handle, and comes in four sizes ranging from roughly 11 by 12 to 16 by 11 inches.

Fish scaler: There are several kinds of patented devices on the market with a handle and a rough-toothed surface for lifting up and removing scales. The scaling end is curved to avoid breaking the skin of the fish.

Fish shears: These rather heavy (12-ounce) scissors make cutting through bellies, snipping around gills, and trimming fins and tails a much easier chore.

Filleting knife: Useful for boning and filleting flatfish. Usually has a 6-inch blade of stainless steel with a serrated section on the dull edge. A sharp point aids in piercing the skin.

Slicing knife: A 15-inch long, narrow bladed knife with a flexibility that permits using it almost horizontally to make paper-thin slices of smoked salmon or *gravlax*.

Oyster knife: A 6-inch knife with a short, sturdy blade shaped like an arrowhead. There are many variations.

Clam knife: Has a blunt blade to avoid cutting into the meat and a rounded tip for forcing open the shells.

Clam opener: A scissors-like gadget that holds the clam vertically and forces the shell open with the pressure of "cutting." A forked tip can be used to remove the clam from its shell.

Lobster pincers: A table utensil for cracking claws. It works on the same principle as a nutcracker, which can be used as a substitute.

Lobster pick: Another table utensil: the pick has two tiny sharp curved tines to facilitate extracting small morsels of meat.

Scallop shells: These can be natural or made of porcelain. They are generally used for creamed shellfish dishes.

Lobster steamers: A large pot with two separate components, one for water below and another larger one above for clams or lobsters. Works on the steaming principle. Generally has a spigot attachment on the bottom for drawing off broth, as from steamed clams.

Fish grills: For open-fire cooking. A curved elongated basket of closely set wires that snaps shut, and has a handle for holding it over the fire. Another open kind, of tinned steel, has short legs for setting directly over a ground fire.

Other general equipment that is useful in cooking fish and shellfish includes:

Cheesecloth: For wrapping fish to be poached.

Bulb baster: For basting baked or broiled fish.

Brush: Of goose feather or natural bristle for brushing on oil or melted butter.

Heavy duty aluminum foil: For baking in foil.

Deep-fat fryer: Electric ones with self-regulating thermostats are available, or you can use a wire French-fry basket set in a heavy, deep aluminum saucepan of 2½–3 quart capacity.

Parchment paper: Sold as "kitchen parchment" in housewares stores, used for baking *en papillote*.

Stiff bristle brush: For scrubbing mussels.

Perforated spoon: For extracting deep-fried fish from oil.

Wooden mallet: To add force to the knife in cutting through shell or bone when splitting lobsters or steaking fish. One weighing about 1 pound 5 ounces and about 12 inches in length is ideal.

Rubber gloves: Useful when shucking clams and oysters or handling lobsters.

Scale: For checking fish weight. Preferably one with a flat, broad weighing tray (not the calorie-counter variety).

Enameled cast-iron pot: With a tight-fitting lid and a 6- to 9-quart capacity for soup and stock-making and steaming open mussels.

Enameled cast-iron gratin *dishes:* A selection of these is almost indispensable—the long oval shape is particularly well suited to cooking fish, the dishes are unbreakable (although a sharp blow can chip the enamel) and may go directly to the table. They come in lengths of 8, 9½, 11, 12½, and 14½ inches. Sides are 1¾ inches deep, a generous depth for sauces.

Timer: One that times accurately in minutes. Precise, to-the-minute timing is one of the keys to successful fish and shellfish cooking.

Electric food processor: An invaluable aid in puréeing, grinding, chopping, grating, mixing flavored butters, mayonnaise. Makes the blender all but obsolete.

Food mill: With interchangeable blades, the food mill acts as a sieve in puréeing. The 2-quart size is handiest.

Wire whisks: For beating and blending sauces.

Mortar and pestle: The non-porous white French porcelain one is what you use for grinding garlic to a paste in the making of aioli.

Pepper mill: There is no comparison between the pungency of freshly ground pepper and preground pepper. It is easy to use and the tightness of the nut governs the fineness of the grind. Have one filled with white peppercorns also, for recipes specifying white pepper.

Large tweezers: To facilitate removal of overlooked fishbones, especially in fillets.

FOOD SHOPPING
BY MAIL

The following list, by no means a complete one, and subject to the vagaries of seasons and price fluctuations, contains the names and addresses of reliable sources that ship seafood, suitably packed. They were culled from *The Food Catalogue: an International Guide to Great Food by Mail,* by Nancy Hyden Woodward, Stonehill Publishing Company, New York, 1977, and *The International Cooks' Catalogue,* Random House, New York, 1977, and private sources.

ABBOTT'S SEAFOODS, INC.
Noank, Connecticut 06340
    Live Lobsters.

ANTON JOSEPHSON COMPANY
Box 412
Astoria, Oregon 97103
    Smoked Columbia River Chinook and chum salmon.

BETTISTELLA'S
910 Touro Street
New Orleans, Louisiana 70116
    Anything indigenous to Gulf waters, including oysters, crab meat, speckled trout, redfish fillets, red snapper, live crawfish, frozen turtle meat.

BLUE CHANNEL COMPANY
Box 128
Port Royal, South Carolina 29935
    Atlantic blue crab, Charleston she-crab soup, white, lump, and claw crab meat.

CAPN'S PICK
702 West Fulton Market
Chicago, Illinois 60606
    Lake Superior white fish, walleye pike, imported French turbot, Idaho rainbow trout, silver salmon steaks, Hawaiian mahimahi, smelt, smoked chub, smoked sable, smoked eel, smoked lake trout, smoked rainbow trout.

CLAMBAKE INTERNATIONAL
8 Greenview Street
Suite 15
Framingham, Massachusetts 01701
    Live Maine Lobsters, Ipswich steamer clams.

EMBASSY SEAFOODS, INC.
Box 268
3 Cottage Park Road
Winthrop, Massachusetts 02152
    Salt mackerel, cod fillets.

ESPECIALLY MAINE
Vinegar Hill Road
Arundel, Maine 04046
    Lobsters, clams.

FEBY'S FISHERY
1111 New Road
Elsmere, Delaware 19805
    Blue crabs, any local fish during its season, from weakfish to oysters.

GARRAPATA TROUT FARM
Box 3178
Carmel, California 93921
    Fresh or smoked trout.

HALVORSON'S FISH PRODUCTS
8290 South Tacoma Way
Tacoma, Washington 98499
    Salmon, octopus, tuna, shrimp, clams, oysters; (some of the above are
    available smoked; all are available canned).

HEGG & HEGG SMOKED SALMON, INC.
801 Marine Drive
Port Angeles, Washington 98362
    Puget Sound alder-smoked salmon; also Dungeness crab meat and red
    sockeye salmon, both canned.

KELLY'S SEAFOODS
RFD 4
Box 112
Bangor, Maine 04401
    Lobsters, clams, scallops.

MURRAY'S STURGEON SHOP
2429 Broadway
New York, New York 10024
    Smoked Nova Scotia salmon, smoked butterfish, smoked winter carp,
    smoked salmon trout.

RED HERRING, INC.
384 Bleecker Street
New York, New York 10014
    Pickled herring fillets, Maatjes herring fillets.

RUSS & DAUGHTERS
179 East Houston Street
New York, New York 10002
    Gaspé Nova Scotia salmon, Lake (Winnipeg) sturgeon, kippered salmon, Selkirk whitefish, Icelandic schmaltz herring.

SALTWATER FARM
York Harbor, Maine 03911
    Live lobsters, clams.

SEY-CO PRODUCTS, INC.
7651 Densmore Avenue
Van Nuys, California 91406
    Columbia River royal Chinook salmon.

TROY SEAFOOD MARKET
11130 S.E. Powell Boulevard
Portland, Oregon 97266
    Smoked salmon, smoked sturgeon.

Ethnic Foods

Japanese

Katagiri & Company, Inc.
224 East Fifty-ninth Street
New York, New York 10022

Enbun Company
248 East First Street
Los Angeles, California 90012

Italian

Manganaro Brothers
488 Ninth Avenue
New York, New York 10018

Indian

Kalustyan Orient Export Trading Corp.
123 Lexington Avenue
New York, New York 10016

Haig's
441 Clement Street
San Francisco, California 94119

Middle Eastern

Malko Bros.
197 Atlantic Avenue
Brooklyn, New York 11201

Mediterranean and Middle East Import Company
233 Valencia Street
San Francisco, California 94103

A GUIDE TO NAMES OF AMERICAN FRESHWATER AND SALTWATER FISH

Ichthyologists will no doubt cavil with the following listing as incomplete and capricious, and the average cook may find it unnecessary. It includes fish names not found elsewhere in this book, and though it is not meant as a guide for fish identification, it may be useful to those who fish or who have access to locally caught fish that do not find their way to market.

SALTWATER FISH

AHI   A Hawaiian tuna with red meat.

AKU   The Hawaiian snapjack, also red-fleshed.

ALBACORE   The whitest of the tuna family (see Tuna).

ALEWIFE   An anadromous member of the herring family. Sardines are often infant alewives.

ALLMOUTH MONKFISH   See Index, Anglerfish.

AMAAMA   The Hawaiian mullet, an important island food fish.

AMBERJACK or JACKHAMMER   A large South Atlantic coastal fish with lean, mild-tasting flesh not seen at market. Check tail for parasites.

ANGLERFISH (French: *lotte, baudroie*)   Other names are goosefish, frogfish, fishing frog, allmouth monkfish, devil-mouth. See Index.

ATKA MACKEREL   Not a true mackerel but a greenling related to the lingcod; found in Pacific waters. Popular in Japan.

A'U   The Hawaiian swordfish.

BARRACUDA   See Index.

BASS   Name for a variety of unrelated fish (see Index).

BELLYFISH   Another name for goosefish.

BLACKFISH   See Index.

BLACK WILL   Another name for black bass.

BLOWFISH   See Index.

BLUE RUNNER, also RUNNER, HARDTAIL, JACK   (see Jack).

BLUE SHARK   See Shark.

BOCACCIO   A rockfish important commercially in California (see Rockfish).

BONEFISH, also SILVER GHOST, PHANTOM   A marine game fish (see Index).

BONITO, also ATLANTIC BONITO   See Tuna.

BOSTON BLUEFISH   See Pollock.

BRILL   (French: barbue) A European flounder similar to turbot.

BRILL SOLE   See Petrale.

BROADBILL   See Swordfish.

BUTTERFISH,   also DOLLARFISH, PUMPKINSEED

CABEZONE   A large Pacific member of the sculpin family. The roe is poisonous.

CABIO   See Cobia.

CALIFORNIA BLACK SEA BASS   Sometimes called jewfish but different from the Florida jewfish (see Index: Bass).

CALIFORNIA SHEEPSHEAD   See Index.

CAPE MAY GOODY   See Spot.

CATFISH   See Index.

CHANNEL BASS   See Drum; Redfish.

CHOGGIE   See Cunner; Wrasse.

CHUB MACKEREL   (See Big-eyed mackerel: Hardhead.) Smaller than Atlantic mackerel—$\frac{1}{2}$–$\frac{2}{3}$ pound average.

COBIA, also LING, CABIO, SERGEANT FISH, CRABEATER, LEMONFISH   A thick-skinned, dry-meat, fish tasting remarkably like chicken or frogs legs, found in South Atlantic and Gulf coastal waters; sometimes miscalled bonito and black bonito.

COD (French: *morue)   See Index.

COD, ROCK   See Rockfish.

CORBINA   A name used for various members of the Pacific sea trout or weakfish genus plus the California corbina, which is the same family but resembles the croaker.

CROAKER   See Drum; Index.

CUNNER, also BERGALL   A small ($\frac{1}{3}$–$\frac{2}{3}$ pound average) member of the wrasse family, related to the tautog. Sometimes called sea perch, choggie (see Wrasse).

CUSK (torsk)   A member of the cod family, average 6–12 pounds.

CUTLASS FISH   A scaleless, vicious-looking, sharp-toothed but delicate-tasting fish found in Atlantic and Pacific waters; miscalled ribbonfish.

DEVIL-MOUTH   See Anglerfish.

DOGFISH   See Spiny Dogfish.

DOLPHIN   A food fish unrelated to the mammal of the same name (see Index).

DORY   See John Dory.

DRUM   The *Sciaenidae* family, including the croakers, banded, black, red, and freshwater drums, corvine, kingfish, silver perch, totuava, and white sea bass (see Index).

EEL   See Index.

ENGLISH SOLE   Also known as sole in the West, but of an entirely different species than the Atlantic lemon sole, or the true English (Dover) sole.

FINNAN HADDIE   Smoked haddock (see Index).

FISHING FROG   See Anglerfish.

FLATFISH (French: *barbue*)   A descriptive term applied to flounder, halibut, gray and lemon sole, plaice, dabs, fluke, all fish having both eyes on one side.

FLOUNDER   A flatfish found in Atlantic, Pacific, and Gulf waters, including the blackback, winter, smooth, sand, and ''see-through'' flounders and the sand dab. Also the gray, lemon, and rex sole (see Index).

FLUKE   A sinistral flounder also known as plaice or summer flounder. Large ones are called ''doormats.'' Delicate flounder-like meat. Available in spring and summer.

FROSTFISH   See Scrod.

GAFF, also called TOPSAIL   A saltwater variety of the freshwater catfish, thought to be too strong-tasting to eat (see Wolffish; Hardhead).

GOOSEFISH   See Anglerfish.

GRAY SOLE   An Atlantic coast sole, also called witch flounder (see Flounder).

GREENLING   A Pacific fish (see Lingcod).

GROUPER (French: *merou*), also called CONEY, GAG GROUPER, JEWFISH, WARSAW GROUPER, RED or BLACK GROUPER, SEANIP, YELLOWFIN   Closely related to the Mediterranean grouper (see Index).

GRUNION   Silversides, a tiny fish that swarms beaches to spawn.

GRUNT   Large ones are called white margate (see Margate; Index).

HARBOR POLLOCK   See Pollock.

HARDHEAD, also SEA CAT, CAT   (see Chub mackerel).

HEE SQUID (Hawaiian)   Should be boiled or curried.

HERRING   A family that includes alewives, spring herring, shad, and sardines (see Index).

HOGFISH   A wrasse miscalled hog snapper but not in the snapper family.

HOUNDFISH   A large needlefish. Fry or broil.

JACK, includes JACK CREVALLE, BLUE RUNNER, BAR JACK, SPANISH JACK, SCAD   Related to the pompano (see Jack crevalle).

JACK   Smelt over 6 inches, and weighing $1/3$–1 pound (see Smelts).

JACK CREVALLE   A game fish with bloody meat, related to the blue runner. Found on South Atlantic and Gulf coasts.

JEWFISH, also SPOTTED JEWFISH, SPOTTED GROUPER, GIANT SEA BASS, WARSAW GROUPER   (see Grouper).

JOHN DORY, also called ST. PETER'S FISH   Found from Nova Scotia to Cape Hatteras, though not abundantly. It is distinguished by a black spot on each side of its body, thought by early Christians to be the fingerprints of Simon called Peter. Most commonly found in the Mediterranean.

JOLTHEAD PORGY   The largest fish in the porgy family except for the sheepshead. Found along the southeast U.S. coast.

JUNKFISH   See Trashfish.

KELP BASS   A California coastal bass.

KINGFISH   A rich, firm-fleshed fish sometimes miscalled mullet or sea mullet. In the mackerel family found along the South Atlantic and Gulf coasts. On the Pacific coast, a variety of kingfish is similar to corbina.

KITTY MITCHELL   See Speckled Hind; Grouper.

LADYFISH, also SKIPJACK   A very soft, bony fish averaging ³/₄–1 pound.

LARGEMOUTH BASS   See under Black bass in section *Freshwater Fish*.

LEMONFISH   See Cobia.

LEMON SOLE   See Flounder.

LINGCOD (cultus cod)   A West Coast fish, not a true cod, available all year.

LITTLE TUNA (false albacore)   Miscalled albacore.

LIZARD FISH   An unattractive panfish with beautiful white flesh and mild flavor.

LOOKDOWN (moonfish)   A panfish similar to pompano.

MAHIMAHI (Hawaiian)   A dolphin fish.

MAKO   See Shark.

MARGATE   The Florida white margate is a large grunt that, freshly caught, has a strong flavor that subsides after being iced. The black margate is another species of the same family (see Grunt).

MARLIN   A large game fish, averaging 50–70 pounds. White and blue marlin differ in color of fin tips.

MOJARRA   A panfish sometimes called shad in southern Florida.

MOONFISH   See Lookdown.

MULLET   A rich, buttery, oily fish averaging 2–3 pounds, found in Atlantic, Pacific, and Gulf waters.

MUTTONFISH   See Snapper.

OCEAN POUT   A sweet, white-fleshed fish resembling eel with a large mouth. Its prime commercial use is as frozen fish. Best poached.

OCEAN TALLY   See Triggerfish.

ORANGE ROCKFISH   See Rockfish.

PALOMETA,   also called GAFF TOPSAIL, POMPANO, LONGFIN POMPANO.

PARROT FISH   Delicious lobster-like white meat, but internal organs can be poisonous. Fry, broil, or bake.

PERCH   Name applied to a number of spiny-finned small, bland saltwater fish, all related, including the surf perch or sea perch (Pacific coast) and deep sea perch (Atlantic coast). The latter is the one true perch. Ocean perch is a catchall name for sea perch and the Atlantic perch, redfish, and rosefish, closely related to several varieties of rockfish. The Pacific Ocean perch is sometimes called the longjaw rockfish. The white perch, also called perch, sea perch, or sand perch, is small (³/₄ pound) with lean, firm, coarse-textured white flesh, similar in appearance to the striped bass. In Europe, perch is a small freshwater fish with spiny fins. See also the listing in Freshwater Fish.

PERMIT, also called GREAT POMPANO   Larger (7–20 pounds) version of the pompano.

PETRALE   A Pacific sole also known as brill sole.

PIGFISH   Often miscalled hogfish. Also Sailor's choice (see Grunt).

PILCHARD   The sardine of California waters, actually a member of the herring family. Occurs in great schools along European coasts. Also any of several types of sardines related to the European pilchard.

POLLOCK   A member of the cod family having darker, less tender flesh that becomes lighter when cooked, and distinguished from that fish by its rounder body and greenish color. Sometimes called green cod or miscalled Boston bluefish. Commercially important, pollock makes up a large percentage of the frozen fish in this country, often purveyed under ambiguous names like "ocean fresh fillets."

PORGY   A family of small fish including the whitebone porgy, red porgy, jolthead porgy, and the pinfish. In Europe these fish and others are part of a large family called bream (see Index).

PORKFISH   Related to the grunts.

PRICKLEBACK   A species of the family *Stichaeidae*, eel-like in appearance but not related to the eel, with delicious flesh not unlike that of shrimp.

PUFFER   See Blowfish.

QUEER FISH   See Croaker.

RAINBOW RUNNER   A member of the jack family. Fry or broil.

RAY   See Skate.

RED DRUM   See Drum; Redfish.

REDEYE BASS   See under Redeye in the Freshwater Fish section.

REDFISH, also called RED DRUM, CHANNEL BASS, OCEAN PERCH, ROSEFISH   The North Atlantic redfish is a type of red drum, which looks like a weakfish without spots. Another variety, the South Atlantic redfish, is a type of rockfish also known as ocean perch and identified by its enormous eye. Averages 1/3–1 pound. Fry, broil, or bake.

RED PORGY, also called PINK PORGY   Miscalled silver snapper, Charleston snapper. Averages 2–5 pounds (see Porgy).

RED ROCKFISH, also known as RED SNAPPER, RED ROCK COD, RASPHEAD.

RED SNAPPER, also SNAPPER, AMERICAN SNAPPER   (see Index).

REX SOLE   See Sole.

ROCKFISH   As a group, a family of fish having stout, heavily constructed bodies and heavily spined fins. There are about fifty varieties in Pacific waters; Atlantic varieties include rock cod, rock sea bass, and grouper.

ROCKFISH   In California a name for the white sea bass and the Pacific Ocean perch. Below the Mason-Dixon Line the name given to striped bass.

ROCK SEA BASS, also SEA BASS, BLACKFISH, ROCK BASS   See Rockfish.

ROOSTERFISH   A Lower California native similar to the jack.

ROSEFISH   See Redfish.

SABLEFISH, also called BLACK ALASKA COD, BUTTERFISH   See Index.

SAILFISH   A South Atlantic coastal game fish, averaging 25–35 pounds. Available in May–October. May be smoked for use as a food fish.

SAILOR'S CHOICE   See Pigfish; Pinfish.

SAND DAB   A tasty Pacific member of the flounder family, available all year, averaging 1/4–1/2 pound. Tricky to bone (see sole; Index).

SAND SHARK, also GROUND SHARK   Sometimes found in mouths of rivers (see Shark).

SARDINE   The young of the herring. Averages 3–6 inches. Called sprats when smoked. European equivalent called brisling (see Pilchard; Index).

SAWFISH   A very ugly fish delicious when steaked or broiled.

SCROD   A cod under 3 pounds. Also called ATLANTIC TOMCOD, TOMCOD, TOMMYCOD, FROSTFISH (see Index).

SCULPIN   A strange-looking scaleless pink-mottled fish with a large, meaty head.

SCUP   Another name for a 1–2-pound porgy (see Porgy).

SEA ROBIN   An Atlantic fish with pectoral fins developed like wings. Largely considered a "trash fish," it is not particularly meaty, but it is tasty.

SEA SQUAB   See Blowfish.

SEA TROUT, GRAY   Another name for a small weakfish, averaging $\frac{1}{2}$–$1\frac{1}{2}$ pounds (see Weakfish).

SHARK, also called SPINY DOGFISH, DOGFISH, DOG   Found on both Pacific and Atlantic coasts. Runs 25–40 pounds with oily, firm, chewy meat similar to swordfish. Other varieties: sandbar shark (brown, 30–50 pounds), black tip shark, spinner shark, blue shark (125–225 pounds), tiger shark (200–500 pounds).

SHEEPSHEAD   See Porgy; Sheepshead in the Freshwater Fish section.

SKATE, also called RAY   Found on both coasts. Only the "wings" are generally marketed, which average 2 pounds (see Index).

SILVER HAKE   See Whiting.

SILVER PERCH, also called SAND PERCH, SEA PERCH.   Sometimes called white perch, from which it differs in the formation of its fin spines.

SKIPJACK TUNA, also called OCEANIC BONITO, ARCTIC BONITO, SKIPJACK, STRIPED BONITO, WATERMELON TUNA   A small tuna averaging 4–8 pound (see Index).

SMALLMOUTH BASS   See Bass; Index.

SMELT   Two saltwater varieties, the silverside (also known as the top smelt) and the grunion, both averaging 2–8 ounces; over 6 ounces they are called jacks (see Index).

SNAPPER   A large family of food and sportfish, the best known of which is the red snapper. Other South Atlantic members are the mutton, lane, silk, vermilion, and yellowtail snappers and the mangrove and schoolmaster. Lower California waters yield Striped, Colorado, Rose and Yellow snappers. Also, a name for baby bluefish (see Red Snapper; Index).

SNOOK   A game fish found in Southern Florida with lean white flesh. Snook can run as big as 50 pounds; small ones have a sweet flesh similar to that of pike. Skin before using.

SOLE   Varieties include petrale, rex sole, sand dabs, and turbot, all are members of the flounder family (see Index).

SPADEFISH   An Atlantic fish also known as bay porgy, porgy, and angelfish (see Porgy).

SPECKLED HIND, also called GROUPER, KITTY MITCHELL   See Grouper.

SPINY DOGFISH   A member of the shark family, often called Harbor Halibut in Maine (see Shark).

SPOT, also called NORFOLK SPOT, OCEAN VIEW SPOT, CAPE MAY GOODY   Similar to silver perch.

SPOTTED SEA TROUT   See Weakfish.

SQUIRRELFISH   A small panfish difficult to clean and handle.

SQUIRREL HAKE   A small hake also known as mud hake, red hake, brown hake, ling.

STARGAZER   Named for placement of the eyes, permanently skyward. Several varieties on Atlantic coast, and one on the Pacific coast.

STEELHEAD   A giant sea-run rainbow trout. Use any cooking method suitable for salmon (see Index under Trout).

STRIPED BASS   See Index.

SUNFISH, also called OCEAN SUNFISH, BREAM, BLUEGILL, and PUMPKINSEED   Called bream in the South (see Index).

SURF PERCH, also called SEA PERCH, BLUE, WHITE, SILVER, SEA PERCH   Not a true perch. Native to the Pacific coast.

SWORDFISH (French: *espadon*), also called BROADBILL   Average size 200–300 pounds, can run to 600 (see Index).

TARPON, also called SILVER KING, SPRAT   A game fish with dark, mushy meat. Not a food fish in the U.S., but in other areas it is dried or made into fish cakes.

TAUTOG, also called BLACKFISH, TOG, SEA TOG, CHUB, MOLLY GEORGE   Similar to the cunner (wrasse family). Found off the middle and north Atlantic states (see Index).

TILEFISH   See Index.

TINKER   Young mackerel.

TOMCOD   See Scrod.

TORO   A panfish.

TORSK   See Cusk.

TOTUAVA   A Southern California fish in the sea bass family, available in winter only. Has mild-flavored, lean white meat. Runs 50–60 pounds.

TRASHFISH   A term applied to any of a number of fish scorned by professional and sportfishermen and thought (until recently) to have little commercial or food value. Fish in this category vary with the region: among them are the anglerfish, sea robin, skate, lizardfish, prickleback, and triggerfish. At one time blowfish, which are poisonous except for the tail, which is now considered a delicacy, were included. The term "junkfish" is sometimes used interchangeably with trashfish but may specifically signify those fish which because of dark meat, strong taste, repulsive appearance, or small size are under-utilized in this country, and hence inexpensive.

TRIGGERFISH   Varieties include the queen trigger and the large ocean tally, sometimes called Turbot. Hard to clean, leathery skin.

TUNA   Has several members, all belonging to the mackerel family (see Index).

TURBOT   In this country the name used for some flounders and occasionally the triggerfish. The true turbot belongs to the same order of flatfish

(Heterosomata) as sole, halibut, and flounder, but is primarily a Mediterranean fish related to the brill and is also found in British waters. It is highly esteemed as the best-flavored of the European flatfish. Its flavor is vastly superior to that of the fish available to us. Can attain a size of 4 feet. The name is sometimes erroneously given to other flatfish resembling it.

VERMILION SNAPPER, also called BEELINE SNAPPER, CALIFORNIA RED SNAPPER   Smaller than the southern red snapper (see Snapper; Index).

WAHOO   A game and food fish belonging to the mackerel family (see Index).

WEAKFISH   A group of fish often called sea trout, including the Pacific corbina and the California white sea bass (see Sea trout; Weakfish in Index).

WHITEBAIT   The small fry of herring, rarely more than 2 inches long (see Index).

WHITE PERCH   See Perch.

WHITE SEA BASS   Not a bass at all, but a croaker and member of the sea trout genus. Ranges in weight from 12 to 20 pounds, with a sleek body shape like that of a salmon. Found in Southern California waters. Usually marketed in steaks. Mild, tender flesh.

WHITING, also called SILVER HAKE   Slender croaker-like fish found in Eastern coastal waters (see Index).

WINDOWPANE FLOUNDER   Differs from the summer flounder in having a fringed dorsal crest (see Flounder).

WOLFFISH, also called OCEAN CATFISH, SEA CATFISH   Averages 10 pounds, has lean, delicate white flesh like that of haddock.

WRASSE   A family that includes the tautog, hogfish, cunner, sea perch, choggie, and California sheepshead.

YELLOWTAIL (Atlantic)   See Snapper.

YELLOWTAIL (Pacific)   See Tuna.

YELLOWTAIL ROCKFISH   See Rockfish.

FRESHWATER FISH

ARCTIC CHAR   See Char.

BLACK BASS, includes LARGEMOUTH BASS, SMALLMOUTH BASS, KENTUCKY (SPOTTED) REDEYE, SUWANNEE   Runs 3–5 pounds, has lean, gamy meat.

BLACK CRAPPIE   See Crappie.

BLOATER   See Whitefish.

BLUEGILL   The most important of the sunfishes, distinguished by the black spot on its dorsal fin. Frequently pond-cultivated for sports fishing.

BLUE PIKE   A walleye related to the perch family.

BREAM   In this country a name applied to freshwater sunfish, though the name is occasionally used to refer to a specific member of the family. Sometimes called brim. The Mediterranean does have a genuine sea bream, the wonderfully gaudy *daurade*, a delicately flavored fish found in the eastern Gulf of Gascony and occasionally the English channel (see Sunfish).

BROOK TROUT   See Trout.

BUFFALO   A lean, coarse-fleshed fish of the sucker family.

BULLHEAD   Brown, black, flat, and spotted—all varieties of catfish. The black bullhead is also known as the horned pout.

BURBOT   A lean, freshwater cod averaging 3 pounds, having delicate white meat. Found in the East and Midwest. Bake, broil, steam, panfry.

CHAR   A genus of the *Salmonidae* family, related to the trout. Has firm, fatty flesh ranging from white to red. Taken in polar waters and northern lakes.

CHUB   See Whitefish.

CISCO   See Whitefish.

CRAPPIE   A large sunfish, also called speckled perch in parts of the South, *sac a lait* in Louisiana, and calico bass, strawberry bass, bachelor perch, and papermouth in the North. Averages 2 pounds, has soft white flesh with a subtly sweet flavor (see Sunfish).

FALLFISH   See Chub under Whitefish.

FRESHWATER DRUM   See Sheepshead.

GAR   A long, heavily scaled fish with sharp teeth and an undistinguished flavor, taken in central and southern waters.

GIANT SEA BASS   See under Bass in Index.

GOATFISH, also called SURMULLET   Related to the well-known *rouget de roche* of France. Distinguished by long chin barbels.

GRAYLING (French: *ombre*)   A delicately fleshed game fish distinguished by a large dorsal fin. A member of the *Salmonidae* family. Cook like trout or whitefish.

LAKE HERRING   See Whitefish.

MUSKELLUNGE   Same family as pike and pickerel.

MUSKIES   See Muskellunge.

PANFISH   A descriptive term for a number of small freshwater fish including the entire sunfish family, crappies, perch, and the smaller basses.

PERCH   A name given to a number of freshwater and saltwater fish only a few of which are true perch, members of the family *Percidae*. (See Walleye, White perch, Yellow perch, and Ocean perch.)

PICKEREL   A market name for the walleye and the sauger, both often called yellow pike.

PUMPKINSEED   See Sunfish.

REDEYE   A small sunfish; also the name given to a certain species of black bass.

SAUGER   Often confused with the walleye, to which it is closely related (both are pikes). See Pike; Index.

SHAD   See Index.

SHEEPSHEAD   A freshwater drum.

SHELLCRACKER   See Sunfish.

SPECKLED PERCH   See Crappie.

SQUAWFISH   An overgrown minnow, like the Eastern chub.

STUMPKNOCKER   Another name for the warmouth, a sunfish. Sometimes confused with the rock bass, which it resembles, it can be distinguished by blue lines extending outward from the eye. Often has a muddy taste.

SUCKER   An important freshwater fish found in many areas and habitats. Divided into three groups, of which the buffaloes are the best known commercially. Other species include the blue and white suckers, carp-sucker, longnose suckers, and spotted sucker. In general, the flesh is sweet though fish is bony. Some prefer sucker, especially the buffalo, to carp. Prepare as for carp.

SUNFISH   Perhaps the most abundant freshwater fish in North America, often called bream or brim because it resembles the European bream (to which it is not related). Sunfish belong to the spiny-finned *Centrarchidae* family; members include the bluegill, the black and white crappie, green, longear, redbreast and redear sunfish, the pumpkinseed, rock bass, and warmouth.

WARMOUTH   See Sunfish.

WHITE BASS   A panfish-sized relative of the striped bass.

WHITEFISH   Members of the *Salmonidae* family to which salmon and trout belong. Related species include the Great Lakes whitefish, mountain whitefish, arctic and American grayling, pilot fish, and the cisco, whose other names include chub, lake herring, and bloater (see Index).

WHITE PERCH   A market name for the freshwater drum. Unrelated to the perch family (see Drum). Also the name of a small freshwater panfish related to the striped and giant sea bass.

YELLOW PERCH   A true perch, related to the walleye and the sauger (see Perch).

YELLOW PIKE   See Index.

Index